revolution squared

Tahrir, Political
Possibilities, and
Counterrevolution
in Egypt

Atef Shahat Said

Duke University Press Durham and London 2024

© 2024 Duke University Press. All rights reserved
Printed in the United States of America on acid-free paper ∞
Project Editor: Michael Trudeau | Designed by Aimee Harrison
Typeset in Portrait Text and Degular by
Westchester Publishing Services

Library of Congress Cataloging-in-Publication Data
Names: Saʻīd, ʻĀṭif Shaḥḥāt, author.
Title: Revolution squared : Tahrir, political possibilities, and
counterrevolution in Egypt / Atef Shahat Said.
Description: Durham : Duke University Press, 2024. | Includes
bibliographical references and index.
Identifiers: LCCN 2023014330 (print)
LCCN 2023014331 (ebook)
ISBN 9781478025504 (paperback)
ISBN 9781478020721 (hardcover)
ISBN 9781478027638 (ebook)
Subjects: LCSH: Protest movements—Egypt—Cairo. | Revolutions—
Egypt—History—21st century. | Egypt—History—Protests, 2011–2013. |
Maydān al-Taḥrīr (Cairo, Egypt) | Egypt—Politics and government—21st
century. | BISAC: HISTORY / Middle East / Egypt (see also Ancient /
Egypt) | SOCIAL SCIENCE / Ethnic Studies / Middle Eastern Studies
Classification: LCC DT107.87 .S24525 2024 (print) | LCC DT107.87 (ebook) |
DDC 962.05/6—DC23/ENG/20230721
LC record available at https://lccn.loc.gov/2023014330
LC ebook record available at https://lccn.loc.gov/2023014331

Cover art by Yassin Mohamed. Courtesy of the artist.

Revolution Squared

Dedicated to the martyrs of the Egyptian Revolution,
most of whom were underclass. They did not die in vain.
And to the memory of my mother.

□

The closer one comes to God,
the more truthfully they exercise freedom.

**THE ITINERANT TEACHER
SHEIKH ABD RABBIH AL-TA'IH**

□

contents

Conclusion. Revolution as Experience, 210

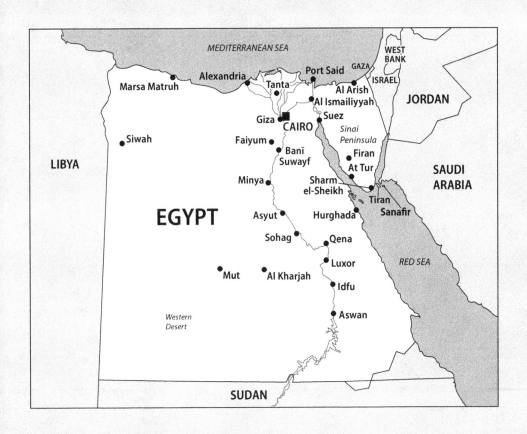

MAP FM.1 Map of Egypt. Map by Omnia Khalil and Iván Arenas.

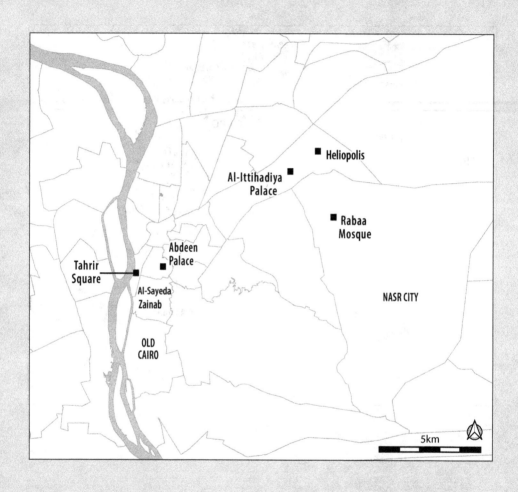

Heliopolis

Al-Ittihadiya
Palace

Rabaa
Mosque

Abdeen
Palace

Tahrir
Square

Al-Sayeda
Zainab

NASR CITY

OLD
CAIRO

5km

MAP FM.2 Map of Cairo. Map by Omnia Khalil and Iván Arenas.

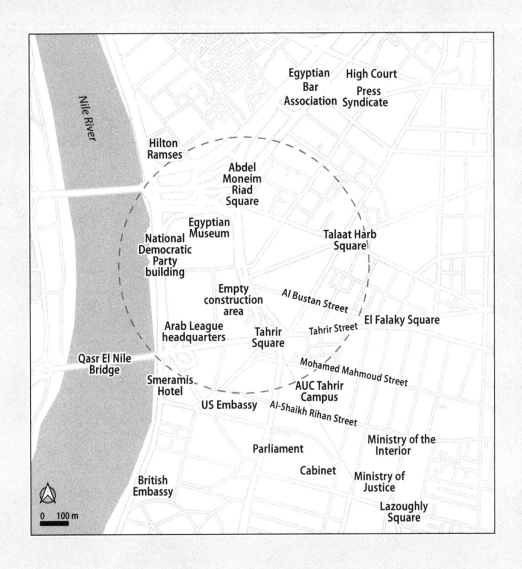

MAP FM.3 Map of Tahrir Square and its surroundings.
Large circle indicates wide action areas. Map by Iván Arenas.

note on transliteration

This book references a sizable number of Arabic source materials, including articles, books, and chapters. The majority of the titles of these sources are rendered in Modern Standard Arabic (MSA) and are thus transliterated in line with the guidelines of the *International Journal of Middle East Studies* (*IJMES*). A minority of titles are rendered in Egyptian colloquial Arabic, in which case they are transliterated using a modified version of the *IJMES* guidelines—for example, *baʾālī eyh*, not *baqiya lī ayh*. Authors' names and periodical titles do not adhere to the *IJMES* transliteration guidelines but are rather rendered according to their salient use—for example, Aly El Raggal, not ʿAlī al-Rajjāl, and *Shorouk News*, not *al-Shurūq*. Likewise, Arabic terms that appear in the body of the text do not adhere to the *IJMES* transliteration guidelines—for example, Midan, not Maydān, and Tahrir, not al-Taḥrīr.

acknowledgments

On January 28, 2011, I was at home in Ann Arbor, Michigan, watching Al Jazeera. I was mesmerized as I stared at masses of protesters marching on Qasr El Nile Bridge in Cairo and battling with police, confronting live ammunition, tear gas, and water cannons with their bare chests. The battle continued, and the protesters marched on to Tahrir Square. That scene later became epic in the memory of many Egyptians. My tears were running uncontrollably, for I had never imagined I would ever watch anything like this in my life: everyday Egyptians defeating the notorious police apparatus of Hosni Mubarak. These events have changed my life. I had never expected that I would be a scholar of revolution, let alone that I would witness one, participate in it, and write about it. Only a few days later, I traveled to Egypt to be part of these momentous events. Indeed, it is cliché to start book acknowledgments with the statement that book writing and production are collective work. This could not be more true in my case. The first group that I want to express my deepest gratitude to are the hundreds of thousands of Egyptians who took to the streets, risking their lives as they called for change. Many of them died, and many others have endured or are still enduring horrific revenge through incarceration, torture, and many forms of persecution. I feel a tinge of bitterness in saying this, for I would rather witness a successful revolution than write an academic book, and become a scholar of revolution, based on a defeated one. But I am grateful to the masses of Egyptians who gave me this historical opportunity of witnessing a revolution. And I ask them for forgiveness if I have not done justice in these pages to their courage and determination.

In addition to the countless revolutionary actors who risked their lives for a better Egypt, I am indebted to many Egyptian comrades and friends for their support and the numerous conversations we had. My utmost gratitude goes to Ayman Abdel Moati, who assisted me in unimaginable ways at many stages of this work. Wael Gamal, Wael Khalil, and Ibrahim Alsahary provided me with love, critical ideas, and conversations and made themselves available on short notice to talk. Tamer Wageih, Dina Samak, Omar El Shafei, Heba Helmi, Ola Shahaba, Yehia Fekry, Moustafa Bassioni, Hossam el-Hamalawy, Aida Saif Al-Dawla, Rabab El-Mahdi, Khaled Abdel Hameed, and Gehan Shaaban answered many questions. Their mere presence assured me that I was not crazy. Other comrades and friends such as Fatma Ramadan, Dalia Mousa, Mohamed Atef, Laila Soueif, the late Seoud Omar, Ahmed Mamdouh, Kareem El-Beheery, Amr Gharbeia, Ahmed Gharbeia, Amr Ezzat, Mahienour El-Masry, Haitham Mohamedain, and Aly El Raggal have been very important in this research. Dina El Khawaga and Choukri Hmed provided critical advice and support, especially when I was awarded a research grant from the Arab Reform Initiative. I had to anonymize the names of many interviewees who played key roles in the revolution, due to the ongoing repressive circumstances in Egypt, and in compliance with institutional review board requirements.

During my time as a graduate student at the University of Michigan, George Steinmetz provided indispensable support and advice and believed in me. He was available at critical moments—most notably, when I saw what was happening in Egypt and decided to jump on a plane just as the revolution was starting. I appreciate all the stimulating discussions I have had with him. He remains an incredible adviser and supporter to this day. Other faculty made unique contributions in terms of mentoring me and this project. Despite his busy schedule, Juan Cole has always been available, and his insightful comments and challenging questions played a crucial role. Howard Kimeldorf has been incredibly generous with his time, providing me with lengthy and critical comments that helped me think through the content of this work. I am indebted to him for my basic knowledge of, and passion for, historical sociology. Müge Göçek's methodological and substantive insights were important throughout my time as a sociology graduate student in Michigan; she has been unconditionally supportive, offering advice ever since I took her SOC 506 seminar in winter of 2005, before I was even officially admitted to the PhD program. Müge Göçek is one of the few sociologists who advised me to embrace my positionality and think of it in a thick way in my work. Her support has continued throughout the years. Sandy Levitsky treated me as a colleague and prodded me not to overlook conventional social movement scholarship. Michael Kennedy has been a friend, mentor, and comrade and a critical supporter in unlimited ways.

The book in its current shape owes a lot to a group of renowned and critical scholars who read the manuscript or parts of it at different stages over the past years. These eminent scholars read either an earlier draft of the entire manuscript or more than one version: Jack Goldstone, Jillian Schwedler, Jessica Winegar, Gilbert Achcar, and Charles Kurzman. All provided me with outstanding advice that critically contributed to the current form of the manuscript. Ann Orloff, James Mahoney, Tony Chen, Marco Garrido, Elisabeth Clemens, Ivan Ermakoff, Rod Ferguson, Damon Mayrl, Eman Abdelhadi, Maryam Alemzadeh, Youssef El Chazli, Ashraf Hussein, Ahmed Abozaid, and Abdou El-Bermawy read one chapter or more at different stages of writing. Norma Moruzzi, Michael Rodríguez-Muñiz, and Andy Clarno read an earlier draft of the theoretical threads of the book. All of them provided valuable feedback. I am especially grateful to Ivan Ermakoff for his very critical engagement, his support, and many conversations about contingency. Mona El-Ghobashy, one of the most prolific experts on Egypt, read more than one chapter. She not only provided critical observations but also offered editorial advice. I cannot thank her enough for her brilliant engagement with my work. I owe so much to our conversations and her friendship.

I presented the ideas that appear here at many academic venues. Among these, in 2013 I attended the Young Scholars in Social Movements Conference organized and hosted by the University of Notre Dame's Center for the Study of Social Movements. Rory McVeigh was a great host, and John D. McCarthy was kind and generous. Sarah Soule was my discussant and provided me with important advice about not overlooking issues of survival and the essentials of the Tahrir revolutionary camp and repertoire. In 2015 I presented a paper at the Annual Seminar at the Bielefeld Graduate School in History and Sociology in Germany. My discussant was William Sewell Jr. As much as this was an intimidating experience, Sewell gave me the most compassionate and critical observations. In January 2016 I participated in the "After Tahrir" conference organized by a group of brilliant colleagues, Sherene Seikaly, Laila Shereen Sakr, and Paul Amar, at the University of California, Santa Barbara. The vibe and the discussion were intellectually and fervently nurturing in unlimited ways. In January 2017 I was invited to give a public lecture hosted by the Institute for Gender, Race, Sexuality, and Social Justice at the University of British Columbia. The audience was engaged, asking very useful questions. Also in 2017, I presented some ideas about the Tahrir revolutionary repertoire at the first Mobilization Conference on Social Movements and Protest, organized by *Mobilization Journal* at San Diego State University. In 2018 I was invited as the keynote speaker at the Annual Graduate Conference of the Department of Sociology of the University of Illinois at Urbana-Champaign. The discussions and the engagement were exceptional. I also presented some ideas from this book at the colloquium of the University of Copenhagen's Department of Cross-Cultural and Regional Studies, and at Goldsmiths, University of London, and the Arab Center for Research and Policy Studies, in Doha, Qatar. And I presented at numerous sociology miniconferences and American Sociological Association conferences, and I especially thank Julia Adams and Cedric de Leon for providing critical feedback when they served as discussants at two occasions in these spaces. Philip Gorski and the Critical Realism Network provided me with support, especially when Phil hosted the postdoctoral seminar in 2015. I also have been fortunate to present my work at important workshops in the Midwest, such as the social theory workshop at the University of Michigan; the Comparative Historical Social Sciences Workshop at Northwestern University; the Politics, History, and Society Workshop at the University of Chicago; and the Politics, Culture, and Society Workshop at the University of Wisconsin–Madison. I am thankful not only to the organizers of these workshops for inviting me to present my work but also to the faculty who were present and provided feedback and, most important, to the great students of history, theory, and sociology in these respective places for their exceptional engagement and useful critiques. Speaking of historical sociology and the Midwest, I am also thankful to the important network of CHAT (Comparative Historical Analysis and Theory) for creating a space for scholars like me who yearn for historical sociology and for inviting me to speak on a webinar about revolutions with an exceptional group including Colin Beck, Xiaohong Xu, and Kristin Plys. Eric Schoon, Ann Orloff, Xiaohong Xu, and Erin McDonnell have been wonderful companions and supporters as co-coordinators of CHAT Midwest. Sherene Seikaly, one of the most critical historians, whose work I admire, made herself available to me on short notice to discuss history and temporalities.

Friends and colleagues on the editorial committee at the Middle East Research and Information Project (MERIP) were great companions and supporters through the last years of my service on that committee. I owe special thanks to the editorial team of MERIP's special issue "Revolutionary Afterlives" (no. 301, Winter 2021) for many important conversations, especially our discussions about temporalities and revolutions, some of which appear in this book. The team included Pete Moore, Stacey Philbrick Yadav, Arang

Keshavarzian, and Michelle Woodward. While we worked on this issue, we led the Practitioners-in-Residence program at New York University's Kevorkian Center for Near Eastern Studies (fall of 2021). Students in this program challenged us and offered many stimulating ideas. Elliott Colla has provided me with invaluable support but, most important, assisted in translating and editing many pieces of poetry that appear in this book.

There were many iterations of writing and accountability groups over the years. I cannot list all of them here, but in the past few years, I have worked with or established different degrees of accountability or support with Naomi Paik, Nadine Naber, Marco Garrido, Eman Ebdelhadi, Nicole Kaufman, Patrisia Macias-Rojas, Xiaohong Xu, Darryl Li, Ghassan Moussawi, Jennifer Jones, Mahesh Somashekhar, Rahim Kurwa, and Amy Bailey. We wrote together, or we shared our work with one another or simply talked about writing. And my special gratitude to the amazing Writers on Site group, especially Lorena Garcia and Marisha Humphries, who organize the group and keep us on track. Another important group of supporters at the University of Illinois at Chicago (UIC) included the following invigorating colleagues and comrades: Ronak Kapadia, Nicole Nguyen, Akemi Nishida, Lorenzo Perillo (before leaving us for the University of Hawaii at Manoa), Patrisia Macias-Rojas, Liat Ben-Moshe, and Michael Jin. Michael and Adam Goodman were great writing companions during our fellowship year at the UIC's Institute for the Humanities.

In 2018 I attended the inaugural meeting of the Du Boisian Scholars Network at Northwestern University. Colleagues at the meeting, including Aldon Morris, Jose Itzigsohn, Michael Schwartz, and many others, reminded me of what engaged and humane sociology ought to be.

Several institutions at UIC provided me with financial support or with venues to write and present my work in its earlier stages. These include the Institute for the Humanities, the Institute for Research on Race and Public Policy, the Social Justice Initiative, and the Great Cities Institute. Mark Canuel and Linda Vavra provided critical support and intellectual care during my fellowship year at the Institute for the Humanities. Also, Amalia Veronika Pallares, the UIC vice chancellor for diversity, equity, and engagement, has been working hard to make UIC a better place for faculty of color. This has helped me and many others.

My department, UIC sociology, provided me with a great space to work and critical support. All my colleagues in the department have been wonderful. I especially thank Barbara Risman, Amanda Lewis, Claire Decoteau, and Andy Clarno for their advice. I am thankful to Barbara, Maria Krysan, and Michael Emerson for being fabulous heads of the department during the process of working on this book. I have talked with Pam Popielarz about our respective projects, and the conversations were very useful. Laurie Schaffner has been one of the most genuine and critical engaged scholars I have ever met. She listened to me for hours, and she was one of the first people to give me unconditional support. Before leaving us to lead the Department of Sociology at Arizona State University, Nilda Flores-González, as associate head, was compassionate and instrumental in providing me with advice about teaching and managing time in the earlier stages of my tenure career at UIC. Tara Williams and Lisa Berube have been more than caring through the years at UIC. Departmental support is one thing, and the privilege of great intellectual engagement with students is another. I owe so much to the students at UIC, both graduates and undergraduates, especially the students who took my revolution class in 2020 and those who took political sociology seminars and social movement classes over the years. Their eager questions and sharp observations were always eye opening and the best gift any scholar can have.

I cannot say enough about how important the Anti-Colonial Machine group has been to me. It is very humbling that some of my intellectual heroes and inspiring interdisciplinary thinkers and theorists have been treating me as a friend, comrade, and intellectual companion for almost a decade and a half. To Fred Moten, David Lloyd, Denise da Silva, Dylan Rodriguez, Sora Han, J. Kameron Carter, and Colin Dayan, I am grateful for your support and intellectual companionship.

Through many years I have worked with a group of wonderful copyeditors. Even though I did not work with Kim Greenwell on this book, I have kept many passages from the dissertation simply because her style is unparalleled. Other superb editors include David Martinez and Andrew Ascherl. Letta Page and Nada Elia especially have been incredible, and no words can describe their extraordinary work with me on this manuscript over the past few years. Boyd Bellinger has been a dream research assistant; without him, I would not have finished. Thanks to Saeed Saffar-Heidari for his work in the bibliography. And I am very grateful to Mohammad El-Sayed Bushra for his exceptional work on the Arabic transliteration. I am thankful to Duke University Press and its editors Elizabeth Ault, Benjamin Kossak, and Michael Trudeau for their engagement and superb care and to Kim Miller, whose copyediting has been very thoughtful. Designer Aimee Harrison was attentive and produced a marvelous cover. I cannot imagine a better press and better editors and designers to work with. I am grateful for Yassin Mohamed for drawing the cover art especially for this work. It is more than special to have an exceptional young artist and former political prisoner produce this piece for me and the book.

Rime Naguib is both a brilliant sociologist and a talented artist. I appreciate her help in reconstructing the layout of the famous Tahrir revolutionary camp. We talked for several hours, we corrected each other's information, and we asked others to make sure we got things right. Ahmed Atif and the Daftar Ahwal project were instrumental in several parts of the book. Omnia Khalil and Ivan Arenas helped me on short notice to create some of the key maps in the book. I am thankful to all of them.

When I moved to Chicago in 2013, it was my second big move since my immigration to the United States in 2004. I experienced a major emotional crisis, as I was moving ever further from Egypt. But a group of incredible humans has made me feel at home in Chicago over the years. These include Barbara Ransby, Peter Sporn, Beth Richie, Dima Khalidi, Khaled Mohamed, Jessica Winegar, Hamdi Attia, Zeina Zaatari, Annie Wilkinson, Camille Odeh, Leena Odeh, Junaid Rana, Maryam Kashani, Tarek Kishawi, Jane Rhodes, Lynn Hudson, Razan Ghazzawi, Hatem Abudayyeh, Muhammad Sankari, Jennifer Ash, Matthew Ash, Noor Shawaf, Rami Gabriel, Henry Liu, Patrisia Macias-Rojas, and John Macias-Rojas. Although they are not technically in Chicago, Rashid and Mona Khalidi have been like family to me, as well as critical intellectual and human companions during their visits to the city. I am thankful to Mona for our long lovely walks. May Seikaly, Khaled Mattawa, Reem Gibriel, and Stacey Austin hosted me at their homes in other states to support me while writing. Without the support of all the above, it would have been difficult for me to finish this book.

During the past few years of completing this book, I lost two humans dear to me. My best friend, Deena Gamil, had been a sister, friend, and comrade for almost a quarter of a century. Deena was the editor of the *Voice of the Revolution*, a newsletter that was distributed in Tahrir in the first few months following Mubarak's ouster. Losing Deena to COVID in September 2020 has caused unparalleled pain. But her love grew in my heart. And in December 2021 I lost one of the most important people to me, the main source of love throughout my life, my mother. I am still grieving her, still grappling with the idea of finding and cherishing all her love after her passing. I know she would have been proud. I find strength every time I think of her love. This helped me through the final stages in this book. All my family members in Egypt have been in my heart when I was writing this book. They supported me, whether they knew it or not. I am hoping that one day all our children and grandchildren in Egypt will live a better life, with unfettered freedom and dignity.

Last but not least, this book would have never been possible without the support of my nuclear family: Nadine, Kinan, and Nile. There are no words to describe how much they supported and grounded me. The revolution has been entangled with my life in numerous ways and forms, many of which were very challenging. Through it all, they lived the cycles of hope and pain with me, while always providing me with support and love. They have been the ultimate source of joy and kindness. Nadine, Kinan, Nile, I am lost without you. I love you more than words can say.

introduction

Revolution as Lived Contingency

I landed in Cairo, Egypt, in the early morning of February 4, 2011. The trip to Cairo had taken almost forty-eight hours because of a curfew imposed by the military. My parents were surprised to see me: I had been in Cairo only three weeks earlier and had not told them I was returning so soon. I worried that my parents, who are not particularly political, would urge me to stay away from the protests in Tahrir Square. As I expected, they were quite upset when I told them I was headed there. For them, Tahrir meant nothing but trouble, violence, possibly even death.

Around eight o'clock in the evening of January 28, 2011, the military had deployed throughout most of the nation's urban centers. The police force had broken down after days of sustained clashes with protesters. At that point, my parents and most Egyptians were subjected to government propaganda telling them there were foreigners and spies amid the wild-headed kids in Tahrir, and all of them were hell-bent on destroying the nation and its stability. I stammered as I made up a story for my anxious parents: "I am not going to Tahrir Square, I am only going to the area near Tahrir, to interview folks from the protest. I have to do this for my PhD research with my adviser." I was lying. I did not know exactly what I was doing. I only knew that I wanted to witness, to take part in what felt, even then, like history in the making. Thinking of their fear and of my spouse and four-year-old child back in the United States, I promised I'd come back and sleep at home every night.

As the days wore on, my parents' reluctance to let me go to Tahrir dissipated. They grew more sympathetic, asking questions about developments in the square. But I felt twinges of shame about returning home every night. I had been a socialist and a human rights activist and knew that important work happens after dark. That's when the serious conversations began, or so I naively believed at the time. At night, when there were fewer protesters, the camp needed the most support. I chastised myself that even though I spent every day in Tahrir, I was not brave enough to be part of the camp at night. Nevertheless, my time near my parents' home allowed me to participate in the interesting workings of what Egyptians called the "popular committees" (*legan shaabiyya*).[1] Egypt was in a security crisis, and the military was ill equipped to take over policing. So while the armed forces focused on hot spots, citizens spontaneously and brilliantly organized neighborhood committees for security. These spread everywhere. Lightly armed citizens stood along main streets and down smaller alleys, keeping a vigilant night watch over their neighborhoods. Citizens—revolutionaries and nonrevolutionaries alike—became both executive authorities and agents of revolution without realizing it. They established checkpoints, used barricades to control traffic, stopped suspicious-looking persons and cars, checked IDs, and, when the need arose, arrested and handed people over to the army. As they rested, committee members engaged in long discussions about these tumultuous days of upheaval.

And so at night I joined my siblings and neighbors in a committee near my parents' home in northeastern Cairo. We talked about Egypt after Hosni Mubarak, about the military and the chaos that seemed to have engulfed our country. They would ask me, the only one spending every day in Tahrir Square, "What happened in Tahrir, what happened with the revolution today?" Repeatedly, I would tell them, "You are part of the revolution," only to be dismissed. For these Egyptians, just like for the regime and millions of others, the revolution was "in Tahrir."

I grew physically and emotionally exhausted, torn between two places. The square was the site of the famous camp where an alternative republic was forming. Northeastern Cairo, about 12.5 miles from Tahrir, was becoming its own alternative government, no matter that most of the actors saw themselves not as revolutionaries but as a neighborhood watch. Both sites embodied astounding formulations and practices of power by everyday Egyptians in a time of revolutionary crisis, yet the global spotlight shone only on Tahrir.

At the time, I could not seem to reconcile the two places into one story. Even as I thought of myself as a bridge between the two, the events were just too overwhelming. It was only in 2012, during the second phase of my research, that I noticed that activists had begun to critique Tahrir. The square was no longer the utopian space where united Egyptian revolutionaries were building an alternative society. Now it seemed that people had realized that the fixation on Tahrir was limiting, that it had obscured other developments during the uprising. New questions swirled: Was Tahrir Square a blessing or a curse for the revolution? Could it be both? Do revolutions have boundaries? What counts as a "revolutionary space," especially in a moment of flux? If the revolution by definition is a moment of rupture, is there one rupture or many? I began to analyze the revolution by blending my ideas around the when and where of the revolution.

This Book

Revolution Squared attempts to answer one key question: How are revolutions defined by their spatiotemporal contexts? I consider this question in relation to the 2011 Egyptian Revolution by asking: (1) How and why did the Egyptian Revolution become solely associated with and, in turn, reduced to the events in Tahrir Square? (2) How did this naming and narrowing affect the developing events? (3) How did all of these processes contribute to the dramatic expansion of political space in the immediate aftermath of the revolution, and the equally dramatic contraction of that space in the years that followed?[2]

I examine how Tahrir Square emerged as the central space and voice of the revolution, as well as how Tahrir related to important modes of action in Egypt's other urban centers, such as labor strikes and popular committees. The revolution was constituted by multiple successes and defeats across numerous intersecting spatiotemporal sites, but I focus on three: the streets and squares, especially Tahrir; digital spaces; and formal political space. I trace how processes within each of these spaces shifted and changed across distinct periods, including the famous eighteen days that preceded Mubarak's February 11, 2011, ouster; the transitional period of leadership by the Supreme Council of Armed Forces (SCAF) from 2011 through mid-2012; Mohamed Morsi's presidency (June 30, 2012, to July 3, 2013); and the current military leadership of Abdel Fattah el-Sisi (May 2014 to the present). Thus, the book includes a very close study of the period from 2011 to 2013, but I also situate this analysis in the context of the battles over political space and democracy in the decade prior to the uprising, the history of protest in Tahrir Square, and the events that followed the 2013 coup. Through a focused investigation of the interconnected forces of space, class, and revolutionary momentum (or its waning), I show how the goals and demands of the revolution were distilled and, ultimately, defanged.

Revolution Squared is also a story about the power of Egyptians who did not fully grasp their immense clout during the days of the revolution. Three major contradictions conditioned how revolutionary actors conceived of their power across spaces and places: ambivalence toward the military and the state coupled with sharp critiques of what they saw as a decoupled Mubarak regime, as separate from the military and the state; the inherent tensions within the cross-class coalition that successfully toppled Mubarak but could not harness the potential social and radical grievances of the uprising; and the lack of unifying political revolutionary organization, despite the presence of an enormous, spontaneous revolutionary mobilization. Together, these tensions shaped the political geography of the revolution. The false impression that the uprising was happening only in Tahrir further aggravated these tensions. By centering and interrogating the revolutionary possibilities that existed during the uprising—even some that were ultimately "squared" by the necessary reduction of the revolution to a list of actionable demands—I demonstrate that the Egyptian Revolution was not doomed to defeat.

My analysis is based on three premises. First, any adequate account of a given revolution's trajectory, especially one that ended poorly, must not overlook the role of counterrevolution. If we agree that every revolution entails two large processes—an expansion of possibilities and also projects of containment—it follows that any fair account of this revolution should include both. By "expansion of possibilities," I mean that the struggle for sovereignty and governance becomes unlimited. And by "projects of containment," I mean different dynamics and ways for counterrevolution to attack. Second, and relatedly, if we agree with what the established sociological and historical research says, namely, that revolutions are messy affairs, we must seriously take into account the perspectives and contradictions of revolutionary actors. Third, to better understand the trajectory of revolutions, specifically defeated ones, it is essential to closely examine what happened on the ground. Bearing these premises in mind, in the following pages I analyze how Egyptian revolutionaries practiced sovereignty and policed Egypt during the uprising, as well as how the revolutionaries ceded power and ultimately their voices in the years that followed.

Squaring can mean different things: to reshape something into a square, to multiply a number by itself, or to regulate or adjust to a standard or principle. The latter is the main connotation I am interested in here. In this book

I use the term to describe how the revolution was discursively reduced to the physical and symbolic boundary of Tahrir Square during the uprising, amplifying the revolution while eclipsing many other kinds of organizing, voices, and more radical possibilities. I also explore how the revolution was squared in the sense of being reduced to a project of elections without democratization. This second process came after Mubarak's ouster, when the counterrevolutionary forces (the military and the Muslim Brotherhood, aided by the complicity of liberal, nationalist, and political elites and the explicit intervention of regional and international powers) contained the revolution's outcomes. The revolution was, in this sense, reduced again—to a project of procedural democracy and free markets, under brutal security and intelligence apparatuses. These two squaring processes were not fated but historically contingent. We cannot understand how Egyptians experienced many cycles of immense outrage, hope, distress, and disappointment without considering possibility and containment (see also Elyachar 2014, 459).

Tahrir as Space, Tahrir as Repertoire

Tahrir Square carries special meaning and symbolism. During the revolution it was described as a "liberated zone" (Holmes 2012), a "quasi-utopian community," a "revolutionary space" (Gunning and Baron 2013), a "self-ruled community" or a "republic" (Van de Sande 2013), and a place that embodied a "time out of time" (Sabea 2013). Most analyses contain the unspoken assumption that the dynamics in and around Tahrir Square were metonymic of the dynamics of the revolution at large. But as Jessica Winegar (2012) suggested, the iconization of Tahrir during the uprising led many observers to overlook many critical components, such as the unequal gendered division of labor and class participation in the revolution.

Given the extraordinary weight of meanings ascribed to Tahrir, it is important to situate it and other key squares in the Egyptian Revolution more concretely, as well as the significance of Cairo as the capital city. Tahrir Square, Midan el-Tahrir in Arabic, is about 11.5 acres of open space in the heart of downtown Cairo, or twenty-two acres if we include its surroundings.[3] Khedive Ismail, the grandson of Mohamed Ali, founded the square around 1869 as a roundabout as part of his vision to modernize Cairo (Ismail had lived in Paris during Baron Georges-Eugène Haussmann's remake of that city). Thus, it was called Ismailia Square. Ismail's vision was to modernize Cairo and create a "Paris on the Nile." (Paradoxically, the wide streets that mimic Parisian squares made Tahrir one of the most policeable spaces in Cairo [Schwedler 2013, 231].) Near the heart of the square is Qasr El Nile Bridge. From 1882 to 1947, British barracks occupied the area near the bridge. Under King Farouk, a huge, all-in-one administrative building known as Mogamma ("the complex") was built in 1951. The name Tahrir Square, meaning "Liberation Square" in Arabic, was first used informally in Egyptian mass protests against British rule in 1919. The name was made official when Egypt became independent and transitioned from a constitutional monarchy into a republic under Gamal Abdel Nasser (Farag 1999; A. Said 2015).

It would be hard to find a place that more neatly symbolizes Egypt's colonial history, postcolonial state formation, and contemporary configurations of power. Jillian Schwedler writes:

> Tahrir Square has long been dominated by the physical embodiments of state repressive capacities. The National Democratic Party headquarters towers over the square, literally and figuratively surveilling activity in all directions. The [Mogamma], a central administrative building that stands at the south of the square, has become such a symbol of impenetrable and crushing state bureaucracy that it has been featured in several films. The National Museum, and the state-sanctioned narrative of national triumph it tells, is located on the northside of the square. The Arab League headquarters, the US Embassy, several major international hotels (and symbols of international capital), and the Ministry of the Interior are all located nearby. As a topography of power, Tahrir Square embodied the oppressive script of Hosni Mubarak's regime and a topographical node of power on constant display and legible to all who traversed the square. The weight of the regime was unmistakable in Tahrir, providing an intimidating environment but also an obvious symbolic location for challenging the regime and reclaiming public space. (2013, 231)

Proximal spaces that were important meeting and resting spaces during the uprising and in its aftermath include opposition-party headquarters, cafés, churches, and mosques. For example, between the Nile Hilton Hotel and the Qasr El Dobara is the Omar Makram Mosque. Named after one of Egypt's revolutionaries during the French occupation (1798–1801), Omar Makram Mosque was, with the Qasr El Dobara, used as a field hospital during the violent clashes of late 2011 (A. Said 2015, 352–53).

I conducted research for this book in three other major Egyptian cities. Mahalla, or Al Mahalla Al Kubra in Arabic, is a large industrial and agricultural city in Gharbiya Governorate in the Nile delta, with more than half a million residents as of 2012. Mahalla witnessed what many considered to be a true rehearsal for the revolution when, in 2008, its textile workers attempted a general strike. Forceful suppression sparked mass riots and later the April 6 Youth Movement, named for the date of the aborted uprising. Suez (as-Suways in Arabic) is located on the north coast of the Gulf of Suez in northeastern Egypt. The first death of a protester in the 2011 revolution (Mostafa Ragab) occurred during the intense clashes there between January 25 and 27. These events galvanized revolutionary anger across Egypt. The third city is Alexandria (al-'Iskandariyya in Arabic), a Mediterranean port city that boasts Egypt's second-highest urban population. Alexandria was key in that it was the home of Khaled Said, the young Egyptian blogger whose torture and death in June 2010 was one of the primary catalysts for the revolution.

In each of these cities, a public square was a significant site of protest (Arbaeen Square in Suez, el-Shone in Mahalla, and Al Qaid Ibrahim Square and mosque in Alexandria), yet at none of these locales did protesters successfully stage a full encampment. The only attempt happened in Alexandria, where a camp at Masr Station Square (the site of the city's central rail station) lasted about two days. In my interview with activist Mara Salim (December 19, 2012), she explained:

> There were many reasons activists thought it does not make sense to stage a sit-in in Alexandria. The first of these is that we do not have the same concentration of government complexes like Tahrir. So if we stage a sit-in, there will be no disruption of the state. The second reason is the geography of Alex[andria]. We have some big squares, but rallies were more important in Alexandria. It is a coastal city, the streets are long next to the Corniche, and rallies are more effective, as they make the revolution reach wider populations. Also, at the time of the revolution Alexandria was way colder than Cairo. If we camped, we would have been simply soaking wet from the rain. Also, Alex[andria] is still, despite its size, a relatively small city. There is no real need for a sit-in. You can protest all day and simply go home in fifteen to twenty minutes, unlike in Cairo, where it is perhaps more convenient to stay in one place versus commuting in horrible traffic.[4]

Of course, sheer numbers are one reason Cairo's protests were so much more successful. Cairo is not only the political capital of Egypt but also its most populous city, with some 10 percent of Egypt's 2011 population clustered there (8.5 million in 2011).[5] Consequently, a mass protest in Cairo can have huge effects. In an unpublished paper, Ellis Goldberg proposes that in the Arab uprisings, capitals that could be considered "primate" cities were crucial: "That the capital is a primate city matters because it allows the possibility of rapidly assembled immense protests that paralyze the administrative and political life of a country. Generally speaking, the primate city is the largest city in a country and frequently contains between 10 percent and 25 percent of a country's population" (2013, 3). The population of Cairo and the concentration of government buildings and centers of power in Tahrir Square made them excellent possible sites of revolution. The so-called million-person rallies that garnered significant domestic and international attention reinforced their primacy. These specific aspects contributed to the contingent factors that made the Tahrir repertoire, or the larger revolutionary repertoire, possible (A. Said 2022, 223).

The Tahrir repertoire refers to a set of available means innovated during the revolution in 2011, including occupying public space, forming a minirepublic that required many forms of organization, keeping the social media focus on Tahrir, and erecting barricades to police the space and protect this republic, as well as planning marches and rallies that ended in Tahrir Square. The ease with which we can identify these aspects of the revolutionary repertoire does not mean that the coexistence of these elements emerged easily or automatically. Indeed, one of this book's goals is to highlight the risk and contingency of this process and so many others in relation to the battle for sovereignty, especially from early 2011 until the military coup on July 3, 2013. The question is why the alternative state in Tahrir did not expand the practice of sovereignty and the enforcement of liberation logics throughout the entire Egyptian territory. Similarly, barricades are also exceptionally critical in revolutionary times. Why did the Egyptian revolutionaries not symbolically, if not physically, extend the barricades erected around Tahrir to those erected elsewhere? Why was the main square not connected to factories and neighborhoods?

There are more puzzling questions. When Egyptians celebrated Mubarak's resignation on February 11, 2011, how could they have trusted the military in that moment? Vice President Omar Suleiman's announcement that Mubarak was transferring power to the military was an odd outcome to hail as a "victory" for a revolution. The army, a significant component of the state, was to "administer" the transition away from the regime of which it was a part and against which the revolution took place. This paradox calls for closer examination. Even if the average Egyptian trusted the military in 2011, how do we explain the fact that revolutionaries in Egypt were "fooled" again and trusted the military in 2013?

My approach is based on what I call *lived contingency*. Let me explain what this means by starting with something one of my interviewees told me. He was a middle-aged man and defined himself as an independent Islamist. We spoke on November 2, 2012, and when I told him that I was conducting research about Tahrir Square and the Egyptian Revolution, he responded, "You should know this: *Every inch of Tahrir has a story, even many stories* [emphasis mine]. Nobody can claim that she or he is capable of collecting all these stories and presenting an accurate account of what happened in Tahrir." His words served as a reminder of the enormous challenge I was already confronting. Despite my best efforts as an ethnographer who was present in Tahrir Square every day from February 4 until Mubarak was deposed on February 11, 2011, I simply cannot do justice to all the stories of Tahrir. This informant's words were with me while I was doing my research in Egypt, and then when I began organizing and analyzing the data back in the United States, as well as when I was writing my dissertation (2013–14), and they remain with me now.

If we juxtapose this interviewee's compelling insight with the idea of revolution as a multifaceted phenomenon with several competing essences (or a peculiar ontology or ontologies), my task would be almost impossible. For example, Tahrir Square meant a myriad of things in the context of the revolution (a site for protest, a central area for mobilization, an icon, or an embodiment of the revolutionary demands), but, most important, some saw it as an embodiment of revolutionary aspiration (idealist view), while others considered it the place where the revolution occurred, reduced to a geographic location, in line with the dominant reformist view of the revolution (pragmatist view). As I collected as many stories as possible about the revolution, I discovered that many revolutionary actors had differing stories about what happened in Tahrir Square, or what happened to the protesters themselves before the revolution. Despite my presence in Tahrir between February 4 and February 11, 2011, I cannot claim that I am capable of generalizing about what happened within the square itself in relation to the revolution.

According to Charles Kurzman (2009, 5), it is critical for scholars of revolutions to incorporate unpredictability and confusion among key actors in the revolution. He states, "Anti-explanation is an attempt to understand the experience of the revolution in all its anomalous diversity and confusion, and to abandon the mirage of retroactive predictability. Anti-explanation begins by comparing the lived experiences of the event with the main explanations offered by studies of revolution" (5–6).

To grapple with these challenges, I turned to one of the most magical terms in historical sociological research: *contingency*. Ivan Ermakoff put forward one of the most useful theoretical elaborations of the concept, suggesting that contingency is indeterminacy and that "indeterminacy is an endogenous property of [historical] processes and conjuncture" (2015, 66). Against accidental or negative perceptions about contingency, Ermakoff proposes that we have to think of contingency in positive and concrete terms in relation to human agency (66) and argues that one of the key dimensions in contingency is mutual uncertainty between actors (100).

To see how this is useful for my inquiry, let us apply notions of contingency as indeterminacy and mutual uncertainty to a very concrete, empirical example from the Egyptian Revolution. One of the critical elements of the revolutionary situation, which perhaps shaped the entire revolutionary trajectory in Egypt, was the interaction between protesters and the military. Neil Ketchley (2017a, 47) examines what he describes as the repertoire of fraternization between protesters and the military during the revolutionary situation. Through a rich analysis, he provides an incisive interrogation of the protesters' use of the famous chant "The people and the army are one hand." While most of Ketchley's analysis of fraternization focused on its performative side, he did not overlook aspects of the political side of the story, namely, that from the protesters' point of view, fraternization was a political move that aimed to win the sympathy of the military through actions such as welcoming the tanks (53). Such actions also had the immediate goal of neutralizing the army at that moment.

But fraternization was only one side of the story. Evidence demonstrates that the relationship between the protesters and the military was also characterized by power testing and was never static. As soon as they realized that the first armored military vehicles arriving at Tahrir, belonging to the Republican Guard, were carrying extra weaponry for the police and were intended to protect the Ministry of the Interior, protesters set them on fire. Protesters also drew graffiti on military tanks cursing the commander in chief, Mubarak, and slept under the tanks to stop them from encroaching on Tahrir. While it is accurate to suggest that protesters performed fraternization toward the military, the relationship between revolutionaries and the military on the ground was full of tension and constituted by mutual uncertainties. In my own ethnographic research in Tahrir, I heard again and again from my interlocutors that the military was like a black box, as they did not know what to expect from it during the uprising. Protesters' speculations about the army varied from day to day until the army clearly distanced itself from Mubarak on February 10, 2011, convening an emergency meeting of the high command without his presence as the ostensible commander in chief.[6] Before February 10, 2011, and especially in the first few days after January 28, 2011, soldiers around Tahrir were begging protesters to stop climbing on the military tanks. I saw this not as a simple practice of fraternization but also possibly as a symbolic power contest about who had ultimate sovereignty in Tahrir. Especially in chapters 2 and 3, I demonstrate how the relation between the two parties was characterized by mutual skepticism and testing of power, and intense and impromptu negotiations over zones of influence and the practice of sovereignty, especially in Tahrir Square but also around barricades in important neighborhoods in key urban centers.

Mutual uncertainty between protesters and the military is but one example of many such indeterminate interactions during the revolution. *Lived contingency* refers to how revolutionary actors practice and experience the revolution, particularly in terms of the actions they do or do not take in relation to the possibilities, unpredictabilities, and practices of power during the course of a revolution. One can argue that contingency only refers to uncertainties and unpredictabilities from the point of view of revolutionary actors. But as I demonstrate in the following pages, *contingency* has a positive connotation as well: experiencing a sense of open possibilities, even while being bold but naive about what is the right action to take in relation to these possibilities. Lived contingency is not limited to the context of a revolutionary crisis, when the revolution is at its peak, but is also relevant during the fluid postrevolutionary context, or the *revolutionary trajectory*, to use the terminology proposed by the authors of *Dynamics of Contention* (McAdam, Tarrow, and Tilly 2001a). I am proposing here that lived contingency matters throughout the entire revolutionary process, from the revolutionary crisis until a decisive outcome takes place, due to the fluctuating politics of this period before new revolutionary institutions are formed, including continuations of the struggle for sovereignty. I now elaborate on three critical aspects of lived contingency: *agential, spatial,* and *radical and/or uncalculated unbounding.*

Agential Contingency

In revolutions many transformations happen in a short window of time, as vividly expressed in Vladimir Lenin's famous phrase "There are weeks when decades happen."[7] This puts revolutionary actors in challenging positions in which they have to make choices. Actors have "inner states" to make sense of macro processes around them, as put powerfully by Charles Kurzman (2004). He proposes that these inner states include "the broadest possible range of mental structures and processes, among them preference structures, motivations, and emotions" (329). I examine how actors in the Egyptian Revolution made (or failed to make) choices during the course of the revolution.[8] One of the most puzzling stories that I aim to investigate is how Egyptian citizens—revolutionaries and nonrevolutionaries alike—became both executive authorities and agents of revolution without realizing it and how they experienced ambivalence about their role and about power during the revolution. I examine this closely in chapters 2, 3, and 4.

Spatial Contingency

A key component of revolutionary agency is how actors experience, appropriate, and remake spaces. Two decades ago, leading scholars of contention such as William Sewell Jr. and Charles Tilly alerted us to attend to the salient meaning of spaces as well as the symbolic and material dimensions of spaces in movements and revolutions. As Sewell (2001, 65) suggests, "While insurgent movements make sure of the preexisting meanings of places, they can also—either intentionally or unintentionally—transform the significance of protest locations." Tilly (2000, 135) has suggested that spaces of contention are textured. It follows, then, that revolutionary spaces are extraordinarily textured. Analyzing Tahrir Square during the revolution, anthropologist Hanan Sabea (2013) states that the everydayness of the revolution "was spatially marked by the carving out of the space of the 'midan' (the square) and the regulation of entry at its multiple check-points." My interlocutors and interviewees shared numerous stories about particular places in Cairo and how they experienced them. Along with Tahrir, other sites gained symbolic status in the revolution and its aftermath. The Qasr El Nile Bridge was a symbol of revolutionary victory because a famous battle took place there on January 28, 2011. Cairo's Zeinhom morgue, where martyrs were taken in many instances, became a symbol of the counterrevolution's victory. Some places, like Abbāsīyah Square, were associated with revolution for some people, and for others with counterrevolution. Human agency always takes space personally, as Edward Soja (2009, 16) puts it. It follows, then, that spaces that connote things like hope, death, and despair are perhaps extraordinarily personal.

During a revolution the assumed difference between place, as a physical location, and space, as a meaning and an idea, no longer makes sense. Sociologists Frances Hasso and Zakia Salime demonstrate how the making and remaking of spaces in revolutions "occur through use (everyday and extraordinary encounters; barricades and checkpoints), memory (of massacres, street battles, sexual assaults, major mobilizations), representations (graffiti, aesthetics, poems, songs, sartorial practices), and Facebook and Twitter wars. This dynamism, emergence, and multiplicity are difficult to control" (2016, 6). Revolutionary actors give new meaning to spaces, such as associating them with victories or defeats, challenging established dichotomies between space and place, and navigating the overwhelming complexities and multiplicities of spaces and their meaning.

Radical and/or Uncalculated Unbounding

Over and over again, my interlocutors shared with me that they were willing to die or felt they had only one choice: to continue their mission. Many told me that they felt like they were on a mythical and persistent mission but without any more specific purpose than achieving freedom or justice. I could not reckon with what this meant at the time, as I was overwhelmed myself. One interlocutor—a thirty-year-old male and self-identified Revolutionary Socialist—said:

> When Tahrir protesters started the sit-in on January 28, 2011, at night, they did not have any other choice. At the time, there was the Mubarak regime and his security apparatus (which seemed to be defeated at the time) on one side, and protesters have this [liberated] square on the other. If we would have left the square, we would have been killed. The protesters will be repressed worse than they were before. We saw it very well in the days from January 25 to January 28 (until late afternoon), when Mubarak and his security apparatus did nothing but arrest leading activists and kill protesters. At the time, we could not think of any big strategies, we just tried to save ourselves and save the uprising. If we could die outside the square anyway, why not die here, for the sake of the uprising? (February 8, 2011)

Many others expressed this same kind of sentiment. One could argue that not all protesters were willing to die, of course, although it is a fact that official documentation suggests that about 846 protesters were killed during the uprising, and about 6,400 people were injured (BBC News 2011). This uprising was deemed peaceful and nonviolent by most observers and analysts. But as I argue and demonstrate in the pages to come, Egyptian revolutionaries not only risked their lives during the revolution but engaged in many spontaneous and uncalculated radical actions that do not happen often in normal political circumstances. These included carrying weapons, even if these were light weaponry; arresting other citizens; arresting police officers; marching in rallies for several hours for distances of up to nine or more miles; storming the headquarters of the State Security Intelligence; resisting the formation of a constitutional assembly; launching a national campaign for citizens to directly draft the constitution; or marching to parliament and asking parliament members to seize power. In this spirit Kurzman suggests that all protests, particularly in revolutions, are "unruly," or "collective actions that do not obey the rules of social behavior, and that do not obey the rules of social science" (2017, 185). He continues, "It is unruly to stand in front of armored personnel carriers and demand that the commander in chief resign? It is unruly to hold up a sign demanding freedom, in a place where people who have held up signs demanding freedom often lose their freedom as a result? These actions are not necessarily raucous or disruptive—although they may be—but they are unruly in the sense that they violate the norms of routine behavior" (185).

When I asked many of my interlocutors what happened to them during the revolution, several told me they were never political before but unexpectedly became radicalized because of specific things they witnessed or saw during these moments. A sixty-year-old mother told me, "The last thing I could have ever imagined is to be part of this, but because I knew that my twenty-year-old daughter was in danger, and I could not stop her, I went to check on her in Tahrir." She continued, "In the early morning hours of what is now known as the Camel Battle [February 2] I became enraged. After that I started to go to Tahrir every day and bring cooked meals for protesters" (interview, October 12, 2012).[9] Another interlocutor I talked to several times during the revolution shared a similar story. He happened to be from Sinai but was living in Cairo. He was not political before the revolution, but something magical happened to him when he saw a specific scene on TV. The scene was aired on Al Jazeera and many other outlets, showing riot police directing water cannons at protesters at close range during what was later known as the Qasr El Nile Bridge battle, on January 28, 2011. During that intense battle, which lasted for more than two hours, protesters decided to pray in an attempt to take a breather, hoping that the riot police would stop shooting and beating them. Instead, the riot police opened heavy water cannons on them. My interlocutor told me he became angry like never before and decided that he now had a new life (or death) mission, that he was following a calling. This idea of a calling was repeated by many of my interlocutors. One interviewee told me that since the revolution and what he experienced on January 28, 2011, he "felt like [he] was developing a new faith during the day, and its name was the revolution" (November 10, 2012).

In short, many told me that they were almost enchanted by the revolution. One other common sentiment I also kept hearing over and over was "Anything is better than what we have now." It is difficult to reconcile that a person is willing to die for the revolution and at the same time not very worried about the revolution's outcome, as they truly believe that nothing could be worse than the present. I tried to reframe this idea in concrete terms related to contingency, the role of agency, and collective action, as any good sociologist/ethnographer ought to do. A lazy critic would conclude that these people were stupid, as they did not care whether the revolution was successful. However, the revolutionary actors I talked to in Tahrir did not completely overlook the question of outcome. They cared quite a lot about the outcome, but they also believed that any outcome would be better than what they had at the time. They did not have any way to measure whether or not a revolution was successful.

I began this discussion to explain what I mean by the third element of living a revolutionary contingency. I describe this as a case of radical or un-calculated unbounding of revolutionary actors, by which I mean how revolutionary actors lose many commitments to the normal, everyday concerns of work, career, family, loved ones, and the future.[10] Or, rather, because of a very dear attachment to these issues, revolutionary actors become willing to take the highest risk of all, to die to make things better on these fronts.[11] In some sense, these issues take on some existential meaning and connotations. Radical or uncalculated unbounding means that an actor is willing to die, feeling that they are undertaking a mythical mission for freedom.[12]

In hindsight, it is clear that actors in the Egyptian Revolution made some major mistakes, such as not considering seizing power and not developing a clear plan for the transfer of power, among other things. After all, in the established literature, revolutions have to lead to complete transformations of state and society to earn this title. In the same vein, to be a revolutionary means one must be capable of and successful at making this transformation.

Throughout this book I demonstrate that it is conceptually accurate to stipulate that revolutionaries are those who claim and seize power to make change. But I also argue that it is equally fair and accurate to acknowledge that part of being a revolutionary actor in the ethnographic sense is experiencing the revolution and taking part in it, with all its uncertainties, unpredictabilities, and unlimited possibilities. Perhaps Egyptian actors were not revolutionary enough, because their revolution did not succeed. This is the stance of the established, teleological meaning of being revolutionary. I propose that a revolutionary is someone who deeply cares about a successful outcome but also someone who lives and relishes, even if painfully, the process of the revolution.

Lived contingency is at the extreme end of a spectrum with teleological analysis at the other pole. The latter focuses on what seems to *happen finally*, discounting other happenings to focus on this sole outcome. The lived contingency approach investigates those happenings but situates them within other possibilities. Between these two approaches, one can imagine different degrees of empirical analysis that focus on what happened and why this happened. *Degrees* here refers to how thickly or poorly the collected data reflect what happened in a complex event such as a revolution, and how far the analysis is tied to theory and brings new findings, rather than focusing only on discrete one-sided data collection to prove a one-sided causal relation.

Settling the Unsettled?

I now tackle how neither scholars nor Egyptians agree on a single narrative for the revolution and further discuss why attempting to present a single definition of revolution is perhaps not a viable project, as it imposes uniformity and coherence on an object that resists any standardization.

The Egyptian Revolution's Identity Crisis

Since the very first protest of January 25, 2011, Egyptians have not ceased debating and reflecting on the revolution. In 2016 the political writer Mohamed Naeem called on fellow Egyptian activists and revolutionaries to reflect on what had happened since 2011 but, most important, advised them to acknowledge that *there is no unifying narrative about the uprising*. This advice has been critical to me while writing these pages. Indeed, narratives about the uprising have been as diverse as the individuals and groups who participated in it, as Naeem writes, and the supposedly organized political forces were themselves contradictory. Among the major challenges of assessing what happened in Egypt in 2011 and its aftermath are the intense and polarized debates around what the revolution was about in the first place. The revolutionaries disagree not only on the ultimate goals or the temporal boundaries of the revolution but also about where it took place, the critical spaces in which revolutionary or postrevolutionary actions unfolded—streets, ballots, negotiations behind closed doors, and digital spaces among them. What's more, different groups have defined the counterrevolution differently, and key actors have constantly changed positions across revolutionary and counterrevolutionary coalitions.

Even if we agreed that political Islamists and liberals were coherent and had one static vision of the revolution, which is not the case, most of the leaders of both camps seemed to want only democratic reform (procedural democracy with free markets and free elections) with some facade of the state being identified as civil/secular or Islamic. Neither objected to the military's control of events in Egypt (see chapter 5).[13]

Taking this wisdom into consideration, it is useful to dig deeper into what can be described as the Egyptian Revolution's identity crisis. Leftist writer Hani Shukrallah (2017) superbly states that "among the shortcomings of the Egyptian revolution is a tendency to faulty self-perception caused by a certain color-blindness: a deeply red revolution that sees itself as orange." The color red here indicates the radical social demands of the revolution, and the color orange indicates the dominance of limited democratic reforms—a formulation that ties the uprising to the revolutions of eastern Europe. Shukrallah clarifies that by "red" he does not mean a socialist revolution but rather the way the social composition of the uprising, as well as its demands for democracy, destined it to clash with the entire capitalist class in Egypt, which is neither capable of nor even interested in democracy. One might argue that Shukrallah, a leftist Marxist, believes that social or socialist revolutions are the only true revolutions. However, the meaning of a social revolution versus a political revolution has never been settled.

About three weeks after Mubarak was deposed, another political writer, Hosni Abdelrehim, wrote that "revolutions start with deposing a tyrant, but they never end until they establish a new order" (2011, 59–60). And only two days after Mubarak's ouster, economic writer Wael Gamal (2011a) suggested that the consensus among the contradictory social forces—which made the revolution possible—was very limited and exceptional. Once Mubarak was ousted, "the social struggle between these forces was open." Soon after ousting

Mubarak, the SCAF and its allies, such as the Muslim Brotherhood and liberal elites, agreed that the social demands should be sidelined and the wheel of production should continue while institutional democracy making took place. Workers' protests did not stop until 2013, and workers' strikes were sometimes attacked with armored vehicles and military tanks.

While analyses were pronouncing that the revolution had already succeeded, or that it was over, Egyptian revolutionaries were still organizing in the streets and storming the headquarters of the State Security Intelligence in Alexandria and Cairo on March 3 and 5, respectively, of 2011 (El Raggal 2019). As I put it with Pete Moore elsewhere, "To the ears of a North American op-ed audience, Arabs waking up in 2011 to demand 'democracy' fit accepted Middle Eastern tropes," and "protesters have been asking for quite some time the important question: democracy for what and democracy for who?" (A. Said and Moore 2021). In short, as I show in chapters 4 and 5, social struggles were a central part of the story and of the momentum shifts throughout the period from 2011 to 2013.

Let me be guided by Naeem's caution while situating this study within the scholarship on the Egyptian Revolution, a literature so immense that it is impossible to cover in these pages. For the purposes of this book, however, it is important to discuss two key terms, *revolutionary situation* and *revolutionary outcome*, which recur throughout. Tilly (1993, 10) defines a revolutionary situation as a moment that has three elements:

1. Appearance of contenders, or coalitions of contenders, advancing exclusive competing claims to control of the state, or some segments of it,
2. Commitment to those claims by a significant segment of the citizenry, and
3. Incapacity or unwillingness of rulers to suppress the alternative coalition and/or commitment to its claims.

Later, Tilly added that a revolutionary situation requires that one of the new emerging centers of power commands "a significant coercive force." He states, "A full revolution combines two elements: a revolutionary situation and a revolutionary outcome. In a revolutionary situation, at least two centers of power emerge, each of them commanding significant coercive force and each of them claiming exclusive control over the state. In a revolutionary outcome, a transfer of power over the state occurs such that a largely new group of people begins to rule" (2008, 126–27). Jack Goldstone (2009) similarly argues for a disaggregated understanding of revolutions, coining the term *revolutionary suite* to highlight the significance of three factors: (1) elite defection and the formation of opposition, (2) polarization and coalition building, and (3) mass mobilization. Where Goldstone puts more emphasis on elite defection and coalition building, Tilly stipulates that contenders must seize control of the state and command "significant coercive force."

The case of the Egyptian Revolution is challenging when applying Tilly's seemingly narrow definition of *revolutionary situation*. Egyptian revolutionaries did not seek to control the state, and while they did seem to command force (defined simply here as aspects of policing), this was limited to certain areas, such as Tahrir Square (and the barricades around it) and the neighborhood committees. The Egyptian Revolution may also fall short of Goldstone's formula in terms of the presence of elite defection. If we interpret *elite* narrowly as referring to people working within the regime, then Egypt did not witness such defection. Others might argue that the military's decision to distance itself from Mubarak was a major defection that weakened the regime and created its severe crisis. Goldstone himself defines *elite* broadly to include many members of the upper class such as politicians, intellectuals, and professionals, not just state officials and military leaders.

Combining elements of Tilly's and Goldstone's formulations, I suggest that Egypt did, indeed, constitute a revolutionary situation that presented the following:

1. Presence of an acute regime crisis, with some elite defection, along with the regime's inability or unwillingness to control the state or suppress the opposition
2. Formation of an opposition with strong coalitions that challenged state power
3. Presence of mass mobilization that supported the revolutionary forces (the opposition)

What about the revolutionary outcome? Conceivably, political outcomes of revolution could include any of the following: a dictator flees; a dictator abdicates power; a new revolutionary government is formed; the military takes over; a presidential council is formed; revolutionary guards are formed, and/or a revolutionary militia rules for a while; and/or the state collapses, with or without plans by the revolutionaries to seize power and restructure the state.

The literature on revolution presumes that *outcome* refers mostly to the general cases of "success" (broadly speaking, the revolutionaries take over) or "failure" (failing to do so) (see Foran and Goodwin 1993). A significant part of the challenge in analyzing the Egyptian case through these terms is that it has been messy: not only did the revolutionaries fail to take power, but the military acted as if it was siding with the revolution, albeit with counterrevolutionary aims. There were also a number of tricky issues, such as the military coup in 2013. The latter is at once interesting and confusing because it seemed like a popularly supported coup, which the military and counterrevolutionary forces dared to call a new revolution. These are all examples of specific empirical challenges in analyzing the Egyptian case.

Now let us see how some notable works have dealt with these issues in the Egyptian case. At the risk of some simplification, one could argue that there are three camps. The first camp favors a narrow definition of the revolutionary situation, defined here as the period of the revolutionary crisis and understood as the eighteen days of the revolution, from January 25 to February 11. A key example here is Ketchley (2017a). Asef Bayat's "refolution" thesis would also fit here, even though he does not use the term *revolutionary situation*. He prefers the notion of revolution as movement, in contrast to revolutionary change, which is analogous to the outcome in the standard literature.[14]

The second camp could be described as analyzing an extended revolutionary situation or long revolutionary situation (e.g., El-Ghobashy 2021; Holmes 2019). In her important analysis of the Egyptian Revolution, Mona El-Ghobashy thoughtfully suggested that the revolutionary situation in Egypt lasted until the coup in 2013 or perhaps until January 2014, when the military decided to explicitly back Sisi's candidacy for presidency. The reason is that this three-year period witnessed a continued struggle for sovereignty. This is an insightful and persuasive claim. Holmes argued that Egypt's revolution went through three major waves of mobilization: against Mubarak in 2011, against the SCAF with a peak of mobilization in January 2012 and throughout 2012, and against Morsi in 2013.[15] This thoughtful formulation has been popular among many Egyptian revolutionaries—including myself—and I only later realized my mistake. I was mistaken, as I demonstrate in chapter 5, because the mobilization for the coup included two contradictory forces: actors from the January Revolution who thought that this new wave of mobilization was an extension of the original revolution and would end up building a new civil republic, and some forces from the old regime. The military and the deep state were part of manipulating the events, as proven later.

The third camp is best exemplified by the works of Gilbert Achcar (2013) and Maha Abdelrahman (2014), who both suggest that the Egyptian case is a long revolutionary process. Not only do they both rightly suggest that it is impossible to separate the social from the political in the Egyptian case—with which I fully agree—but they also suggest that these tensions would not be resolved in the short term. I believe that the latter makes good sense as well because it takes into account how the revolution was a series of contentious conflicts and revolved around the entanglement of political and social issues, which have been decisive factors in shaping the troubled revolutionary trajectory.

My analysis in the pages to follow is closer to the second and the third camps. It is closer to the second (extended revolutionary situation) because that camp rightly highlights the fluid political struggle for sovereignty over a long period from 2011 to 2013, and perhaps shortly afterward (El-Ghobashy 2021). It is also close to and overlaps with the third camp (long revolutionary process) in its affirmation that it is a major mistake to overlook the social grievances underpinning the political struggle in Egypt's revolution. My own research has been enlightened by the work of these respected scholars. Yet it also differs from theirs in various respects. First, it centers revolutionary actors' role and experience, on the ground, and how they thought about matters such as the struggle to seize power and viewed the state and the regime as they evolved over time (specifically from 2011 to 2013). My approach, guided by the notion of lived contingency, demonstrates how those actors experienced a long chain of indeterminacies and unpredictabilities and made sense of possibilities and containments throughout this period. Second, it provides a temporally sensitive account of the counterrevolution in Egypt.[16] Third, it provides a grounded historicization of the revolution over a long span (from 2000 to 2015).

I interrogate four phases of the revolution: the decade prior to the revolution (prelude to revolutionary possibilities), the period of the revolutionary crisis (peak revolutionary possibilities), the so-called transition to democracy (the waning of revolutionary possibilities, combined with counterrevolutionary coercion), and the events of the military coup in July 2013 (which I describe as the destitution of revolutionary possibilities). I argue that each phase was characterized by unique conjunctures of indeterminacies, mutual uncertainties, and sometimes crisscrossing and overlapping uncertainties between the pro-democracy opposition and the Mubarak regime, followed by the intervening political regimes in the postrevolutionary period, until the military takeover in 2013. I argue that indeterminacies and mutual uncertainties have been *spatialized*. These uncertainties created a dialectical leverage for both the regimes and the opposition, where each party could claim political gravity/sovereign control in the form of temporarily seizing the upper hand in one or more of these spaces: formal political space, street political space, and digital space. Through an analysis that centers lived contingency, I argue that a true understanding of indeterminacies insinuates that revolutionary actors are open to different possibilities and outcomes and not preoccupied with certain outcomes.

To demonstrate briefly why an approach that centers contingency is needed in this messy case, let us see how this analysis differs from the first camp, which is the one that I diverge from the most. I will start with Ketchley, who provides a rich event analysis of the revolution and its aftermath. He describes his approach as follows: "a conjunctural and interactive account of the 25th January Revolution and the post-Mubarak political process, grounding my explanation in a series of relationships: between collective violence and nonviolent activism, protestors and security forces, elections and contentious collective action, elites and street protest movements, and repression and mass mobilization. In doing so, I show how a relational ontology can be employed to interrogate several key assumptions of the literature on civil resistance, emotions, democratization, authoritarian retrenchment, and repression" (2017a, 9).

Ketchley's engagement with the literature is very clever, especially in relation to issues of violence/nonviolence and coalitions during elections in the aftermath of the revolution. But the most interesting and novel contribution is his thesis of fraternization between the military and protesters. Ketchley also provides many sharp observations, such as how "revolutionary aspirations were efficiently harnessed and redeployed on 30 June 2013" (2017a, 6). In spite of all these strengths, one of the key problems in this analysis is the examination of these contentious episodes from 2011 to 2013 separately from one another but also frequently separate from the revolution itself. Most important, despite the rich event analysis of the revolution and the political process in its aftermath, including a series of mobilizations and countermobilizations, one cannot see where these (seemingly) isolated events fit within the contingencies of revolution *and* counterrevolution. In short, many of these events are ambiguous in relation to the original eighteen days.

I turn now to Bayat, giving his argument more attention because of its sophistication. Bayat suggests that the Egyptian Revolution was neither "revolution in the sense of the twentieth-century experiences (i.e., rapid and radical transformation of the state pushed by popular movements from below) nor simply reform (i.e., gradual and managed change carried out often from above and within the existing structural arrangements)" (2017, 17–18). The Egyptian Revolution—like the Tunisian and Yemeni uprisings—was, according to Bayat, a "refolution," which refers to "revolutionary movements that emerged to compel the incumbent states to change themselves, to carry out meaningful reform on behalf of the revolution" (18).

The term *refolution* was coined by British historian Timothy Garton Ash in his analysis of the events in Hungary and Poland in 1989.[17] The notion of refolution has been taken up and variously defined by a number of authors. Goldstone (2009, 19) emphasizes that it is a type of democratic revolution in which changes are limited to electoral reforms, while Jeff Goodwin (2001, 260) defines refolution as negotiated reform and specifically suggests that refolutions result from collaboration between reformist movements and factions of old Communist parties (see also Lawson 2017). Both specifically discuss the concept in relation to the eastern European revolutions of 1989. Bayat (2017), in contrast, discusses the concept in the context of the Arab uprisings.

Thus, it seems that there is no consensus about what *refolution* means. I propose that it is crucial to distinguish between three different definitions of a refolution: (1) a revolt that is motivated by and includes calls for political and electoral reform, (2) a revolt that is based on negotiated reform that mostly takes place between reformist movements and factions of the old regime, and (3) a revolt that ends with factions of the old regime leading the transition. These subtle differences can have huge impacts on the outcomes of a given uprising. Some of the three criteria existed in Egypt, with notable variance. For instance, there was no negotiated reform; perhaps only the Muslim Brotherhood was seriously engaged in negotiations with Mubarak during the uprising. But the most important element was that the uprising ended with the military seizing power. People celebrated after Mubarak's resignation speech, delivered by his vice president, Omar Suleiman. In some sense, February 11 was both a military coup and a transition imposed by the military (with international support). That it was celebrated by Egyptians as a revolutionary victory complicates the picture.

Bayat's take on refolution is useful in certain aspects. First, it accurately points to the most central paradox of the revolution: having a force of the old regime managing the transition to "democracy."[18] Second, it highlights some of the structural limitations of the uprising, including an essentially conservative global context that opposed radical change, and the ways that most revolutionaries in the Arab Spring "were rich in tactics of mobilization but poor in vision and strategy of transformation; they adopted loose, flexible, and horizontal organization but one that suffered from fragmentation; they espoused civil opposition but overlooked the danger of restoration; they were concerned more with democracy, human rights, and rule of law than reallocation of property and distributive justice" (Bayat 2017, 18).

However, my twofold critique of Bayat is not only of his forceful claim that the Egyptian Revolution was about recognition more than redistribution (something I critique in chapter 4) but also of the teleological nature of his argument—limiting his analysis to what happened on February 11, 2011—in addition to the fact that he downplays the role of counterrevolutions. From the perspective of contingency, Bayat seems to present a case of predestined outcome (what happened on February 11) and ignores the possibilities that presumably existed before this date. Put differently, it is not clear whether the Egyptian refolution was born as a refolution or became one on February 11, 2011. Both cases are problematic. The first is problematic because it ignores the possibilities that existed during the uprising but also seemingly presumes the homogeneity of revolutionary actors: they are all "refolutionaries" in this case, perhaps. But Bayat (2017, 25) himself was explicit about the variety of classes that participated in the revolution. But through the focus on the idea that the uprising "emerged to compel the incumbent states to change themselves" (18), it seems that Bayat is indicating that Egyptian refolution became such on February 11, 2011. This is problematic because it assumes a final closure of the events on that day. Bayat also does not explain why the state (the military) decided to make reforms, if the uprising did not reach a revolutionary situation in the first place and was only a movement. According to his analysis, events in Egypt in 2011, 2012, and 2013 all were refolutions, without any difference. In short, Bayat's analysis is rich in discussing the limits of the revolution, while not giving proper attention to its possibilities. Most important, he downplays the role of counterrevolution. Bayat states, "The question is not whether the counterrevolution was responsible for stalling or hijacking the Arab revolutions; all revolutions carry within themselves the germs of counterrevolutionary intrigues. The question is whether the revolutions were revolutionary enough to offset the perils of restoration" (16).

Not only does Bayat not provide us with any satisfactory analysis of counterrevolution, but he also assumes that it is a given or static thing, born within the revolution with the goals of restoration.[19] One cannot deny that Egyptian revolutionaries made many mistakes, including overlooking the vicious nature of counterrevolution and being naive about the true aims of the military. However, the key problem here is not that he puts the blame mainly on the side of the revolutionaries but that he assumes that the relation between revolution and counterrevolution is static and happens in a vacuum, and the question of momentum almost does not exist.

A challenging anonymous reviewer asked me to define *revolution*. That has proven to be an extremely difficult and interesting task, as one cannot separate the definition of *revolution* from the changing knowledge about the concept. Yet this question has helped me to clarify how I approached the Egyptian Revolution. There are at least two reasons it is extremely difficult to define *revolution*, despite the bounty of definitions in the scholarly library. The first is what I describe as the problem of the peculiar ontology (or ontologies) of revolution, meaning the fact that revolution has many competing essences. Scholars and theorists have attempted to answer the question of revolution's essence by suggesting that revolutions should be understood in terms of dualities. One way is to look at revolutions as aspirations (for a desired ideal or better society by idealists) and as reality (how it actually happened or how pragmatist actors made it work). In this duality, there would be a tension between idealistic revolutionary actors and pragmatic revolution actors. Another duality is looking at revolution as an emancipatory project, or liberatory experience, and as a totalizing experience (Lawson 2019, 16). In this sense, successful revolutions can lead to an emancipatory society, but they also have the potential to pave the way to an autocratic regime (such as in France in the early 1800s and possibly Iran a few years after the Iranian Revolution in 1979). A third way is to look at revolution as a movement or as a change (Bayat 2017, 15), which speaks, with some slight difference, to the established terminology of *revolutionary situation* and *revolutionary outcome*. Of course, these dualities overlap in any given revolution. In reality, certain actors who seem to adopt one perspective may change their position over time. I argue that these multifaceted realities of revolutions create tensions that could coexist, overlap, and change all the time. This creates an enormous challenge for scholars of revolutions, for all these dimensions matter and shape the making and the trajectory of revolutions. No matter how sophisticated one scholar's analysis is, they will never be able to present a comprehensive account of what happened or what is relevant in a revolution.[20] The peculiar ontology (or ontologies) of revolution is the first main challenge of defining revolutions.

The second is the continual change in the meaning and practice of revolutions, leading to new paradigms to make sense of them and their changes. Revolutions have happened throughout history, and they continue to happen. The production of knowledge around revolutions is constantly trying to keep up with revolutions (see Beck 2018; Goldstone 2003; Kumar 2007). Scholars have distinguished among premodern revolts, revolutions that created what we describe as modernity, and revolutions in the postmodern world. Other distinctions have included social/classical or political and anticolonialist or third world revolutions and revolutions in the late-capitalist or neoliberal era. Thus, we are dealing with a moving object. Indeed, some major claims are made in the literature, for example, that the age of social/classical revolutions is over. While this is a reasonable claim that could be supported by evidence, it is also problematic because it presumes some primacy of classical revolutions as a category, and it also implicitly invokes end-of-history arguments. In today's world, more than at any previous time in history, revolutions and counterrevolutions have become a global phenomenon. Thus, a more reasonable concept that exists in the literature today is that revolutions have not become obsolete, yet their meaning is changing.

This is why I argue that it is not easy or even viable to present a new definition of revolutions. Yet I believe that the classic definition proposed by Theda Skocpol is still relevant and useful insofar as it rightly highlights that the real issues at stake in revolutions are states and classes. Skocpol defines social revolutions as "rapid, basic transformations of a society's state and class structures; and they are accompanied and in part carried through by class-based revolts from below" (1979, 4). Skocpol famously distinguished between political revolutions, which entail a change in state institutions, and social revolutions, which entail a change in both state institutions and social structure. If defining revolutions today is an impossible task, a more feasible one is to present some parameters or theses about understanding revolutions today. The following are four theses that guided my thinking in this book.

The first is that the terms *revolutionary situation* and *revolutionary outcome* are critical and still matter in our understanding of revolutions. They matter because they tell us about the moment of revolutionary explosion and about the revolution's supposed fate, or, to use the positivist terminology, the origins or causes and outcomes of revolutions. But while these remain critical, it is important not to treat them as technical jargon, without giving sufficient attention to why a certain situation would lead to an outcome. Indeed, there seems to be a problem in the canonical literature, which emphasizes successful revolutions. As Goldstone (1998a) and the authors of *Dynamics of Contention* (McAdam, Tarrow, and Tilly 2001b) famously argue, there are many overlaps among collective action, social movements, and revolutions: "Successful revolutions share some characteristics with social movements, rebellions, failed revolutions and cycles of protest" (194).

The second thesis relates to the broader context of the current neoliberal global order or neoliberal capitalism. It is impossible to do justice to this broad context in a brief discussion like this, but I echo scholars (Armbrust 2018; Bayat 2017, 20; Kutay 2022) who maintain that neoliberal capitalism has contradictory effects on revolutions. By *contradictory effects*, I mean that neoliberal capitalism enables revolutions and also works to contain them. On the one hand, neoliberal globalization increases poverty and inequality, enables corruption and cronyism, and sponsors police brutality and racism. Thus, it motivates revolts. On the other hand, neoliberal globalization is complex, cutting through many levels in any given society and worldwide. It appropriates radical thinking and action, commodifies revolutionary ideas, and has been internalized by neoliberal subjects. It is important to attend to both dimensions—the enabling and the limiting—in our analyses and not to focus on one at the expense of the other. I also argue it is almost analytically impossible to compare the enabling factors of neoliberalism with its appropriating and damaging effects when one is studying revolutions. Yet we must acknowledge both effects in our research and do our best to attend to both aspects in our analysis.

The third thesis relates to the established wisdom in the literature about the dichotomy of social revolution and political revolution. Whether we agree with the statement that the age of great social revolutions is over (Drescher 1992)—a statement that I see as laden with modernization theory thinking and perhaps entailing an underlying acquiescence to the end-of-history thesis—and regardless of why we have taken this established dichotomy for granted for years, I argue that the social dimensions of revolutions and their political aspects have become more intertwined than ever, because neoliberalism does not work without the facilitation and support of political regimes. The very idea of the disappearance of the role of the state under free markets is erroneous. The state regulates and/or deregulates, and enables heavy policing and repression, for the sake of the markets and profits. This has been the case with the Mubarak regime and continues to be the case under the current military rule in Egypt. The social and political aspects have been more intertwined than ever because revolutions and counterrevolutions have become transnational processes in which many global actors are involved, reflecting arrays of politics, economies, and conflicts about social ways of living. One good example of these issues is transnational repression and the way counterrevolutions became regional and transnational in the context of the Arab Spring (see Allinson 2022; Lawson 2015b; Moss 2016). Recent critical democratization analyses affirm that democratization won't work or succeed without categorical equality. It is also not possible to progress without a global environment that supports and contributes to sustaining democracy, not containing or limiting it to the most superficial levels of procedural democracy under a free market. In the context of the erosion of liberal democracy as we know it (see Brown 2015; Castells 2018), even in the most established democratic nations, it becomes all the more difficult to conceive of a successful democratization process in developing nations.

The fourth and last thesis is that revolutions do not follow paradigms but contribute to creating new paradigms, waiting for this newly created paradigm to be dismantled. By *paradigms*, I refer to theoretical and analytical frameworks that are used in scholarly disciplines to analyze social phenomena. One could argue that only a successful revolution can earn this name and can create a paradigm, an important discussion that I cannot resolve in these pages. Here I agree with Mohammed Bamyeh and Sari Hanafi, who remind us that "revolutions are opportunities to learn something new. The worst analytical insult to a revolution is to use it as an opportunity to apply mechanically an existing theory or model" (2015, 343). Similarly, sociologists Frances Hasso and Zakia Salime observe that "revolutions fit uneasily within totalizing ideology, strategy, theory or method" (2016, 6). Charles Kurzman (2009, 5) famously argued against explanations, calling them retroactive predictions. Jack Goldstone (2014, 6) notably suggests that revolutions are like earthquakes—we cannot predict them with any precision. The only thing social scientists can do is to gain new knowledge and improve their analyses for the future. Indeed, some scholars have argued that the age of volcanic or explosive and radical revolutions is over. The idea here is that classical revolutions are radical and violent (and explosive) and postmodern or contemporary revolutions are not. Yet I would like to distinguish between the idea of revolutions being explosive as an analytic model and the description of revolutions being explosive as a historical argument.[21] The distinction is useful analytically. Nevertheless, given the excessive global militarization and the police violence that has become almost a global norm, it is difficult to imagine that at least some future revolutions won't happen without profound eruptions, possibly radical violence. This is also a great example of the complex relation between revolutions and paradigm making, neither of which is settled. Even within the same categories, such as anticolonial revolutions, or even in the same context, revolts have different characteristics, despite scholars' effort to establish commonalities and laws.

What Lies Ahead

Historical ethnography, which employs archival and ethnographic research simultaneously and in conversation, is at the core of my interdisciplinary approach. Throughout, I sought to produce not only a rigorous account of the famous eighteen days of the revolution but also an analysis attentive to the historical context and the constantly shifting spatial and social dynamics. I explain in detail how this worked in appendix 3, which includes a detailed description of my interviews and the informants' demographics, as well as information on my historical and documentary research.

In chapter 1 I present a historical overview of the politics of street protest in Egypt, especially in the decade before the revolution, along with an overview of previous protests in Tahrir Square in relation to the evolution of neopatrimonial police state in Egypt. I also demonstrate how this history informed the 2011 revolution and discuss the rise of social media in political dissent, particularly in the decade before the uprising. In chapter 2 I examine the rise of Tahrir's revolutionary repertoire and consider how and why Tahrir constituted a physical and symbolic boundary of the Egyptian Revolution. More specifically, I examine how specific processes drove the squaring of the revolution in Tahrir, such as the physical sites of battles and clashes near Tahrir, the "virtual" making of Tahrir through social media, the establishment of the Tahrir camp, and the mutual recognition by the regime and the protesters. In chapter 3 I investigate key modes of action outside Tahrir, especially the popular committees. I provide an anatomy of the popular committees in Egypt and situate these committees within a triangle of power that existed in Egypt at the time: the military, Tahrir revolutionaries, and the popular committees. In chapters 4 and 5, respectively, I present and investigate my claim that the Egyptian Revolution had two sets of demands, or souls: political and social, analyzing why the former became more visible and eclipsed the latter. The tension between the revolution's two souls impacted the trajectory of the uprising, especially in the transitional period. Specifically, in chapter 4 I provide a historicization of how the democratic reformist demands became dominant in the revolution but also demonstrate how radical social demands and grievances existed during the revolution. I present key pieces of evidence to demonstrate the existence of the latter (the radical soul), such as working-class strikes, and present new data on the demographics of the martyrs and the injured of the revolution. And in chapter 5 I examine Egypt's troubled transition to democracy, which involved, I argue, elections without democratization. I provide a short and close historization of the period from 2011 to 2015 in Egypt with a focus on the intersection of revolutionary mobilization and electoral and constitutional politics.

Finally, in chapter 6 I analyze the dramatic closure of political space in the aftermath of the 2013 military coup—a moment seen by many as the death of the revolution. I present a historically sensitive and disaggregated account of the counterrevolution in Egypt. I examine Sisi's rise to power, and I propose the notion of the paranoid regime to make sense of Egypt's new authoritarianism today. I also demonstrate that activists chose to withdraw and did not give up their agency despite the unlimited repression in Egypt today.

Ultimately, *Revolution Squared* is a story about the power of Egyptians—both the power they had and their inability to recognize its vastness in the moment. One sentiment that pervades the book is that the praxis of revolution is like love. Egyptians have a proverb "Ein el hobb amiyah." It's a bit like saying "Love is blind." This book is about how much we loved the revolution, as well as how blinded we were to the ways power, including our own, was even then met by the dynamism and the viciousness of counterrevolutionary forces. Revolution moves forward, and the outcome is never certain. It is action, with all the upheaval and uncertainty and possibility one can imagine.

prelude to revolutionary possibilities

I

TAHRIR AND POLITICAL
PROTEST IN EGYPT

I saw myself marching in a large demonstration
    that filled the streets and squares
At the front of the march, someone raised a huge
    banner with images of Ahmed 'Urabi,
Saad Zaghloul and Mostafa Al-Nahhas
Demonstrators raised their voices, shouting for a
    new constitution to suit our era
The riot police were not able to break it up
The march seemed like it was determined to
    continue on toward victory
—NAGUIB MAHFOUZ, *THE DREAMS
OF DEPARTURE*, DREAM 217

A mere twenty-four hours before the tragic events of September 11, 2001, a small protest took place in Tahrir (Liberation) Square, organized by the Egyptian Popular Committee in Solidarity with the Palestinian Intifada (EPCSPI), which had formed in the wake of the 2000 Al-Aqsa Intifada. Most of the EPCSPI's activities revolved around collecting medical aid and food, which they delivered in caravans to Palestinians in Gaza and the West Bank. Sometimes the EPCSPI convened political education events, but they were unable to organize public protests due to excessive police repression. Therefore, despite its small size, the September 10 protest was an escalation. The EPCSPI announced that they planned to march with a small delegation to the American embassy in Cairo, a couple minutes' walk from Tahrir Square, to submit a letter condemning the United States' unconditional support of Israeli aggressions against Palestinians. The embassy was known as a fortress in downtown Cairo, one of the most secure places in the capital. As protesters reached the square, they faced the heavy presence of riot police in the area, especially around the Mogamma governmental complex and Simone de Beauvoir Street, blocking access to the embassy (see Dawoud 2001). This time, however, the police presence did not deter EPCSPI members from protesting, even if it meant they had to be very careful in navigating their way through the highly controlled space. A few members walked separately into the Mogamma, pretending to be regular citizens seeking bureaucratic services, and then they suddenly all gathered at once at the front of the building. The police were taken by surprise, an important element in forming any protest under Hosni Mubarak's autocratic rule. Once the protest was underway, the police established a heavy cordon around it. As a rule, the government never approved legal requests for protests, as required by the 1914 Assembly Law, enacted by British colonial officials.

I was present at this protest and recall how, when I arrived at Tahrir, all I could see was the very substantial police cordon blocking any view of the entrance to the Mogamma. I had walked from the nearby American University in Cairo (AUC) campus, where I was studying for my master's degree, toward the protest. When I arrived, the police cordon had already been formed. I mustered the courage to ask the officers to let me through. In most cases, they were forcing people away. They tried to intimidate me too but eventually let me through after much verbal harassment and dirty looks. When I was finally able to join the protest, I realized there were no more than two hundred to three hundred protesters, with the antiriot police outnumbering us three to one. Protesters were squeezed in the area outside the Mogamma, with very little room to breathe and walk around. I knew almost every single protester, including leaders of the EPCSPI, individuals from leftist parties and groups, a few trade unionists, and some young members of the Revolutionary Socialists. I walked around, greeting protesters and enjoying quick interactions amid the chanting.

I vividly recall my contradictory feelings while participating in this protest. On the one hand, I felt that the group was victorious in liberating this small space, an area no larger than one hundred square feet. They owned the space, albeit very briefly. I remember walking around the liberated space, talking to people and reading the signs they held. On the other hand, when I looked over at the edge of the protest, I confronted the repressive ring of riot police, a reminder that Mubarak's police state had the upper hand over both Tahrir Square and the country as a whole. The very dense police cordon signified that our liberation of this small area was both partial and temporary. The tension between this brief liberation and the police line controlling it embodied the ongoing standoff between Mubarak's dictatorship and control of political space, including the physical space of Tahrir Square, and the Egyptian opposition. The two-hour protest was a short-lived demonstration of the possibility of people power.

Ironically, from my childhood and teenage years, I recall Tahrir Square as a large, welcoming space with generous patches of lawn, an open plaza where citizens enjoyed the green space and iconic pedestal. Friends and families met there for picnics, especially on Fridays, the weekly day of rest. I recall how much I enjoyed sitting there and generally being around that area. When the first line of the underground metro opened in 1987, the square lost some of its charm; the pedestal was removed, and only a few benches remained. Yet people still enjoyed sipping tea ordered from the many stands and street vendors around the square. Over the next few years, in the early 1990s, the remaining benches were also removed, and fences were erected at various points, presumably to facilitate car traffic. But this also restricted human traffic, further reducing the public's access to the square. In the late 1990s, a project was launched to build a public parking garage, but construction did not start until 2015. Yet for almost a quarter of a century, overlapping with the time of the 2011 revolution, some twenty thousand square meters of the physical space of Tahrir Square were fenced off (Tariq 2014). Despite these changes, Egyptians still found ways to protest and seize the square on a few occasions. I first experienced the change in my own relationship to Tahrir when I joined the September 10 protest: instead of a space for hanging out and relaxing, I now saw it as a place for protest and public dissent.

This chapter discusses the different manifestations of Tahrir as a site of protest, focusing on a core relational dynamic: the regime learned new methods of repression, only for protesters to challenge them with new tactics. In the September 10 protest, officers preemptively blocked the public area before a planned protest, and the protesters then surprised the police by going to another area and then erupting in spontaneous protest. In other words, the relation between regime and public political dissent was never static or uniform.

Let us step back to contemplate this odd experience of temporary liberation within a police cordon. Most social movement literature assumes a dichotomy between democratic and authoritarian regimes, based on which scholars propose generalizations about the emergence of political dissent. One such thesis is that authoritarian states restrict dissent in public space, while such space is mostly open in democratic states. Against this dichotomy, I propose that we should think of democratization and de-democratization as contentious processes (Markoff 2015; Tilly 2007a). I argue that both democratization and de-democratization are contingent outcomes of interactions among a number of claims and counterclaims. Democratization is contested directly and indirectly, on ballots and in the streets. Democratization in general is a complex process, conditional on key developments, such as the integration of interpersonal trust networks into public politics, the insulation of public politics from categorical inequalities, and the elimination or neutralization of autonomous, coercion-controlling power centers in ways that augment the influence of ordinary people over public politics and increase the control of public politics over state performance (Tilly 2007a, 78).[1]

Here I also deploy the formulation of the contentious politics framework, where repertoires of contention are understood to be in dynamic relation with regimes (McAdam, Tarrow, and Tilly 2001a; Tilly and Tarrow 2015). For example, Charles Tilly and Sidney Tarrow suggest that regimes may be generally classified according to the mix of political repertoires they engender; each regime has prescribed, tolerated, or forbidden political performances. They also suggest that a critical understanding of regimes should look at two dimensions: capacity and democracy. Thus, roughly speaking, regimes can be located on a continuum of four ideal-typical configurations—high-capacity undemocratic, high-capacity democratic, low-capacity undemocratic, and low-capacity democratic—that produce specific types of contention (Tilly and Tarrow 2015, 58). However, I suggest that this way of looking at regime-repertoire relations remains too unidimensional, focused on what the state will or will not allow. I argue that through this interaction, which is undoubtably asymmetrical, the relation is much more dialectical, with both regime personnel and dissenters learning from each other and eventually finding new means of control (by the regime) or dissent (by protesters).

Thus, we should think of protests and dissent in public spaces as dynamic processes contingent on both external and internal factors. The external factors include colonial and postcolonial relations. Both the regimes and the opposition deployed these against one another, and global superpowers often used both support and pressure—though mostly support—of the regime. And protests always depend on internal factors (economic, social, and political) that are always shifting and contingent. Protesters have to make choices under these changing circumstances, whereby opposition forces and pro-democracy protesters always try to challenge the confinement of public political space, expanding it through formal channels (elections), street protests, or internet and social media activism. Besides, contention/opposition actors also practice curiosity, risk-taking, and daring.

When looking at this dialectical relation between the temporary liberation of the square and the heavy police presence, one must necessarily examine the reason for the protest. The immediate goal of the September 10, 2001, protest was to express solidarity with Palestinians, but it was met with repression. In fact, during that protest and for a few years afterward, many pro-democracy activists in Egypt knew that the repressive authoritarian state was entangled with regional and global politics. Later in this chapter, as we look at the history of protest in Tahrir Square itself, we will realize how the postcolonial state, ostensibly formed as an anti-imperialist state, became implicated in US imperialism in the region and developed into an unremittingly authoritarian state.

This chapter has three goals. First, I present a historical overview of the politics of street protest in Egypt, especially in the decade before the revolution. Second, I present an overview of protests in Tahrir Square in relation to the evolution of the postcolonial state in Egypt, as well as demonstrate the ways in which this history informed the 2011 revolution. Third, I analyze the rise of social media in political dissent, particularly in the decade before the uprising, and situate it in the broader composition of political space, which I argue includes formal politics, street politics, and social media spaces. I conclude with some remarks about how this composition changed over time and how this change was interpreted during the revolution.

The Rise of "Street" Politics in Egypt

The September 10 protest happened in a broader context of the rise of street politics in Egypt. The main temporal marker was the Palestinian Intifada of September 2000. From that year onward, major shifts began to transform the battle between the opposition and the Mubarak regime over public political space. "Street politics" thus emerged, marking not only new sites of protest but also new strategies on both "sides." I use the term *street(s)* here to refer to actual physical streets but also other public spaces of protest such as the steps of public buildings, squares, bus stations, police stations, and court-rooms. Whether staging large-scale street rallies or merely occupying the steps of key government buildings, protesters used their bodies and their mere presence to politicize public spaces and register their opposition to the regime. For their part, state security forces became increasingly aggressive and violent in their attempts to repress and control these spaces, developing new tactics and specific targets along the way. Over the years, all parties involved began to recognize just how much was at stake in these spatialized struggles. It is important to stress, however, that the relationship between street politics and formal politics is complex. To the extent that Egyptians began to seek out new public political space, their goal was not so much to sidestep or oppose formal political channels as to challenge and expand the latter, to expose them as corrupt and demand that they be made more democratic.

Street Rallies since 2000

The first major street rallies in Egypt since 1977 were sparked, in fact, not by domestic conflicts but by regional politics.[2] On September 28, 2000, Israeli defense minister Ariel Sharon visited the Temple Mount / Al-Aqsa Mosque, the most important religious site in Old Jerusalem. The visit was seen by most Palestinians and other Arabs and Muslims in the region as deeply provocative. The Israeli army arrested some protesters and dispersed others using force, triggering the Second Intifada, which was met, in turn, by further violence from Israeli authorities. Before long, Arabs and Muslims throughout the region and in various parts of the world launched protests in solidarity with the Palestinians. In Egypt the protests began spontaneously. A group of Egyptian activists and intellectuals formed the EPCSPI and began collecting donations to be sent to Palestinians. The group also sponsored protests in the street, which were joined by other spontaneous protests, especially on Fridays after prayers in the mosques. These large spontaneous rallies lasted for a few months.

The first few protests were very surprising to the regime. Indeed, the huge numbers of participants were a surprise to both the protesters themselves and the police. I myself participated in some of these protests and saw tens of thousands of people gathered in the streets of downtown Cairo, met by similar numbers of security forces, who were ultimately unable to prevent the rallies. Street protests occurred almost every day for the first few weeks of

October 2000 in front of the Press Syndicate and the Egyptian Bar Association headquarters in downtown Cairo. Police used violence and arrests, but the sheer number of protesters created a momentum that buoyed the rallies and encouraged others to join.

Protests spread to colleges and even to elementary, junior high, and high schools, where kids and teenagers started to carry small signs and chant against Sharon and in solidarity with Palestinians. Faculty at the AUC formed a Faculty for Palestine group that met and worked with student groups to organize protests and solidarity events on campus. One rally organized by AUC faculty in the first week of October 2000 was seen as a particular success by activists because faculty and students dared to walk outside campus, carrying signs of solidarity with Palestinians. Around that time, on October 8, 2000, Hossam el-Hamalawy, a socialist student and activist at the AUC, was arrested and went on to become one of Egypt's most famous bloggers.[3]

Protests in solidarity with the Intifada continued for a few months until they finally died down and eventually vanished, with a few exceptions primarily in response to subsequent attacks by Israeli occupation forces on Palestinians in Gaza or the West Bank. This diminishment of public protests could be explained by the continuing police assaults on protesters as well as protesters' own feelings of exhaustion and the movement's dwindling momentum.

Large-scale street rallies were not seen again until 2002 in reaction to Sharon's reinvasion of the West Bank. Then, in March 2003 external events again prompted widespread public reaction—this time, the US-led invasion of Iraq. Activists in Egypt announced their plan to gather in protest in Tahrir Square. Once again, AUC students were key participants, as the university's main campus is located right on Tahrir Square. Indeed, AUC students were the first to arrive at the square, and though they numbered but a few hundred, the police were reluctant to disperse or attack the protesters because so many AUC students are from upper-class and elite Egyptian families or the children of high-ranking military or police officers and other government officials. This created just enough leverage in terms of time. While police hesitated, thousands of protesters from mosques and elsewhere joined the rally, and the antiwar protests of March 20–21, 2003, soon grew to become the largest sit-in in the history of Egypt prior to the 2011 revolution.

Both protesters and police learned important lessons as a result of this reemergence of street rallies in the early 2000s. According to many activists I spoke with, the 2000 protests and the violent police response served as a turning point, after which they became increasingly critical of the Mubarak regime and determined to organize against it. Many wondered why the regime was attacking them with such force when they were merely protesting in solidarity with the Palestinians. Between 2000 and 2003, and then after the March 2003 sit-in, street rallies did not disappear entirely; rather, protesters began to adapt their strategies. Youth activists in particular learned the value of extremely sudden, spontaneous rallies in populous neighborhoods. As one youth activist explained to me about protests occurring in 2010, by which time such tactics had become common, "The main reason the police could attack rallies is that they knew the time and the location of the protest. Hence, we decided to surprise them."[4] The tactic involved small groups of activists gathering in centrally located neighborhoods that often suffer from terrible social and economic conditions. The protesters would suddenly start to chant and sing, confident that the public would join in. The rallies generally lasted sixty to ninety minutes, at the most, before the police arrived, but by then the protesters had achieved their modest purpose: to carve out, if only temporarily, new public political space.

For their part, police also began to adjust their tactics. From 2000 onward, it became common to use plainclothes officers and informants to infiltrate and spread chaos among protesters, spy on activists, and even assist in dispersing rallies by force. The police also learned that it is best to stop rallies at their source before they can gather momentum. In many cases, the sources were mosques, and thus these were increasingly targeted by police, who would occupy the space or prevent worshippers from leaving as a group, forcing them to head out single file between two columns of riot police. Police were also quick to recognize the threat posed by student activism, and they began to work closely with AUC security to prevent a repeat of the 2003 sit-in. Some AUC students received threats from the police and warnings from their parents that such protests would not be allowed again. Many foreign students at the AUC were threatened with deportation if they participated in future protests.[5] Activist students were highly surveilled in almost all Egyptian public universities by Egyptian security. Perhaps the most pernicious new repressive strategies, however, were those the police developed targeting female protesters in particular.

"The Street Is Ours"

In 2005 the Mubarak regime decided to hold a referendum on a few constitutional amendments, opening the door to multicandidate presidential elections for the first time in Egyptian history. However, the changes also established extremely difficult requirements that candidates, both within and outside of the party system, had to meet. Ultimately, the changes were designed to pave the road for Mubarak's son to run in the future, or to give Mubarak himself a chance to run for a fifth term. Recognizing this, pro-democracy activists gathered in Cairo on May 25, 2005, in front of the Egyptian High Court Building (Dar Al-Qadaa Al-Aaly) and in front of both the Press Syndicate and Egyptian Bar Association headquarters. The police responded with organized widespread sexual harassment and rape of female protesters, many of whom were arrested and dragged through the street by both uniformed and plainclothes police. Some were kidnapped and left out on remote desert highways after being sexually assaulted. The assaults reflected sexist and patriarchal assumptions that women should not be in public space to protest and that they are "weaker" and need solidarity and help. From the police point of view, attacking women protesters was effective for two main reasons: it discouraged women from protesting in public in the future, and it rendered men easier targets for violence, as they would be busy "protecting" women, or the overall number of protesters would simply be lower, thus making men easier to isolate and attack.

Perhaps not surprisingly, some of the leaders of the pro-democracy Egyptian Movement for Change (Kefaya, or Enough) movement decided to stop protesting in the streets for a while due to the risks involved. Resisting this attack on women, as well as the Kefaya leaders' decision, many Egyptian feminists and activists launched a new campaign named "The Street Is Ours."[6] On June 1, 2005, the group organized a protest outside the entrance stairs of the Egyptian Press Syndicate headquarters in downtown Cairo, carrying banners with the slogan "We will not be scared." The police force stood outside, cordoning the syndicate. In the years leading up to the revolution, being cordoned or arrested by the police while protesting on the syndicate's stairs became common experiences for protesters. The movement lasted for a while, organizing a few more small protests and releasing documents about the rights of women and pro-democracy movements in Egypt to have access to public political space. Many female activists who participated in the revolution told me that the police attacks of May 25, 2005, and the subsequent "The Street Is Ours" campaign in June changed their lives. Indeed, since May 25, 2005, feminist and progressive activists in Egypt have continued to organize an annual conference or protest every year to commemorate the attacks and the movement. As even the name of this group revealed, the "streets" had become a potential political symbol and site for both police and protesters, yet the actual spaces in which "street" protests took place gradually began to change, along with the specific repertoires of protest.

After 2005 a new pattern began to emerge. In the face of intense police repression and the development of specifically gendered tactics, large-scale street rallies subsided, and protests took on smaller, more diffuse forms. Activists launched petition campaigns around various issues and organized boycotts—not only of the elections but also of big corporations such as cell phone companies, to protest bad service and constantly increasing bills. In some cases, people simply refused to pay their electric bills, to protest bad service and the constant lack of power in various areas of Egypt, especially in urban centers. In other cases, individual government officials were sued for corruption, or to try to force a release of information about a detainee. But the most visible forms of protest were those that involved crowds of people using their bodies and their mere presence to politicize public space.

As large street rallies declined, lower-profile tactics such as sit-ins and stand-ins became more common, targeting not only streets and outdoor spaces like squares but also the indoor and outdoor premises of key buildings concentrated in urban centers. The most common targets were court buildings, police stations, and particularly the headquarters of the Press Syndicate and Egyptian Bar Association in downtown Cairo.[7] The range of spaces was captured in a 2010 study conducted by Essem Syam that mapped the main sites of protest in the decade before the revolution, particularly between 2005 and 2010 (see table 1.1).

Protesters would gather in front of, or around the steps of, buildings, knowingly drawing the police but also hoping that their efforts would encourage the public to join or the media to cover the event. Protest signs were specifically crafted to speak to the public, featuring slogans such as "We are here for you and us" and "Our people, listen to us, we are standing here for you and us." Other signs even addressed the police officers themselves, targeting the lower ranks of the riot police by telling them, "You are poor or marginalized and oppressed like us, and one day you will join us," or "Do not do violence to or shoot at your people."

One of the most important protests was a stand-in in front of the Ministry of the Interior in June 2010, in response to the killing of the young activist Khaled Said. The initial protest drew no more than a hundred protesters yet was surrounded and cordoned off by thousands of soldiers and riot police. Pictures of this protest later became iconic for many activists after the revolution, who looked at the image and often commented something along the lines of "Remember, we were once as small as this."

Table 1.1. New Spaces of Political Protest in Egypt before the Revolution

Places of Protest	Examples
In front of court buildings	The High Court Building (Dar al-Qadaa Al-Aaly) in downtown Cairo The Supreme Administrative Court in Dokki Inside lawyers' rooms in the courts
In workplaces	Bus and subway stations Schools and colleges Headquarters of education districts Hospitals Main railway station in Cairo
In front of government buildings	Government cabinet headquarters in Cairo Parliament buildings in Cairo Specific ministry buildings Police stations Governorate headquarters Local government buildings
In front of trade unions and syndicates	Egyptian Trade Union Federation headquarters Various professional syndicates' headquarters (e.g., doctors, engineers, lawyers, press)—all near Tahrir Square in downtown Cairo
In streets and public spaces in general	Various streets, highways, and squares, especially Tahrir Square in Cairo

Source: Adapted from Siyam (2010, 74).

The other forms of protest that emerged prominently during this period were strikes and labor sit-ins (see El-Merghany 2009). Between 2006 and 2008, there was a particularly steep increase in labor protests in Egypt. Joel Beinin and blogger Hossam el-Hamalawy (2007) observed, "The longest and strongest wave of worker protest since the end of World War II is rolling through Egypt." In 2006, there were 200 strikes, and in 2007, 850 strikes and sit-ins.[8] Many of the labor sit-ins were against factory closures brought on by neoliberal policies, and most of them targeted the state-chartered Egyptian Trade Union Federation headquarters in downtown Cairo, near Tahrir

Square. One particularly important event was in December 2007, when a group of real estate tax collectors staged a sit-in at the headquarters of the ministerial cabinet, steps from Tahrir Square. Around three thousand men and women participated in the eleven-day sit-in, effecting a 90 percent drop in tax collection. Protesters even managed to occupy the space in front of parliament, though not the building itself. Ultimately, the sit-in was successful because it was backed by a parallel strike of fifty-five thousand real estate tax officers throughout the country and culminated in the launching of an independent union. The formation of the union was celebrated widely across the opposition in Egypt, as it was the first independent trade union formed outside state control in contemporary Egypt.[9]

I participated in many sit-ins and stand-ins, and around 75 percent of the activists I interviewed told me that they also participated in these kinds of protests. Based on my field observations and these interviews, I note that these protest methods shared the following three features. First, the protests tended to be small and short-lived. Protesters focused on occupying very limited spaces, for an average of one to two hours. Multiple squares were the sites for such sit-ins and stand-ins: Tahrir Square (most important) but also Al-Sayeda Zainab, Shobra Circle (Dawaran), Talaat Harb Square, and Mataryya Square. The smallness of the protests was oftentimes a self-fulfilling prophecy; as one protester put it, "This is like a vicious circle. The public does not participate in the first place because the small place and small crowd do not guarantee protection." That is, the limited space often had an antimobilizing effect. In a 2006 piece titled "The Anatomy of a Downtown Demo," leftist writer Hani Shukrallah described these protests as "invitation-only" demonstrations and noted the way police sought to control (and literally compress) protesters' space: "At last, I felt, I had uncovered the full subtleties of the police counter-demonstration strategy. It was brilliant in its simplicity. Huge contingents of riot police laid a tight siege to the demonstrators, who, squeezed into a small corner of the square, were surrounded by wider circles made up of hundreds of civilian-clad and uniformed policemen. The encirclement was nearly 10 tight circles deep."

Despite such tactics, often accompanied by violence, these protests continued. Part of their resilience can be linked to the second feature of the protests: their concentration in urban centers, most specifically in Cairo, in or near Tahrir Square. The focus here was hardly surprising: the area near Tahrir has more governmental buildings and centers of power than anywhere else in Egypt. But by targeting such central locations, protesters held out hope that some of their sit-ins and stand-ins might transform into rallies that could move around downtown and/or expand to fill the square. Importantly, such central locations also provided protesters with multiple spaces to stop and rest, and also multiple escape routes. Finally, many human rights nongovernmental organizations (NGOs) have offices downtown. Hence, protesters could seek legal aid or assistance when the police became abusive. Many of these offices, like the headquarters of the syndicates, became central places for protesters to meet, plan logistics, and seek medical aid.

The third feature shared by these protests is the fact that, regardless of how small or peaceful they were, they invariably provoked an intense and aggressive police response. The police intentionally cordoned protesters into limited spaces, and once this was achieved, they started to crush and squeeze them in an effort to break the protest as quickly as possible. In the simplest terms, this was a battle over a small amount of public political space, and the state came to the battle prepared to use violence. Shukrallah (2006) describes how police not only tried to limit protests to well-known activists (thus enforcing a strange form of elitism) but also tried to literally control who could enter the protest space and who could leave it.

Having participated in many protests, I recognize the pattern Shukrallah discusses. I also argue that things began to change after 2006, in the years leading up to the revolution.[10] Protesters were gaining confidence, and some started to challenge and even break down cordons. Some protesters, especially in the year before the revolution, started to intentionally stand outside of the cordon and talk to the public. Thus, the use of specific protest repertoires reflected the battle over physical space in Egypt between the regime and the opposition. The opposition movements also tried to find venues for their grievances that were alternative or parallel to the street. One such venue was social media, discussed in the following.

Tahrir: History of Protest and Inspirations

It will be useful at this point to situate the rise of street politics in the decade before the revolution within the deeper history of protest in Tahrir Square, particularly in relation to the development of the coercive apparatus of the postcolonial state. Without this historical depth, we cannot fully grasp the immense role of Tahrir during the revolution, nor, perhaps, the limitations of this mobilization, as it played out after the revolution.

Soon after Britain occupied Egypt in 1882, the colonial forces decided to locate their Qasr El Nile British Army Barracks on the borders of the square—known at the time as Ismailia Square—where they remained from 1882 until 1947 (see figure 1.1). This period witnessed a number of anticolonial protests in this area, including on February 21, 1946, when the National Committee of Workers and Students called for the evacuation of British troops and a general strike against the British occupation. The same day, a massive demonstration of students marched from Giza to the center of Cairo. When they reached Ismailia Square, they were confronted by British troops, who opened fire; twenty-three demonstrators were killed and some 120 injured (Farag 1999). The day was later chosen as National Students' Day in Egypt. Earlier that month, on February 9, the Egyptian police, collaborating with the British, raised the Abbas drawbridge near Cairo University to stop protesters from reaching the square. This led to the drowning of dozens of students who were rallying from Cairo University to the square.

According to a treaty between Egypt and Great Britain signed in 1936, British troops were to have withdrawn from all Egyptian territory and relocated to the Suez Canal area in 1946. In 1947 the square was expanded, and the Qasr El Nile British Army Barracks was replaced by the Egyptian Army Barracks. Between 1947 and 1951, British colonial officials refused to negotiate regarding a complete withdrawal from Egypt. Anticolonial protests continued in Egypt during this time, often taking place downtown and in the square.

For example, an important protest took place on November 14, 1951, which the newspaper *Al-Ahram* estimated at one million people. The protest demanded a complete withdrawal of British troops from Egypt; at the time they were still located in the Suez Canal area. The protest began in Ismailia Square.[11] Other major protests took place the same day in Alexandria and other cities in Egypt. The rally started at 11:00 a.m. in the square and moved to Abdeen Palace, the official government headquarters of King Farouk I, seen by many Egyptians at the time as a colonial puppet (see K. Fahmy 2011; see also Al-Shamaaa 2015; Shaaban 2018).

Following the July 23, 1952, military coup against King Farouk, the Egyptian officers who carried out the coup negotiated the British withdrawal from Egypt, which finally took place in 1954. I should note here that the Free Officers (military) regime founded the first republic in Egyptian constitutional and political history. This republic was announced through a constitutional declaration on June 18, 1953. The Free Officers coup (known also as the July 23 Revolution) had several goals, which included ending the feudal order, ending colonialism, and establishing social justice and democracy. In public critical culture in Egypt and among many political dissenters

FIGURE 1.1 A memorial service to welcome King George V of Britain in 1936 at the Qasr El Nile barracks in Ismailia Square (known as Tahrir after 1952). Source: Wellcome Library.

in the past few decades, the consensus is that the first republic perhaps was successful in ending the British occupation of Egypt and ending the feudal order and monarchy but never succeeded in establishing democracy. The epigraph at the beginning of this chapter, by Naguib Mahfouz, a notable Egyptian writer who was the 1988 Nobel laureate in literature, reflects this sentiment in a dream: that anticolonial national movements in Egypt had continued, establishing democracy. Now back to Tahrir: after the complete withdrawal of British troops from Egypt, the July regime officially changed the name from Ismailia Square to Tahrir Square.

The space became a site of festivities organized by the new regime. For example, in January 1953 the military leadership announced an end to party politics in Egypt and their plans for a one-party system, which took place in the square while celebrating the six-month anniversary of their military coup. The rally soon turned chaotic, as "the regime could not control the crowd. The police force had to intervene to protect Mohamed Naguib, a military general and the first president of Egypt after the coup, and assist him in leaving the square safely" (K. Fahmy 2011).

In the 1960s and beyond, citizens gathered in Tahrir to protest the republican regime's lack of democracy and transparency, which led to Egypt's defeat in the Arab-Israeli War in 1967, as well as its lack of will to liberate land that Israel occupied in 1967. Other notable struggles were the student occupation of Tahrir in 1972 and the rallies against the war in Iraq in 2003. Egyptian bloggers occupied Tahrir for most of one night on March 16, 2006, to express solidarity with pro-democracy judges prosecuted by Mubarak. In sum, the square has historically been an important site of national protests. It was no surprise, then, that the main organizers for the January 25, 2011, protest called for the uprising's demonstrations to converge in Tahrir.

The history of protest in Tahrir Square informed mobilization for the 2011 revolution in at least three ways. First was the identification of Tahrir Square as a known target for protest. During the revolution in 2011, protesters knew to a certain degree that they should head to Tahrir, and the planned protest of January 25, 2011, also included Tahrir as the main gathering point. In addition to its symbolic and historical power, Tahrir has a number of physical features that make it a convenient and strategic location. These include the massive width of the space; its location in downtown Cairo; its proximity to numerous cafés, where activists and intellectuals can meet and write statements; and the square's centerpiece—a pedestal until the mid-1970s and then, by the time of the Egyptian Revolution in 2011, a simple green mound that revolutionaries called *al-sinyiia* (the tray). It is Tahrir's central location, then, in both literal and historical space that leads some analysts to say, "Whatever happens in Tahrir immediately becomes a national concern" (Farag 1999).[12]

The second aspect of how the history of protest in Tahrir informed the revolution is the repository of strategies it offered, specifically providing the revolutionaries with the idea of establishing an encampment in Tahrir. Prior to the 2011 revolution, Tahrir had only been occupied three times, in 1972, 2003, and 2006 (A. Said 2015). These three attempts were briefly successful but never lasted for more than one day. The decade before the revolution also witnessed many sit-ins organized by Egyptian workers in the area around the Egyptian cabinet, close to Tahrir.

The idea of occupying Tahrir Square became a significant symbol in Egyptian intellectual and cultural history because of a student occupation in January 1972. Shortly after this protest, Amal Dunqul penned the famous poem "Oghneyet El-Kaaka El-Hagareya" (The song of the stone cake) (Dunqul 1987, 274–80). In the poem, Dunqul refers to the pedestal, which was circular in shape and resembled a multilayered cake. The pedestal was located at the center of the square, around which student protesters were gathering. In the same poem, Dunqul describes the protesters' chants and determination against the tyranny of President Anwar Sadat. The poem enjoys a powerful place in Egyptian memory and was cited by participants in later events. The history of sit-ins in Tahrir provided protesters in the 2011 revolution with not only the idea of occupying the square but also concrete strategies for doing so. Experienced activists who had participated in previous sit-ins knew that focusing on issues of survival, such as food, water, and sleeping equipment, would be crucial. Even though Tahrir was announced as the site for a protest assembly before the revolution, nobody knew or expected that protesters would decide to occupy the square. But the first statement released from Tahrir ended with this statement of the protesters' strategy: they would occupy the place until Mubarak's resignation (see chapter 2 for the full statement).

The third way that the history of protest in Tahrir impacted the 2011 revolution lies in the square's inspirational symbolism, which fueled new narratives about the liberation of the square. During my research many of my interlocutors remembered past unsuccessful attempts to occupy the square, emphasizing with a sense of pride that the occupation during the revolution was the longest period anyone had held the square and that this represented a new form of liberation. One of the most important components in protesters' narratives was the idea that Tahrir should finally live up to its name: "Liberation." Their hope was that the liberation of the square would lead to the liberation of Egypt from dictatorship. The idea of borrowing meanings from the past to encourage more newcomers to join the protests was an important aspect of the first eighteen days of the revolution.

One of the best examples was the use of important political songs from Egypt's history. Protesters sang old national songs, particularly those advocating resistance against occupation and/or the liberation of lands. One of the most significant songs appropriated and redeployed in Tahrir in 2011 was a song written by poet Ahmed Fou'ad Negm and composed and sung by Sheikh Imam.[13] The song, titled "Il-gada' gada' wi-'l-gabān gabān" (The valiant is valiant and the coward is a coward), was written in 1969 in the context of what is known as the War of Attrition between Egypt and Israel.[14] Protesters in the 2011 revolution appropriated the song to refer to their occupation of Tahrir. The message was clear: Tahrir is for those who are valiant.

A Neopatrimonial Police State

Why was the Mubarak state exceptionally repressive? How can we make sense of Mubarak's gigantic repressive apparatus in the context of his regime's neoliberal economic agenda? The Egyptian state under Mubarak has been described variously as a neopatrimonial state, a failed state, a crony capitalist state, and a police state (Achcar 2013; Brumberg and Sallam 2012; Ismail 2011, 2012; Jerzak 2013; Lazard and Diwan 2012; Lesch 2011; Teitelbaum 2012). All these descriptions focus on only one element of a broader picture, and they are by no means mutually exclusive. But I argue that neopatrimonialism, advanced by Gilbert Achcar (2013), is the most relevant to the analysis addressed here. Achcar updated the notion of patrimonialism, famously developed by Max Weber, in the context of the Arab state. According to him, "Patrimonialism is an absolute, hereditary type of autocratic power, which is, however, capable of functioning with an entourage of 'kith and kin.' The patrimonial power appropriates the state for itself, specifically: 1) the armed forces, dominated by a praetorian guard whose allegiance is to the rulers, not the state as such; 2) the economic means at the state's disposal; and 3) the state administration. The species of capitalism that tends to develop under this type of government, to the detriment of market capitalism, is 'crony capitalism,' dominated by a state bourgeoisie" (59). Compared to patrimonialism, in neopatrimonialism, the state achieves some degree of institutionalization of the republican authoritarian power, even operating with a significant "rational-legal" bureaucratic dimension (59). Per Achcar, it is possible for a neopatrimonial state to regress to a higher degree of patrimonialism when an autocratic neopatrimonial regime has achieved long-term stability and when an autocrat chooses his successor. Raymond Hinnebusch defines neopatrimonialism as "a hybrid regime mixing pre-modern practices of clientelism and primordial solidarities with modern bureaucratic and political technology" (2014, 42). Both definitions are useful, but for the purpose of this book, I favor Achcar's because it centers the role of the ruler, as well as the relationship between the ruler and the local bourgeoisie, and addresses the connection of cronyism to the ruler and his family. In the last decade under Mubarak, his family, especially his wife and his son Gamal, had some direct influence on the cabinet. In the last few years before the revolution, Mubarak Jr. controlled the ruling party almost entirely. The interior minister, Habib El-Adly, was one of the sponsors of the plan for Gamal Mubarak's succession. This is a critical factor, as state coercion was directly deployed in relation to the succession plan as much as it was used for the benefit of state elites, as well as targeting political dissent.

The neopatrimonial state under Mubarak included an expansive, sprawling police apparatus that developed out of the state's repeated collisions with various sectors of society. From the mid-1990s onward, militant Islamists, fueled by their belief that the state was not Islamic enough, launched a new campaign of attacks that aimed to destabilize the "infidel" state and punish it for not complying with what they saw as "true" Islam. Tourists, state officials, and Egyptian Christians were among their targets. In response, the Egyptian state launched its own "war on terror," and the police were granted enormous resources and both legal and extralegal powers. Arbitrary detention, killing, and torture became pervasive and even normalized. This had two important outcomes for the state and its police. The first was the strengthening of the repressive apparatus. Notably, when Habib El-Adly started his career as minister of the interior in 1997, the ministry's primary objective was combating "terror." Framed as such, its actions were typically considered beyond critique, except for some pesky voices in the emerging human rights movement who criticized torture, military trials for civilians, and arbitrary detentions.[15] The second outcome was that the state concluded that a security-based solution worked. Some immediate successes led to the premature assessment that expanded state repression was effective in controlling militants, an assessment no one in the state apparatus seemed to question. To this day, notwithstanding accumulating evidence to the contrary, this remains the fundamental logic behind repressive state security as the solution to all problems.

With the escalation of structural adjustment programs, crushing the protests of peasants and workers resisting the new so-called economic reform laws became a major task of the police. These programs officially began in 1991 but were applied gradually, with their tempo increasing steadily from 1997 onward. It bears emphasizing here that the police apparatus in Egypt cannot be separated from or seen as operating independently of the interests of the privileged elite. A significant portion of high-ranking police officers come from the middle class, and many of them joined the police to maintain the interests of this class; some actually entered the police academy through corruption and bribery (Immigration and Refugee Board of Canada 2005; Lindsay 2011; Nice 2006).[16] Of course, there is nothing new about the police becoming an apparatus for the privileged, but human rights groups and experts studying torture in Egypt noticed the emergence of new categories of torture, most notably what may be described as *complimentary torture*—instances in which powerless individuals are tortured at the request of or as a favor for a powerful, influential person, usually to force the torture victim to sign certain papers or give up some rights (see A. Shahat Said 2008; see also Markaz al-nadīm li-taʾhīl ḍaḥāyā al-ʿunf wal-taʿdhīb 2007).

By the time the pro-democracy movement Kefaya was founded in late 2004, opposing Mubarak's apparent plan to hand power to his son Gamal, the police state had crystallized and became practically synonymous with the protection of Mubarak's family and interests. As protests challenging Mubarak grew, the security apparatus kept pace and suppressed resistance whenever and wherever it was apparent. As the back-and-forth struggle between police and protesters continued, both sides learned important lessons and developed strategies for dealing with each other. As we already saw, the regime's new tactics included deploying plainclothes police to infiltrate protesters and using organized sexual harassment and assault to disperse female protesters.[17]

This brutality did not deter citizens and activists from fighting back in different ways as they took their demands and their politics out into the streets. This happened in physical as well as virtual spaces, which expanded the political space for democratic opposition and provided a critical site for contesting the regime. Interestingly, the fight to expand public space took place only minimally through electoral means and mostly in the streets and in virtual spaces.

The Rise of the Virtual and the Changing Composition of Political Space

Perhaps no issue has garnered more scholarly and public attention than the role of social media in the 2011 revolution (Bhuiyan 2011; Choudhary et al. 2012; Eltantawy and Wiest 2011; Khondker 2011; Tufekci and Wilson 2012; Zhuo, Wellman, and Yu 2011). Yet much of this literature has two flaws: first, the analysis is too often ahistorical, failing to examine the longer history of social media in Egypt; and, second, not enough attention has been paid to the dynamic relationship *between* online and offline forms of activism.[18] In the following I briefly historicize this relationship by tracing the interaction between social media and street protests over time. I argue that whenever street protests took place, social media served more of a supportive, backseat role, but in the absence of physical protests, social media emerged as an alternate space in which political protest could be staged. In other words, I show that the rise of social media activism in Egypt is a story about public political space.[19]

Social media in general has a very strong presence in the lives of Egyptian youth. According to a report about Facebook usage in 2010, Egypt had the largest Facebook community in the Middle East and North Africa region. Of North Africa's 7.7 million Facebook users, Egypt accounted for 3.4 million users (or 44 percent of all North African users) (Malin 2011b). Egypt also had the largest number of users of Facebook's Arabic interface (2.2 million Facebook Arabic users in Egypt, versus 1.8 million in the Kingdom of Saudi Arabia), and 30 percent of Egypt's 17 million internet users were Facebook subscribers: up from 20 percent in May 2010 (Malin 2011a).

But as impressive as these numbers are, social media's political impact is even more significant. Most scholars of social media in the region, as well as bloggers in Egypt specifically, affirm that social media in Egypt—especially blogging, which started before Facebook and Twitter—was politicized from the very beginning. Three main factors were involved. The first is that social media constitutes an alternative to official media, most of which is heavily censored. The second reason is the general exclusion of youth perspectives from mainstream politics, social and political talk shows, and printed mainstream media. Youth were eager for a medium to express themselves, making them, not surprisingly, the most frequent and enthusiastic early adopters of blogging and social media. According to the same report on Facebook usage cited above, nearly two million of Egypt's Facebook users in 2010 were under twenty-five years of age, representing 61 percent of its total users (Malin 2010, 8). Finally, the third factor was the concomitant rise of pro-democracy protest movements, particularly after 2005. Prior to 2005, blogging existed and was somewhat political, primarily insofar as it provided a forum in which people broke taboos by discussing politics, religion, and sex. A key shift began in late 2004, however, as bloggers increasingly began to lend support to and collaborate with pro-democracy protests in Egypt, especially the Kefaya movement. Some bloggers assisted Kefaya with its website, while other bloggers actually started to organize themselves in support of the movement.

Based on my own observations and participation in activism in Egypt, as well as the recollections of many of my interlocutors, I have identified the following seven moments or events as particularly crucial in shaping the relationship of social media and politics in Egypt before the revolution of 2011. In each of these instances, the internet and social media served as mobilizing tools for protest.

The first significant instance of activists using social media was in 2003, during the protests against the US-led war in Iraq. Though the blogger movement had not yet developed, these protests marked the first expansive use of cell phone texting to mobilize people for protests. In addition to widely circulated emails at the time and the use of Yahoo Groups, most antiwar and anti-imperialist activists in Egypt used their phones' short message service (SMS) to send the following text: "On the day the US attacks Iraq, let us gather and protest at noon in Tahrir." Such use of texting for mobilizing purposes has since become a regular feature of Egyptian activism, especially given the high number of cell phones in Egypt.

Second, in late 2004, with the formation of the Egyptian Movement for Change, otherwise known as Kefaya (Enough), a new method was developed: blogs. In 2005 some of the key founders of the blogging movement in Egypt joined Kefaya and its campaign to mobilize for democracy. These bloggers assisted in launching Kefaya's website and became its web administrators. By matching Kefaya's protests in the street with activities online, bloggers brought new energy and expertise to promoting Kefaya's ideas and helped to build a network for the movement across different regions of the country.

Third, during a March 2006 sit-in in solidarity with judges, bloggers took organizing to the streets. When Mubarak put two prominent judges challenging electoral corruption on trial for ostensibly violating their impartiality and discussing politics, pro-democracy activists in Egypt launched campaigns and protests declaring their solidarity with the judges. Bloggers were pioneering forces in these campaigns, both online and offline, using their sites and virtual connections to organize a sit-in in Tahrir Square to support the judges.

Fourth, social media was a key factor shaping the April 2008 strike at the Al-Mahalla Textile Spinning and Weaving Company, when a Facebook page was used for the first time for mobilization in Egypt. Mahalla is a public sector company located in the Nile delta. In the spring of 2007, workers there staged a strike that led to an increase in their bonuses. A year later, in April 2008, workers announced a new strike demanding a minimum wage (for themselves and for workers across Egypt) of no less than 1,200 Egyptian pounds a month. Many activists—including Kefaya and other pro-democracy and socialist activists—seized on the Mahalla workers' plan for a strike as a nationwide call for strikes and civil disobedience across Egypt. A group of activists launched a Facebook page to promote a one-day general strike in Egypt. The police intervened at Mahalla, this time storming the factory and preventing the strike, but citywide riots lasting three days broke out, and one protester was killed. Many activists describe the riot at Mahalla as the true rehearsal for the 2011 revolution. On April 6, 2008, protests in solidarity with the Mahalla workers were staged in Cairo and a few other cities, where the police arrested Israa Abdel Fatah, one of the administrators of the previously mentioned Facebook page. The April 6 Youth Movement was formed and named after this event. While the group started as a way to support striking Mahalla workers, it expanded its role to become one of the main pro-democracy youth groups in Egypt and one of the groups providing on-the-ground assistance during the 2011 revolution's initial days.

The fifth moment of activist use of social media I want to emphasize is not so much a single instance but rather the growing trend of using blogger-led campaigns to publicize and protest police brutality and torture. In 2008 many groups and individuals working on human rights tried to draw attention to police brutality and the issue of torture. The most notable of these was a group called Egyptians against Torture, formed in 2008 by individual human rights activists. The group led a number of campaigns that sought to document cases of torture, raise awareness about police torture in Egypt, and file actual criminal and civil cases against police torturers. Bloggers played (and continue to play) an important role in these campaigns, devoting significant space on their blogs to writing about torture.

Sixth, the return of Mohamed ElBaradei, the former director general of the International Atomic Energy Agency, to Egypt in February 2010, and his announcement of his willingness to run for the presidency, had a hugely energizing effect on pro-democracy groups. After Mubarak amended the constitution in 2005 and extended his power for another term (moving the new end date to 2011), many Egyptian activists grew depressed and discouraged. While the constitutional amendment allowed multicandidate elections for president *in theory*, in practice, the amendment actually instituted stipulations that made candidacy far more difficult for opposition candidates. It was a gloomy time for pro-democracy organizing, so when ElBaradei returned and was very vocal in criticizing Mubarak, many Egyptian youth started Facebook groups and Twitter accounts calling for his presidency. Bloggers wrote extensively about ElBaradei's return, and a special campaign was created offline to collect a million endorsements by Egyptians for ElBaradei's bid. According to many activists I talked to at the time, ElBaradei's return and campaign were like throwing a stone in stagnant water.

The seventh and final moment of social media mobilization that I wish to highlight is the June 2010 creation of the We Are All Khaled Said Facebook page. On June 6, 2010, a young blogger and activist named Khaled Said was tortured to death because he posted a leaked video about police corruption in Egypt. Soon after Said's death, blogger Wael Ghoneim created a Facebook page not only to commemorate Said but also to draw attention to the circumstances of his death and mobilize others against police brutality.

Abdel Rahman Mansour, another activist, was the other page administrator alongside Ghoneim. Despite being anonymous, the two were targeted by the police, but they managed to remain unknown until after the revolution. The page's membership reached about half a million the day before the revolution, and the page itself became the central site for mobilizing the protests that eventually culminated in the revolution.[20]

Note here that the shift from one tool to another (Yahoo Groups, then SMS, then blogs, then Facebook and Twitter) was full of contingencies, influenced by many complex intertwined factors (such as political, technological, and economic aspects). For example, it was the rise of Kefaya that attracted bloggers to become more explicitly political in 2004/5. It was the bravery of bloggers in 2006 that took social media organizing to the streets, when they organized a sit-in in solidarity with prosecuted judges under Mubarak. The wide use of Facebook in 2006 and after facilitated the use of this tool for activism. Blogs became less influential after the emergence of Facebook and Twitter simply because the latter tools had a wider audience. In an interview with Noha Atef, one of the main bloggers in Egypt from 2002 to 2008, she mentioned, "I stopped being active in my blog due to the rise of Facebook" (November 2, 2012).

Overall, social media activism was intertwined with organizing in the streets, emerging during the decade prior to 2011 as a key venue through which political activists of many different kinds could connect, share information and resources, and mobilize for offline activities. Through this interconnection social media was a major force in expanding public political space under Mubarak's authoritarian rule. Given the difficulty of censoring social media, compared to the strict censorship of most mainstream media, the blogosphere and later Facebook and Twitter further developed into spaces in which alternate voices could speak and alternate ideas could be expressed, even when activism was repressed in the streets and in official political spaces. This was especially important in 2008–11, given the almost complete absence of serious and organized venues for free political discussion at the time.[21]

That the spaces of formal, street, and virtual politics were all intertwined can be seen clearly with a closer look at formal politics. Establishing political parties and running for elected office or fighting for the right to form unions are rights that were supposedly protected by the 1971 Egyptian constitution and laws, but in practice, these rights were so eviscerated under Mubarak that they didn't exist at all in any meaningful sense. Laws, statutes, and administrative regulations severely hampered Egyptians' rights to form or join a political party, NGO, or union. To form a political party, for example, one had to get a license from a committee chaired by a member of the ruling party. Not surprisingly, the license was rarely granted; indeed, most of the political parties that existed before the revolution gained their licenses only after suing the government and challenging the committee's prior refusal. Even after obtaining a license, political parties were not really allowed to practice politics. Often, their work was reduced to small gatherings of people in closed rooms, struggling simply to publish a newspaper criticizing the government. But the newspaper could be banned if it dared to criticize Mubarak himself or talk about his health or his family. Similarly, to form an NGO, one needed to obtain a license, in theory granted by the Social Affairs Ministry. In practice, such decisions were made by the police (Stork 2005). The law in Egypt also restricted union activities during elections, and nonunion members could be arrested if they practiced politics. Active union members known to be critical of the government often were confronted with many barriers to running for office in trade union elections in the first place—or, rather, they could run, but it was understood that they would never win thanks to the police's and corrupt officials' control over the electoral process.[22] Many of these practices can be traced to Gamal Abdel Nasser's rule. What was new under Mubarak was the expanded use of police forces and the security apparatus—compared to the Military Intelligence and Reconnaissance Administration and national security agencies—to manipulate domestic politics.

Conclusion: Tahrir, Ready for the Burst

I started this chapter with a short account of my experience participating in a small protest in Tahrir Square on September 10, 2001. I highlighted the tension and the relation between this short-lived, temporary liberation of a very small place in the square and the heavy policing around it. Throughout, I discussed how Egyptians took their politics to the streets in the form of sit-ins and other demonstrations and used digital spaces when formal politics were controlled by their repressive rulers. The analysis in this chapter shows that the decade prior to the revolution not only paved the way for what happened during the revolution but provided revolutionaries with many protest tactics that they developed during incessant interaction and struggle with the authoritarian regime and its agents.

A close analysis of the history of mobilization in Egypt before the revolution reveals that formal political space, social media space, and the space of street politics have been intertwined and that together they constituted a more dynamic and broader public political space. By examining the history of mobilization in these three spaces, I have identified a pattern whereby Egyptian activists turned to social media space and street politics when formal political space was all but closed. The general logic is that street politics was used as an alternative to and against the restrictions on formal politics. Social media in general was subordinate to street politics, but it sometimes came to the fore when street politics was blocked or banned. But the aim was always to expand and push the limits of formal politics. Interestingly, street politics and virtual spaces contributed to paving the road to revolution in Egypt.

The preceding discussion also demonstrates how Tahrir Square was central in Egypt's history of political protest. The very name of the square was associated with liberation, through colonial and postcolonial times. And according to many Egyptian political dissenters, Tahrir does not live up to its name unless people are able to access it freely, if not to seize it for themselves. It is not a surprise then that Egyptian revolutionary actors chose Tahrir as the main gathering point during the 2011 uprising. But it is one thing to rally to Tahrir, or even control it briefly, and another to make the square a center of a revolutionary repertoire, which included creating an alternative republic, sustaining a revolutionary camp surrounded by barricades that was policed by protesters, and making this square a messenger of revolutionary demands, among other things, as I demonstrate in the next chapter.

2 | peak of revolutionary possibilities

My dear Square—where have you gone?
You broke through walls, you brought forth light
You gathered around you a broken people
We were born again. A stubborn dream was born.
When we disagree, it is in good faith
Sometimes the picture was unclear
We will protect our nation and our children's children
And redeem the rights of our martyred youth
—FROM "YA EL MIDAN" (OH, SQUARE),
A SONG BY AIDA EL AYOUBI AND CAIROKEE

When I first entered Tahrir Square on February 4, 2011, I realized that what might look chaotic to outsiders was actually extraordinarily organized and coordinated. The uprising had begun on January 25, with a sit-in. At the stroke of midnight, police violently forced the protesters out. On January 28, Egyptians took to the streets again, rallying and battling throughout the country and eventually reconvening and reestablishing their camp in Tahrir Square. Hosni Mubarak ordered the military to restore order in the streets, which included a mandatory daily curfew from 6:00 p.m. to 6:00 a.m. For five days, the military prevented food, medicine, and camp supplies from reaching protesters in the square, and on February 2, pro-Mubarak supporters, protected by the police, attacked the protesters with sticks, rocks, Molotov cocktails, and live ammunition. The military was complicit in facilitating this crackdown, which would become known as the Camel Battle, after the horses and camels the militia brought. Despite twenty hours of fierce fighting, the sit-in survived.

When I reached Tahrir Square, there were two stages with huge speakers, along with impromptu field hospitals manned by volunteers to treat protesters' injuries. Barricades protected the square from intruders. My mind flooded with questions: *How had this been achieved? Who built those stages, and how did they get sound equipment into a square so recently under siege? When and how were the field hospitals set up? Who was coordinating food, water, and hygiene for a crowd reportedly reaching one million during the daylight hours? And how, in the midst of it all, did mobilization continue?* Over the next week, I moved in and out of Tahrir Square, talking to people both within the square and on the outside, looking in. By February 11, 2011, when Mubarak was ousted from power, Tahrir was firmly established in the media and in the minds of Egyptians as *the* site of the revolution.

In this chapter I analyze how Tahrir Square became the main liberated zone in Egypt and the main site of the revolution, associated with its famous revolutionary camp. This liberation happened in the context of a revolutionary situation, in which the regime was no longer capable of stopping protest by force, where revolutionary possibilities were at their peak. I argue that Tahrir Square represented a physical and symbolic confinement of the revolution—the focal point of a process of containment and boundary making I call *squaring the revolution*. By virtue of being the most visible site of action, it bounded the revolution physically, but by containing the bulk of the revolutionary demands, Tahrir was also made a symbolic boundary of the revolution. My use of the phrase *squaring the revolution* calls attention, too, to the fact that all boundaries are double-sided: mobilizations and actions within this limit were marked as part of the revolution, and mobilizations and actions outside the boundary were marked as not part—or, at least, not an important part—of the revolution.

Four processes drove the squaring of the revolution: the physical sites of battles and clashes, the "virtual" making of Tahrir through social media, the establishment of the Tahrir camp, and the mutual recognition by the regime and the protesters that the other was, in fact, its main contender.

Battling at the Boundaries

As we learned in the previous chapter, historically, Tahrir has been an important, "if unattainable (or, perhaps, because unattainable) meeting point for demonstrations" (A. Said 2015, 356). Still, converging in the square is one thing; seizing control of it is another thing entirely. On January 25, 2011, the first day of the uprising, protesters were able to control the square until about midnight. They would fight throughout the day on January 28, the Friday of Rage, as they attempted to reach and "liberate" the square. The battles and clashes throughout that critical day contributed significantly to defeating Mubarak's police apparatus, and they led up to protesters seizing the square. One of my interviewees described fighting to reach Tahrir that day: "The police's plan A was to prevent protesters from reaching the square, and then plan B was to seize the square if some or many were able to reach it. But what happened is that due to the huge number of protesters, the police were exhausted and defeated in many confrontations around Tahrir. It was protesters who surprised the police, and indeed surprised themselves, to reach Tahrir from different entrances coming from many routes, at the same time, all in the afternoon of January 28."[1]

The day involved fighting between the protesters and the police apparatus in both pitched battles and individual clashes.[2] Among the major battles that took place near the square, the battle over Qasr El Nile Bridge started when thousands of marchers met with heavy configurations of Central Security Forces (CSF). Soldiers deployed water cannons and fired guns. They used electric sticks and live ammunition. As the enforcers' fury rained down, thousands of protesters began to pray. In response, the soldiers used armored vehicles to drive through the protesters. Five hulking armored units blocked the bridge, but protesters—those who hadn't been killed or injured as the vehicles moved in—scaled the machines and burned them. In the end, the police withdrew, and the long, hard-fought battle, much of which was captured in video footage, became emblematic of both the Friday of Rage and the revolution itself.[3]

My interlocutors' and interviewees' testimonies revealed other important battles that they witnessed or took part in as they fought to regain Tahrir Square on January 28: in Qasr El Eyni Street, over May 15 Bridge, in Ramses Street, in Abdel Moneim Riad Square, and over Al Galaa Bridge before protesters reached Qasr El Nile Bridge. Another important battle took place in front of the Opera House, in Borg Gezira Street, before protesters reached Qasr El Nile Bridge, while smaller battles erupted in Talaat Harb Street and

Square, in El Falaky Square, and in the downtown streets. Smaller clashes took place at the locations where marchers set off or on the main roads as the protesters processed toward Tahrir Square.

Seizing Tahrir Square was no simple task. It was the culmination of a long and bloody process that entailed intense determination, bravery, and action. The battles that paved the way to Tahrir became a significant part of the memory of the victory over the police apparatus that day. One interlocutor told me that he will "never forget the young protester dying in my lap," who had been run over by a military vehicle on Qasr El Nile Bridge. He recalled the elation of successfully taking the square: "I was over the moon when I entered Tahrir. I forgot how much I endured—tear gas, blood, and very, very long confrontations." No single group liberated the square, and a full takeover was elusive as battles and clashes continued in Tahrir until about 9:00 p.m. Confrontations would erupt near the parliament and near the Ministry of the Interior for days to come while the military stood by, feigning neutrality, complicit in that it allowed violence from snipers and security forces, who targeted protesters with live ammunition. Many protesters were injured, and several lost their eyes in these clashes.

One participant told me, "The most brilliant thing about the battles on January 28, 2011, is that there were so many clashes and battles taking place at the same time, which we didn't know about. Every group of protesters attempted to rally, reach Tahrir, and engage in combat with police, and we thought that we were the remaining group." Each group fought as though theirs was the only group fighting in the streets. The police apparatus, particularly the CSF, spent three days between January 26 and January 28 in the street, battling rallies on many fronts. Even if they succeeded in preventing one group from proceeding to the square, another group would rise up in a different area. Multiple large groups of protesters were moving in different places. Some rallies were longer than others. Some groups broke off from a rally due to its intensity, only to find themselves swept up in another. For example, some of the protesters who started their rally at Mostafa Mahmoud Mosque faced clashes all the way to Al Galaa Bridge, where they fought a pitched battle. After breaking through the military forces, the protesters arrived at Qasr El Nile Bridge, where they took part in its epic battle (see map 2.1 on the routes of rallies on January 28, 2011).

Despite the difficulties inherent in establishing a chronological retrospective of the day's progress toward the square, it seems that the marching rallies and their attendant clashes lasted for three to four hours, and then the battles near Tahrir took about four hours. The police were defeated and started to

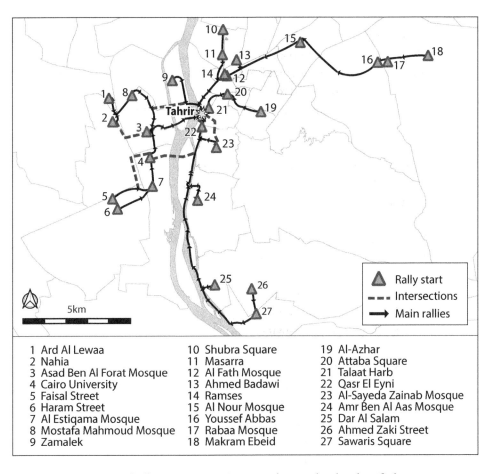

MAP 2.1 Routes of rallies on January 28, 2011, with major battles identified. Map by Ahmed Atif and Daftar Ahwal.

1 Ard Al Lewaa	10 Shubra Square	19 Al-Azhar
2 Nahia	11 Masarra	20 Attaba Square
3 Asad Ben Al Forat Mosque	12 Al Fath Mosque	21 Talaat Harb
4 Cairo University	13 Ahmed Badawi	22 Qasr El Eyni
5 Faisal Street	14 Ramses	23 Al-Sayeda Zainab Mosque
6 Haram Street	15 Al Nour Mosque	24 Amr Ben Al Aas Mosque
7 Al Estiqama Mosque	16 Youssef Abbas	25 Dar Al Salam
8 Mostafa Mahmoud Mosque	17 Rabaa Mosque	26 Ahmed Zaki Street
9 Zamalek	18 Makram Ebeid	27 Sawaris Square

Rally start
Intersections
Main rallies

5km

withdraw sometime between 6:00 and 8:00 p.m. This process was chaotic and not organized. The army intervened in Tahrir around 9:00 p.m. The military vehicles that had arrived earlier, around 6:00 p.m., carrying military police and republican guards, live ammunition, and tear gas to aid the police, were burned by protesters. This was the first actual move to set the boundary between protesters and the military in Tahrir. Now the army controlled the area around the square, while protesters controlled the square itself. Military tanks formed a border from Talaat Harb Street to Tahrir Street, Qasr El Nile Bridge, and Abdel Moneim Riad Square.

It is useful here to situate the clashes and battles at Tahrir within the larger context of nonviolence and violence in the Egyptian Revolution. Against the simplistic labeling of the Egyptian Revolution as entirely nonviolent (see

Batstone 2014; Lawson 2015a; Nepstad 2013), I agree with scholars (Kadivar and Ketchley 2018) who propose that the uprising witnessed the dominance of "unarmed collective violence," especially on the Friday of Rage, when protesters were all but forced to respond to the use of violence against them. From midnight on January 25, 2011, when the police used force to evacuate Tahrir Square, through January 26 and 27, when Mubarak's security apparatus began using excessive force and live ammunition to disperse protesters, those in the uprising continued to use both nonviolent and violent tactics in their own defense against escalating crackdowns. As of January 28, however, the protesters had largely united around the use of unarmed collective violence (compared to nonviolence).[4]

My interviews bear out the idea that both nonviolent and violent episodes took place in these days. Some testimonies recall even large crowds chanting the famous chant *"silmiyya"* (peaceful). Others told me about myriad on-the-ground, impromptu negotiations, especially during the clashes and battles of January 28. One interlocutor present at the battle on Qasr El Nile Bridge described trying to convince a big crowd to attack the CSF. The protesters refused. But he successfully convinced them to confiscate the troops' equipment and use it for self-defense. He also was able to convince his fellow protesters to use simple tools—nails and rocks, the CSF's metal sticks, and sharp, broken street signs—to slash the tires on the security forces' vehicles. It was, the protesters agreed, a matter of self-defense: these vehicles were being used to run over protesters.

Another tactic that could be described variously as violent or nonviolent, depending on one's perspective, is evidenced by the testimony of several interlocutors and interviewees from the Revolution Youth Coalition (RYC). They told me they had prepared by assigning rally volunteers they called *sayadeen* (catchers). This group's job was to walk along the outside edges of a marching rally, speedily collecting the tear gas containers thrown at protesters and throwing them back at the CSF. Police stations and courts, along with the headquarters of the National Democratic Party, were burned—targeted violence, but, again, these were attacks on buildings and property rather than bodily interpersonal violence.

It is important to consider, alongside these accounts, the police plan for responding to the uprising. One of the few glimpses available comes in the form of a classified document from the State Security Intelligence titled "The Scenario of the Events the Country Witnessed and Its Developments." In fifty-one pages, the document describes the revolution as the crisis that began with an unprecedented uprising on January 25 and peaked with the

Friday of Rage. The report states that these protests were characterized by the continuous flow of large crowds of citizens and representatives of different political powers, noting that, on January 28, the crowds included masses of citizens who had no political allegiances.

I was able to locate another important document, known as "Plan 100." It was developed in 2010 by the Cairo Security Directorate (Modeyriat Amn Al-Qahira) and was meant to be used to "confront riots" (see Arab Republic of Egypt 2011). The plan, which was mobilized in the Arab Spring, included elements concerning organizing police communications and securing key security locations with the goal of controlling urban borders, especially in capitals, and strategic roads, main squares, and central gathering places for labor, union, and political party crowds. More specifically, armed configurations would be launched in twelve squares and city spaces: Attaba Square, Talaat Harb Square, Abdel Moneim Riad Square, Garden City, Ahmed Maher Square, the Cairo Marriott Hotel area, the Safir Hotel Cairo area, the Egyptian Museum, Corniche El Nile, the Cairo Security Directorate, Rabaa Al-Adawiya Square, and Revolution Square in Heliopolis. Of these, ten surround Tahrir Square, a key location in the plan (Mawqee al-ahdaath). Explicitly, "Plan 100" calls for the use of live ammunition to control riots in the area of Tahrir Square.

As for violence in Tahrir *after* January 28, it is fair to say that clashes and confrontations continued on the edges of the square and the streets leading to it. These occurred mostly at night, and with lower frequency than in the last few days before Mubarak's ousting. In the days immediately following my arrival in Tahrir Square on February 4, I witnessed street skirmishes outside the square—in Mahmoud Bassiouny and Talaat Harb Streets—in the afternoon. I would see bloodied protesters arriving for treatment in Tahrir's field hospitals while others threw rocks back at Mubarak's militia. My respondents confirmed that the same scenes were playing out, especially in the afternoons and evenings and despite the military curfew, from Talaat Harb Square itself to Champollion Street, Khairat Street, Rihan Street, the end of Mohamed Mahmoud Street, and all areas going to Abdeen and Al-Sayeda Zainab. All these squares and streets are located in three administrative districts—Qasr El Nile, Abdeen, and Al-Sayeda Zainab—and these three districts surround Tahrir. Tahrir Square technically is part of the Qasr El Nile district, which is at the heart of downtown Cairo. Pro-Mubarak militia and paid thugs were sent to block these streets and to track and attack protesters coming into or leaving Tahrir. Protesters—especially female protesters—told me they walked in groups, ready for action. As public support grew for the uprising

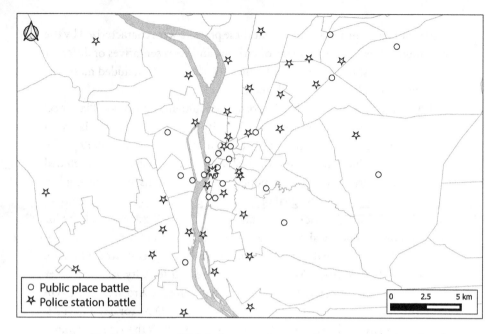

MAP 2.2 Key battles around Tahrir Square on January 28, 2011. Map by Ahmed Atif and Daftar Ahwal.

and revolutionary mobilization, sit-ins and checkpoints moved out from the square, extending the boundary of the protest's core to include some of the surrounding streets, such as Talaat Harb and Mahmoud Bassiouny. Now protesters fought to protect the square, the camp, and the revolution. (See map 2.2 on key battles around Tahrir on January 28, 2011.)

Protesters' Victory

Four factors have been cited in the protesters' success in these days. The first was the unexpectedly large number of protesters, and the second, stemming from the first, was the overextension of police forces. The third factor was, ironically, the communications blackout imposed at midnight on January 28, which continued until early in the morning on February 2. People were curious and lacked information. They came into the streets to see what was happening and check on the safety of their relatives and loved ones. Those who were actively fighting could not know what was happening in other places. One told me, in the absence of real information about the progress of the protests, "I was fighting as if I am the last one, and so was my group.

Table 2.1. Distribution of Key Protest Events on January 28, 2011, as Documented by Selected Egyptian Newspapers in Cairo, Giza, and Alexandria

	Cairo	Giza	Alexandria	Total
Battles in front of police stations	23	12	9	44
Battles in streets and squares	18	6	9	33
Looting/riots	4	4	0	8
Violence in jails	2	0	0	2
Main rallies	11	8	7	26
Sit-ins	1	0	1[*]	2
Total	**59**	**30**	**26**	**115**

[*] Only one attempt, and it was dispersed on February 2, 2011, as mentioned in the introduction of this book.

We thought we were the last group that will save the revolution." Fourth, the burning of police stations and the protesters' success in liberating and then controlling Tahrir provided an enormous boost to their morale. Many Egyptian activists I interviewed maintain that the battles in front of police stations were more important than battles elsewhere in Egypt. One scholar (Ketchley 2017a, 37) seems to agree with this conclusion. However, I contend that it is very difficult to make any generalizations about the relative importance of different battles between protesters and police forces during the uprising. Table 2.1 sums up the key protest events during January 28, 2011. As the table demonstrates, about forty-four instances of battles in front of police stations took place on that day in three key governorates (Cairo, Giza, and Alexandria), while thirty-three battles took place during marching rallies. There is no big difference between the two figures. More accurately, *regular police forces* were defeated in the battles in front of police stations, and the CSF (the main antiriot police in Egypt, comprising no less than 300,000 soldiers) were defeated in other battles during marching rallies throughout Egypt, including key battles near Tahrir.

In sum, the protesters' victory not only meant the defeat of the police apparatus but also entailed key battles near an important political and symbolic place: Tahrir Square.[5] Its legacy made it a site of protest in the first place, but the battles to retake Tahrir, and the social and international news media cycles that broadcast it to the world, made it the crucible of the revolution.

The Virtual Making of Tahrir

Many analysts have emphasized the significance of social media in the Egyptian Revolution. To be sure, the impact of social media warrants attention as a relatively new and potentially powerful social phenomenon. Yet, too often, analysts have exaggerated the role of social media, at the risk of reducing the complex dynamics of the revolution to a simple outcome of technological determinism. These analyses have failed to explore the ways social media connects with various forms of offline activism and to broader historic political dynamics. Even within the eighteen days of the revolution, the role of social media shifted over time. So the more accurate and productive question is not whether the Egyptian Revolution was a "social media revolution," but in what ways social media facilitated, impeded, and/or influenced the revolution in the streets.

What I call the virtual making of Tahrir was a unique process whereby the sit-in was connected both to the larger Egyptian population and to an international audience via new communications technologies. Yet the relationship between the physical space of Tahrir and the forms of cyberactivism mobilized before and during the revolution was more multilayered and dynamic than has previously been acknowledged. First, while cyberactivism was significant in both the initial mobilization that led to the occupation of Tahrir Square and the subsequent iconization of the sit-in there, the physical square itself must also be remembered as a major site of bloggers' and activists' organizing efforts and campaigns during the revolution. It is this reciprocal dynamic between online and offline dimensions of activism that I seek to emphasize as I argue against technological determinism. I must affirm the insistence of many of my interlocutors that, for all their virtual dimensions, revolutions are ultimately fought out on the ground, spelled in blood as well as bytes.

Second, the role of social media in the revolution was dynamic. It took different forms and shifted through various phases that, for my analytic purposes, I divide into three periods: (1) June 2010 to January 27, 2011; (2) January 28 to February 1, 2011; and (3) February 2 to February 11, 2011. Social media contributed in various ways to expanding and transforming public political space in Egypt in the years leading up to 2011 (Herrera 2014; Hirschkind 2011; Lim 2012). Here I focus more specifically on the revolution itself, noting how social media facilitated mobilization at key moments, provoked government responses, and sometimes produced paradoxical effects.

Social media arguably played the most decisive role in the Egyptian Revolution over several months leading up to the revolution. The most important and obvious example is the We Are All Khaled Said (WAAKS) Facebook page, which was central in the initial mobilization for the revolution. Between June 2010 and January 2011, the page brought widespread attention to the issue of police brutality, in general, and the case of Khaled Said, specifically. Activists used this virtual space to organize demonstrations, and over this seven-month period, the page attracted more and more visitors and built up credibility—in large part by avoiding association with any particular political party. By the time of the revolution, the page had almost half a million members.[6] And in the weeks immediately preceding the revolution, it would be *the* virtual meeting place for discussions and publicizing of protest events—including, most crucially, the protests in Tahrir Square slated for January 25, 2011.

As activists discussed various details regarding where, when, and how to stage protests, the WAAKS page provided an important space for participants to develop patterns of online communication that then transitioned to off-line and to institute collective forms of discussion and decision-making. Members of the page proposed ideas about places and slogans. They shared practical strategies. The administrators facilitated discussion and highlighted conclusions reached through some form of consensus. Some of my interviewees, especially the founders of what later became the RYC, described to me how, in the weeks leading up to the revolution, they regularly interacted with the then-anonymous administrators of the WAAKS page. Members of the RYC sent the admins emails and Facebook messages, and they discussed tactics and ideas for the prospective protest. This mediated relationship between participants who eventually gathered in mass numbers makes it very difficult to assert a rigid dichotomy between the virtual and the real. It also indicates that social media was providing participants with an opportunity to practice and produce new forms of dialogue and interaction in anticipation of on-the-ground protest. And for all my interlocutors' insistence that the revolution absolutely *could not* be contained or enacted online, neither would it have been possible without the planning and mobilization that took place in these virtual spaces.

The Social Media Blackout: January 28–February 1, 2011

Egyptian authorities shut down the internet and all cell phone communication in Egypt at midnight on January 28, 2011. For almost a week, Egypt was plunged into a predigital age. The measure was described by the US-based internet-analysis firm Renesys as "an action unprecedented in Internet history" that rendered "every Egyptian site inaccessible, from any part of the world" (Toor 2011). And yet, despite this drastic action, the revolution continued.

The significance of this period cannot be overemphasized because it obviates any analyses that attempt to reduce or dismiss the revolution as the simple outcome of technological advances and online activism. The protests may have been planned online, but the protesters were prepared to fight regardless of the technology at hand. They seamlessly returned to using predigital methods of communication, from landlines to satellite phones and, perhaps most important, word of mouth, as the blackout took effect. Additionally, they developed "backdoor" social media strategies whereby they would speak to friends and family outside of Egypt and have those interlocutors post to social media on their behalf. More important, the blackout had an unanticipated galvanizing effect: as the communications ban took hold, more and more people were angered and mobilized to protest, and the blackout compressed their energies into a physical space, Tahrir Square. Thus, the Friday of Rage and its decisive events came right in the middle of the blackout. Mubarak's brutal CSF suffered a major defeat in the street battles, and the relatively more restrained army troops were deployed in the streets (Cole 2011). These two things—the defeat of the police and the deployment of the army—signaled an important victory for the revolution, and that victory depended, in large part, on the massive turnout of protesters, all of which took place under the communications ban.

Even more ironic is the possibility that the *absence* of social media actually helped to increase protester participation on January 28. I interviewed many activists about their participation in the revolution, but it was my interviews with everyday citizens that proved revealing in this regard. They didn't identify as activists prior to the revolution but ended up in the streets, participating in it nonetheless. These interviewees told me: *We and many others we know just went to the streets to check things out.* The lack of news and social media communications pushed these interviewees to want to see with their own eyes what was going on. One interjector said bluntly, "This was the decision that made a critical mass participate in the revolution." And so the crowds came.

By the morning of February 2, 2011, when internet and cell phone communications were restored, it was clear that the plan had backfired. Further, the return of the internet, which pro-Mubarak forces believed would show the world their cause, instead enabled protesters to show the world the regime's brutality and authoritarianism. Worldwide, images of protesters being beaten in Tahrir, being attacked with camels and live ammunition, dominated news cycles. The shutdown had stirred international sympathy for the protesters in Tahrir, and the ill-timed return of the internet demonstrated the brutality they were enduring. It made Tahrir Square the indelible icon of the Egyptian Revolution, transforming it into the most potent symbol of the revolution.

From the start, Egyptian bloggers, activists, and newly politicized citizens used their smartphones to take pictures and post messages about Tahrir. Then hashtags arose, helping to organize communications about the uprisings across social media channels: #Tahrir, #Egypt, #Jan25, #revolution, and #Mubarak helped sympathetic activists around the world find and share words and images from Tahrir. The phrase "Tweets from Tahrir" became widespread in the days immediately preceding the ousting of Mubarak on February 11.[7]

The first time I saw an image of Tahrir Square teeming with protesters was on February 1, 2011. A colleague sitting next to me as I looked at Facebook somewhere in the American Midwest commented, "This is what democracy looks like." I was leaving for Egypt the very next day, and I had this idea in my head that the revolution was happening mainly, maybe exclusively, in Tahrir. The globalized image, as much as it contributed to creating global solidarities and spreading revolutionary fervor and inspiration, was also detrimental and conceivably limiting to the events themselves. In a sense, the revolution was reduced to the borders of the square, to the borders of a stunning, impressive image detached from the bloodshed and sacrifices being made beyond those borders. The image circulated across the globe at lightning speed.

To the extent that this "making" of Tahrir was effected through virtual channels, the process highlights the immediate modularity of the repertoires that converged at Tahrir. The sit-in may not have been replicated elsewhere in Egypt, particularly not at the same scale or with the same level of success, yet through social media and the iconization of Tahrir, I suggest that we might find in this example new ways of thinking about repertoires and their modularity (transferability/transposability), as highlighted by Sidney Tarrow (1993). But, unavoidably, the virtual making of Tahrir would not have taken place without the actual presence of the Tahrir camp.

How, despite being under siege in the early days of the uprising, did Tahrir Square become synonymous with the Egyptian Revolution?[8] The actions and events that unfolded in the Tahrir camp were characterized by a complex interplay of organization and spontaneity, and they were centrally concerned with issues of *both* basic survival and political mobilization. I show how this worked for the goal of constructing the camp as the main site of the revolution. But, first, it is useful to discuss briefly how the camp came to be and how it developed over time.

Several of my interviewees told me about a meeting that took place in Tahrir Square on the evening of January 25, 2011. Conflicting reports put the number of protesters present in the square at that point between five thousand and twenty thousand, but most interviewees said that at its peak about two hundred people were present at the meeting. Different people focused on different elements. Some were even wary of calling it a "meeting." For my purposes, I will use the name *tree meeting*, as it was later dubbed (in reference to a tree near the KFC restaurant and the entrance to Talaat Harb Street from Tahrir).[9]

The tree meeting began about 8:00 p.m. There was no agreed-on agenda, set structure, formal speakers, or even start or stop time. Rather, the gathering was relatively spontaneous. Some people called for it; others came. Not everyone stayed the whole time; people joined and left over the course of an hour. (This fluid participation is normal given the culture of coalitions among political factions in Egypt in the decade before the revolution.) The main purpose of the meeting was to exchange information, particularly pertaining to when and where the police would focus their energies next. Participants agreed on just two clear goals: to stay in the square—in short, to stage a sit-in—and to release a statement of the protesters' demands. Among other things, the statement was titled with the famous slogan "The people want the downfall of the regime." It clearly linked the establishment of the camp with the demand to oust Mubarak.

One of the founders of the RYC corrected one point of confusion, noting that in fact the tree meeting was more like a *series* of meetings:[10]

> The meeting took place three times, at 7:00, 9:00, and 12:00 p.m., before the square was evacuated by force. At 7:00, in the first meeting, the following forces were there: Youth for Justice and Freedom [a leftist coalition of youth, not to be confused with the Freedom and Justice Party, the political

arm of the Muslim Brotherhood formed after the revolution], some youth from the Muslim Brotherhood, youth from the Democratic Front Party, youth from the ElBaradei Campaign, from the April 6 Youth Movement, and some members from the Revolutionary Socialists. In the meeting we talked about what to do next. It was surprising that so many people showed up in the protests that day. And we suggested that we would meet in two hours to assess the situation and see how many people were in the square. At 9:00 we met another time. And we decided that the next step would be to call for collecting donations and food and blankets and equipment for forming a sit-in in Tahrir. In the second meeting, some political figures attended too, such as Ibrahim Esssa [a journalist and critic of Mubarak], Kamal Abu Eita [a Nasserite and labor organizer], and Kamal Khalil [a radical socialist]. At the end of the meeting, we issued a statement in which we called for firing the minister of the interior, all the cabinet, and all those who were responsible for torture in the police in Egypt. At 12:00 we met one more time, but after a few minutes . . . the police started to attack the square, and we ended up leaving.

Several activists would tell me that there were no efforts to develop a plan for the revolution. Nor did the protesters attempt to reconcile their considerable differences: these were not seen as immediate stumbling blocks or even as issues in need of resolution before the revolution could move forward. This awareness, the activists would say later, meant that nobody dared to claim in retrospect that they had been in control of the events that came later. So there was no guarantee of any sort about how things were going to unfold. Short of agreeing to simply stay in the square until Mubarak was gone, the tree meeting did not result in a grand plan. And yet people did meet, and there was, from the start, a collective sense of the need to coordinate and support one another. People were talking not only about political issues but also about blankets and food and equipment.

It is important to affirm here that Tahrir's occupation was not *developed* until at least January 28, 2011, thus throwing into question the accuracy of the oft-cited reference to the "eighteen days of the revolution." Nonetheless, from January 28 to February 2, despite the continuation of violent clashes, more and more people came to sleep in the square at night, bringing blankets, tents, and food. Conditions were difficult in these days, because Mubarak's thugs in nearby areas, as well as the military, were stopping protesters carrying food, medicine, or blankets into the square. Under military siege, protesters continued to get supplies through to the square. The military started to appear more neutral after the Camel Battle on February 2. Another important development after February 2 was erecting barricades surrounding Tahrir.

I asked many protesters to estimate the population sleeping in the square at night. They all had different estimates, but many said that between five thousand and ten thousand protesters stayed overnight in the days until February 2, when the numbers would climb to an estimated ten thousand to twenty thousand occupiers. In the last days before Mubarak's ouster, there may have been as many as two hundred thousand people sleeping in tents clustered at the center of the square and spreading out to its boundaries. (Media descriptions of million-person rallies referred to daytime assemblies.) I estimated that there were several hundred tents when I arrived, ranging from ready-made tents designed for hiking and camping to handmade lean-tos fashioned from pieces of cloth and sticks. Other protesters simply slept on the ground with sheets, plastic mats, or cardboard beneath them. The scene was incredibly dynamic. As tents moved and people joined and left over time, the visual image of Tahrir Square shifted day by day. A protest calling for radical change itself changed, radically, as events unfolded.

Organization and Spontaneity

With thousands of people under extreme duress, pressured by a militarized siege and an influx of new protesters each day, why didn't the square descend into chaos? These days were characterized by a complex interplay of organization and spontaneity. From my own observations during the revolution and my discussions with activists and protesters who participated, I can vouch that there was no *central* organization for anything. Rather, multiple simultaneous organizing efforts took place before and during the key eighteen-day period of revolution. These efforts included organizations that had existed prior to the revolution, mostly political parties, activist coalitions, and other interest-based groups, including Egyptian Movement for Change (Kefaya), the National Association for Change, and the Muslim Brotherhood.[11] Another interesting extant set of groups was the "ultras," or organized groups of soccer fans who had plenty of experience of fighting with police in violent clashes related to football games. These prerevolution groups played an important role in protecting the square, particularly during the first week of the uprising.

But new organizations also sprang up as the revolution developed. These primarily arose in response to the need to accomplish specific tasks, like taking care of the wounded, providing art and entertainment, or ensuring ongoing mobilization. The most important of these organizations was the RYC, which announced its founding just five days after the start of the protest, on January 30, 2011. It had, in fact, been several months in the making: youth organizers had been working together to plan large-scale protests in the run-up to the revolution, and they made the initial call for protests on January 25. The coalition included five youth groups: Justice and Freedom Movement (leftist), the April 6 Youth Movement (liberally oriented), Youth for ElBaradei / NAFC (liberally oriented), youth of the Muslim Brotherhood, and youth of the Democratic Front Party (liberally oriented).[12] The RYC later launched a Facebook page and put out press releases, but from the beginning the tents and the corner claimed by the coalition provided an important center for spreading news inside Tahrir. Another group that formed in Tahrir was called the January 25, 2011, Movement. It was based on individual membership and was more radical, refusing membership to liberal and/or Islamist members. The RYC was arguably more effective because it was a coalition of strong, already existing groups.

Other specialized groups that formed during those first days in Tahrir included Physicians for Tahrir, which managed and staffed the field hospitals; Artists for the Revolution, tasked with boosting morale and filling the square with creative art to inspire and sustain revolution; and Journalists for the Revolution, who organized displays of martyrs' pictures, newsstands, and art in the square. Scriptwriters, filmmakers, and workers in Egypt's cinema production also organized in the square and made their own statements.

Grouped loosely according to the coalitions to which they belonged, protesters claimed "corners" to display their work, offer assistance, and talk to members of the public who came to Tahrir to learn about what was going on. To deal with morale, there was more of a fluid network of activists who circulated through the crowd, especially at night, singing to boost people's spirits or even creating false alarms to ensure people were remaining alert. Other protesters took it on themselves to clean the square and establish garbage collection sites.

In other words, organization in Tahrir Square emerged organically, both from existing networks and practices and in innovative responses to unique pressures. Some people came to the square as part of groups, but once there, they interacted within the space as part of a larger whole. People volunteered to do things all the time, with little, if any, concern for who was in charge.

The general feeling was that what was happening was too large for any one group to control, but that was seen not as an impediment but as a boon.

One of the founders of the RYC emphasized that what was going on in Tahrir was way bigger than the RYC or any other organized group. Perhaps the most telling phrase was one uttered by many protesters and activists during this period: "Tahrir has no owner." Or as others said to me, "Tahrir only belongs to the revolution."

Survival and Mobilization: Or Revolution as Survival

Organization and spontaneity were critical for addressing the immediate, pressing goals: survival and mobilization. On the one hand, protesters within the square were faced with the very real logistical problem of how to ensure the basic survival of so many people in a space not designed to accommodate day-to-day habitation. On the other, protesters also needed to ensure that those within the square *and* those who might join in the future remained mobilized, committed to the cause of holding Tahrir and insisting that their demands be met. Both goals were imperative, and each served to counterbalance the other. If either fell apart, the whole endeavor would unravel. Protesters thus needed to maintain a persistent double vision, attentive to both short-term practicalities and long-term visions for Egypt's future. Neither the *physicality* nor the *politics* of Tahrir could be ignored.

The problem of survival was both individual and social: How could the protesters ensure the survival of the movement *and* its members under the constant threat and regular reality of violence? And how could they address seemingly banal needs like food, water, and bathrooms for tens of thousands, even a million people, with limited resources and no top-down organization in a space never meant as housing? For a one-day rally, this is a manageable problem. A sit-in lasting over two weeks is a totally different thing. *No one* in Tahrir had previous experience managing a community without central services. As with so much else that took place in the square, these issues were managed on a dynamic, ad hoc basis, combining elements of organization and spontaneity.

The simple provision of blankets, tents, and food was a contentious issue from the very beginning. On the first night, after the tree meeting, activists began bringing these to Tahrir. The police attacked at midnight and evacuated the square by force. In the days that followed, the pattern became familiar: people would bring supplies to the square, and the military and Mubarak's thugs tried to block them—whether by arresting their bearers before they could reach Tahrir or by periodically using force to disperse those set up in the square. Over time, arguably *because of the siege*, the protesters' numbers swelled. An informal network connected protesters within the square with a more fluid group of people who moved in and out, bringing what they could, when they could.

Water provides an interesting example. There were many ways to get drinking water, and these varied in terms of class and preferences. Some people drank only mineral water and were careful to always bring water with them. Visitors and protesters also brought boxes of mineral water to share with others, either distributing the bottles personally or giving them to one of the survival committees to distribute later. Other people just drank tap water, and many protesters volunteered to collect, wash, and refill reusable water bottles at nearby taps. The many cafés and restaurants around the square could have served as resources, but most were closed: the police had warned them, in no uncertain terms, to shutter. Ever adaptive, protesters went to nearby churches and mosques. Omar Makram Mosque and the Qasr El Dobara Evangelical Church became water stations and sites for two of the major field hospitals. Other small mosques were used in similar ways: in one case, a long hose was connected from the back of a small mosque, or simple *zawyia* (corner in Arabic), connecting a site for prayer with a hose that would carry water to Tahrir campers.

Strategies around sanitation and hygiene evolved over time as well. For example, there was no central plan to collect garbage; after a few days, some people just volunteered to collect it, gathering it all in a couple of corners of the square. Bathrooms were another major issue. There are no public restrooms in the square. Only a small number of stores violated the police order and stayed open, and protesters' other option remained the church and mosques mentioned before. Thus, attending to the most basic human need could become a time- and energy-consuming proposition. Protesters walked up to a mile to find a bathroom. Some told me they would get up at 4:00 or 5:00 a.m. or even earlier to stand in line to wash in the Omar Makram Mosque. Others went home to take showers, risking not being able to return to the besieged square. Pictures circulated later, showing activists carrying signs reading, "To Mubarak, you should leave because I want to take a shower." By the second week, protesters had begun to build public restrooms in the square, but their efforts were never completed.

Sleep was not an issue for the daily visitors, but for members of the core sit-in that held the square, it was a nightly concern. It rained twice during the eighteen days of the sit-in—once during the Camel Battle and then again on Friday, February 11, when Mubarak left. Amid the tents, there were still many protesters who simply slept on a blanket in the open air. A number of female protesters told me they slept at the headquarters of the leftist political party Al Tagamoa, about half a mile from the square, while many activists and interviewees said they slept at friends' homes nearby. Many activists were renting apartments in downtown Cairo, which would become handy during the uprising.[13]

I detail these practical matters to emphasize that survival was not a simple thing. The sit-in in Tahrir was a mode of collective action, yes, but it was also a social and physical space in which revolutionaries needed to attend to basic human needs in order to survive.[14] All too often, social movement theories (and perhaps also revolution theories) give scant attention to such issues in their analyses. Social movement theorists ask how social movements endure, but they are referring to the challenges associated with maintaining or reviving mobilization, or the issue of continuity between two movements (Rupp and Taylor 1990; Taylor 1989). Such questions are concerned with movement organization and structure, not the mundane tasks of providing food, water, and safe places for people to sleep and go to the bathroom. And yet, for an action as large as that staged in Tahrir Square, survival issues *were* mobilization issues. They spoke to not only meeting people's basic physical needs but also ensuring that people would remain in the square, either sleeping there or returning on a daily basis, despite discomfort and the constant threat of violence.

Four features of the actions in Tahrir addressed these issues of survival and simultaneously contributed to keeping the movement alive for over two weeks. The first is the existence of a culture of survival aid that was strengthened in the decade before the revolution. Some of my ethnographic notes from the years before 2011 are telling here. In 2003 I was the director of a research unit at the Hisham Mubarak Law Center (HMLC), an NGO that offers legal aid to victims of human rights abuses in Egypt.[15] In addition, the HMLC offices provided space for meetings of antiwar and pro-democracy activists. The office was messy—not just full of legal files but also crowded with blankets, cans of food, and medicine. Sometimes you couldn't even walk in without tripping over blankets and packets of medicine—donations for political prisoners. When Mubarak was detained a few months after the Egyptian Revolution, activists mocked his detention, saying, "Perhaps we should contact the HMLC to offer him legal aid and send him food in jail."[16] In short, Egypt was already equipped with a culture of assistance, especially around practical issues related to basic survival. Protesters were able to draw on these existing networks *and* spontaneously develop new ones.

The second feature that facilitated both survival and mobilization in the camp was the emergence of parallel patterns of organization to deal with practical issues. Older activists, experienced with sit-ins and protests, quickly and systematically began to deal with logistical issues in the square. More newly politicized, often younger participants simply volunteered to solve problems they saw: they would collect garbage or bring food and water, sometimes on a daily basis, sometimes just once. In other words, people helped out according to their own prior experience, preferences, and abilities. On February 11, for example, a friend and I decided to bring sandwiches to the sit-in, along with bottles of water that we planned to distribute. When we got to the square, we were told to leave everything at one of the central distribution sites.[17] It would be difficult to characterize these actions as purely spontaneous *or* organized. Yet they clearly worked.

The emergence of multisite networks of volunteers, both inside and outside the square, is the third feature that developed in and sustained Tahrir. Much attention has been given, understandably, to the people who were *in* Tahrir Square, but equally important were the many people who sent assistance from outside. Many interviewees reminded me that families and people who could not participate directly in the revolution for various reasons—some of them upper-class people or people with ties to the ruling regime—organized campaigns to collect donations of money and/or food to send to the square. The sit-in represented in many ways, then, only the tip of an iceberg kept afloat by unseen people and resources beyond the square.

The fourth feature of the sit-in that highlights the intertwined organizing for survival and mobilization is the division of labor that not only emerged among the protesters themselves but also manifested in how resources were used. As already noted, there were preexisting organizations and political and/or interest-based groups in the square but also random volunteers who simply started to assist with tasks needed in the camp. Regardless of who initiated the action, a division of labor always developed. Some people took care of food and tents, while others took care of political negotiations, meetings, and mobilization. Big organizations, such as the Muslim Brotherhood, played an important role in collecting food and blankets and in staffing the checkpoint system established at entrances to the square, while the RYC helped with food and tents, while also giving speeches and maintaining mobilization.

The first stage was erected in the square by the RYC on February 3; the next day, the Muslim Brotherhood installed another.[18] Each stage had huge speakers broadcasting messages throughout the square. The space underneath the stages was also crucial for protecting and storing food. This was a profoundly telling image, for it captures the way that survival and mobilization efforts reinforced one another. A stage serves as both a platform from which to politicize a crowd of people *and* a place to keep food safe and away from the eyes of police who might otherwise have targeted such resources. It speaks, in other words, to the multiple ways in which a movement needs to be nourished.

Before proceeding, it is important here to briefly discuss how the military's intervention affected the course of events on the ground. Some scholars and media commentators at the time would note, without explanation, that the military sided with the Egyptian protesters (see, for example, Barany 2011). My ethnographic and documentary work, however, suggests that this is far from accurate. I divide the military's role during the eighteen days of revolution into three stages. In the first stage, January 28 to February 2, the army intervened in clashes in Egyptian streets based on orders from Mubarak. The army assisted the police, and after the withdrawal of the police, the army took over as the main coercive force. In some cases, the army even assisted the police by providing them with weapons in Tahrir, as confirmed by multiple eyewitnesses. During this stage the army forces near Tahrir also prevented food, tents, and medical supplies from reaching the square. On January 30 the army flew two F-16 fighter jets loud and low over the square to scare protesters. The army, at this point, was not neutral: it was operating in accordance with the orders of the regime. Throughout this period conversations between protesters and military officers around the square revolved around a common question: "Are you here to protect us, or are you contributing to the siege of the square?"

Then came the second stage, from February 3 to 10. On February 2, pro-Mubarak thugs and armed police and militia came to attack protesters in Tahrir. Army forces surrounded Tahrir but did not intervene to prevent the attacks. On the contrary, the army seemed to be complicit in facilitating the attack. Only one officer violated orders and intervened to help protesters, by shooting in the air to scare the militia. Protesters began to form their own security system to protect the square, and the checkpoint system became more rigid. While the incident highlighted the army's complicity with the regime, it also prompted the army to begin trying to appear neutral—an effort that would define the second stage. After February 2, the army's hostility toward Tahrir dissipated. They allowed food and tents to enter the square. Still, an army leader was sent to Tahrir as a messenger on behalf of Mubarak, an important incident that I discuss later on.

The third stage included the last two days of the revolution (understood here as the eighteen days), February 10 and 11. The army released its first statement on the revolution the day before Mubarak was ousted, acknowledging the demands of the Egyptian protesters. I argue that only during this stage can we see the army actually distancing itself from Mubarak. In other words, to say simply that "the military sided with protesters" is an extremely generous—if not wholly inaccurate—reading of the revolution. I would counter that the military would have liked to control the events but could not. In the simplest terms, it had guns on its side, and thus it retained the upper hand in terms of literally policing the situation. But far from facilitating the protesters' revolutionary agenda, the military merely replaced the regime. It shared power with the protesters only when it couldn't avoid doing so.

Protesters had a complicated view of the military's role throughout. Many saw the army presence as a good thing, symbolic of the extent to which Mubarak and his police force were incapable of controlling the situation—and how important the situation really was. When I talked to protesters at the time, they told me the army was like a black box. They did not know what to expect from it and worried about what role it would assume in both the revolution and the future of Egypt. At the same time, they preferred not to chant against the army so as not to antagonize it while events were still uncertain and unfolding. A leading blogger, Adel Wagdy, told me in an interview on April 5, 2011, "It is this mix of feelings/actions toward the army that sums it up: on the one hand, we have chanted 'The people and the army are one hand,' and on the other, protesters decided to sleep under tanks and block them from encroaching on the square or dispersing the Tahrir sit-in."

Obviously, the Tahrir camp was no ordinary camp. It was a place for battles (life and death); a place for sleeping, eating, and treating the wounded (resting, survival); a place for practicing revolutionary art (enjoying the revolution, celebrating the revolutionary moment); a central place for communication (conferring with other revolutionaries about the revolution); a place for protecting the revolution; and a symbolic center of liberation. Its complexity only underscored its centrality. Protesters drafted their first statement (figure 2.1) in Tahrir Square on the afternoon of January 25, 2011, and distributed it widely across Egypt. It circulated globally in social media. The statement highlights the main slogan of the revolution ("The people want the downfall of the regime"), calls for ousting Mubarak, and states that protesters are determined to occupy Tahrir, calling for rallies and strikes everywhere until their demands are met.

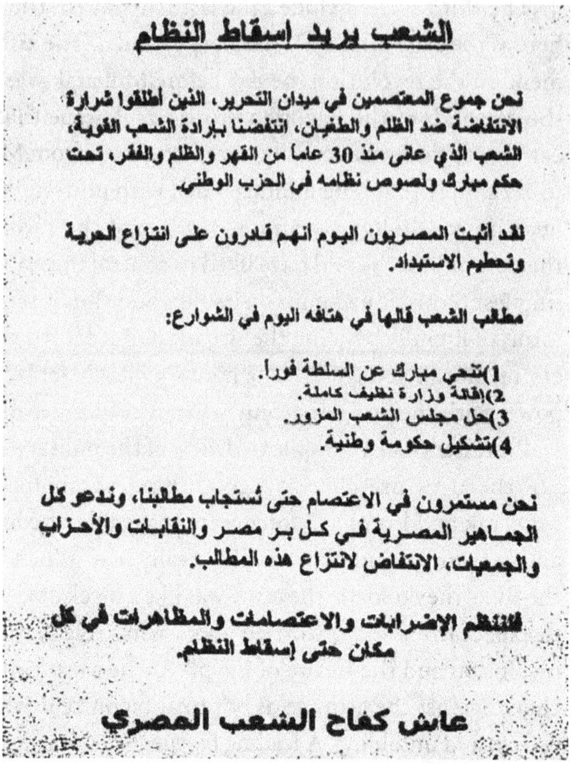

FIGURE 2.1 First statement issued by protesters in Tahrir Square, distributed on the evening of January 25, 2011. In the statement protesters announced that they would start a sit-in in Tahrir and would not leave until Hosni Mubarak's ousting.

الشعب يريد إسقاط النظام

نحن جموع المعتصمين في ميدان التحرير، الذين أطلقوا شرارة الانتفاضة ضد الظلم والطغيان، انتفضنا بإرادة الشعب القوية، الشعب الذي عانى منذ 30 عاماً من القهر والظلم والفقر، تحت حكم مبارك ولصوص نظامه في الحزب الوطني.

لقد أثبت المصريون اليوم أنهم قادرون على انتزاع الحرية وتحطيم الاستبداد.

مطالب الشعب قالها في هتافه اليوم في الشوارع:

1)تنحي مبارك عن السلطة فوراً.
2)إقالة وزارة نظيف كاملة.
3)حل مجلس الشعب المزور.
4)تشكيل حكومة وطنية.

نحن مستمرون في الاعتصام حتى تستجاب مطالبنا، وندعو كل الجماهير المصرية في كل بر مصر والنقابات والأحزاب والجمعيات، الانتفاض لانتزاع هذه المطالب.

لتنظم الإضرابات والاعتصامات والمظاهرات في كل مكان حتى إسقاط النظام.

عاش كفاح الشعب المصري

Mutual Recognition

The fourth process that contributed to squaring the revolution was the mutual recognition between Tahrir protesters and the regime. They understood each other as the opposition during the uprising.

The regime's attitude toward Tahrir shifted over the eighteen days of the square's occupation. They were forced to mix strategies as they contended with the uprising. First, they used force: they brutally attempted to prevent protesters from reaching Tahrir, they sent armed supporters to attack protesters within the square, and they blocked internet and cell phone access. Then they attempted to isolate the square, using the army to help prevent food and medical supplies from reaching the encampment. Third, they attempted to incite the public against Tahrir through media campaigns, and, fourth, they attempted to engage, sending invitations for negotiations and sending messengers to Tahrir. All these strategies ironically led to a recognition that Tahrir was an equal and opposing force going toe to toe with the regime. It was a process of unintended interpellation of Tahrir by the state.

Amid the examples of the regime using force against Tahrir protesters, I witnessed attempts at conciliation. One involved the arrival of a high-ranking military general in the square on February 4. He talked on the main stage, as protesters wondered who he might be. The general's voice came through the speakers, saying, "The regime has heard you, and your demands are respected, and it is now time for you to leave the square."[19] The protesters refused to listen. They chanted back, "We will not leave; he [Mubarak] should leave." Later we learned from the media that the speaker had been General Hassan Al-Rouiny, the head of the Central Command in Egypt. His rank underscored the unintended message of recognition and acknowledgment. Even asking the protesters to leave the square seemed to validate the idea that Tahrir *was* the revolution—if only it would empty out, perhaps the uprising would be over. Other messengers were sent by the regime to ask the protesters to accept Mubarak's offer, which included allowing him to continue his term, supposed to end in six months.[20]

The regime's announcement of its willingness to negotiate for reform, which came on January 30, 2011, was another attempt to disperse the movement and to isolate the square. Mubarak announced that he had given a mandate to his new vice president, Omar Suleiman, to discuss terms and ideas for implementing reform in Egypt.[21] Political parties and some important groups such as the Muslim Brotherhood were invited to Suleiman's meetings, but the protesters in Tahrir were not properly invited.[22] After the talks started, a few youth figures were invited, most of whom later wrote testimonies stating that they were marginalized at the meetings.[23] The regime was obsessed with Tahrir to the point of suggesting that the negotiations with political forces and parties be displayed on big screens for the protesters in Tahrir (presumably in a show of transparency).

Meanwhile, official media targeted Tahrir, labeling protesters as infiltrators and troublemakers and disseminating images purportedly showing violent instigators and groups of irresponsible, destructive kids.[24] Many prominent conservative actors, politicians, and state intellectuals were interviewed extensively on state TV, praising Mubarak's reform while demonizing Tahrir. Over and over again, the protesters were referred to in a reductive and pejorative manner as "the kids of Tahrir." Yet again, the ironic effect of the excessive propaganda against Tahrir was to construct and inadvertently acknowledge Tahrir as a legitimate counterpart to the state. The political climate had become acutely polarized, such that society was essentially divided into three main camps: pro-Mubarak/regime, pro-Tahrir/revolution, and "the couch party"—reluctant to participate in the revolution and overwhelmed with anxiety and worries about the stability of the country. As several activists pointed out to me, the obsession of the official media with Tahrir was ironic and contradictory: If the Mubarak regime was as strong and stable as it asserted, why so much concern over a "bunch of kids"?

Mubarak gave three speeches in response to the protests (on the evenings of January 28, February 1, and February 10). Neither of the first two mentions the word Tahrir, but the third speech invoked Tahrir in the very first sentence: "In the name of God, the Most Gracious, the Most Merciful, dear citizens, I am addressing the youth of Egypt today in Tahrir Square and across the country."[25] But this belated attempt to appeal to the protesters was too late; Mubarak's third speech was the last time he would address the country as its president.

From the regime's perspective, focusing on Tahrir was a way to isolate the square and contain the nationwide protest. That it set up Tahrir as its symbolic contender was unintentional but incendiary. Tahrir protesters responded by acting as the embodiment of the revolution. As mentioned before, Tahrir not only was a sit-in and a symbolic site of the revolution but became a very real and strategically effective center of mobilization, given its proximity to all of the major political power centers of Egypt, from the cabinet and the parliament to no fewer than ten ministries. There was a constant sense of struggle between the regime and the protesters in Tahrir about occupying this important national space. For many protesters, their successful occupation of Tahrir both symbolized and literally demonstrated their ability to shut down the government. As writer Saad El-Qersh conveyed, "Who occupies Tahrir Square grasps the nation's neck and controls the rhythm of life. If the regime loses this control, this will be this regime's end" (2012, 123–24). Protesters used this as fodder for mobilization: the occupiers of Tahrir were the future of Egypt. On February 11, 2011, a protester who was also a lawyer carried a sign that read "This is the Tahrir state, it is based on justice, dignity, liberty and respecting diversity. Outside this square is Mubarak's state, which is based on corruption, despotism and humiliation" (related in Saad 2012, 53).

Simply put, the regime, the media, and neighborhood committees all contributed to the sense of a dichotomy between the regime and the revolution; the former was reduced to Mubarak, and the latter to Tahrir.

Conclusion: Tahrir as a Revolutionary Boundary

Tahrir's identification with the revolution was not just a metonymy. It reflected that Tahrir was constituted as the physical and symbolic site of the revolution, that its boundaries became the boundaries of the revolution.

It is useful here to comment briefly on social boundaries. Boundaries are simply methods of separation, of inclusion and exclusion. Social boundaries entail categorization and identification of who is in and who is out (see, for example, Georg Simmel's [2008] notion of the stranger; see also Lamont and Molnár 2002; Mayrl and Quinn 2016; Tilly 2004). I argue that spatial analysis of revolutions and movements should not be limited to how the geographic environment enables or disables protests. We also ought to think about how claim making is itself spatial and how a movement is bounded by a specific network and an idea about specific place(s). Of particular relevance here is Charles Tilly's (2000, 137) idea about spatial claim making in contentious politics. Tilly argued for two types of contention: contained and transgressive. In the latter, claim making involves new actors and employs innovative means of collective action (138). Tilly argues the distinction is important "because transgressive contention more often disrupts spatial routines in its setting, and more often involves deliberate occupation, reorganization, or dramatization of public space" (138). As my research shows, however, Tahrir was an instance of *both* contained and transgressive contention.

Tahrir was contained in the sense that the most critical pieces of the revolutionary modes of action were associated with Tahrir (the battles to reach Tahrir, after which the police apparatus was defeated, and the sit-in that became the revolution's camp); also, the revolution was thus literally located in and symbolically represented by a relatively contained space in the center of Cairo. But Tahrir also represented a case of transgressive contention insofar as it was constructed as the center of action and mobilization for a nationwide revolution. It was understood as the symbolic seat of a worthy adversary to the Mubarak regime.

Tahrir was made a boundary of the revolution through the discourse on the ground and the actual demarcation of the square through barricades. Over and over again, I heard protesters in Tahrir say things like, "When you enter Tahrir you are in the revolution," or "You are now in the most important liberated zone in Egypt," or simply "Welcome to the revolution." Indeed, some of my interviewees noted that despite the dangers, they "never felt safer" than when they were in Tahrir. Outside the square, they said, they were anxious and worried about the future of the revolution and the future of the country. Inside the square, all their fears and worries ceded importance to the cause of revolution itself.

Barricades first appeared in the afternoon of January 28, 2011. A leading activist told me, "It was the evacuation by force on January 25 that gave us the idea to erect barricades on January 28, after seizing the square for the second time." Initially there were just a few barricades. But after the Camel Battle on February 2, 2011, Tahrir was completely surrounded by barricades. Protesters brought tires, broken trees, rocks, and traffic barriers and constructed these barricades. Map 2.3 shows the spread of the barricades and the location of tents in the famous camp, as well as of key banners that carried the revolution's demands in Tahrir during the uprising.

During a revolution, I argue, barricades not only divide physical space and indicate control but also assert the *authority* to control and separate zones. Barricades, in revolutionary times, are associated with liberated zones and alternative authorities. In my research I show how protesters erected barricades to protect their republic in Tahrir Square from intruders, going so far as to establish checkpoints and inspect visitors. I argue that any satisfactory analysis of revolution should include an analysis of the composition and the distribution of barricades, whether or not checkpoints were associated with these.

But beyond suggesting that barricades still matter in revolutions, I also argue that barricades' usage varies, such that there were three critical differences between barricades in Tahrir and barricades elsewhere during the Egyptian Revolution. First, the barricades in Tahrir were established after brutal confrontations. Second, there was a difference in the rhythm of the barricades in Tahrir compared to the barricades elsewhere (especially the popular committees, discussed in chapter 3): barricades in Tahrir were busy, with people coming and going all the time, and inspections continuing apace. The action did not stop in Tahrir until the day Mubarak was ousted, while barricades erected by the committees saw just a few days of intensity, from the night of January 28 until roughly February 3. Third, the materials that constituted barricades differed: protesters in Tahrir used traffic barriers and fences seized from construction sites but also extended their barricades to include the burned-out police trucks and armored vehicles near Tahrir's entrances. These objects gave the square and its entrances added symbolic power, marking them as the site of the victorious party on January 28. The barricades enclosing Tahrir thus came to serve as symbols of the division between revolutionary and nonrevolutionary space, demarcations of the square, both literally and figuratively, as something that protesters controlled.[26]

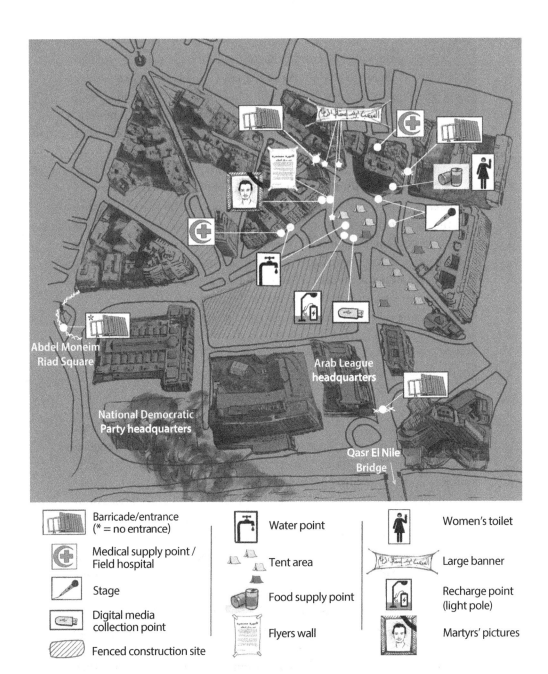

Abdel Moneim
Riad Square

Arab League
headquarters

National Democratic
Party headquarters

Qasr El Nile
Bridge

Barricade/entrance (* = no entrance)	Water point	Women's toilet
Medical supply point / Field hospital	Tent area	Large banner
Stage	Food supply point	Recharge point (light pole)
Digital media collection point	Flyers wall	Martyrs' pictures
Fenced construction site		

MAP 2.3 Layout of Tahrir's revolutionary camp on February 11, 2011. Map by Rime Naguib.

Speaking of the barricades in relation to the Tahrir camp, it is useful here to correct a common confusion about the larger revolutionary repertoire. Many observers reduced the larger revolutionary repertoire to the camp in Tahrir.[27] I define the Tahrir repertoire, or the larger revolutionary repertoire, as a set of available means, which included the occupation of public space, the formation of a minirepublic that required the presence of many forms of organizations, the social media focus on Tahrir, and the erecting of barricades to police the space and protect this republic, as well as the presence of marches and rallies that ended in Tahrir Square.[28] The protest in Tahrir and the encampment in the square were inspired by past protests in Tahrir. But the larger combination of all these means of action was invented during the revolution in 2011 (see A. Said 2022). Yet many of the important pieces that made the revolutionary repertoire successful the first time were missing during attempts to repeat it in the aftermath of the uprising.

I also argue that the creation of a revolutionary boundary in Tahrir did not start in 2011. Rather, a diverse yet specific set of historical conditions constituted Tahrir as the center of the revolution. These conditions included its historical significance and political prominence, both of which made it a target for protest, as well as the regime's attempts to limit mobilization to Tahrir and its paradoxical endorsement of Tahrir as its central counterpart; the media's obsession with Tahrir; and the reliance of the revolution on the continued sit-in in Tahrir. Together, these conditions created a convergence of processes that made Tahrir the most powerful center of gravity of the Egyptian Revolution, the pivot point around which a revolutionary boundary was established. Indeed, because Tahrir Square became a metonym of the revolution, many artistic compositions were created during the uprising by revolutionary actors and artists that carry this meaning, in songs, graffiti, and poetry. The epigraph at the start of this chapter is part of a song by the famous singer Aida El Ayoubi with the band Cairokee. It was composed and widely circulated after the ousting of Mubarak.

Of course, the very idea of Tahrir becoming the center of the revolution means that there existed other revolutionary modes of action and perhaps important possibilities—alternately beyond or even within Tahrir—that were *not* central; voices, modes of action, and forms of political imagination that, unlike Tahrir, did not come to be understood as *the revolution* but remained on the *margins of the revolution*.

3 | sovereignty in the street

POPULAR COMMITTEES,
REVOLUTIONARY
AMBIVALENCE, AND
UNREALIZED POWER

I wish the whole world was mine
Together, my love and I
I really, really wish
But "I wish" never built a home
—FROM "YA RAYTNY TAYR" (I WISH I WAS A BIRD),
A SONG BY SYRIAN-EGYPTIAN SINGER FARID AL-ATRASH

I'd had a long trip to Egypt and a long day in Tahrir Square, breathing in the
air of revolution, by the time I found myself sharing a meal with my siblings
at our parents' house in Cairo. It was the evening of February 4, 2011, and
I was trying to absorb as much as possible. The news media's focus on the
square, on Hosni Mubarak and the military, had me prepared for one sort
of study—and it had taken a full half hour to convince my parents to let me
go to Tahrir, so great was its reputation at this point. But my siblings' din-
nertime revelations about their involvement in the popular committees were
suddenly opening up an unanticipated avenue. When I pressed for details,
they explained that the popular committees were groups of people walking

the streets to protect the neighborhood at night. "Why not join us and see for yourself?"

Out in the street, people sat on folding chairs and perched on the apartment complex stoop. A tray of tea was brought from my parents' home to the committee members. My brother-in-law mentioned, "We even smoke hookah here. Do you want me to fix one?" and we happily smoked, eating sunflower seeds as the folks shared stories of their recent exploits. This, they told me, was a very different night from the intense ones they had seen since January 28. On that night they heard the news and rumors that prisons had been opened, that many convicts had escaped from jails, and that Egypt's police seemed to have vanished. Now all the streets in the entire neighborhood had committees, they reckoned.

"We started a popular committee like them," they said.

I asked the people outside my parents' home to describe those formative days. They mentioned stories about shootings and people carrying guns. They told me that the committee in the next street, closer to the highways, saw more "action," because theirs is a main street that divides and connects two neighborhoods. They told me that other committees swapped stories about arresting police personnel, who were supposedly hiding out rather than engaging with the revolutionaries throughout the country.[1] They told me that the committees had erected checkpoints because the mass police withdrawal had created a security vacuum—now *police* and *criminal* were synonymous. And as they told me all this, I marveled that my siblings, generally disinterested in politics, were among these men, sharing anxieties about the future of Egypt and discussing, in great detail, large questions such as Mubarak's fate, activism, political forces, and the prospect of regime change in Egypt. The revolution had dramatically politicized them, like so many other everyday Egyptians, *yet they did not see themselves as revolutionaries.*

That police officers were hiding out and being arrested like common criminals was shocking: as an Egyptian; a person interested in torture, security, and human rights; and a scholar of states and social movements, I could not imagine what the seeming disappearance of a police apparatus meant. As the world's eyes were on Tahrir Square, self-appointed popular committees were practicing power, taking up functions usually associated with the state (but with an assertion of middle-class logic of protecting property, while the committees' members hailed from every class).

The paradoxes I explored in the previous chapter involved understanding why Tahrir Square became both a symbolic and a physical site of revolution, the pivot point around which a revolutionary boundary was established—

that is, understanding how the revolution was "squared." In this chapter I consider another set of paradoxes. Why were the popular committees peopled by average citizens, from different classes, engaging in radical acts? Why did their members see themselves not as revolutionaries enabling an uprising but as protectors of homes and property? How did the protesters in the square understand their relationships to the committee members patrolling the streets? And how did the squaring of the revolution obscure or truncate transformative possibilities *outside* Tahrir as the eighteen days of the revolution wore on? Most important, and unfortunately, if both parties, the Tahrir actors and the actors in the committees, were practicing power, why did they not realize the immense power they had? And, overall, are there varieties of power to be practiced on the ground during the time of revolutionary crisis?

The Road Untraveled: Possibilities beyond Tahrir

Before talking about revolutionary possibilities outside Tahrir Square, I would like to briefly recap what was going on in the rest of Egypt during the fast-moving days of the 2011 uprising. Prior to January 25, pro-democracy protests had focused not on regime change but on the problems of corruption and police brutality. When Mubarak refused to offer concessions and deployed violence against protesters, their demands shifted to the downfall of the regime. The main modes of action—and media depictions of revolution— soon centered around Tahrir, to the detriment of a holistic understanding of this social movement.

My days in Cairo and conversations with friends and interlocutors reveal a lot about what was happening outside the square. The media tried, for the first two days, to downplay the protests, but people were talking about these every day and everywhere. As events escalated, news coverage remained hostile to the protests, and people grew increasingly anxious. Society became sharply politicized as media-fueled rumors circulated through covert conversations in cabs, cafés, and family homes. People heard that the protesters were foreigners and spies intent on destabilizing the country. They worried about when they could go back to work, about how to protect their homes, and about not having enough cash (the banks had closed on January 28, the same day army checkpoints were established in Cairo's main squares and along its highways). Divisions soon emerged between those in favor of Mubarak and stability and those in favor of revolution and change; a broad middle fervently hoped they might remain neutral and uninvolved. As the government media blamed the uprising for stock market losses, class divisions were revealed: some people sympathized with urban riots by the poor, while others were hostile to the revolution and Tahrir.

Drawing on both documentary research and interviews, I have identified five critical modes of action that occurred beyond Tahrir as the Egyptian Revolution unfolded. I do so not to reduce but to expand the analysis around what was actually happening on the ground—to demonstrate the significance of these possibilities and to make a case against teleological understandings of revolution that focus only on materialized and notable outcomes. These modes are (1) the January 26 and 27 battles in Suez between the protesters and the police and ruling-party militia; (2) attacks on centers or symbols of power, such as the January 28 burning of the ruling party's headquarters, of police stations, and of courts; (3) urban riots by the poor that erupted in several parts of suburban Cairo, the Nile delta, upper Egypt, and some Suez Canal cities; (4) the formation and operation of popular committees in urban centers from January 28 onward; and (5) working-class strikes that started on February 6 and continued beyond Mubarak's ouster.[2]

Here I focus on the neighborhood popular committees. These modes of action took organized forms involving large, cross-class sectors of the population. I argue that their organization held potential for an expansion of the political and dynamic density of the revolution, if not its radicalization. This mode of action also played an important role in providing security for revolutionaries and for the revolution, understood even then as focused on Tahrir Square and on the removal of Mubarak. At a time when the state—except the army, which would distance itself from Mubarak—simply was not present in the streets, the popular committees partially filled the power vacuum in ways that effectively supported the revolution while appearing mainly conservative.

Popular Committees

Egypt's security vacuum arose in this period because most of the police force was immediately focused on attempting to crush the protests. Significant portions of the force were involved in major battles with protesters, especially in Tahrir and in other major urban centers. The most important of these battles, on January 28, ended with the apparent defeat of the police. They were exhausted, unable to match the mass of protesters. Further, many police stations were, like the streets of so much of Egypt, left unattended. There was evidence, too, that many prisons had been left unattended (or, according to the police narrative, stormed, mainly by "foreign spies"). As rumors about escaped convicts spread, people formed committees to protect themselves and their homes.[3]

Mohamed Fayez, a thirty-year-old professional and self-identified Revolutionary Socialist, told me about this moment: "The security vacuum may or may not have been a plot, but it is a fact that the entire police apparatus did focus on the protests at that time. And on January 28, 2011, following its defeat, the police force withdrew from most streets in Egypt. The defeat of this apparatus affected the entire network and communication among police forces. The police force simply lost direction and were clueless about what to do. I do not deny the plot. I am just saying that the police were defeated and withdrew due to the heroic actions of protesters too" (interview, November 29, 2012). Whether the police withdrawal was planned—an effort by the police to deter protests or an effort by the protesters to gain control—or simply happened when the police lost their cohesion and communications, the protesters' role in creating the security vacuum cannot be denied. That means the rise of the popular committees is also, undeniably, connected to the actions and aims of the protesters. Fayez, one of the organizers in Tahrir, helped coordinate the popular committees outside the square. He told me:

> After we organized ourselves in Tahrir, we realized the significance and the need for protection beyond Tahrir. . . . [We] asked protesters to go to neighborhoods, especially those who are in touch with or have networks there, and talk to them. Groups of two or three went to these neighborhoods. We learned that committees were quickly formed in Ard alliwaa, Almatariya, Roud alfarag, Ain chams, Almarg, Helwan. And then the idea spread to many other areas. The independent media caught the idea and started to circulate it widely after the media showed images of people protecting their areas. This was a revolutionary moment; ideas and initiatives were spreading like wildfire. People were empowered, and they were the authority.

Fayez's account was confirmed by several other interlocutors in Tahrir. Yet another account of the committees' formation has them starting in Suez. There is a historical precedent for such committees in Egypt: in an Al Jazeera documentary (see Che Batikha 2012) about the committees, Shaikh Hafez Salama, a Salafi elder in Suez who enjoyed political and popular credibility because of his role during an anticolonial popular resistance movement in 1956, claims the committees of the revolution arose in Suez, and the idea transferred to Cairo and Alexandria. Salama also notes that Egypt witnessed similar committees during World War II, as well as during the 1956, 1967, and 1973 wars. In the committee that I participated in, located in northeastern Cairo, participants told me, "We just started like everybody else in Egypt." They meant that the committees of the revolution had formed just like the other committees in other eras: to fill power vacuums and serve state functions.

A common thread in these stories about the initial spread of the committees in 2011 is that they spread *quickly* and *voluntarily*, and their spread was *expansive* to all urban centers in Egypt. Most of the committees started late in the night on January 28 and in the early morning of January 29, when there was neither cell phone service nor internet throughout the country. Basically, Egyptians took the security role on themselves, within twenty-four hours, without complex methods of communication.

Committee members armed themselves with whatever was at hand—sticks and batons, swords, and guns—as they stood in their streets and established checkpoints and barricades to protect their neighborhoods and control the flow of vehicles and pedestrians. They inspected cars and the IDs of anyone who seemed to be from outside the neighborhood. They arrested people and turned them over to the army. When checkpoints were attacked, the committee members reacted with violence, sometimes coordinating with other committees.

My interlocutors told me about arresting thugs and police personnel—not within Tahrir Square, as was being reported worldwide, but in the streets of Cairo and other urban centers. By this time, police personnel were not wearing their uniforms in the streets. Many had gone into hiding. And though there is not much documentation for the claim that the committees detained police in these days, some videos do show committee members stopping, inspecting, and/or arresting police.[4] One of my interviewees told me that in their neighborhood in Nasr City, an off-duty officer joined the committee at night. He was, they said, "seeking protection by being in the committee."

Police stations were targeted in this period, with large groups of armed thugs attacking police stations to release their friends. Not all police stations were burned; some remained open with a light police presence. One interviewee told me that he witnessed an incident in which police officers were besieged in their station, cordoned off by a civilian militia. The popular committee in the area knew that one of the officers was unable to leave the station in his uniform, and so "the officer here was protected by the committee," escorted into the night. The irony, of course, was that civilians had blockaded the station, yet civilians also "released" the familiar officer.

On January 31, BBC Arabic aired a report where it interviewed members of a popular committee in Cairo (BBC Arabic 2011). In the segment, one member affirmed, "Starting today, there is no government; we are the government." According to the report, most members of the committees believed that the security withdrawal was planned by senior government officials, to sow fear among citizens due to the absence of the state, which was supposed to be providing protection and security. This was also the common sentiment I heard from many popular committee members I talked to. Many members in the BBC Arabic report also emphasized that the committees had the power to arrest anyone, rich or poor, "al-ghafeeer wa-al wazeer" (literally, "the doorman and the minister"). Thus, the committees were groups of citizens doing neighborhood watch, which included the power of arrest.

Here it is important to note three important details. First, the military tanks and larger military configurations were unable to go into the streets. Instead, they had spread around Tahrir, on highways, in main squares, and along the borders of cities and governorates. Second, the military was not ready or equipped for daily policing, at a time when the public largely felt betrayed by the police force. Third, the processes of coordination between the military and the members of the committees, while seemingly simple, were in reality complex and laden with mutual power testing.

From my notes and based on conversations with many interlocutors, people were angry and frustrated at the failure of the police apparatus, in what felt to them like a major betrayal. A common refrain went "As if torture and abuse were not enough, how dare the police apparatus and Ministry of the Interior do this to us," meaning abandon their job of "protection." In many locales the committees were extremely well organized, not only establishing networks of communication (including the use of walkie-talkies and cell phones for coordination), but also dividing the city into numbered districts. In a story published in *Shorouk News*, one committee member explained that they had developed passwords so that trusted citizens could use those codes to avoid inspections at other committees' checkpoints.[5]

My interviews revealed numerous examples of the committees taking important action. On January 30, 2011, committee members in New Maadi and Zahraaa Maadi confronted and arrested two armed escaped convicts from nearby Tora Prison and arrested five low-ranking police officers (*umanaa shorta*). The day after, committee members in New Maadi and Zahraaa Maadi also arrested some informal police personnel (*mokhbreen*) as they tried to rob an apartment. All these captives were turned over to the military.[6] Another neighborhood committee, in Al-Ayaat (Giza), arrested fifteen escapees from

Fayyoum Prison on January 29, the same day committee members in the Asa-fraa and Victoria areas in Alexandria stopped five informal police personnel who were terrorizing citizens by opening fire in residences; fought them with sticks, rocks, and knives; and arrested the men.[7] *Almasry Alyoum* and *Shorouk News* asserted that on that day they also arrested fifteen armed thugs, while committee members in the Imbaba neighborhood (Giza) arrested three in-formal police personnel (*mokhbreen*).[8] Committee members even reclaimed stolen property from police stations, so that on January 31, 2011, members in Bandar Damanhour (lower-western Egypt, seventy kilometers from Al-exandria) confronted thugs who had taken nine hundred weapons from Damanhour Police Station. Both the thugs and the weapons were turned over to the military.[9]

Mohamed Fayez conceded that there were cases in which committee members abused their power to enact revenge against the police: "Yes, this happened. It was impossible to control things in this chaotic situation." According to one leftist writer, "People have found their inner (or suppressed) prosecutor" (El-Merghany 2012). One committee member stated, "Commit-tee members enjoyed stopping other citizens to check their IDs. The funny thing is our doorman participated in the process of checking IDs, despite the fact that he cannot read" (interview, March 16, 2011).

Through gathering primary sources—my ethnographic notes, my inter-views with activists and personal contacts—along with secondary sources like newspapers and social media posts, I was able to document that popular committees had operated in twenty-six of the twenty-seven Egyptian gover-norates during the 2011 revolution. Table 3.1 demonstrates the distribution of popular committees across the Egyptian governorates during the eighteen days of the revolution.

Based on this documentation and analysis, I provide a simple anatomy of the committees in table 3.2. Some of their key features include being armed and handing over detainees to the military. As the table shows, the com-mittees were not connected to the Tahrir camp, though some individual protesters, like myself, moved back and forth from the committees to the camp. Perhaps the greatest evidence of the committees' significance and "revolutionary" potential is that, immediately after Mubarak's ouster, *both* revolutionaries and state officials rushed to try to work with the committees—whether to further radicalize them or to co-opt them. After ousting Mubarak, socialist activists and revolutionary youth tried to form a national network for these committees. They held a gathering in Tahrir, attended by many people from within and outside of Cairo, at which the committees were re-

Table 3.1. Distribution of Popular Committees across Egyptian Governorates during the Eighteen Days of the Revolution (as Documented in Selected Egyptian Newspapers)

Governorate	Documented Popular Committees	Governorate	Documented Popular Committees
Cairo	37	Faiyum	5
Giza	23	Banī Suwayf	5
Alexandria	21	Minya	2
Qalyubia	10	Asyut	1
Dakahlia	4	Sohag	0
Sharqia	1	Qena	1
Gharbiya	2	Luxor	3
Minufiyah	6	Aswan	1
Beheira	9	North Sinai	2
Kafr El Sheikh	2	South Sinai	1
Damietta	1	Marsa Matruh	3
Port Said	4	Red Sea	2
Ismailia	3	New Valley	1
Suez	2	**Total**	**152**

Note: See appendix 3 for more information on documentation methods.

formed under the name Popular Committees to Defend the Revolution.[10] Fayez, my interviewee, was one of the key activists in this effort.

Meanwhile, the state and the police pursued a double strategy. First, they tried to push some of these committees (or committees comprising state informants) to use more aggressive measures. That is, they tried to get the committees and their members to abuse their power, in an effort to increase people's fear of such committees and turn the public against them. Additionally, they disseminated a discourse that referred to the committees as militias and criminals (a strategy offset by largely positive media coverage that framed the committees as Egypt's great protectors).[11] Some funding agencies saw the committees as an opportunity to build a culture of civic engagement in Egypt—one that would last beyond the democratic revolution—and tried to find ways to fund them, though some activists worried that accepting such funding might lead to the committees' co-optation and corruption.[12]

Table 3.2. An Anatomy of the Popular Committees

Method of formation	Spontaneously and voluntarily after hearing rumors that prisons were open and convicts had escaped.
Start date	Mostly late in the night of January 28 and early in the morning of January 29, 2011.
End date	February 11, 2011. But some newer versions of the committees started after the revolution for a short period.
Location	Most neighborhoods and most urban centers in Egypt. A committee's mobility was limited to walking its own neighborhood and borders, sometimes chasing escaped convicts and criminals within these areas.
Demographics	Youth and middle-aged persons (average age, 17–50); mostly male.
Use of barricades	Yes, large rocks, tires, and traffic barricades. Sometimes there were no barricades in use, simply the committee blocking the street with chairs and/or standing there.
Arming	Lightly armed: mostly with large wooden and metal sticks and also swords. But sometimes guns, and in some cases machine pistols or automatic weapons, were used.
Tasks	Main tasks involved the patrolling and protection of neighborhoods, including the guarding of churches, banks, and museums, as well as policing price gouging and other social and economic activities. Some committees protected rallies.
Class	Diverse, but mostly they were composed of the middle and working classes.
Organization	Localized formations; had no hierarchy and were democratically based.
Communication	Relied on direct communications, but cell phones (after February 2) and walkie-talkies were used in some cases to coordinate among different committees.
Relation with the military	While committee members handed over some criminals and suspects to the military, committees were chiefly responsible for their areas. Military tanks were deployed on the main roads and highways only.
Relation with Tahrir revolutionaries	Disconnected. But some actors participated in both Tahrir and the committees.

So the popular committees constituted one of the most important forms of mobilization during the revolution. They practiced policing power. They had considerable potential for further politicization, especially through expanding the political and dynamic density of the revolution. There are four main aspects to their potential. First, they were fundamentally democratic, having formed spontaneously and without hierarchy. They were like small communities or congresses that gathered to talk about politics daily. Second, the committees were forced by the pressure of the revolutionary situation, and the need for security, to continue for a considerable period. Unlike the attacks on centers of powers, such as burning the headquarters of the ruling party and police stations on January 28, popular committees were a collective form of organization and lasted for about thirteen days. Third, the committees exercised a form of collective authority—actual power, practiced on the ground. They had the authority to stop "strange" people in the streets and in neighborhoods. They targeted and arrested police officers and personnel—many of whom were in hiding. The committees developed a coordinated form of power that increasingly resembled and took responsibility for the operations of the state. Members of the committees volunteered to organize traffic and control checkpoints. It could be said that actual power in Egypt at the time was divided among the army, which was dispersed in the streets; the popular committees; and Tahrir. Table 3.3 documents key committee events and activities to emphasize the ways that these committees were not basic unarmed neighborhood watches but armed groups that engaged in conflict and practiced the power to arrest. Committee members fought, were injured, and sometimes died in the course of their work.

Fourth, the committees were doing the state's job. In contrast to the historical committees described by Sheikh Hafez Salama, the committees of 2011 were not backing the state but substituting *for* the state. Enraged at the state's failure to do its job, they formed an alternative government without knowing they had done so.[13]

The committees were the de facto authorities in their districts. One interlocutor mentioned that a couple of days before Mubarak's ousting, the commissioner of Omrania Police Station (Giza) came to the popular committee at night and asked *permission* to reopen the police station. And as I circulated in Tahrir Square, I frequently heard that the revolution would not have continued without these committees. By this logic, Tahrir represented the political arm of the revolution while the committees protected Egyptians' homes (the revolution's back).

Table 3.3. Events among the Popular Committees in Different Governorates during the Eighteen Days of the Revolution (as Documented by Selected Newspapers)

Governorate/ Type of Action	Committee Members Dying during Security Confrontations	Committee Members Injured during Confrontations	Arresting Escaped Convicts or Thugs	Stopping Vandalism	Recovering Stolen Property	Calm Activities*	Total
Cairo	2	1	12	1	1	20	37
Giza	6	0	8	1	0	8	23
Alexandria	1	0	6	5	0	9	21
Qalyubia	1	1	4	2	0	2	10
Dakahlia	1	0	2	0	1	0	4
Sharqia	0	0	1	0	0	0	1
Gharbiya	0	0	1	0	0	1	2
Minufiyah	2	1	3	0	0	0	6
Beheira	0	0	0	0	2	7	9
Kafr El Sheikh	1	0	0	0	1	0	2
Damietta	0	0	0	0	0	1	1
Port Said	0	1	1	1	0	1	4
Ismailia	1	0	1	1	0	0	3
Suez	0	0	1	0	0	1	2
Faiyum	0	0	2	0	0	3	5
Banī Suwayf	1	0	0	4	0	0	5
Minya	1	0	1	0	0	0	2
Asyut	0	0	0	0	0	1	1
Sohag	0	0	0	0	0	0	0
Qena	0	0	1	0	0	0	1
Luxor	0	0	0	2	0	1	3
Aswan	1	0	0	0	0	0	1
North Sinai	0	0	0	0	0	2	2
South Sinai	0	0	0	0	0	1	1
Marsa Matrouh	0	0	0	1	0	2	3
Red Sea	0	0	0	0	0	2	2
New Valley	0	0	0	1	0	0	1
Total	**18**	**4**	**44**	**19**	**5**	**62**	**152**

* These activities include conducting neighborhood watches or simply conferring among members, rather than arrests and other confrontations.

Among the most critical information I gained from several of my interlocutors was how members of the committee thought of the military and of their regular communication with military personnel during these times. One interlocutor was very clear in asserting, "When we coordinated with the military, I knew we were doing it from a position of power, not of weakness." He added, "We—both the military and us—knew that there was a security vacuum in Egypt and that the military could not claim they were guarding Egypt without us." Several other revolutionary interlocutors confirmed this view. It seems that the main priority for the military at the time was to guard strategic places, that is, key government buildings and the headquarters of the Egyptian Radio and Television Union. It was the first thing the military tended to in the afternoon of January 28, 2011, when it deployed in the streets. After that, it guarded key highways and the main entrances to the capital, as well as the borders of governorates. But most of Egypt was in practice guarded by the committees.

My findings and analysis are supported by several lucid testimonies by Egyptian revolutionaries. For example, in 2014 Egyptian leftist writer Mohamed Naeem wrote an extensive Facebook post about his participation in the popular committee in the southeastern Cairo neighborhood of Mukattam, where he went after spending the day in Tahrir.[14] Naeem shared his vivid memories about the cross-class composition of the committee and the arming of the committee members with knives and other bladed weapons. He emphasized that the committee members engaged in serious political conversations, despite the different class backgrounds of the members. He also highlighted that doormen were key parts of the committees and recounted that on his own street, it was the committee members who protected the street and its surrounding areas, while two military officers who also resided on that street merely watched. Naeem emphasized, "One of them showed up for fifteen minutes on the first night. He otherwise watched us from his balcony at night."

Furthermore, if we agree that policing in general (and *especially* during a time of unrest) is a crucial component of state authority, then the power accrued by the committees—even those that were not pro-revolution— represented a revolutionary practice. The committees presented an opportunity that could have led to a much more decentralized form of revolutionary power *outside* of Tahrir. One of the main factors that limited the further development and radicalization of these committees was their ambivalent relationship with the revolution (and with Tahrir). Again, in the committee in which I participated, the members did not think of themselves as revolutionaries but as protectors. Many interviewees told me that some of the committees were more radical than others, yet the overall common denominator was that the committees were united not by any particular political stance but by anger toward the police and by their commitment to protecting their homes. The ambiguity regarding the committees' positions vis-à-vis the revolution meant that encounters between committees and protesters were often tense.

Friends and protesters in Tahrir talked often about being stopped by the committees, never knowing whether the committee was sympathetic with the revolution or not. When asked, "Are you coming from or headed to Tahrir?" the answer was always a gamble. Still, though the committees constituted an alternative to state power in the streets and could be seen as sharing power with the military, and although many committees became more sympathetic toward the revolution as events escalated, their members did not see themselves as part of, let alone representative of, the revolution. They kept their distance from the revolution, thus limiting their role in the change to come.

Ambivalence and Agency

I argued in the previous chapter that Tahrir Square and the mobilization around it constituted a boundary of the Egyptian Revolution in 2011 during the days of the uprising. In this chapter I have shown how this boundary worked through ambivalence in relation to those events and activities that were beyond or outside of Tahrir. By *ambivalence*, I mean the failure to resolve the relationship between Tahrir and various spaces of mobilization, particularly the popular committees.

One important question arises about the agency of protesters in Tahrir. Did they intend to marginalize certain voices within Tahrir and to overlook opportunities outside? If we agree that diverse factors led to the constitution of a revolutionary boundary, then things like the ambivalence of protesters and the nature of compromise within Tahrir are just individual factors among many. The making of the revolutionary boundary cannot be attributed to any particular group or decision; instead, the process by which the revolutionary boundary was constructed was replete with contingency. At multiple moments a different configuration of events and actors might have shifted the boundary, and changing any given factor alone does not guarantee a different outcome. This is to say: it is the wrong question to ask whether protesters in Tahrir intended to marginalize actors and events outside the square. Some of the complex and contingent factors that contributed to creating a revolutionary boundary in Tahrir preceded the revolution, such as the history of mobilization in Tahrir Square, which contributed to making Tahrir synonymous with the revolution.

In Tahrir, and at the peak of the revolutionary crisis, the revolution was overwhelming for nearly everyone involved. Protesters suddenly had to contend with issues of basic survival and continued mobilization. As many of my interlocutors and interviewees told me, most people simply didn't know *what* to do. The Revolution Youth Coalition (RYC) was deciding things on a daily basis. Adel Wagdy, a leading blogger and activist, described the makeshift nature of the revolution: "What I can describe as our 'revolutionary psyche' shifted not only from one day to another but also within the same day. The typical daily curve was as follows: in the morning, concern that not enough people would show up; by noon, confidence upon seeing mass numbers turning up, then later, as people start to leave the square, anxiety and eagerness to know what is really happening outside the square" (interview, April 10, 2011). Likewise, Nadia Sleem, a fifty-six-year-old pro-democracy activist and university professor, stated, "Things were fluid and in flux all the time, from the first moment. On the night of January 25, for example, if Mubarak had made some reforms, things may have been different. But instead they attacked protesters. The more they attacked, the more things escalated. People on January 28 were angrier and more determined and in way bigger numbers than January 25. The more the regime resisted reform and attacked, the higher were the demands of the people. This was a revolutionary moment where intensity and unpredictability [were] ruling the situation" (interview, November 20, 2012). In contrast to how Tahrir Square was constructed globally, as a peaceful and organized camp, things were fluid and unpredictable all the time (see figure 3.1).

Sleem, like other interviewees, told me stories about people from southern Egypt and the Nile delta cities coming to Tahrir and joining the sit-in with their own tents, and I saw tents in Tahrir bearing the signs of many different Egyptian cities (see figure 3.2). Poor villagers, people who belonged to the Muslim Brotherhood and the Salafis came, too, supported financially by these networks. So did people from other major cities and movements, including the leaders of the 2007 working-class strike at the Al-Mahalla Textile Spinning and Weaving Company. The presence of people from outside Cairo gave more representative power to Tahrir but also negatively affected mobilization outside the square and Cairo by concentrating action in this

FIGURE 3.1 Tahrir Square on February 3, 2011, one day after the famous Camel Battle. Photo by Sebastian Scheiner, AP.

one place, rather than diffusing it by retaining the power of leading activists and unionists within their own major cities and constituencies across Egypt.

Another reason Tahrir revolutionaries did not think to look to the popular committees as a revolutionary possibility relates to the fact that the popular committees closest to Tahrir were frequently hostile to the camp and the revolution. Neighborhoods like Abdeen, Al-Sayeda Zainab, and Qasr El Nile included huge networks of thugs who had long worked with the ruling party leadership or the police apparatus. For example, Ragab Helal Hemeida, a former member of parliament in Abdeen, had a close connection to the security apparatus and a huge army of thugs. Ahmad Fathi Sorour (a former speaker of the parliament) had his own large army of thugs and supporters in Al-Sayeda Zainab. And the network of spies and informal police in Qasr El Nile was often used by the police apparatus to deal with protests in the downtown area. Given the proximal hostility, many revolutionaries in Tahrir assumed that popular committees were generally hostile to the revolution.

Meanwhile, the ways of life emerging within Tahrir were overwhelming, even to me. I consider myself equipped with some decent organizing skills,

FIGURE 3.2 A sign on a tent in Tahrir. The sign reads, "This is the camp of the peasants of Faqous Ash Sharqiyah." Faqous is a town in Ash Sharqiyah province in the Nile delta of Egypt. Picture by the author, taken on February 9, 2011, two days before Mubarak's ousting.

having organized in different spheres in Egypt under Mubarak from 1995 to 2004. And yet, when activists running the RYC stage asked me to speak, I declined, feeling perplexed and intimidated by the tens of thousands of people present. In my field notes, over and over again, I find some variation of the following comment from protesters: "We were just walking around and looking at the faces, enjoying the moment, but also directionless." Yes, protesters were talking about Tahrir as a utopia and "the safest place in Egypt," but they also experienced it as a disorienting, overwhelming space. Tahrir's protesters were *ambivalent* and were dealing with constant challenges to find the right balance between pressing but often opposing issues. How could they balance the protection and survival of the camp and the need to continue mobilization, or the need to sustain Tahrir's camp as the center of revolutionary action and grievance, while expanding the revolution and its demands elsewhere? They had to balance maintaining and performing unity in Tahrir for Egypt and the rest of the world, amid hysterical pro-government propaganda playing on divisions; simply getting rid of Mubarak and taking other radical approaches, especially proposals for the future; responding to the army's hostility to the square while working to neutralize the army; and making judgments and deciding about the relationship between the regime and the state amid their ambivalence toward the military.

The main goal of Tahrir revolutionaries was to keep the revolution going until its demands for political change and the ousting of Mubarak (and, over time, maybe even just the latter) were met. Some of my interlocutors were experienced organizers and tried to bridge the gap between Tahrir and the popular committees (and even some of the working-class strikes). Especially in the early days of the revolution, they told me, it was understood that the greatest danger was that Tahrir would be isolated from the rest of society. Shokry Ahmed described forming an impromptu organization in Tahrir, the January 25 Youth Movement. One of the first tasks they discussed was the need to reach out to neighborhoods, especially the popular committees. In my interview with Ahmed on November 21, 2012, he stated, "Our main discussion was how to reach out to people outside Tahrir. Then we decided to talk about the division of labor, and we divided the [new] movement into groups and decided which groups were to work on which issues. There were four groups: provinces, labor, media, and legal issues. If you notice, three of the committees were about reaching out outside Tahrir." The group's first action was issuing a statement, which was distributed in neighborhoods and working-class areas both within and outside Cairo. The statement talked about unity:

> The main focus of the statement was to explain to the public what Tahrir was all about. Who the people in Tahrir were, and what their demands were. We tried to tell the public, either the laborers or the people in the neighborhoods, that Tahrir's demands were also their demands. We distributed sixty thousand copies of the statement, in seven heavily working-class areas inside and outside Cairo. Labor entered the revolution strongly with strikes in the last few days of the revolt. I cannot say this is because of our statement, of course, but I would say that our statement was important in mobilizing labor.

Mohamed Fayez worked with others to form the Egyptian Committees to Defend the Revolution a couple of months after the ousting of Mubarak. Intended to continue to defend neighborhoods, these committees were based on networking the popular committees that had been established during the eighteen days. He told me how many activists in Tahrir worked to spread the idea of popular committees:

> Tahrir had been liberated by protesters but was still under attack. The protesters came up with the idea of establishing checkpoints and security committees. And some said we have to inform our neighborhoods and networks about the idea. The idea then started to spread. We simply were hoping to spread the [logic of the revolution in the] square to these neighborhoods, not only the idea of the popular committees. There were many groups and open discussions in the square about the need to spread the idea of popular committees to neighborhoods. I cannot confirm that we in Tahrir were the only reason the idea spread outside. But we wanted to reach out, both to make sure that people were safe and to spread the revolution.

The idea of "spreading" the square or making all Egyptian squares mimic the main square (Tahrir) existed among many activists, but activists remained ambivalent about the relationship between the square and its surroundings. One common slogan at the time is very telling: "Do not come to Tahrir empty handed." On the surface, this was just a message: daily visitors to Tahrir should bring food, water, blankets, medicine, and other supplies, or, better yet, other friends, family, or neighbors. But as another activist pointed out to me, that imperative begged the question: "How do you want to spread the revolution everywhere and at the same time focus mainly on Tahrir to make it stronger?"

In sum, Tahrir's effect on the Egyptian Revolution was complicated and paradoxical. As one interviewee, Noha Sameh (a thirty-one-year-old IT expert and self-identified revolutionary Marxist), put it:

> This specific charm of the square comes from many things. Yes, we lived together there. We saw people dying there. But the media was insisting that the revolution was only in Tahrir. It is like we were admitting this and were acting accordingly. There was a construction of a myth about Tahrir, and we all contributed to it, not only the media. I would not say there is a conspiracy, but the insistence of the regime and international media that the revolution was only in Tahrir created this myth. It was unfortunate that we were not very critical of that at the time. (November 19, 2012, interview)

At the same time, it was difficult to be critical. As Nadia Sleem stated, "The power of Tahrir was not from the few hundred thousand or so sleeping at night in the last few days. It was from the millions coming every day, and from the sometimes ten million people or even more protesting all over Egypt. Tahrir was not authoritative to the rest of Egypt. But Tahrir was kind of bragging about its power. Tahrir was telling the regime, we are those millions. We are the true representation of the nation. And our message is the people's message."

Triple "Sovereignty"

In chapter 2, I argued that protesters in Tahrir controlled the entire space of the square. I also discussed how this worked in relation to the spread of the military on the ground in the aftermath of January 28, 2011. In theory, the military controlled (and policed) most of Egypt, but, in practice, the protesters controlled and policed the space of Tahrir Square. How can we reconcile this with the role of the popular committees, taking into consideration that the military theoretically *could* have policed Egyptian neighborhoods and streets?

Leon Trotsky's concept of dual power is useful here. *Dual power* refers to a situation in which revolutionaries establish institutions that perform the same functions as the government. Trotsky is clear that dual power

> does not presuppose—generally speaking, indeed, it excludes—the possibility of a division of the power into *two equal halves*, or indeed any *formal equilibrium of forces* whatever. It is not constitutional, but *a revolutionary fact*. It implies that a destruction of the social equilibrium has already split the state superstructure. It arises where the hostile classes are already each relying upon essentially incompatible governmental organizations—the one outlived, the other in process of formation—which jostle against each other at every step in the sphere of government. The amount of power which falls to each of these struggling classes in such a situation, is determined by the correlation of forces in the course of the struggle. ([1932] 2008, 150, emphasis mine)

The popular committees in Egypt represented some form of power in Trotsky's sense, given that they were like true parliaments in the streets and they claimed the power of arrest. Yet I argue that Egypt during the uprising witnessed a form of *triple sovereignty*, with subtle caveats, compared to Trotsky's famous formulation.

This triple form of sovereignty included (1) Tahrir protesters, whose camp constituted a form of minirepublic, the main liberated zone or the main revolutionary space in Egypt; (2) the popular committees, which claimed policing power and established a form of alternate state in neighborhoods throughout Egypt; and (3) the military, which nominally controlled key strategic areas in Egypt.

Keeping these three powers in mind, we can compare the Egyptian case with Trotsky's formulation. Similar to Trotsky's thesis, the equilibrium found among the three forces in Egypt was a revolutionary fact. It was practical in nature, not constitutional. Further, these three forces were doing the government's work, defined here as policing, with obvious variations in the ways this function was performed: the military practiced its authority to protect itself, its interests, and the state apparatus (the focus was strategic places); the committees controlled the streets and neighborhoods in key cities in Egypt; and the Tahrir protesters controlled and policed Tahrir.[15]

Departing from Trotsky's formula, in which the dual power was based on a crystallization of class antagonism, with the old government representing the interests of the dominant class and the new emerging government the interests of the dominated, Egypt's triple sovereignty was more complex and did not reflect a clear class antagonism. Each of the three parties reflected a mix of classes with subtle differences. The military as an institution is the backbone of the state, and its generals are part of the ruling class. The military was based on conscription, however, and at the time of the uprising, most soldiers could be considered working class, at least during their conscription period, and lower-tier officers could be seen as middle class. Both the Tahrir revolutionaries and the committees were a mix of classes, but while the former represented the revolution, the latter were divided. See map 3.1, showing the rough class differences in Cairo's main districts.

Besides, if we agree that sovereignty is always a relative concept, then the actual practice of sovereignty is also a matter of degrees, which can fluctuate all the time, rather than existing in an absolute manner (see, for example, Stoler 2006).[16] To be most accurate, the committees and Tahrir revolutionaries embodied a sovereign practice in an embryonic sense, according to Trotsky's analysis. To meet Trotsky's criterion, one important thing was lacking in the Egyptian case: mass defection in the army. The potential of this scenario to happen was real and not hypothetical, if the army leaders decided to shoot at protesters, because the army is based entirely on conscription of citizens (see Nepstad 2013). In the example I mentioned earlier, it was a civilian militia who besieged a police station, with its officers, and it was civilians who liberated from the siege a specific officer who was familiar to the committee in the area. If this example does not reflect a degree of sovereignty of civilians in the revolution, what else can? Finally, not only was there a complication related

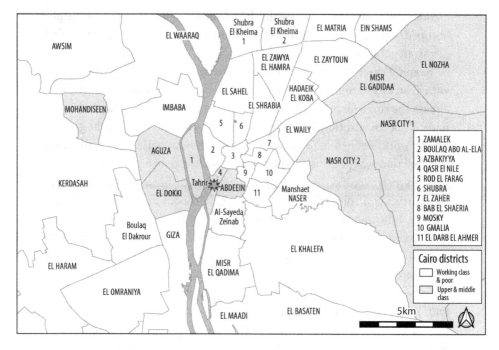

MAP 3.1 Rough class differences in Cairo's main districts. Map by Ahmed Atif and Daftar Ahwal.

to the class composition of these powers and the degrees of power, but each of these parties also saw the revolution in different ways. For the army, the revolution was an opportunity for the generals to maintain military rule and thwart Gamal Mubarak's succession (see also Kandil 2014). The army took advantage of its ambiguous position to maneuver: it intervened on behalf of the Mubarak regime initially but also attempted to take advantage of the revolutionary situation and then initiated its role as a counterrevolutionary force from the first day after Mubarak's ouster. Tahrir's protesters articulated themselves as the revolution and the voice of the revolution, while the committees remained divided about the revolution.

On the surface, the committees shared power over the streets with the military, in the same way the Tahrir protesters shared control of the areas near Tahrir with the military. That they and the Tahrir protesters handed detainees over to the military may suggest that the military had power over both, but neither the committees nor Tahrir had jails.[17] Also, in practice, the military was not in control of Tahrir itself, nor of the committees' spaces. As I discussed earlier, the committees spread quickly and voluntarily and expanded into all the urban centers in Egypt, claiming the power of policing without any authorization. The need for security was an outcome of the revolutionary situation, and each party started to do its job in policing by practicing its authority in its spaces. Committee members repeatedly told me that they had simply taken up their positions when Tahrir was occupied, and "a day or two days later, some military officer came to us, exchanged phone numbers, and asked us to be in touch if we needed help." In some cases, they did not call the military at all, and in others, they got in touch with the military to send them detainees. Something similar happened in Tahrir, where the military controlled the surrounding areas but not the square itself.

As for the power of the military, note that the military was dispersed into the streets based on Mubarak's order as commander in chief. Its primary mission was to restore order. The military had the actual power of coercion and acted as a representative of the state in crisis. But the ambiguous status of the military and its claim to be on the side of the protesters—never actually the case until February 10—gave the military more credibility and more room to maneuver. Many protesters believed that as long as the military claimed distance from Mubarak and did not actively enact violence against the revolutionaries, it could be assumed to be on the side of the protesters.

The discontinuity among Tahrir and the committees was not a result of their cross-class bases but of the committees' general lack of revolutionary articulation. As Trotsky theorizes, the amount of power gained or to be gained by competing powers depends on "the correlation of forces in the course of the struggle." The equilibrium among the three powers in Egypt did not last for long: it ended on February 11, 2011, when Mubarak stepped down and delegated his powers to the Supreme Council of Armed Forces (SCAF).

In short, it is critical to differentiate between three instances in relation to the practice of power on the street in Egypt at the time: (1) practicing power on the ground, while lacking both an interest in and a vision for seizing it; (2) practicing power while having a vision and articulation about the revolution, while being ambiguous about seizing power, a fact that prevented Tahrir revolutionaries from achieving this goal; and (3) practicing power while cultivating an interest in and actually seizing power. The military obviously had an eye on all three. Tahrir revolutionaries practiced the first, while formulating some parts of the second (conceiving themselves as the representatives and the embodiment of the revolution but lacking a vision about seizing power). The popular committees practiced only the first. Ultimately, the ambivalent relationship between the Tahrir revolutionaries and the committees prevented the coordination that could have led to greater radicalization and power for both. Indeed, the missed opportunity for coordination between the committees and Tahrir protesters (and perhaps also with working-class strikes) was part of the collective sentiments shared by many revolutionary actors in 2012 and beyond. In the introduction of this book, I mentioned the idea that revolution and love have much in common. In the epigraph to this chapter, from a romantic song by Farid al-Atrash (composed in 1937), "I wish" never built a home in love, so lost opportunities would not make revolutions succeed.

Conclusion: Power's Enigma and Revolutionary Disjunction

It is important to differentiate between different degrees and iterations of practicing power or seizing power during revolutionary crisis. One example of the revolutionaries' confusion and lack of interest in seizing power can be helpful here. I discussed earlier that revolutionaries in Tahrir and elsewhere targeted government buildings during the uprising—notably by attacking and burning the headquarters of the National Democratic Party, many police stations, and some courts. Other attempts to storm government buildings were less successful.[18]

During the uprising on February 3, a group of protesters decided to move from the main camp in Tahrir to a nearby space in Hussein Hegazy Street. The group, which activists told me numbered about two thousand, aimed to occupy the area in front of the parliament and the headquarters of the Egyptian cabinet, and their minicamp continued until the day Mubarak was ousted. Surprisingly, this group did not storm and occupy the buildings—perhaps their disinclination symbolized their general disinterest in seizing state power. After the uprising I asked several leading activists from the RYC and other witnesses about this group. They told me that this specific action was started spontaneously by a group of revolutionaries who saw this as an important escalation and expansion of the Tahrir camp. One leading activist in the RYC later told me, "There were ongoing daily conversations between the RYC and the group that occupied that area." He stated, "The key component of these conversations was the next step for this minicamp [presumably a plan to storm the parliament building, for example, and occupy the cabinet]. The discussions about the escalation were serious. This discussion was also shaped by concerns and careful consideration of this proposed action given that the military was guarding the building as well." He added, "On the morning of the day of Mubarak's ousting, I and many other key members in the RYC as well as the campers in the minicamp were considering the escalation, but the announcement of Mubarak's stepping down ended this idea" (Facebook private communication, May 10, 2019).

Of course, occupying a government building is one thing, seizing state power quite another. While some could argue that the revolutionaries in this minicamp were just crazy activists who did not reflect a larger stance in the uprising, I note two important pieces of information here: First, I witnessed and heard many announcements from the stages in Tahrir about the need to support *and expand* the minicamp. My sense was that there was no opposition in the main camp to this minicamp. Second, this minicamp was in place during the peak of a revolutionary crisis, and there were plans for its escalation. This was not just an idea about occupying a government building but about doing so during a revolution, at a time when the government itself and the existing parliament were incapable of doing their jobs and practicing their power. In fact, on February 11, 2011, Egypt was in a state of comprehensive mass disobedience. As stated by Amnesty International, "On 11 February, as a general insurrection looked increasingly likely, the army stepped in and President Mubarak resigned" (Amnesty International 2011, 9). In sum, perhaps it is no exaggeration to suggest that the military's decision to take over on that day was intended to stop any further radicalization, due to the escalation of working-class strikes and evidence on the ground that Tahrir revolutionaries were considering an actual occupation of important buildings such as the parliament, even while being confused or lacking interest in actually seizing power.[19]

As I have argued in the introduction, agential and spatial elements are some of the key aspects of lived contingency in the revolutionary context. I also discussed in chapters 1 and 2 that Egyptian revolutionary actors' relation with the military on the ground was far more complex than the basic fraternization story promulgated by the Egyptian elite and the military after the uprising against Mubarak. Despite the prevalence of the slogan "The people and the army are one hand," revolutionary actors and the military were deeply suspicious of each other, and the revolutionaries had to make decisions accordingly.

Unfortunately, there was also a disconnect between the main camp in Tahrir and other modes of action outside the square, such as the popular committees; also, some voices within Tahrir itself were marginalized during the uprising. The squaring of the revolution, physically and symbolically, as the boundary of the Egyptian Revolution happened even as activists maintained ambivalence about Tahrir's relation with other key modes of action outside its barricades.

4 | the two souls of the egyptian revolution

DEMOCRATIC DEMANDS,
RADICAL STRIKES

In Egyptian, bread means life
Egyptians have lived this for many years
Even if the Nile were to ever go dry
It will flood then and fulfill its promise.
Bread, freedom, social justice.
—RAMY ESSAM, EGYPTIAN SINGER

Every day from February 4, 2011, until the ousting of Hosni Mubarak on February 11, I was in Tahrir Square. Things were in constant flux, including the protesters' relationships with the square itself. As these grew increasingly comfortable and confident, they began to integrate more of the square and its surroundings into their sit-in. The protesters even expanded the camp to some of the nearby government buildings.[1] Soon people were climbing buildings and traffic lights not only to hang banners but to provide a form of security. When intruders, mostly armed thugs aligned with the Mubarak regime, attempted to enter the square, the sentries would sound an alert. Posters covered many surfaces. The grounds were filled with tents, communication centers, and impromptu field hospitals, and barricades protected the square's borders.

On February 6, I saw protesters atop one of Tahrir's tallest buildings unfurl a banner that ran the length of the entire building, to the cheers of hundreds of thousands of demonstrators below. The banner was a list of demands (see figure 4.1) that read:

OUR DEMANDS:

1. Ousting Mubarak
2. Dissolving the illegitimate parliament and upper house (Shura Council)
3. Ending the state of emergency immediately
4. Forming a transitional national unity government
5. Electing a parliament to enact constitutional amendments, based on which a presidential election would take place
6. Immediate trials for all officials responsible for killing martyrs (protesters) of the revolution
7. Immediate trials for all corrupt officials and those who stole the nation's wealth

Signed: The Youth of Egypt in the Sit-In (in Tahrir)

Over time, the banner's demands and the revolution's demands would become synonymous in public discourse. Yet I cannot point to any process by which these demands were drafted, were voted on, or became the consensus. What made thousands of individuals in Tahrir and beyond accept these as *the* (minimal) demands of their revolution? How did the broader and potentially more radical slogans of the revolution, such as the demands for bread, liberty, social justice, and human dignity, stand alongside the narrow democratic agenda of the banner?

When the banner was unfurled, I cheered along with everyone else. It was thrilling—the largest banner yet in the square—and was embraced as a rallying point for all our efforts. I didn't even think to seek out who was behind it; no one really did. In hindsight, this may seem like curious indifference, but it is difficult to overstate the extent to which no one seemed to know *or* care during the event. Even when I began to inquire, the answers sidestepped authorship: "We don't know who hung it. It has our demands; it belongs to Tahrir and the revolution." Months later, as I turned to social media, the banner's authorship was still unfindable. When I returned for more fieldwork in the summer of 2012, my contacts among leading bloggers

FIGURE 4.1 The banner hung in Tahrir Square, displaying the demands of the Tahrir protesters. The building, the balcony, and some journalists on top are also shown. Picture by Hossam el-Hamalawy, used here with his permission.

and activists suggested that I ask Pierre Sioufi, whose apartment was on the top floor of the building from which the banner was hung. He had allowed many bloggers and activists, along with international and local journalists, to use his home's windows to capture wide-angle pictures of Tahrir in the days of revolution.[2]

Even Sioufi had little concrete information. He revealed:

> I really don't know. There were a few youth from Tahrir, and [they] came to ask me to hang it from the top of the building. At the time, I was receiving a lot of police harassment. The police told me to prevent journalists and foreign nationals from taking pictures of the square from my apartment. After this harassment, I stopped allowing journalists. But I made an extra effort to know who was filming or taking pictures from my balcony. Eventually, I did not prevent anybody who seemed to belong to or be sympathetic with the revolution. I saw the banner, and I did not say no.

The issue was all but moot by the time one of the older activists from the National Association for Change (NAFC) told me their organization had hung the banner. In the moment, the banner's unknown provenance had probably fueled its acceptance and power.

The Most Visible Banner and the Problem
of the Democratic Revolution

If the power of the banner did not rest in its authorship, what about its content? What made this set of demands widely acceptable to what was, as I elaborate in the following, a diverse group of protesters? The story of the banner reveals much about what can be described as the revolution's democratic reformist agenda, as well as the role of Tahrir's sit-in in the larger revolution. My argument in this chapter is that what we know now as the Egyptian Revolution of 2011 carried two sets of demands, or had two "souls."[3] One centered on political grievances, defined here as demands for a competent representative democracy based on a new constitution. The other focused on demands for economic justice, at the center of which was ending or reducing the severe damage of neoliberalism in Egypt. This second set included ending state corruption, guaranteeing a decent minimum wage, and stopping the further privatization of the public sector. For many reasons, one of these sets became the most visible and seemed paramount. The reasons for this include (1) the history of political coalitions in Egypt, which revolved around democratic reform; (2) the cross-class nature of the revolution, which made political demands and the end of Mubarak's cronyism the minimal consensus between the conflicting classes; (3) the role of social media and media in general, which focused on these demands at the expense of the other set; (4) the neopatrimonial nature of the Mubarak regime, which deluded many revolutionary actors (myself included) into believing that ending Mubarak's rule would put an end to the corrupt political regime as a whole; and (5) the active role and class privilege of certain actors in Tahrir Square, which made them more visible than others, as they were able to engage more actively with social media. Because of these intertwined factors, the more visible actors were public figures and revolutionary youth, while the poor and underclass folks in Tahrir were sidelined.

I offer an ethnographic-cum-historical account of the rise of democratic-reformist demands, defined here as demands for a constitutional democracy and a fair electoral system, tracing the story of the banner back to a decade of demands for political reform. I explain how many Egyptian revolutionaries, understandably but in a misguided way, collapsed the entirety of the regime to Mubarak alone. I situate the dominance of the democratic demands of the revolution within the context of the coalescence of three types of coalitions: political, cross-class, and youth, despite their different temporal trajectories. Together, the processes of coalition building and the high-profile creation of political messaging in the square fed into the squaring of the revolution. Though a critical factor in the initial success of the revolution, the democratic consensus played an enabling role in the counterrevolution, as the next chapter takes up.

My claims about the two souls of the revolution, political and social, rely on three pieces of evidence: the uprising's radical and general slogans, the escalation of explicitly working-class strikes in the last few days of the eighteen days of the uprising, and the class makeup of the revolution's martyrs and casualties. We cannot declare a dichotomy in which procedural democratic demands stood against the social demands of the revolution, nor should we stop at saying that the two coexisted during the uprising. Instead, I argue that the prevalence and the dominance of electoral reform over social reform was the result of crucial dynamics that shaped the revolution's trajectory over time. Some of these key dynamics included the ambivalence of the revolutionaries toward the military and the state, the cross-class coalition that existed during the revolution, and the lack of unifying political revolutionary organization that could link the practice of power on the ground with developing and articulating a centralized intention to seize power, as I demonstrated in the previous chapter.

A word about what I mean by *democratic revolution*, a notion that has not been stable historically: it is often invoked in contrast to the more radical or classic *social revolution*. In fact, so-called classic social revolutions established the first waves of democracy. They cannot be separated. Democratic revolutions are, and always have been, pregnant with radical social grievances, and they are, and always have been, necessarily incomplete. The United States, whose version of democracy is critiqued as a federalist republic masquerading as a direct democracy, as well as having oligarchic and plutocratic features, excluded women and most racial groups other than "white" people from the vote until recent decades. In short, the making or the achievement of democracy in the so-called democratic revolution is never separate from social issues.

Three Roads to Consensus: Why the Democratic Demands Became Dominant

To properly answer the question of how the reformism expressed in the Tahrir banner came to stand in for the political voice of a majority of Egyptians, it is useful to step back and ask who exactly participated in the Egyptian Revolution. To my knowledge, there has been no rigorous demographic analysis of the revolution. Various studies have focused on groups of participants and coalitions of groups (Amar 2013; Goldstone 2011; Holmes 2012; Shehata 2012), but it is vital to avoid conflating the various levels of coalition politics. I examine political, cross-class, and youth coalitions separately, to show how and why the various groups that formed these types of coalitions arrived at a consensus on democratic reformism via distinctive but overlapping processes. Political coalitions were a decade in the making, whereas cross-class coalitions intensified from 2005 to 2010, with 2011 representing a "final straw" moment in which economic elites also became alienated from Mubarak. Meanwhile, youth coalitions emerged first as part of larger umbrella political coalitions such as the Egyptian Movement for Change (Kefaya) but went on to become more independent after 2008, the birth of the April 6 Youth Movement. Youth organizing peaked with the birth of the Revolution Youth Coalition (RYC).

I define a coalition as a temporary agreement between social and/or political movement organizations to work together to achieve a common goal. A coalition does not entail the dissolution of the individual groups and their reconstitution as a single new group; rather, each party may continue to work autonomously under its own banner at the same time that it is involved in a common project. The dynamic is similar to what Leon Trotsky (1938) called the strategy of the united front, in which the Bolshevik Party established a temporary common platform with reformist parties.

Jack Goldstone (2011) spells out the benefits of cross-class alliances:

> If a protest draws support mainly from just one class or group (peasants, workers, students, urban shopkeepers, professionals), the state can confront that group as a disruptive force, and seek to unify elites from other sectors against that threat. However, if protestors represent many different groups, it is much harder for the state to find allies against them. Moreover, while a state can claim to be preserving a society by acting against isolated disruptive elements, it is far more difficult to maintain legitimacy when acting against a broad cross-class coalition. Elites are more likely to

desert the state, creating crippling divisions, if protestors represent a broad spectrum of society. In addition, a broad cross-class coalition facilitates further mobilization by creating "mega-networks" linking prior, tightly linked within-group networks to each other. The impact of public media in favor of the protestors is also greater if media representation shows protestors as representative of the whole society, rather than as one particular group seeking partisan advantages for itself. (457)

Yet coalitions are often necessary but insufficient conditions of revolution—their emergence does not set the stage for revolution but may be crucial to it. What coalitions do offer is the seemingly paradoxical benefit of unity in diversity. But if diversity and appeal increase, so too does the difficulty of arriving at a consensus.

Road 1: Political Coalitions

Scholars of the Egyptian Revolution agree that political coalitions were important during the uprising but seemed to fail in its aftermath (Abdelrahman 2014, 92–93; see also Fadel 2014), especially after the ousting of elected president Mohamed Morsi in 2013. To understand how the political coalitions of Tahrir arrived at a set of reformist demands, we need to study the history of political coalitions in Egypt, particularly in the decade *before* the revolution. Drawing on a variety of primary and secondary sources, I compiled a list of thirty-three political coalitions and/or temporary collaborative campaigns in Egypt from 2000 to 2010 (see appendix 4). All demanded democracy, whether through explicit calls for political and electoral reform or general calls for increased freedom of organizing.[4] I identify two key organizations in this history of coalition building that illustrate not only peak moments of mobilization but also the process by which demands became increasingly focused on the removal of Mubarak and the institution of political reforms. A quick comparison of the respective platforms of Kefaya in 2004, the NAFC in 2010, and the Tahrir banner in 2011 reveals significant similarities (see table 4.1). The platforms are almost identical, with two principal differences: the 2011 addition of ousting Mubarak and a focus on punitive measures for those associated with his regime.

Table 4.1. Comparison of the Platforms/Demands of Political Coalitions in 2004, 2010, and 2011

Kefaya (2004)*	NAFC† (2010)‡	Tahrir Banner (2011)
1. The constitution (of 1971) should be amended to allow a multicandidate presidential election, and the presidency should be limited to two terms for one person. Presidential power should be reduced to guarantee some sort of separation of powers.	1. End emergency status.	1. Oust Mubarak.
2. End emergency status and all despotic laws in Egypt as well as releasing all political prisoners and prisoners of conscience.	2. Grant the Egyptian judiciary full supervision of all the stages of the electoral process.	2. Dissolve the illegitimate parliament and upper house (Shura Council).
3. Amend election laws in Egypt to allow full supervision of the judiciary over all stages of the electoral process.	3. Grant national and international NGOs the right to monitor the election process.	3. End the state of emergency immediately.
	4. Ensure equal opportunity in the media to all candidates in elections, especially in the presidential election.	4. Form a transitional national unity government.
	5. Ensure that Egyptians abroad have the right to vote in Egyptian embassies and consulates abroad.	5. Elect a parliament to enact constitutional amendments, based on which a presidential election would take place.

(continued)

Table 4.1. *(continued)*

Kefaya (2004)*	NAFC† (2010)‡	Tahrir Banner (2011)
	6. Ensure that the right to run in presidential elections is not restricted with tough stipulations, according to Egypt's commitments with the ICPR.** Also restrict presidents to two terms.	6. Hold immediate trials for all officials responsible for killing martyrs (protesters) of the revolution.
	7. Ensure voters vote only with their national ID.	7. Hold immediate trials for all corrupt officials and those who stole the nation's wealth.

* For Kefaya's original statement, see Popular Campaign for Change 2004.
† NAFC = National Association for Change.
‡ As outlined specifically in the 2010 "We Will Change" campaign. See National Association for Change 2010.
** ICPR = International Covenant on Civil and Political Rights.

KEFAYA

On September 9, 2004, a cluster of organizations affiliated with political parties, civil society networks, and individuals issued a historic statement against Mubarak's plans to run for a fifth term in 2005. The statement launched the Popular Campaign for Change, with the slogan "No to the Extension of Power and No to Succession." The campaign opposed Mubarak's seeming plan to pass power on to his son Gamal, and demanded multicandidate presidential elections. By September 23, 2004, the statement bore the signatures of twenty-six organizations and 489 individuals. It required great courage to sign and circulate this manifesto. Most political parties had been co-opted by Mubarak and the security apparatus, and it was dangerous to go against them, no matter how simple the statement's demands may seem.

This statement gave birth to the Egyptian Movement for Change, or Kefaya (Enough), signaling the unequivocal opposition to Mubarak's continued hold on power. The new coalition was built on existing movements, its platform representing a process of both refinement and compromise over time (Howeidy 2005a, 2005b).[5] It offered a broad, flexible tent built on years of joint work but was dominated by Nasserists, socialists, and the traditional working-class left. The Muslim Brotherhood (MB) was not officially part of Kefaya, though individual MB members joined. It was led by middle-class professionals and offered a space for professional syndicates to come together. A series of Kefaya offshoots included Lawyers for Change, Artists for Change, Youth for Change, and so on—what some writers and Egyptian intellectuals would come to call "Kefaya and Its Sisters" (Essmat 2010). Last but not least, it took opposition to the street, sending a clear signal that Egypt's formal opposition, the political parties co-opted by Mubarak, had failed. Its weekly protests in 2005 insisted that no reform would come to this broken system without pressure and protest.

When I interviewed Yasser Ahmed, a leftist organizer and founding member of many of the coalitions listed in appendix 4, by phone in March 30, 2014, he noted that the biggest problem in coalition building was "mostly about who will join in," rather than "the political ceiling of the coalition." In other words, priority was given to building a critical mass over any rigid conception of the coalition's goals. This quantitative strategy, I argue, led to the adoption of a relatively watered-down reformist agenda, to appeal to the greatest possible number of people and groups. This is not a critique but an important corrective: the mass-appeal strategy emerged as a rational response to the authoritarianism of Mubarak's regime. Protesters were pushed to form coalitions for reasons of safety and amplification, and that meant compromises. Compromises, in turn, meant a relatively generic agenda focused on political reform.

Ahmed noted that one of the biggest recurrent questions in Kefaya was whether to include the MB and, if so, how. The MB was an outlier, in a sense, in that it preferred to work on its own. When it did form coalitions, it tended to dominate them given its sheer numbers.[6] Appendix 4 shows that many other coalitions were created for the same purposes. Their proliferation often resulted from disagreements regarding whom to include in each group. For example, there were two different attempts to unionize socialists during 2005 and 2006; likewise, two or three other groups had the same aims as Kefaya—one initiated by Marxists and another by the MB—but Kefaya succeeded because it managed to unite most of the opposition under a single umbrella. The MB-led coalition was the National Campaign for Change, which it formed with the Revolutionary Socialists—a new Trotskyist group that justified its partnership with the MB with the slogan "With the Islamists?—Sometimes. With the state?—Never!" (Abdelrahman 2009). The short-lived National Campaign for Change formed in 2004 and had the same goals as Kefaya, yet it failed because it was seen as dominated by the MB. This illustrates how it was crucial in those years for successful coalitions to be seen as expansive rather than exclusive.

The NAFC was formed after Mohamed ElBaradei, the Egyptian diplomat and former director of the International Atomic Energy Agency, arrived in Egypt in February 2010 and announced that he would join the movement for change in Egypt.[7] Within a week he hosted a meeting that included leaders from Kefaya and the MB and numerous important politicians from across the opposition. In addition to convincing ElBaradei to run in the scheduled 2011 presidential election, the meeting founded the NAFC. It would become, with the inclusion of the MB, the biggest political coalition in the decade before the revolution.[8]

The NAFC got to work, releasing a founding statement, "Together We Will Make Change," which clearly connected the group's seven demands (see table 4.1) to the multiple deteriorating arenas of Egyptian life.[9] It took just seven months to gain one million signatories—an unheard-of achievement in a country where a police state had long stymied even such symbolic political actions.

The NAFC marked a renewal of the reform-minded politics that had stagnated from 2006 to 2010. The regime saw it as a serious threat, no doubt heightened when, in November 2010, the NAFC sponsored a bold idea—the formation of an alternative parliament. This counterparliament included a number of former members of parliament who had been ousted in corrupt elections, and it met at least twice before the revolution. Its very existence underscored the opposition's claims that the regime lacked legitimacy. The NAFC's million-strong petition whipped up enthusiasm and momentum on the streets. Many youth joined the campaign for ElBaradei's election and worked in organized groups to collect more signatures. When the protests began in Tahrir, it was the secretary-general of the NAFC, Abdel Galil Mostafa, who drafted the first formal statement, on the night of January 25, 2011. Later, as I learned, NAFC activists would make and hang the famous yellow banner discussed in the beginning of this chapter.

Road 2: Cross-Class Coalitions

Though political coalitions were working in the decade before the revolution, there was no reason to expect the kind of wide, cross-class coalition that developed in and around Tahrir in 2011. The opposition had long highlighted the inequities of Mubarak's political economy, yet the regime proclaimed satisfaction with the economic indicators it presented (or fabricated) and pointed to "complimentary" reports from international financial institutions such as the World Bank and the International Monetary Fund (IMF).[10] The unprecedented participation of people from all class backgrounds in the revolution, however, reveals the reality of widespread dissatisfaction and disillusionment across Egypt's class structure.

Prominent Egyptian blogger Hossam el-Hamalawy (2011b) described the cross-class mobilization: "Mubarak managed to alienate all social classes in society. In Tahrir Square, you found sons and daughters of the Egyptian elite, together with the workers, middle-class citizens and the urban poor. But remember that it's only when the mass strikes started on Wednesday that the regime started crumbling and the army had to force Mubarak to resign because the system was about to collapse." As el-Hamalawy suggests, the mobilization of the working classes provided what we might consider the crucial foundation of the revolution. Labor strikes between 2006 and 2008 and a series of working-class sit-ins in downtown Cairo and in front of the Egyptian cabinet and the parliament signaled organizational know-how. Labor strikes would prove key in the days leading up to Mubarak's ouster. On February 9, 2011, for example, public transportation workers announced a strike in solidarity with the revolution's demands. They released a statement calling for an end to the state of emergency, a national minimum wage of 1,200 Egyptian pounds, and the drafting of a new constitution—echoing the demands hung on the banner in Tahrir Square (el-Hamalawy 2011c). The statement was critical in that it came at a time when a general strike seemed imminent, especially in the last days of the uprising, when many similar statements were made in a context of spreading strikes. It was also one of the few statements released by workers that explicitly forwarded political and economic demands.

As I walked through Tahrir, the presence of working-class and labor organizations was easily detectable. The newly founded Independent Tax Collectors Trade Union, for instance, hung its own prominent banner, important evidence that even a critical sector of the state bureaucracy was against the regime. I saw many other banners hung by workers who hailed from beyond Cairo. Key organizers included Waleed Haleem and Karam Fahmy, two of the workers who planned the April 2007 labor strike at the Al-Mahalla Textile Spinning and Weaving Company. Haleem, speaking with me on November 15, 2012, described participating in the uprisings as its own sort of job: "I joined the protests in Mahalla on January 25, 26, and 27, and then I went to Cairo. I was at the Tahrir sit-in constantly until the ousting of Mubarak. I left Tahrir for only a couple of hours each day, and when I needed to go to the bathroom. In Tahrir I saw workers from Mahalla, from Suez, from Ismailia." Despite their presence in Tahrir, however, workers did not visibly mobilize *as* workers or join the protests until February 8 and 9. Haleem told me that, at first, workers felt that participation in the street protests was the best way to contribute to the cause. It was when they saw the numbers in Tahrir that they felt encouraged to attempt to organize strikes. Hossam el-Hamalawy (2011c) writes of this period:

> From day 1 of our uprising, the working class has been taking part in the protests. Who do you think were the protesters in Mahalla, Suez and Kafr el-Dawar for example? However, the workers were taking part as "demonstrators" and not necessarily as "workers"—meaning, they were not moving independently. The govt had brought the economy to halt, not the protesters by its curfew, shutting down of banks and business. It was a capitalist strike, aiming at terrorizing the Egyptian people. Only when the govt tried to bring the country back to "normal" on Sunday [was it] that workers returned to their factories, discussed the current situation, and started to organize en masse, moving as a block.[11]

Mohsen Bassem, a labor organizer and journalist, told me that the military's implementation of a curfew also hindered workers' plans to strike during the eighteen days. With the curfew, as well as the closing of banks and government buildings, they feared that a strike—particularly one involving government workers—would be ineffective. Then, when businesses opened on February 6, it took labor leaders at least two days to organize. The strikes started on February 8, 2011.

If working-class participants were present but not visibly involved in Tahrir's leadership, middle-class participants were hypervisible. In 2012 I interviewed a total of fifty people who participated during the eighteen days of the revolution.[12] Of those, only ten clearly identified as working class, while the rest identified as middle class. Certainly, my sample may not be representative; indeed, it is likely impossible to construct in hindsight a clear picture of the exact class composition of the protesters in Tahrir. Nonetheless, many of my interviewees were middle-class professionals. Middle-class protesters—including journalists, doctors, and lawyers—set up stages and banners and established professional association tables in the various corners of Tahrir. As many of them acknowledged, participating in an ongoing action for eighteen days required the freedom to miss work or simply quit—a luxury the working class and poor could not afford. Thus, the prominence of middle-class protest leaders was unsurprising. It paralleled the composition of Kefaya and many other core opposition groups and coalitions in the decade prior to the revolution.

Middle-class participants went to Tahrir not out of altruistic solidarity with workers and the poor but because they, too, were weary of economic disparities and the lack of opportunities under the Mubarak regime (Kandil 2012). The application of structural adjustment programs since the mid-1990s, followed by Mubarak's excessive neoliberal reforms, had negatively affected both the lower and middle classes. Where once there had been the protection of the welfare state under Gamal Abdel Nasser, there was now an increasingly repressive police state and crony capitalism that offered few opportunities for those outside the ruling inner circle.

Talking to people in Tahrir Square, I got the sense that the working classes welcomed the politicization of the middle classes, even if it was bittersweet. Some working-class leaders recalled a sense of betrayal, traced to the complacency of the middle class in years past. They had not supported strikes in places like Mahalla, for instance. Yet those same working-class leaders noted that in Tahrir it was enough for workers to come and be part of the story without necessarily being visible; if middle-class protesters assumed leadership roles in Tahrir, that was fine. Ultimately, it was the revolution that mattered. Perhaps most remarkably, Tahrir gained support among the upper classes, including many key Egyptian businesspeople. Why? How did so many classes harbor so much anger toward Mubarak's regime?

Here it is useful to situate the cross-class coalition within the larger picture of the Egyptian political economy under Mubarak. The late political economist Samer Soliman (2012a) identified three main features of the political economy of the Mubarak regime: (1) the transition from a semi-rentier state to a predatory tax state (in which taxation increases constantly without true representation); (2) the decline of the regime's public purchasing power; and (3) the "bourgeoisification" of the ruling party.

The third feature is especially relevant to the question of upper-class Egyptians' participation in the uprisings. Soliman was naming a major shift in the practices of the Egyptian state, especially after the rise of Gamal Mubarak in politics. Historically, Hosni Mubarak, who rose through the army's ranks to inherit Anwar Sadat's bureaucratic economy, had acted as an arbiter between the military and the upper classes. As Gamal Mubarak became increasingly involved in politics, however, this formula changed. The ruling party and its relation to "business" shifted such that the regime's inner circle contracted around a small group of cronies close to Gamal Mubarak. Not only the military but also wider segments of Egypt's upper classes were threatened by this shift toward Gamal Mubarak's inner circle. Soon only small segments at each level of Egypt's class structure stood to benefit from connections to the Mubarak family network.

The upper classes' participation in and support for the sit-in in Tahrir differed from the ways the lower and middle classes mobilized. Some business tycoons, for example, Naguib Sawiris, the CEO of Wind Telecom and Orascom Telecom Holding, offered their private TV channels to cover the protests, thus violating the government ban and censorship on news featuring Tahrir. Tawfeeq Kamel Diab and Ibrahim El Moallem, owners of the two main independent newspapers, *Almasry Alyoum* and *Shorouk News*, tried to offer perspectives from the ground, covering the protests within and beyond Tahrir even under threat (journalist friends told me these papers received the ire of Mubarak's thugs throughout the days of revolution). And other prominent Egyptians, including Mamdouh Hamza, the founder of a major engineering company in Egypt, helped to finance the protests in Tahrir and offered assistance with logistics (*Jadaliyya* 2011). Several members of the RYC would tell me later that Hamza directly contributed to the cost of building their stage within Tahrir, while another mentioned that funds from sympathetic businesses allowed the NAFC to rent an apartment overlooking Tahrir Square for meetings.

Businessmen within the MB and its networks also supported the sit-in. Soha Shehata, the key organizer of the survival committee of the RYC, told me that she asked MB contacts to provide her with money and donations for the square. The MB even set up their own survival committees and provided tents and blankets to their poorer members who traveled to Tahrir from the countryside. I personally witnessed such assistance, and my interlocutors confirmed that the MB and the Salafis brought in and supported members from outside Cairo who wanted to help. Indeed, on my second day in Tahrir, February 5, 2011, I helped two old men who appeared to be Salafis or MB members carry in huge piles of blankets and tents for the sit-in.

Political coalitions in Egypt were a decade in the making, but the widespread participation of different classes in the revolution was sparked by more recent changes in politics and the economy occurring mainly after 2005. The cost of such cross-class coalitions, however, was that the only agenda capable of uniting everyone focused on political, as opposed to economic, reform. While for working-class Egyptians, the Egyptian poor, and leftists, for example, ousting Mubarak was entangled with reducing or even ending poverty and reaching social justice, for upper-class and many middle-class Egyptians, ousting Mubarak would guarantee basic liberal democracy, without necessarily achieving social justice. As I discuss throughout this book, one of the main problems of the revolution was the reduction of the revolution to Tahrir and the reduction of the regime to Mubarak.

Road 3: Youth Coalitions

Many of my interviewees were young; thirty-nine out of the fifty interviewees I interviewed in 2012 were under the age of forty. If the NAFC was the most important political coalition prior to the revolution, the RYC would be the most effective group during the uprising. It was crucial in the mobilization for the revolution and presented the most solid, concrete coalition during the uprising in Tahrir. But to understand the role of youth in the revolution, we must locate them in their political and economic context (Korotayev and Zinkina 2011).

Scholars have described Egypt's "youth bulge" (LaGraffe 2012; Shahine 2011; Shehata 2011). Youth in Egypt—those between the ages of eighteen and twenty-nine—stood at about 24.3 percent of the population in 2012, according to the Central Agency for Public Mobilization and Statistics (Middle East News Agency 2012). The Carnegie Middle East Center puts that number higher, reporting that two-thirds of the Egyptian population is under the age of thirty (Achy 2010). Still, before the revolution, a number of studies had suggested these youth were excluded from politics and lacking in opportunities (Assaad 2008; Assaad and Barsoum 2007; Assaad and Roudi-Fahimi 2007; Hassan and Sassanpour 2008). In a 2009 survey, the Egyptian Population Council found that nine out of every ten jobless people in Egypt were under thirty years old and estimated that 51.3 percent of young adults were living in poverty. And although most young Egyptians are educated, only 1 percent are members of political parties (Achy 2010; see also Population Council 2010). Amid this combination of education and unemployment, sociologist Asef Bayat (2011) calls for studying the new uprisings in the Middle East with a focus on what he calls the "poor middle class," who have the aspirations and expectations of the middle class but are frustrated by economic hardship at every turn. Many of the young people I spoke with echoed Bayat's logic and suggested that they saw politics as hopelessly corrupt. This set the stage for their participation in the revolution.

When it came to patterns of mobilization, this young generation was heavily influenced by the coalition politics of the early 2000s. Kefaya's offshoot Youth for Change became, like its predecessor, an umbrella for myriad groups. By the time the RYC was created in 2011, it included six youth groups: the April 6 Youth Movement, the Youth for ElBaradei / NAFC, the youth of the MB, the youth of the Democratic Front Party, the Justice and Freedom Movement, and Youth from Al-Karama (Dignity) Party.[13] Many of the young people I interviewed belonged to at least one of these groups.

Adel Qassem, one of the RYC's founders and a key member in the Youth of the MB, violated MB orders when he joined the sit-in—and the revolution—on January 25, 2011 (an action for which he would later be fired by the group). I cite Qassem at length here, as his narrative reveals the subtle way in which the growing authoritarianism of the Mubarak regime itself pushed youth to gravitate toward a more coalition-based form of politics, focused on building numbers and strength rather than adhering to any rigid ideology or agenda. This excerpt is from our November 9, 2012, interview:

> I was an active member of the MB in college in the 1990s. My father is a scholar in Al-Azhar. I studied in Dar El-Oloum College, one of the main centers of Islamic studies in Egypt.
>
> The 1990s were unique in college activism for many reasons. First, it was obvious that Mubarak's regime was very authoritarian, and getting worse. Also, we were very strong as Islamic student activists on campus (Cairo University). The regime was very hostile to us and to student activism. True, the Islamists were the strongest group on campus, but we realized that coordinating with other groups would make the student movement stronger.
>
> The years 2004 to 2008 were very crucial in the making of our generation and the experience of working together. In the context of Kefaya, some of us, the young MB, became very interested in joining the movement and working with others. Also, we participated in something called the International Cairo Conference against the War and Zionism. This was coordinated by the MB, socialists, and Nasserists. This grew out of the efforts against the war on Iraq and then continued for a few years in Cairo. In this conference I was one of the organizers of panels on student activism and antidiscrimination. In 2006 I participated with others in the protest in solidarity with the prosecuted judges.

When I asked why he did not follow MB instructions, Qassem responded:

> I cannot attribute this to one factor. Some of us were not really so committed to the rigidity of the orders and instruction of our senior folks in the MB. I was arrested many times. And I was [prosecuted and put on trial] in the military trial against the MB in the 1990s. And I did not like some aspects of this disciplining way, perhaps. And probably these experiences

of working with others affected me. I have always valued the experience we shared with others, and perhaps also this context of participating in the streets that made our experience unique, as an MB member and also working with others. Then the April 2008 strike occurred, followed by the movement that took its name. In other words, these years created a unique generation, those who had graduated earlier and politics absorbed them

Many members of the RYC expressed similar ideas to me. By the time the RYC was organized in Tahrir, it had brought together a generation of youth uniquely predisposed to building consensus across traditional political lines. They had witnessed the growth of authoritarianism under Mubarak. They were depressed about their lack of economic opportunities. And they came to believe that their voices would only be heard if they worked together. As a result, the RYC was the most visible organized coalition in Tahrir and the revolution. From Marxists to liberals to Islamists, this diverse group's membership, like the diverse class coalitions already described, was predisposed to focus on political reform. Anything else was unthinkable amid so many divergent voices. Once focused on this goal, though, the RYC held fast—they remained the only organized voice insisting on Mubarak's ouster as a precondition for negotiations during the eighteen days, in contrast to groups such as the MB, which engaged in negotiations with the regime before Mubarak was out.

These, then, were the three roads that led to a consensus around political reform as the main goal of the revolution: the history of political coalitions in Egypt, the creation of an impromptu cross-class alliance, and the crystallization of youth coalitional experiences in the RYC. All three pathways help explain how the revolution became confined to a specific list of demands that represented, in many ways, compromises for everyone. In reality, of course, these three roads overlapped—they are only separated here for analytic purposes, to avoid conflating the different dynamics at work. The point is that many factors shaped what came to be seen as *the* demands of the revolution—demands spelled out on a banner that hung over Tahrir Square and embraced because they seemed to belong to no one and everyone at the same time.

The Social Soul of the Revolution

The banner's simplest and most powerful demand was its first: ousting Mubarak. At the time the idea was radical, not reformist like the subsequent demands. Far from dismantling and rebuilding Egypt's political system anew, those demands sought to make the existing system work properly. Nevertheless, the revolution also carried truly radical social demands, such as raising the minimum wage, ending structural adjustment programs, or even granting workers ownership of projects that were previously privatized or capitalist but neglected by their owners.

I build my claim here on three pieces of evidence: the slogans of the uprising, the significance and escalation of working-class strikes, and my analysis of the class makeup—mostly poor, working class, and lower middle class—of the martyrs and the injured in the uprising.

Social and Radical Slogans

The revolution's main slogans stood in contrast to the reformist banner discussed earlier: "The people want the downfall of the regime" and "Bread, freedom, and social justice." The first slogan was also displayed prominently on a banner in the square, but its deceptive simplicity likely prevented it from being seen as outlining an entire agenda. In actuality, of course, it went beyond the demand to oust Mubarak, calling for a radical dismantling of the entire ruling regime.

Elsewhere, I examined how there is no strong consensus in political science or political theory about the meaning of *political regime* (A. Said 2021). There are at least two meanings of the term. The first comes from Alexis de Tocqueville's classic *The Old Regime and the French Revolution* (2010 [1856]) and defines the *old regime* broadly, to refer to the entire social and political order and the state itself, not just the royal regime or royalists. The second dominates the political science and political sociology literature and differentiates among the state, the government, and the regime. The latter is often understood as the *ruling networks*, sets of rules for deciding how political offices are filled. Accordingly, it is unclear how we can ascertain what Egyptian revolutionary actors meant by the *political regime*. In hindsight, it became obvious that during the Egyptian Revolution, many revolutionaries saw the old regime only as Mubarak and the Mubarakists. While this later proved to be a distorted vision, one cannot blame Egyptian revolutionaries for an ambiguity that exists among scholars themselves.

Here is what happened on the ground. In the first few weeks after the uprising, I witnessed many activist debates about the meaning of *regime*. For many, it meant the government, as well as Mubarak, the networks of corruption around the Mubaraks, and the ruling party and its security apparatus.

Still, it did not mean dismantling the *state*, in Vladimir Lenin's terms (see also Achcar 2016a). A number of writers at the time noted the "civilized" or "peaceful" nature of the revolution, pointing to the ways that it targeted only some, particularly abusive centers—police stations, for instance—but not other institutions, like the Egyptian Museum in the Tahrir area, which was guarded by the protesters.[14] But this was a narrow definition of both *regime* and *revolution*. As Samer Soliman (2012b) maintains, Egyptians during the uprising could not see that the military was part of Mubarak's regime.

The common sentiment in Tahrir revolved around Mubarak and his networks. The relationship between the military and protesters was shaped by mutual uncertainties and ambiguities. As I discussed in chapter 2, while the protesters chanted "The people and the military are one hand," they doubted that the military had been involved in the abuses of Mubarak's regime. Most of the protesters, for instance, did not see how the military connected to the regime's corruption.[15] This can be traced to the dominance of *illusions* about the anticolonialist and postindependence role of Nasser's military regime as well as ideas about the military as a backbone of the modern nation-state. Several activists circulated leaflets warning protesters that the military would take over, but these fell on deaf ears. Even the radical slogan about a complete regime change was interpreted narrowly to focus only on Mubarak, stripping it of its practical and effective power.

The revolution's other headline slogan, "Bread, freedom, and social justice," goes further, articulating the specific components of an imagined future, which included increasing the minimum wage and ending privatization, among other things. This slogan was crafted into a song, composed and sung in Tahrir, the words from which serve as an epigraph to this chapter. The breadth of its terms was more radical and emphasized the social component of the uprising, in contrast to the demands of the banner, and its general spirit was manifested by working-class strikes.

Working-Class Strikes

Most analyses of the role of the Egyptian working class, with few exceptions, look only at the period before the revolution, not the ways the revolution played out (see A. Alexander and Bassiouny 2014; Beinin 2012). But working-class strikes were critical and worked in tandem with other important modes of mobilization to oust Mubarak. Working-class activists also brought the tantalizing prospect of radicalization—opening different possible outcomes for the revolution even as they were foreclosed through compromise.

An organized working class has a long history in Egypt, stretching back to the nineteenth century, but truly hit its stride after 2000, which witnessed an expansion of the role of the private sector and the labor market and increased Egypt's ties to the global market (El-Merghany 2009). According to unionist and labor analyst Elhamy El-Merghany, Egypt had 21.7 million workers in 2007. Forty-eight percent were employed in the private sector, 46 percent in the government, and 2 percent and 1 percent in the investment and cooperative sectors, respectively. The Egyptian government employs about 5.4 million workers, 2.7 million of whom work in urban centers and 2.6 million in rural areas. Of those, 69 percent are men and 31 percent are women. In Egypt 32 percent of workers work in agriculture and fishing, 13 percent in mining, 11 percent in small businesses, 10 percent in construction and education, 7 percent in communication and transportation, 5 percent in the service sector, 3 percent in health and social work, and 2 percent in hotels and restaurants (El-Merghany 2009). Only about a quarter of this labor force is organized in unions.

Most of the organized workers have been subject to a one-union-per-sector policy, implemented under Nasser in 1959. This policy resulted in a very hierarchical union system, on the top of which sat what is known as the Egyptian Trade Union Federation (ETUF). This body became essentially a front under Mubarak; most of its leaders were members of Mubarak's ruling party. Things changed with the December 2007 real estate tax collectors' strike, an eleven-day strike of 55,000 workers that resulted in the birth of Egypt's first independent trade union outside the ETUF (Azouz 2007). The strike ground tax revenues to a trickle, causing a 90 percent drop in tax collection (el-Hamalawy 2008). Alongside the 2008 Mahalla uprising, this strike and the creation of the tax collectors' union stand as major prerevolution turning points in Egyptian labor history.[16]

Industrial labor dominated the groups striking against prerevolution neoliberal policies, but the tax collectors and other state employees slowly gained prominence among the activists. And while most analyses focus on 2006–8 as a peak for workers' protests in Egypt, these protests in fact continued beyond this period—with minor interruptions—until the revolution. According to a report by the Egyptian Center for Economic and Social Rights and the Awlad Al-Ard Center for Human Rights, 2010 was an especially important year for labor protests, with workers' actions serving as a "prelude to the revolution." In that year alone, there were 209 labor sit-ins, 135 strikes, eighty demonstrations, eighty-three stand-ins, and twenty-three unplanned rallies. Some six thousand workers were injured at labor sites, forty thousand were compelled to resign from their jobs, and fifty-two workers committed suicide in protest of economic hardship.[17]

The role of the Egyptian working class during the eighteen days of the revolution can be divided into two main phases. In the first, from January 25, 2011, to around February 5, workers participated in the revolution as protesters but not as an organized force. In the second phase, workers joined the revolution as an organized force, with many critical labor sectors staging actions in support of the revolution. Mohsen Bassem, a journalist and labor organizer, explained to me why workers' participation was not as visible in the early days of the revolution:

> Labor action didn't stop throughout the eighteen days. It just was not visible until the final days before Mubarak's ouster. Workers came to Tahrir and participated in rallies. They couldn't participate in actions for two reasons. The first is that many jobs were closed for security purposes, especially government employees, where Mubarak's regime ordered the closing of government buildings and they paid workers. They assumed that this would negatively impact the protests by reducing workers' interaction with protesters and reducing their chances of participation. Government workers are a significant proportion of the workforce in Egypt. Then there was simply no government work. In that context, workers simply could not go to work and then strike at a workplace that is already closed. That would not make sense. And the second reason was the curfew, imposed by the military since January 28, 2011. The curfew restricted movement to limited hours in the day. This limited their ability to organize in these days, until February 6, when jobs and banks were opened again. During that time, workers just participated in rallies and in Tahrir. (Phone interview, February 28, 2014)

Haleem, another labor organizer, also spoke about the relationship between workers and the events in Tahrir:

> The leaders of the official union participated in the Camel Battle on February 2, 2011. The numbers were funny; it was only thugs and corrupt unionists. But the workers boycotted this, as they did not feel they belonged to the official union. When the government decided to open government offices on February 6, 2011, their plan was to bring [so they thought] society back to normal life. And they intended to isolate Tahrir.

The prime minister at the time, Ahmed Shafik, said we don't mind the Tahrir folks, and we can even make Tahrir a Hyde Park. Workers first participated in the rallies. But work resumed in government and banks on February 6. It took workers a few days to organize. This included workers releasing statements about the revolution or raising their demands and linking them to the revolution. In addition to this, some political forces released statements asking labor to intervene by joining and supporting the revolution. (Interview, December 18, 2012)

On February 4, 2011, the Egyptian Federation of Independent Trade Unions (EFITU) issued a call for a national strike. The EFITU is a very important organization in Egypt's labor history because it was the first federation of independent trade unions, as independent union organizing had been banned in Egypt since the 23 July Revolution in 1952.[18] Before the EFITU's creation in 2011, the only trade union federation in Egypt, the ETUF, was controlled by and tied to the state. On February 6, public transportation workers announced a strike in Cairo. They issued a statement in which the first demand was Mubarak's ouster. They went on to demand that the minimum wage be increased to 1,200 Egyptian pounds a month and that corruption within the Cairo Transport Authority be stopped. Workers in the Suez Canal Authority and Egypt's Railway Authority followed with their own calls for strikes. The Railway Authority saw strikes in railway workshops in Banī Suwayf, Sharabiya, and Alexandria as severe threats to the economy. Workers in Tanta went on strike in its cement factories and chemical manufacturing plants. Hossam el-Hamalawy tweeted on February 9, 2011, that four military production companies were on strike. Amid a near-universal focus on Tahrir in the final days before Mubarak was forced out of power, few local and international media even mentioned these strikes (see, for example, Al Hussaini 2011; Beinin 2011; Lee and Weinthal 2011). But on February 11, the day Mubarak stepped down, there were at least sixty strikes strategically deployed across Egypt (Beinin 2012, 7).

Did the mobilization of the working class represent an alternate revolutionary path in 2011, one that was at least as important as Tahrir? My aim here is not to speculate in the abstract but to discuss the actual modes of action taking place at the time. I suggest that working-class mobilization constituted a revolutionary center of gravity, so to speak, which had links to Tahrir but remained distinct and potentially radical. Working-class action did not stop; it intensified during the revolution, until April 2011 (NPR

2011). The strikes in the last few days before Mubarak's ouster, especially, put substantial pressure on the regime and arguably were key to his downfall.

According to Khaled Ali (2011), a prominent labor lawyer, strikes averaged thirty to sixty per day between February 12 and February 16, 2011—*after* Mubarak was out. Fatma Ramadan (2011), a unionist and organizer, wrote on the day after Mubarak's ousting about a series of strikes in different places in Egypt, including one company, Grain Mills Company of the East Delta, which has branches in Ismailia, Suez, Port Said, and Mansoura. Egypt's post office workers and laborers at the Daqahlia Sugar and Refining Company in Mansoura walked out. The workers of the Petro Trade Company, which belongs to the Ministry of Oil, continued a sit-in in front of the ministry (see figure 4.2). And on February 16, Suez Canal workers went on strike (Shadid 2011). According to a report by the International Development Center, workers' strikes and protests numbered 2,210 in 2010 but 2,532 in 2012 and 2,782 in 2013 (*Youm7* 2013). In short, Egypt was almost experiencing a national strike during the last three days before Mubarak was ousted, and strikes continued after ousting Mubarak. Banning strikes was one of the first actions the

FIGURE 4.2 Workers of Petro Trade Company, run by the Ministry of Oil, announcing a sit-in and strike, on February 13, 2011 (two days after the ousting of Mubarak, despite the SCAF ban on strikes). Photo by Hossam el-Hamalawy.

Supreme Council of Armed Forces (SCAF) took on February 13, but strikes continued for a while despite this ban.

Ousting Mubarak obviously occasioned a temporary halt to the social aspect of the revolution, as many forces did not want strikes to continue in the aftermath and were pleased with only ousting Mubarak. But one could argue that there was some continuity between workers' strikes during the revolution and those in its immediate aftermath. The strikes in the final days of the revolution rose to a level that might be considered a national strike. Given their focus in critical, strategic sectors, these were crucial to Mubarak's ouster.[19] Strikes after Mubarak's resignation also raised slogans such as getting rid of "Mubaraks" (corrupt CEOs in the public sector). Strikes both during and after the uprising leveraged economic demands for a minimum wage but also some political demands about political accountability for existing corruption in the privatization program. Some of the striking workers' demands were far more radical than the demands articulated by the famous banner in Tahrir Square. They called, for instance, for the confiscation of public sector factories that had been sold under privatization programs and the formation of workers' committees to supervise these factories. The Iron and Steel Workers in Helwan released a statement on February 9, 2011, in which they called for the following:

1. The immediate resignation of the president and all officials of the regime.
2. Confiscation of funds and property of all personnel of the previous regime and everyone proven corrupt.
3. The resignation of all workers from the regime's and ruling party's workers' federation, the announcement of independent unions, and the planning of general assemblies to freely establish each sector's own independent union without prior permission or consent of the regime, which has fallen and lost all legitimacy.
4. Confiscation of public sector companies that have been sold, closed down, or privatized, as well as the public sector that belongs to the people, and its nationalization in the name of the people and formation of a new management by workers and technicians.
5. Formation of a workers' monitoring committee in all workplaces, monitoring production, prices, distribution, and wages.
6. A general assembly of all sectors and political trends of the people to develop a new constitution and elect real popular committees without waiting for the consent of or negotiation with the regime.[20]

As economic writer Wael Gamal (2011a) emphasized, only two days after ousting Mubarak, the revolutionary forces included "businessmen and workers, youth and older generations, educated and illiterate people, state employees and unemployed, farmers, fisherman, professionals and professors." The consensus among these contradictory social forces was very limited and exceptional. Once Mubarak was ousted, the social struggle between these forces was open, not closed. While conservative forces were pleased with limiting the revolution to ending Mubarak's dictatorship, others wanted "to dismantle the conditions of poverty, unemployment and barriers to gain living bread" (Gamal 2011a). While many observers and scholars suggested that the social struggle was secondary, or over after ousting Mubarak, workers' struggle was afoot throughout roughly all of 2011.

Halting workers' strikes was one of the first goals of the SCAF. On February 13, 2011, only two days after Mubarak was ousted, the SCAF responded to the escalation of labor strikes by issuing a statement denouncing strikes and labeling them as chaotic, "illegitimate works that aim to damage the nation . . . disrupt citizens' lives . . . and disturb the economy and the wheel of production" (Egypt State Information Service 2011; see also *Marefa* n.d.). However, the strikes did not stop. On March 24, 2011, the SCAF issued another decree, this time banning strikes throughout the country. The SCAF and government media, still under the SCAF's control, launched an antistrike campaign, describing (and dismissing) them as *mataleb faaawyeea* (sectional demands).[21] Many of the Egyptian elite joined the campaign; pro-government writers and, ironically, the MB and some liberals who were part of the revolution joined in the denunciation, arguing that national interests should take priority over sectional demands (see Gamal 2011b; Qabil 2014). In some of the protests I witnessed against the law to ban strikes, workers raised the slogan "It Is Social Justice, Not Sectional Demands" (*Masr Al-Jadida* 2011). The SCAF and the transitional government used force to apply this law, in one instance using armored vehicles to attack workers at the Shebeen El-Koum Textile Factory on April 7, 2011.

The strikes as well as the speed with which workers organized demonstrate how social struggle has been central in the revolution and its aftermath. Before the revolution there were only three independent trade unions. By October 2012 there were 507 (see table 4.2). One of my interviewees, Mohamed Haleem, confirmed that in February–April 2011 he "was assisting trade unions to form a new union almost every day." Two particularly important groups formed: the EFITU officially announced its formation on March 2, 2011 (Gaber 2011), and the Egyptian Democratic Labor Congress (EDLC) was formed in April 2013 (Al-Tawy 2013).

Table 4.2. Labor Union Federations in Egypt in Relation to the Labor Force, 2012

	No. of Affiliated Unions	No. of Workers (in millions)	% of Labor Force*
ETUF	23	3.8	16.2
EFITU	261	2.4	10.2
EDLC	246	not available	not available

Source: Abdalla (2012, 2).
Note: ETUF = Egyptian Trade Union Federation; EFITU = Egyptian Federation of Independent Trade Unions; EDLC = Egyptian Democratic Labor Congress.
* The total labor force numbers 23.346 million. This number includes those working with and without salaries. Workers without salaries are family members who work in family-owned businesses where there is no way to document them. Some of these yet may join unions.

This level of labor organizing would have been impossible without the revolutionary context that developed in 2011; as my interviewee Haleem put it, this "massive organization was like a fervor." Outside of but connected to Tahrir, it nonetheless left Tahrir without significant challenge. One reason was that workers were ambivalent about the center of the revolution. They knew that their strikes were important and part of the revolution, yet they did not see their efforts as separate from Tahrir. Two of the main organizers of the public transportation workers, Taha Samy and Fathy Mohamed, affirmed this view in their interview with me. Both said, "Our strike was complementing Tahrir" (interview, December 19, 2012). The workers were also not as adept as the youth in Tahrir at using social media. They organized separately, on their own, to support the revolution, but they did not have independent media tools or the sophistication of Tahrir's young protesters. Consequently, their strikes received less media attention. Though my interviewees, as well as analysts such as Joel Beinin (2011), suggested that the social media gap has closed since the revolution, it certainly shaped the relative impact of the Tahrir sit-in and the workers' strikes.

In short, the revolution's cross-class basis should not make us overlook that the working-class strikes presented a serious challenge to the regime and constituted one of the most critical components of the social soul of the revolution. The strikes posed real economic threats to the state, such as stopping the Suez Canal revenues as well as preventing the government from functioning, given that state employees (including the real estate tax collectors union) had become involved in the revolution.

The notion of the underclass does not have a coherent and unified definition in sociology. The rubric of the underclass, in conventional and critical
research, includes groups such as people experiencing long term unemploy
ment (Aponte 1990), people who live in slums in urban areas (Mohanty and
Mohanty 2005), and people who live in highly impoverished and segregated
areas, known commonly as inner cities (Wilson 2012). While most scholars
have emphasized the significance of middle-class youth in general or the
middle-class poor (educated but unemployed youth), per Asef Bayat's terminology (Bayat 2015, 35), in the Egyptian Revolution, some of the most important actors were underclass. Some of these were poor youth who worked in
gas stations, for example, or street vendors or street kids. My research shows,
for example, that street children played an important role in Tahrir Square,
particularly in the battles between protesters and the police. Street kids were
crucial given their mobility and their knowledge of materials available in
the streets. Several of my interviewees told me stories about the role of street
kids in battles in Ramses Street and in Qasr El Eyni Street on January 28, 2011.
Many street kids came to the sit-in and lived there during the eighteen days
in Tahrir. One interviewee told me that the street kids were very excited to
fight alongside the protesters: "They told me they finally got a chance to
get revenge for the police violence and the abuse they receive all the time."
He also said, "I have tried to give them money and help. And many of them
refused, and they told me: we are here to fight with you, we are not beggars"
(interview, October 17, 2012).[22] In short, to argue that the Egyptian Revolution
was carried out by middle-class youth is a simplistic claim. A more accurate
claim would be that the revolution consisted of a cross-class of protesters,
whereas the middle-class voices were more dominant, and workers and the
underclass were in front of key battles during the uprising.

The following four tables provide descriptive statistics about the revolution's martyrs and injured, with information specific to the eighteen
days of the uprising. Across the country the official total is 1,082 killed
and 1,072 injured. There are many discrepancies, however, and because
of the difficulty in documenting cases outside Greater Cairo, I focus my
analyses on Cairo, Giza, and Qalyubia, where the total number of martyrs
was 658, and the injured stood at 831. Both the occupations of the martyrs
and their home neighborhoods are critical indicators of the uprising's class
composition.[23]

In short, the majority of those injured and killed during the uprising were poor. Among the injured, the poor represented about 50 percent, with 65 percent hailing from poor areas. These included workers from the private sector and small businesses, as well as peasants, nonskilled workers, and day laborers. Among the martyrs, some 34 percent resided in poor areas, and almost 40 percent were underclass. They, too, included private sector workers alongside small business owners, peasants, and nonskilled laborers. Among those whose residency and occupation were difficult to determine, many were also likely poor. Those in the lowest classes have little access to courts; therefore, many more, unlikely to join in lawsuits related to protester deaths and injuries after the revolution, surely remain uncounted.

The youth killed in the uprising were even more likely to come from the city's slums (*ashwaiyyat*) and informal housing—writer Mohamed Aboul Gheit (2011) documented several of these martyrs' stories. Many were in their twenties, had not gone to college, and were economically responsible for entire families. Many others were simply poor orphans. About 40 percent of Egyptians were living in poverty in January 2011, so the poor were necessarily part of the uprising. Aboul Gheit documented actual stories of heroism on January 28, 2011, on Qasr El Nile Bridge and in battles in front of police stations. He even joined protesters in defending Tahrir Square during the Camel Battle on February 2, 2011. Aboul Gheit criticized the dominant narrative in the Egyptian media, which focused narrowly on political factions and overlooked the poor people who died in the actual battles and violent confrontations, who defeated the police apparatus in Tahrir, and who rallied and marched through the city and laid siege to police stations. They *could not* and *should not* be silenced in history, he urged. Aboul Gheit's position is supported by the data I present here. It is heart-wrenching to consider

Table 4.3. Place of Residence of Those Injured in Greater Cairo during the Eighteen Days of the Uprising

	No.	%
Downtown Cairo and middle-class areas	64	7.70
Popular neighborhoods (working-class areas)	543	65.34
Countryside centers	25	3.01
Countryside villages	45	5.42
Unidentified	154	18.53
Total	**831**	100.00

Table 4.4. Occupations of Those Injured in Greater Cairo during the Eighteen Days of the Uprising

	No.	%
College faculty	2	0.24
College students	60	7.22
High school students and lower levels	19	2.29
Lawyers	21	2.53
Media and journalists	4	0.48
Professionals (doctors, engineers, and others)	46	5.54
Private-sector workers and small-business owners	206	24.78
State employees	22	2.65
Working-class and day laborers, peasants	217	26.11
Police and related positions	6	0.72
Unidentified	228	27.44
Total	**831**	**100.00**

Table 4.5. Place of Residence of Martyrs in Greater Cairo in the Eighteen Days of the Uprising

	No.	%
Downtown Cairo and middle-class areas	23	3.50
Popular neighborhoods (working-class areas)	225	34.19
Countryside centers	12	1.82
Countryside villages	18	2.74
Unidentified	380	57.55
Total	**658**	**100.00**

that these underclass folks died for empty procedural democracy and empty recognition.

According to Aboul Gheit as well, "the martyrs in the Egyptian Revolution represent those Egyptians (40 percent of Egyptians) who live under the poverty line, and those twelve million Egyptians who live in slums, and about 1.5 million who have no homes and live in and around cemeteries, because they cannot afford rent in normal homes" (Aboul Gheit 2011). Most of the battles near police stations were led mostly by these underclass poor. Aboul Gheit affirms, "These people did not care at all about the constitution, or the

Table 4.6. Occupations of Martyrs in Greater Cairo during the Eighteen Days of the Uprising

	No.	%
College faculty	1	0.15
College students	33	5.02
High school students and lower levels	25	3.80
Lawyers	5	0.76
Media and journalists	2	0.30
Professionals (doctors, engineers, and others)	16	2.43
Private-sector workers and small-business owners	91	13.83
State employees	5	0.76
Working-class and day laborers, peasants	44	6.69
Police and related positions	41	6.23
Unidentified	395	60.03
Total	**658**	**100.00**

election of the system of governance. All of this stuff is newspaper talk. What matters only to them is improving their living conditions."

An important ethnographic note is critical here to demonstrate how and why middle-class voices prevailed. Despite the atmosphere of solidarity and unity in Tahrir, the dominance of middle-class voices sometimes led to targeting of street vendors. The presence of street vendors in Tahrir is a complicated story.[24] (See figure 4.3 for a photograph of a street vendor in Tahrir Square during the uprising.) In part, after the revolution some protesters said the police had been using the vendors to spy on them. But during the eighteen days, their presence was normal and accepted: they were part of the culture of Tahrir. However, as increasingly hostile media tried to portray Tahrir not as a place of protest but rather as an arena filled with kids doing drugs and engaging in other illegal activities, some protesters began to think it would be better to force the street vendors to leave the square. I discussed this issue with many protesters at the time, and they were divided. Some agreed it would be better to let the vendors stay, since "Tahrir belongs to all"; others said, "No, it would be better if Tahrir had no street vendors."

Eventually, however, the revolutionary youth developed the view that it would be better if street vendors were all concentrated in one area. The nearby Qasr El Nile Bridge was suggested as one possibility. In one video a

FIGURE 4.3 A street vendor in Tahrir. The vendor was selling tissues, but he was also very creative, making up chants such as "Mubarak: Leave, you traitor, you made us survive by selling tissues." Picture taken by the author, February 8, 2011, three days before Mubarak was ousted.

youth can be seen talking over a speaker, saying, "The street vendors issue is getting out of control, and we ask them to go now, and we ask people to show restraint, and please do not offend them, but please, we ask the vendors now to move to Qasr El Nile Bridge."[25] Some of my interlocutors criticized this decision and suggested that the upper-class participants were just romanticizing Tahrir. One of my interviewees, a journalist who defined himself as an independent Islamist, stated:

> The diversity of Tahrir as a social space came from different factors. But I would say that one of the main factors is the dominance of the discourse of the upper middle classes who participated in the revolution. Those people have a specific self- and class-centered perspective about social networking and social interactions. They talk exclusively about consumer culture and themselves, unlike people in poorer neighborhoods, who have

different perspectives about social interactions, where they experience more communality and share life in a sense. The upper-class people were more impressed with Tahrir's shared community, where you can talk with strangers as if they are close friends you trust. In other words, they became obsessed with Tahrir because they miss this intimacy. (Interview, October 11, 2012)

Of particular relevance to the question of classes in Tahrir, and the dominance of some voices over others, especially in the media, was the prominent usage of the phrase "our image in the world" among many participants in the revolution.[26] Some informants saw this as reflecting the dominance of a middle-class respectability mindset, while others simply saw it as a necessary focus on strategic unity in order to gain support. Members of the former group blamed middle-class participants for obscuring a more complex reality with their concern over image. In one instance, for example, one of my interviewees criticized middle-class kids who returned after Mubarak's ousting to clean and paint the square. In his view, "they reduced the power of celebrating ousting the dictator to some painting action" (interview of a twenty-eight-year-old journalist and self-described democratic and independent Islamist, November 10, 2012).[27] Others supported the emphasis on unity and emphasized the idea that the whole world was watching. Another interviewee, Nadia Sleem, stated,

> Part of mythologizing Tahrir is this idea of "our image in the world." My nephew has this fascinating phrase. He said: Tahrir was a show. And I agree with him. Everybody in Tahrir was making an effort to be part of the show. We knew we are sending a message to all Egypt, all those who are not yet with the revolution. And also we were sending a message to the world, that we are doing something right. We are telling all, we know what is right, and we can do it, we are doing all the right things here. (Interview, November 20, 2012)

It seems to me that these two points of view are not actually contradictory; the performance of unity was indeed largely middle-class driven, but it was also designed to portray a positive image of the revolution, given the regime's rigorous campaign of vilification. The larger picture here was one of overall unity, not just class unity, with an emphasis on portraying Tahrir as a great community. In the same interview, Sleem added, "Part of the show also was the emphasis on showing the peacefulness of the uprising. Protesters also wanted to emphasize unity and show off unity to the world. Look at the emphasis on taking pictures of different people, for example, showing nonveiled women next to the *niqabi* [women with a face covering]. The point here in the show was to send a message to all that we are united and nobody can separate us."

Conclusion: Fracture Under the Revolution's Oneness

I opened this chapter with a story about a banner that conveyed an electoral democracy agenda for the uprising and closed with a discussion illuminating the social soul of the uprising. My aim is to demonstrate that one cannot separate the two souls, the democratic and the social. I noted that a big factor in the priority accorded to the democratic demands was their high visibility, the ready reception of middle-class voices in Tahrir, and the history of political coalitions prior to 2011, which revolved around democratic reformist demands. Besides, global social media, in circulating appealing images, fixated on the middle-class kids with iPhones in Tahrir. More important, many could not reconcile the contradiction between the existence of a cross-class coalition in the uprising and the fact that working-class strikes were critical in ousting Mubarak. The cross-class coalition was the most visible in Tahrir. Working-class strikes were crucial in placing political and economic pressure on the ruling regime, especially when the strikes targeted key locations and industries that generated revenue for the state. Working-class activists also carried the radical social demands of the uprising. The tension between the souls of the reformist and the social sides of the uprising played an important role in the trajectory of the uprising. While the cross-class coalition was critical during the uprising, in the days after Mubarak's fall the tension between the middle class and the working class appeared. About this tension, el-Hamalawy (2011a) states:

> When Mubarak was toppled on the 11th of February and the middle class and most of the youth groups were more than happy to suspend the Tahrir sit-in, and there were calls for everybody to go back to work amidst all of this nationalist propaganda—you know, "let's build a new Egypt" and "put 110 percent of your effort into work"—the working class did not go. A journalist like myself, I can afford not showing up to work for 18 days, but then go back to my editorial position where I earn several thousand Egyptian pounds a month. But a public transport worker cannot basically suspend his strike and go back home to his kids and tell them, "I'm still getting paid 189 Egyptian pounds after fifteen years of service; let's wait for another six months while the ruling military junta gives us a civilian cabinet so as to solve all our problems."

I also demonstrated that certain historical contingencies led to the dominant tunnel vision about the nature of the regime and the state, where the regime was narrowly defined around Mubarak. It is one thing to argue that one set of demands / one soul dominated or was more visible and another thing to analyze why and how it dominated. Let me offer one more example from circumstances on the ground in Tahrir Square to further clarify why one vision dominated over the other. As I already mentioned, two stages were built in Tahrir Square. One was managed by the MB and was known as the stage that belonged to all national forces (*quwaa wataniya*). The second was managed by the RYC, composed mainly of leftists and liberals. Most of the speeches on the main stage were about unity and consensus, reform and inclusion, and so on. Most of the speakers were national figures from all political factions. The speeches on the second stage focused on the demand for a minimum wage, social justice, and ending privatization. Unlike on the first stage, most speakers here were labor organizers, socialists, and radical artists. Yet the national and international media focused almost exclusively on the first stage, which was often described as the main stage.[28]

The tension between the two sides, the two souls, was later used against the revolution during the so-called transitional period, to suppress social grievances. During that period most of the political actors—especially liberals, the SCAF, and the MB—were hostile to workers and insisted that the revolution was about electoral reform alone. Beyond the old story of the betrayal of the poor who made the uprising, the tension between the two sides of the uprising was also reflected in narratives about the nature of the revolution. Reducing the revolution to its reformist agenda and electoral politics contributed to polarization and allowed the SCAF to use its legal apparatus and experts to constrain and control the power of elected bodies after Mubarak. Social demands were silenced thanks to the SCAF and the MB, as reformers coalesced around electoral, procedural, and sectarian battles, as we shall see.

5 | waning revolutionary possibilities

SQUARED II: COUNTER-
REVOLUTIONARY
COERCION AND
ELECTIONS WITHOUT
DEMOCRATIZATION

In the last Parliament, we counted many dealers
The real job is wheeling and dealing, hidden behind representation
The dealer has immunity that shields him
Just as it protects hell-bound criminals.

They say that we now need free elections in this country
This is what the constitutions say, stipulating limited terms
To do a forty-truck rally
"Vote for Mr. So-and-So" with drums and horns
The people stand, breast exposed to bullets
The state is afraid, and wrapping itself behind walls.

—"FI-L-BĀRLIMĀN ILLI FĀT" [IN THE LAST PARLIAMENT],
BY BAYRAM AL-TUNSI (EGYPTIAN-TUNISIAN POET)

On October 12, 2012, I was on my way back to Tahrir Square. According to social media, this day was the "Friday of Accountability." There would be a protest against Mohamed Morsi, the first democratically elected president after the revolution, who had failed to deliver on a campaign promise that his hundred-day program would end some of the most immediate social and security-related problems in Egypt.[1] Activists charged that now-president Morsi was equivocating and relying on former regime figures. As my taxi approached Tahrir, we realized that the square had been closed off for the protest. The cabdriver dropped me off at Qasr El Nile Bridge. I walked through the Nile Corniche to Qasr El Eyni Street, then wound through the Garden City area. Barriers, erected by the military to obstruct entrances to Tahrir and divert traffic, sent me off onto side streets and forced me to improvise my route. When I finally approached the square, I heard loud clashes erupting from within. I decided to sit in a café and ponder my next move.

There were very few civilians in the café, where a TV tuned to Al Jazeera droned with news of the square. Posing as an ordinary citizen, I approached a pair of Central Security Forces officers sitting there, close to the clashes and seemingly ready for action. One scoffed, "Let them kill each other." For just a second, I imagined these two among the security men who had stripped off their uniforms and fled from protesters nearly two years before. *So much has changed*, I reflected, *that now men in uniform can feel at ease in this place speaking as these two are.*[2]

Returning to the situation at hand, I tried to figure out who the men were talking about. It seemed that Muslim Brotherhood (MB) supporters were involved in the clashes, but the protest had been planned by revolutionaries. Now I began to understand: apparently, MB supporters did not appreciate the protest and were fighting *against* leftist revolutionaries. The police officers probably hoped the MB would win without their help—or at least that the MB and the revolutionaries would wear each other out.

I decided to make my way to the square. Near the old American University of Cairo campus, I saw that Qasr El Eyni Street was blocked off by a huge metal gate, allowing only a few pedestrians in at a time. I walked through, then stopped by Mogamma El Tahrir (a gargantuan government administrative complex) to watch. It seemed like a safe zone, but soon bloodied protesters were running past me, and hurled rocks were reaching me. I determined that it was unsafe to walk farther and headed back home.

Almost nine months earlier, a mere three days after the first anniversary of the uprising, another clash had taken place in Tahrir, also between Islamists and leftists, who had been part of the same camp during the 2011 revolution.[3]

On January 28, 2012, a group of leftist revolutionaries had marched to parliament. This was the first parliament after the revolution, with 75 percent Islamist members of parliament, and its first session was about to start. The protesters came with a list of demands, with one overarching goal: Egypt's first postrevolution constitution must not be written while the Supreme Council of Armed Forces (SCAF) was in power. The protesters demanded that all power be transferred over to the new parliament, Egypt's only elected body at the time, and that presidential elections be held as soon as February 11, 2012 (*Almasry Alyoum* 2012a). When they reached Tahrir, the protesters were surprised to see that the MB youth had formed human shields in certain areas, including around, the parliament building in Majlis El-Shaab Street. They were blocking the way to the parliament. The MB youth told the media their goal was "to protect the Parliament from subversive elements" (*Almasry Alyoum* 2012a). Forty-three protesters were injured in the subsequent confrontations (*Almasry Alyoum* 2012a). At the time, MB leaders in the parliament had announced their commitment to the road map drawn by the SCAF after the March 2011 constitutional referendum, discussed later on. They suggested that the parliament had consensus on how to achieve revolutionary goals and that there was no room for party politics in the parliament. They also announced they would not form a coalition government after the election but would continue working with the government appointed by the SCAF. An MB majority leader remarked that the MB opposed the "leftist revolutionaries' demands for complete power transfer to the parliament," which would strip the SCAF of all power (quoted in Yassin 2012).

Skirmishes like these challenge the conventional narrative about protest and Egyptian politics in the aftermath of the revolution. Many accounts drew divides, at most admitting a static tension between mobilization in the street and electoral politics.[4] And a simplistic portrayal of Egyptian politics drew a binary divide between two parties: unseasoned and unorganized secular and leftist revolutionaries, young and uninterested in party politics, and a better-organized group of electoral democracy adherents, mostly Islamists led by the MB. Partially because of these tidy narratives, many outside Egypt believed that from 2011 through the coup in 2013, Egyptians had not given institutions and elected bodies a chance to establish reforms and institutionalize the revolution. The July 22, 2013, cover of *Time* magazine was an elegant encapsulation. Split into two halves, the cover showed on the left an image from the Egyptian Revolution of 2011 emblazoned "World's Best Protesters," while on the right was an image of the June 30, 2013, protest that paved the way to the coup, captioned "World's Worst Democrats."[5] All over the world, politics in Egypt was misread as either a mismatch between protest and election or a betrayal of democracy.

The picture was more complex, as the so-called transition had started while the military—the leading antidemocratic, counterrevolutionary force—was in charge.[6] In that context, many asserted that Islamists, not the leftist and revolutionary youth, prioritized organizing for elections—and that they were good at it, given their electoral gains in the first ballots after the revolution. Yet such analyses fail to resolve a key paradox: If Egyptians revolted in 2011 to establish democracy, why did they revolt again in 2013 to end this "democracy"? I contend that the question is not whether or not democratization took place in Egypt after Hosni Mubarak was ousted but rather what type of democratization took place. As I discuss here, the 2011 revolution arose against the fraud-based parliament of 2010. In 2012 and beyond, many activists and critics who participated in the Egyptian Revolution had begun to echo Jeff Goodwin's claim: "The ballot box is the coffin of revolutionaries" (2003, 67).

My goal in this chapter is to answer these complex questions. Specifically, I chart and historicize the relation between political mobilizations and electoral and constitutional politics from the uprising in 2011 through to 2015. By interrogating the shifts in the relation between political protest and electoral and constitutional politics, I argue that Egyptian revolutionaries consistently strove for electoral democracy but were disconcerted by the meaning and limitations of this democracy in the aftermath of the revolution. I agree with some critics (Adly 2012; El Raggal 2012) that the SCAF and its allies used proceduralist democracy—namely, simple electoral and constitutional reforms—as a tool to absorb and neutralize demands for more substantive democratic change, yet I argue that Egyptian revolutionaries persisted in mobilizing for reform, as well as with regard to electoral and constitutional politics. In chapter 4 I analyzed how the Egyptian Revolution had two souls, meaning both a democratic agenda *and* more radical and social demands. In this chapter I analyze how the SCAF and its allies retroactively used the reformist agenda of the revolution *against* the revolution. The military's goal was to reduce democratic demands to their most minimalist components so as to establish an electoral system *without democratization*.

In my analysis here, I synthesize two threads from the literature and advocate a central claim. The first thread is the focus on democratization as a contentious process, and the second the analysis of electoral politics as contentious politics. The central claim is that it is impossible and perhaps erroneous to study democratizations in the aftermath of a revolution separate from the revolution itself. First, leading scholars of democratization establish that *democratization* is *a contentious process* and that "'democratization' is not A Single Thing, but the contingent outcome of interactions among a number of claims and counterclaims" (McAdam, Tarrow, and Tilly 2001a, 268; see also Whitehead 2002). The core of this approach is the understanding that democratization is "not a finite and linear process" (McAdam, Tarrow, and Tilly 2001a, 268) but is contested directly and indirectly, on ballots and in the streets. This scholarship emphasizes democratization as a complex process, conditional on key developments. Charles Tilly, a pioneer in this field, wrote, "Democratization never occurs without at least partial realization of three large processes: integration of interpersonal trust networks into public politics; insulation of public politics from categorical inequalities; and elimination or neutralization of autonomous, coercion-controlling power centers in ways that augment the influence of ordinary people over public politics and increase the control of public politics over state performance" (2007a, 78).

As my analysis shows, the so-called transition process in Egypt started and continued under the control of the military. In other words, a key coercion-controlling power in Egypt was never neutralized in the transition process, except for a fleeting moment during the uprising. Democratization also entails four key components: *breadth* of coverage to all polity members, *equality*, *consultations*, and *protection* (McAdam, Tarrow, and Tilly 2001a, 266). The transition process took place while there were continuous violent attacks on protesters on the streets, along with restrictions on political parties. It is more accurate to say that after the revolution, Egypt experienced elections without democratization (see Elgindy 2012). I describe this as the project of procedural democracy. A critical understanding of democratization as a contentious process shows that democratic and antidemocratic tendencies always coexist. Besides, processes of democratization sometimes involve delays "as a function of institutions set in place in the past" (Tilly 2007a, 78). As this chapter demonstrates, the military and deep state have relied on their legal experts and the Egyptian judiciary as well as the legal apparatus to obstruct more substantive democracy, even to end the life of elected bodies.

Second, I bring the electoral contention framework here and join its key theorists, Doug McAdam and Sidney Tarrow, who rightly suggest that the separation between scholarship of social movements and of elections is untenable (2010, 531–33). By *electoral contention*, they refer to a "set of recurring links between elections and movements that powerfully shapes movement dynamics and electoral outcomes" (2013, 328). I expand their framework to include not just elections but electoral and constitutional politics, including politics and grievances related to electoral and constitutional reform and the demand for accountability of elected officials. In Egypt the 2011 revolution produced fluidity, instability, and uncertainty in electoral politics. Electoral politics and constitutional politics became intensely intertwined, forming a large contentious space of democratization. One can argue it was the natural outcome of the dominance of the reformist agenda during the uprising, which never included a demand about transition under military rule.

The central claim is the significance of the context of a revolution relative to democratization. The revolution in Egypt was the causal mechanism to start democratization. It "should" have worked, among other things, "to produce protected consultation" (McAdam, Tarrow, and Tilly 2001a, 268) but did not. Yet one cannot ignore the revolutionary context. I propose that the fluctuating revolutionary momentum from 2011 through to 2013 significantly impacted the practice of politics in the streets and the large contentious space of democratization as well. If separating mobilization from constitutional and electoral politics is fruitless in a normal political order, this separation makes even less sense in revolutionary and postrevolutionary contexts, in which the dynamics of mobilization and the contested space of democratization are highly intertwined. I demonstrate throughout this chapter how this (limited and) specific form of democratization process was always unpredictable because it was shaped by the fluctuating and contingent circumstance of the revolutionary and postrevolutionary mobilizations. In these circumstances, revolutionary mobilizations have raised unusual grievances, such as asking an elected parliament to seize complete power, or called for early elections, or challenged the composition of constitutional assemblies, or resisted constitutional declarations, among other things.

In proposing that we ought to investigate *democratization* as a *contentious historical process*, shaped by the revolution, I argue against the relevance of the scholarship on the transition to democracy because this literature does not attend to the pace, quality, or contradictions within the so-called transition itself. I uphold that overlooking that the so-called democratic process in Egypt started with revolutionary mobilization is a grave mistake that many scholars of transition and democratization have committed.[7] Revolution played a critical factor in starting the presumed democratization, not only as a causal mechanism for this process but also as an aspiration and ideal, presumably for the desired democracy.

In this sense, I argue against what I describe as *transitionologists without transitionology*, meaning scholars who criticize the transition paradigm for its mechanistic inadequacies or linearity, while failing to consider the moving turmoil that started the whole thing: revolution. As one writer emphasized, "Arguably, protesters in Tahrir square did not call for democracy as the political scientist [Robert] Dahl defines it or an Islamic state as Hassan Al Banna, founder of the Muslim Brotherhood, envisioned it; instead, they called for Bread, Freedom, and Social Equality" (Oraby 2018). The tension between the proceduralist understanding of democracy and its substantive meaning, let alone the significance of the social justice piece in the wanted democracy, proved to be part of the tensions and polarizations that existed in this period.[8]

In the introduction of this book, I argued that along with studying the origins and outcomes of revolutions, we must consider the dynamics and processes that take place *within* revolutions. Specifically, I argued that a key component in revolutions is the proliferation of possibility and the processes of containment. In this book I analyze two instances of containment: the self-containment of the uprising, as discussed in chapters 2 and 3, where we saw "the squaring of the revolution," and now the transitional period's containment of the revolution into a project of procedural democracy, free markets, and the retention of a brutal security and intelligence apparatus. This second "squaring" was led by counterrevolutionary forces, namely, the military apparatus, with the MB, liberals, and political elites in tow.[9] Thus, throughout the chapter I categorize the short but intense period from 2011 through 2015 as a series of processes:

1. The upsurge of revolutionary mobilization as the center of political gravity (January 25, 2011–February 11, 2011)
2. The emergence of the project of procedural democracy, pulling political gravity from the revolutionary street (March 2011)
3. The emergence of polarization in political mobilization, reflecting polarization with regard to procedural democracy (April–October 2011)
4. The emergence of acute tension and complex entanglements between political mobilization and the project of procedural democracy (November 2011–December 2012)
5. The collapse of the project of procedural democracy and the establishment of a system of farcical electoral democracy over crushed mobilization (January 2013–January 2015)

The first four processes speak to the developments from the revolution to the coup in 2013, and the fifth speaks to the coup and the developments that followed. In analyzing these processes, I show how the SCAF orchestrated the legal and constitutional apparatus and used the project of procedural democracy to absorb and kill the fervor of the revolutionary street. I also analyze how the revolutionary street worked in tension and entanglement with, but also in the expansion and protection of, the project of procedural democracy. They were never separate.

Before proceeding, two interrelated notes should be stated here. First, in analyzing the short but intense period from January 2011 to January 2015 in terms of these five processes, and in charting it temporally and nominally, I discuss many episodes of contention within each process, which took place between streets and elections. I do not seek to compare or equate these processes, or contentious episodes, or determine which ones had more impact with regard to the revolutionary possibilities. Through the periodizing of these processes, I also intentionally avoid making forceful claims that some of these episodes were more conjunctural (presenting turning points) than others. In fact, all of them could be viewed as conjunctural depending on the angle of analysis. But as I show later, it is fair to say that the rigged election of 2010 was one of the important triggers for the revolution. The revolutionary mobilization in 2011 was one of the most critical conjunctures in launching political change—whatever form that may have taken—not only in this relatively brief period but perhaps in all of recent Egyptian history. The constitutional referendum on March 19, 2011, was a critical conjuncture in starting the formal political process and granting the military (in alliance with the MB) more power to control the political process in Egypt, a development that proved to be one of the most critical factors in derailing the so-called transition to democracy in Egypt. Dissolving the first parliament after the revolution, on June 16, 2012, also gave the SCAF more power to do as it pleased in the process, even if this parliament was paradoxical: it came out of free elections, but then its MB/Islamic-dominated majority blessed and expanded the privileges of the military and contributed to giving constitutional powers to the military's expanded rule. The military coup on July 3, 2013, and the Rabaa Massacre on August 14, 2013, were turning points in sealing the military's grip on power in Egypt. Many of these episodes, and others I discuss in the following, have been very critical in different ways, and all contributed to and came out of the context of a gradual decline in revolutionary momentum. Some important factors that contributed to this decline are the use of lethal force, the fatigue of the revolutionary street, and the strategic exhausting, by the military and its allies, especially the MB, of the Egyptian public with procedural democracy. Second, beyond presenting this modest charting of these contentious episodes, I aim to demonstrate how the political center of gravity was shifting and contested all the time between the revolutionary street and the project of procedural democracy. As I suggested in the introduction of this book, revolution has presented an explosion of open political possibilities for change. In this chapter I examine the waning of revolutionary possibilities, defined here as the uncertainties concerning who and which institutions really ruled Egypt, in the period between Mubarak's ouster and the enabling of the military's domination.

Revolutionary Mobilization: The Center of Political Gravity
(January 25, 2011–February 11, 2011)

As I walked around Tahrir during the uprising in 2011, I looked at the surrounding images and banners. In addition to pictures of martyrs, there were images of the enemies of the revolution. The most notable was, of course, Mubarak, but there were also images of key figures in the National Democratic Party (NDP), such as Gamal Mubarak and Ahmed Ezz, a steel tycoon who headed the ruling party's organization committee. Ezz and the NDP's security apparatus had been key in creating the last preuprising parliament. Egyptian revolutionaries had not forgotten the first session of that parliament, on December 13, 2010, when Ezz had spoken at length, bragging about his party's electoral gains (see *Egypt Today* 2010) and roasting other parties whose adherents had failed to mobilize and retain their seats.

In this parliamentary election, the NDP won about 81 percent of the parliamentary seats (91 percent if we include NDP members who ran as independents). The NDP now controlled 473 out of the total 518 seats, and the parliament gained the nickname the "businessmen's parliament" (Eddin 2010). There had been seven parliaments under Mubarak's rule, but the 2010 parliament was the most fully controlled by the ruling party. And no wonder: before and during the election, NDP leadership and the security apparatus had opposing candidates arrested, preventing them from campaigning, and threatened opposition-party supporters. They forged ballots and prevented opposition-party supporters from reaching their polling stations. They gerrymandered districts. In short, the 2010 election made it clear there was no real representative democracy in Egypt.

In the face of this widespread election fraud, about 120 former members of parliament and activists formed a symbolic parallel or alternative parliament. It was a bold move and a first in Mubarak's three decades of rule. Suddenly, a new space for radical politics and revolutionary mobilization had opened (Zidan 2010; see also Khayal 2016). As some of my interviewees suggested, the election alienated not only the opposition but also many members of the ruling party, who were marginalized in the process. Some shared that youth groups were invited to join, and participated in discussions at, the first meeting of the alternative/parallel parliament, sponsored by the National Association for Change. These groups would become key forces in the uprising, including the founders of the Revolution Youth Coalition.

In chapter 4 I discussed the famous yellow banner of demands (see figure 4.1). These demands confirmed that the fraudulent 2010 parliamentary election was one of the main immediate reasons for the uprising in 2011 (H. Fahmy 2012; Lesch 2011). The revolutionary mobilization, then, not only was a corollary to the fraudulent election (Kuntz and Thompson 2009) but also carried calls for electoral democracy. Thus, the revolution was not only a protest against rigged elections but also an embodied claim to be the center of political gravity for the revolutionary street. Legitimacy was in the street, the revolutionaries insisted, where the old electoral system had collapsed. On February 13, 2011, two days after ousting Mubarak, the SCAF issued a statement suspending the Mubarak-era constitution and dissolving the parliament and the Shura Council (*New York Times* 2011). The process of institutionalizing change—however that is defined—would not be so simple. Tensions between the street and political institutions emerged around the March 2011 constitutional referendum and then grew over time as the SCAF's control and its counterrevolutionary role solidified.

The Emergence of the Project of Procedural Democracy (March 19, 2011)

On February 13, 2011, the SCAF issued a decree delineating a road map, presumably for a transition to democracy, in which it declared itself the supreme administrative authority over Egyptian affairs and announced its intention to remain in power for six months, "or until completing the election of a new parliament and Shura as well as a new president." In short, the military promised not to transfer power *except* to a democratically elected government. It would retain control of the entire constitutional and electoral processes until such an election could take place. Accordingly, the SCAF authorized a committee to draft amendments to the 1971 constitution, which remained in force. The committee was chaired by former counselor Tarek El-Bishry, an Islamic thinker and senior retired judge of the Supreme Administrative Court.[10] The proposal was confusing, as it *suspended* the existing constitution even as it authorized a committee to draft amendments to it. Many activists were shocked and angered: they believed that Egyptians should formulate a new constitution, not amend the old one. This revolutionary demand, however, did not resonate with a conservative body like the SCAF.

The constitutional amendment committee accomplished its task, putting the amendments to a general referendum on March 19, 2011. Those in favor suggested the amendments constituted a first step toward creating a clear road map for a new permanent constitution, based on a constitutional assembly chosen by an elected parliament. The road map would shorten the period of SCAF control, thus hastening the process by which civilians would take power. Opponents maintained that the revolution had aimed to overthrow the old regime and its constitution; the amendments represented extremely limited constitutional reform, when the country needed *radical* change. If anything, opponents charged, the amendments actually invigorated the old constitution and made reform less likely. With fewer than 1 percent of ballots counted as null votes (in which voters did not clearly mark a choice), that referendum saw 77.3 percent in favor and 22.7 percent against (Egypt Government, Higher Election Commission, 2011).

The referendum's passage had four important outcomes with regard to the democratization process. First, it established a sort of start date for *formal* democratization in Egypt. Second, it created a misleading distinction between people committed to democracy and those opposed to it, with the SCAF and MB leaders insisting that anyone who continued to protest, or rejected the referendum, was against democracy. Only two days before the referendum, El-Bishry published an article titled "Those Who Are Scared of Democracy" (2011), in which he compared referendum opponents to those who rallied in support of Gamal Abdel Nasser and his totalitarian plans in 1954. The rift between street and electoral politics thus took on a new, albeit falsely constructed cast, as a conflict between democratic and undemocratic camps.

A third outcome of the referendum was that it again shifted the political center of gravity. It was no longer the province of the revolutionary street, as now it was shared by the street and the electoral/constitutional political space. Only one day after announcing the road map, the SCAF issued "Statement Number Five," in which it insisted that honorable citizens should stop protesting and disrupting production in all sectors. Protesting, the SCAF declared, "create[s] a climate for irresponsible elements to carry out illegal acts; whereas all honest citizens should join all efforts to lead the homeland to safety and not affect the wheels of production and progress" (for SCAF statements, see *Marefa* n.d.). As socialist writer Tamer Wageeh (2017) put it, "The most critical goal of the March 19 referendum was to rob or empty the momentum and centrality of street power and transform this into the trajectory of counting votes. The street was replaced by the political weight of the referendum." On the day of the referendum, a small, symbolic protest of about three thousand took place in Tahrir (Al Jazeera 2011a). The millions of protesters were gone. The discussion had shifted to the millions of *voters* in the referendum. In my field notes at this time, I wrote:

> There is much confusion among revolutionaries. One of the main reasons is that things are not happening the way many actors had hoped for. For example, a constitutional assembly directly chosen by the people would symbolically reflect the idea of the revolution. But this is not happening. There is anger and confusion, mixed with uncertainty, because of the intense conflict and debates happening between those advocating saying no and those advocating saying yes in the referendum. The referendum seems to provide a road map, which gives it more power among the conservative voices of stability. At the same time, I and most revolutionary friends are worried about the waning of the power of the street. (Field notes, March 15, 2011)

Fourth, the referendum meant the fragmentation of the revolutionary camp. On the third anniversary of the referendum, for example, the April 6 Youth Movement issued a statement suggesting that the SCAF and the MB had colluded on the referendum in order to secure the upper hand in the process of transition (April 6 Youth Movement 2015). Additionally, some leftist activists had voted yes in the referendum, adding to the tension and confusion within the larger camp of the left. I wrote in my field notes:

> I voted no, but I am really skeptical about the romanticization of the "no" vote. I am also skeptical about the growing narrative that those who voted no are revolutionaries and those who voted yes are nonrevolutionaries. It is a mistake to associate voting with the status of being revolutionary or not! I have close radical friends who voted yes. Their logic was that it is important to shorten the period under military rule. They suggested that this plan was the main guarantee at the time to ensure a democratic transition and shorten the period of SCAF control. But it seems to me that the heart of the problem is as follows: while many revolutionaries believe that Egypt witnessed a revolution, and change should happen with some revolutionary methods, whatever those be, others believe that all that Egypt needs now is a transition to democracy, whatever that is. Both camps are unclear about their vision. (Field notes, March 20, 2011)

I wrote an op-ed, whose Arabic title translates to "The future beyond the referendum," published in the independent newspaper *Shorouk News*. Naively, I stated, "We should continue to think in a unified way to implement the demands of the revolution" (A. Shahat Said 2011).

The unity that had prevailed in Tahrir now fragmented into conflict about Egypt's identity and religion. One day after the referendum results were announced, a well-known Salafi preacher would frame the conflict between yes and no votes as a confrontation between Islam and non-Islam: "Egypt is the land of Islam and Muslims. And the ballots said yes to religion" (Elhady 2011). The MB, too, used misleading slogans asking voters to say yes to maintain sharia in Egypt. Banners sponsored by the MB were emblazoned, "Say yes to the amendments. Endorsement of the amendments is an Islamic obligation." Meanwhile, a statement from the April 6 Youth Movement affirmed, "Both SCAF and MB contributed to transforming the political battle in Egypt from a battle about aspirations and liberalities of Egyptians into a battle about the identity of Egypt and Islam" (Agamy 2016; April 6 Youth Movement 2015; see also M. Said 2011).[11]

Most actors I talked to did not doubt the free nature of the referendum procedure. Some went so far as to say this was possibly the first in Egypt's history whose outcome Egyptians could not anticipate. However, it was conducted in a climate where the SCAF was in power, with pro-stability discourses leading the chorus of the main media. Thus, it is accurate to say that while it was conducted freely, the climate was not conducive to a fair process. The referendum brought tension and confusion and established a long-lasting division between so-called secular and civilian parties on the one hand and political Islamists, mainly the MB and the SCAF, on the other. As put by El-Ghobashy, "The military council ignored all the proposals, especially calls for a joint civilian-military council to manage the transition. Rushing the process to leave no room for debate and deliberation reinforced their command of the situation and prevented any counterproposals from gaining traction" (El-Ghobashy 2021, 106). In my field notes, I noted how the government media were not only consistently pro-SCAF and pro-stability but also started to launch an aggressive discourse against those who continued to protest. Some of the key themes in this discourse were that the youth of the revolution were peaceful and civilized, *shabab taher* (pure youth), while anybody who was still protesting was a troublemaker and an enemy of the revolution and the state. Other key themes were that "good" Egyptians who wanted to adhere to the revolution and its values had to model this by driving automobiles safely, cleaning their streets, and working hard to build

FIGURE 5.1 Poster on subway station states, "Moralities first, Respecting traffic laws is part of the goals of the January Revolution." March 20, 2011. Photo by the author.

Egypt. The revolution's main goals of democracy and economic justice were not the core of this discourse. Cairo's streets were full of small signs that carried empty slogans on Egyptian nationalism and being a civilized nation; see, for example, a poster (figure 5.1) hung at the metro station. The small sign states that morality comes first and that respecting traffic laws is part of the goals of the January Revolution.[12] In short, the MB and the SCAF had transformed revolution and all its radical possibility into an endless stream of procedural and sectarian battles to barely alter the status quo.[13]

Polarization in Street Politics and Polarization about Procedural Democracy (April–October 2011)

After the March referendum, the SCAF inserted itself as a mediator between the so-called secular and civil parties and the Islamic parties—even as it controlled the transition process (with SCAF legal experts, tanks, and military tribunals for civilians). Revolutionaries understood that the SCAF and the MB were on the same side: the victorious one. Mobilizations were more sporadic, occurring perhaps once or twice a month, for a total of thirteen major protests in Tahrir between April 1, 2011, and the end of October 2011. They were no longer gatherings of millions but smaller uprisings that splintered the civil parties and the Islamic parties, if the latter were present at all.

The conflict between the SCAF and the MB on one side and leftists, liberals, and many revolutionaries on the other was crystallized in two proposals for the transition. One argued that a new constitution must come first, the other that a new parliament must come first. The "constitution first" camp included the Democratic Front Party, Al Tagamoa Party, the Arab Nasserist Party, the Free Egyptian Party, the Youth Coalition for the Revolution, and several liberal groups. They intimated that the revolution had established a new republic in Egypt ("the second republic"), whose revolutionary legitimacy should be reflected in a new constitution. While power relations were murky, they believed, it made no sense to elect a parliament and president. The "election first" camp, on the other hand, suggested that their approach was the most respectful of the people's will as expressed in the constitutional amendments endorsed in the March 2011 referendum (which should, after all, make the road map clear). The elected parliament would then choose a hundred members to form the constitutional assembly (Dunne 2011).

On July 22, 2011, the "constitution first" camp rallied in Tahrir. The "election first" rally came a week later. The former rally was organized by leftists and liberals and was boycotted by the Islamists. The latter was organized by Islamic forces led by the MB. The July 29, 2011, rally was one of the most notable postrevolution rallies. All Islamic forces, the MB, Salafis, and a wide range of Islamic groups, even some called jihadist by activists and journalists, came together on that day in Tahrir. The crowd chanted Islamic slogans, including that Egypt should be an Islamic state. Another key chant was "O Field Marshal, you are the guardian."[14] Activists and revolutionaries at the time referred to this rally as the Friday of Kandahār, a reference to the second-largest city in Afghanistan, because there had been so many jihadist flags on display.[15] Now, where there had been unity, the disunity of the Tahrir coalition was reflected in opposing visions of procedural democracy in Egypt. From March 2011 to October 2011, mobilization was shaped by polarization, in which procedural democracy had gained political weight over street politics.

Acute Tension and Complex Entanglements
(November 2011–December 2012)

While the center of political gravity oscillated between the street and procedural democracy, mobilization remained entangled with electoral politics in complex ways. Protests erupted against the parliamentary election as well as the newly formed parliament. Other rallies sought to strengthen the elected body against the SCAF, called for impartiality of the presidential election committee, or demanded public accountability for elected officials.[16] Four episodes highlight the tensions and entanglements between political mobilization and the project of procedural democracy in Egypt from November 2011 until December 2012: the Mohamed Mahmoud Street battles in November 2011, revolutionary leftist protests calling for the empowerment of parliament against the SCAF in January 2012, a pair of June 2012 protests calling for fairness in the presidential election, and the varying reactions of political forces to a constitutional declaration the SCAF issued on October 2011 and one issued by President Morsi in December 2012.

November 2011: Mohamed Mahmoud Battles
(Mobilization Opposed to Election)

As polarization teased apart the secular/civil and the religious camps, a corresponding divide was opening between street and electoral logics. It had become obvious that the SCAF had no intention of abdicating power, as it deftly played political forces and parties against one another. Meanwhile, the revolutionary leftist youth were still mostly immersed in mobilization in the streets, as secular and civil forces demanded that the new constitution guarantee the civil/secular nature of the state. These forces expressed their concerns over the exclusionary politics of the MB, emphasizing the need for guarantees on principles such as international human rights, freedom of expression, and the democratic nature of the state in the new constitution (Abu Seada 2011). These so-called supraconstitutional principles were drafted by a group of constitutional law professors and politicians, as well as representatives from Al-Azhar (Abu Seada 2011).[17]

The principles, approved by the SCAF, were announced by Deputy Prime Minister Ali El Selmi (a senior member of the liberal Wafd Party) on November 1, 2011 (CNN Arabic 2011). Ahead of the announcement, the MB and

Islamic parties organized one of the largest rallies in Tahrir, the Friday of "unity of demands." The MB and Islamic parties charged that the principles ignored the public will, represented in the March referendum, yet the rallies continued, mostly organized by non-Islamic forces insisting on reclaiming the revolution and opposing the SCAF's control in Egypt.[18]

On November 19, 2011, the protests took a bloody turn. The Mohamed Mahmoud Street battles started with police and military forces attacking a group of campers in Tahrir who were peacefully protesting the slow trials of the police officers responsible for killing and violence during the uprising. In the evening of November 19, revolutionary youth gathered in solidarity with those who were injured that day. The clashes wore on, with the military and the police using rubber bullets, tear gas, and live ammunition against protesters.[19] Snipers directly targeted protesters' eyes.

The battles ended on November 25, only days before the parliamentary election began. This election took place between November 28, 2011, and January 11, 2012, and the Mohamed Mahmoud battles created a significant clash of narratives and meaning making between the protest in the street and the making of the parliament.

Today the Mohamed Mahmoud battles rank among the most important episodes in the revolution and its battles of narratives and memory (Abu Ghazy and Mubarak 2016). Some revolutionary actors even labeled it a "second revolution," connecting the protesters' heroism in the streets and their willingness to die for the spirit of the revolution. For revolutionaries, the poor, the marginalized, and street kids, the Mohamed Mahmoud battles offered an opportunity to reclaim the radical image erased by the dominant media and the SCAF since Mubarak's ouster. They were not the peaceful, middle-class youth that media and elites claimed, and they did not want to be forgotten.[20] More important, a new narrative emerged after the battles, in which radical leftists claimed, "The MB betrayed us on Mohamed Mahmoud" because MB leaders had publicly entertained the idea that the incidents were part of a plot to delay a democratic election. Leftists also said the new parliament was "founded on the blood of the martyrs."[21] As one writer put it, the Mohamed Mahmoud battles established "a case of revolutionary romance" (Adam 2013).[22] Even in street art, Egyptians saw their compatriots' claims: "People have forgotten the image of the martyr and are only uploading images of the candidates." Revolutionary artists drew antielection graffiti and portraits of martyrs; the walls of Mohamed Mahmoud Street soon became an improvised gallery of revolutionary street art (El Shimi 2012; see also Ryzova 2011). In the months that followed, the tension between the street and the parliament became intertwined with mobilization in the street for the parliament itself.

January 2012: Mobilization for the Parliament and Tension between the Streets and the Parliament

As seen earlier, the first parliamentary election after the uprising was a big win for the Islamic parties. Of the 332 seats available, the MB won almost 50 percent, and the Salafi parties took 22 percent. Four coalitions of parties and forces participated in the election. The coalition whose slogan was "The Revolution Continues" won only eight seats (2.4 percent).

The parliamentary offices were formed. The Speaker of the parliament was from the MB and had two deputies, one from the liberal Wafd Party and one from the Salafi party, Al-Nour. The media at the time described it as the "parliament of the revolution."[23] But soon after its formation, this parliament faced an immense test, the "Transfer of Power Initiative." This initiative was formed in January 2012 by independent leftists and socialists (including members of the "Revolution Continues" coalition) and aimed for a peaceful transition. Members of the initiative marched to the parliament on January 28, 2012, and asked it to seize all powers and to strip the SCAF of its authority, as already described. But members of the Freedom and Justice Party (the MB) clashed with the Transfer of Power Initiative. While the leftist protesters chanted against the MB, the MB protesters said they were making shields to protect the parliament (*Almasry Alyoum* 2012b; also see *Almasry Alyoum* 2012a). It had only been three days since, on January 25, 2012, an enormous protest featured banners reading, "Down with military rule," "Power to the people," and "Sovereignty is for Tahrir and the revolution" (El-Khouli and Youssef 2012).

Unfortunately, this parliament was short-lived. It lasted nearly five months before it was dissolved by a verdict from the Supreme Constitutional Court (SCC) on grounds of irregularities in the election law. It was only days before the June 30, 2012, transfer of power to the new president.[24] Shockingly, the SCC's decision to dissolve the parliament—one of the most impactful decisions in the transitional period—was not met with strong protest, except from MB members and political Islamists. At the risk of some simplification, one of the main reasons for the lack of public support of the parliament is that it became associated with political Islamists rather than the revolution at large. As mentioned earlier, this parliament came out of a free election, but its Islamic-dominated majority blessed the privileges of the military and contributed to granting constitutional legitimacy to the military's increased rule. Egyptians have a long history of mistrusting representative bodies due to the long history of manipulating elections, not only under Mubarak but also since the formation of the republic in 1953, and even before, under the monarchy, as shown in the epigraph by Bayram al-Tunsi.

The revolution had been launched to terminate a parliament formed after a rigged election and a president who was out of step with his people. Yet after the parliamentary elections, heated discussions centered on a presumed conflict between "electoral legitimacy" and "revolutionary legitimacy." The regime, now controlled by the SCAF and the MB, argued that revolutionary legitimacy had come to the fore with the election of the new parliament (Kirkpatrick 2011b). But many activists and protesters continued to suggest that revolutionary legitimacy was still embodied in the space of Tahrir and had not dissipated when the protests subsided and the SCAF took power. As such, it should guide in the transition period.

June 2012: Mobilization for the Dissolved Parliament and for the "Revolutionary" Integrity of the Presidential Election

On May 23 and 24, 2012, Egypt's first round of presidential elections produced a surprising outcome. The top two vote getters were Mohamed Morsi, the MB candidate, with 5,764,952 votes, and Ahmed Shafik, Mubarak's last prime minister, with 5,505,327.[25] The former secretary-general of the Arab League, Amr Mousa, a moderate candidate favored by civilian forces, placed fifth, when most polls had expected him to be in the runoff. And even though the revolutionary votes were split among several candidates, Hamdeen Sabahi, associated with the left, came in third. Nobody had expected this (*Sky News Arabia* 2012; see also Salam 2012). The second round of voting would pit an MB candidate against one from the old regime. It was suddenly clear that voting dynamics are different from revolutionary dynamics: compared to mobilization, which is dominated by radicals and activists, voting is dominated by conservative voices.

Revolutionaries faced a stark choice.[26] Many predicted that a Shafik win would mean the end of the revolution, while few knew what a Morsi victory would entail. The April 6 Youth Movement, for example, suggested that a Shafik presidency would deal a death blow to the revolution, while endorsing Morsi would keep options open. For other revolutionaries, a vote for Morsi was anathema (BBC Arabic 2012d). Consequently, revolutionaries and political forces met with Morsi at the Vermont Hotel in the Heliopolis in Cairo. Morsi promised he would be a president of the revolution, standing up to the SCAF and ushering in a new era of Egyptian unity (Deutsche Welle 2012). Yet legal controversies were swirling, raising questions about the election results and the validity of Morsi's victory even before the second round of voting. Others questioned whether Shafik could legally run in the election and whether the elimination of popular candidates such as Salafi candidate Hazem Salah Abu Islamiel had been legitimate (Qassem and Aly 2018).

The Supreme Constitutional Court's June 14, 2012, decision ended the short life of the first postrevolution Egyptian parliament. It declared the elections unconstitutional on the grounds that independent candidates had not been given the same opportunities as political-party candidates (Qassem and Aly 2018). The Speaker of the parliament called the SCC's decision itself unconstitutional (BBC Arabic 2012c). One political observer described the SCC decision as a blow to democracy and an outrage to Islamists (Kirkpatrick 2012; see also Hearst and Hussein 2012). The SCAF announced it was seizing the legislative power in Egypt until the election of another parliament (Al-Hurra 2012; also see Hassan 2012), while two hundred gathered in Tahrir, agitating against the SCC verdict.[27]

Legal instruments, relying on old laws and reviving the old constitution and the SCAF's control of legislative power, were used in this period as restraints on revolutionary mobilization and demands. The judiciary played an important role as a "destabilizing factor in the transition," as well as a tool to "undermine institutions produced by electoral process" (Al Jazeera 2012a; Darwisheh 2018). It is accurate to say that political protests in the transitional period and under Morsi were about elections, constitutional decrees, and larger demands that relate to the revolution. Throughout this period mobilizations and countermobilizations were important features of political protests as well. In late November 2012 the MB protested in front of the SCC, denouncing a possible dissolution of the constitutional assembly—charged with drafting the new constitution—by the court (Abdel Hameed 2012). From June through November 2012, civilians mounted scattered protests against the MB's dominance of the constitutional assembly (*Almasry Alyoum* 2012c). These protests intensified during the last two weeks of November and the first week of December after Morsi issued a constitutional declaration to expand his power, while protecting the constitutional assembly.

On June 17, 2012, one day after the second round of the presidential elections but a week before the results were announced, the SCAF issued the "Complementary Constitutional Declaration," seen by many as a preemptive step toward controlling the power of the elected president.[28] Its points included the following:

1. The SCAF has exclusive rights to govern all military affairs, with the head of the SCAF acting as the commander in chief until a new election goes into force. (This stipulation provided SCAF members with immunity from being ousted before the new constitution took effect.)
2. The SCAF also has legislative power, including approval of the state budget, until the election of a new parliament.
3. The SCAF claims the power to appoint a constitutional assembly should the parliament fail to form one.
4. The SCAF—as well as the president and the prime minster, and/or one-fifth of the constitutional assembly—has the right to veto any article in the constitution in the event that this article "opposes the goals of the revolution and its principles, or if these articles violate the common principles in Egypt's previous constitutions" (*Official Magazine of Egypt Laws* 2012; see also Al Jazeera 2012d; Ayman 2012).

On June 30, 2012, Mohamed Morsi took office. He was modern Egypt's first democratically elected president, its first Islamic president, and its first nonmilitary president. On November 22, 2012, he issued a constitutional declaration granting himself unlimited power (for the text, see *Ahram Online* 2012b). The decree included the following:

1. Investigations and trials related to the killing of protesters during the revolution will be reopened.[29]
2. Presidential decisions made between June 30 and the time when a constitution is approved by the people's assembly are "final and binding" and cannot be appealed in any way by any entity.
3. The president has the right to appoint a prosecutor general.
4. The constitutional assembly is granted an extension to complete the drafting of the constitution.
5. No judicial body can dissolve the Shura Council (the upper house of the parliament) or the constitutional assembly.

The radical street viewed Morsi's election as unsatisfactory. Now even the moderate Islamic politician Abdel Menem Abu Al Fetouh described Morsi's decree as "passing a revolutionary demand within a package of autocratic decisions" (quoted in Kirkpatrick and El Sheikh 2012).

The first constitutional assembly, formed on March 24, 2012, was dominated by Islamic members (sixty-six out of one hundred) and included scant representation for workers, trade unionists, civil society representatives, women, and Christians. That assembly was dissolved on April 10, 2012, with the court order clarifying that while the parliament was responsible for forming the assembly, parliamentary members could not appoint themselves to the constituent assembly (thirty-eight of the fifty parliamentary members of the constituent assembly were members of the MB's Freedom and Justice Party). Another assembly was formed on June 13, 2012, with slightly better representation for unions, women, and Christians but still plagued by the accusation that Islamists were appointing parliament members and MB loyalists. All this provided the backdrop to Morsi's inauguration. The parliament had been dissolved; the second constitutional assembly was embattled. Now Morsi's constitutional declaration aimed to protect the constitutional assembly from being dissolved by the judiciary (helmed by Mubarak-era judges).

It is ironic that the SCAF's and Morsi's declarations used similar terminology, especially the commitment to protecting the revolution. Yet both declarations were authoritarian. They were both issued without consulting the public. And they were both met with protests.

Interestingly, the protests against Morsi's declaration were larger than those against the SCAF's. On June 22, 2012, for example, in response to the SCAF's declaration, the MB organized a rally in Tahrir that drew thousands. The majority were Islamists and Salafis, including the Salafi youth group Hazemoon (attributed to Hazem Salah Abu Islamiel). Some members of the April 6 Youth Movement and Revolutionary Socialists rallied, too. The rally raised slogans such as "No to the coup" and "Yes to legitimacy" (BBC Arabic 2012a).[30] Another protest took place in Alexandria, outside the Northern Military Command (A. Hafez 2012). Many protesters in Alexandria and Cairo carried pictures of Morsi, and some Islamists in Tahrir carried banners that stated "From Giza to Aswan, Morsi is the winner" (A. Hafez 2012).

Morsi's declaration, in contrast, spurred significantly larger protests. Within two days of its issuance, a mass protest began in Tahrir (Al Jazeera 2012b). Some of Morsi's advisers, including Christians, liberals, and Islamists, resigned, specifying that Morsi had not consulted with any of them prior to his decree. The SCAF called the declaration an attack demeaning the power of the judiciary. The April 6 Youth Movement suggested that Morsi's declaration aimed to reestablish authoritarianism in Egypt. The protests included a sit-in in front of the Al-Ittihadiya Palace in Heliopolis (Ramzy 2012). And on December 5, 2012, what became known as the Al-Ittihadiya Palace clashes erupted between MB supporters and protesters and campers in the area (Ramzy 2012). The protests escalated for two weeks until Morsi withdrew the declaration on December 8, 2012.

Activists I asked about the different responses to the two declarations suggested that many did not view the SCAF's declaration as authoritative, despite the bloody and troubled transition under the SCAF, while they agreed with the April 6 Youth Movement's claim that Morsi was attempting to reestablish authoritarian rule. Many Egyptians still trusted the military, believing it to be a stabilizing force committed to safeguarding the nation's interests. Others suggested that secular forces were pleased with the SCAF's declaration, which represented a step against the MB's aspirations and toward "constitution first," whereas Morsi's decree was an obvious betrayal of the promises he had made before his election (Al-Shereef 2014; Facebook correspondences, February 1, 2019). Nevertheless, in both cases Egyptians took their opposition to the street.

It bears repeating that toward the end of December 2012, Egypt was totally polarized. This was different from the polarization that had taken place during the uprising, between Mubarak's regime and the revolutionaries. This time, the antagonism was constructed as between Morsi / the MB and the Egyptian people. Everyday people were exhausted: the political process had failed to deliver *either* stability or democracy. The SCAF's control and the MB's exclusionary politics alike fanned the flames, but the anger focused more on the MB, thanks to the infiltration of the deep state.

The Collapse of the Project of Procedural Democracy and the Establishment of a System of Farcical Democracy (January 2013–January 2015)

How did we get to the coup on July 3, 2013? It is ironic indeed that a mobilization embodied by the Tamarod ("rebel") campaign paved the way to the coup. The Tamarod campaign is best understood as an "infiltrated" mobilization used to oust an elected official and force an earlier presidential election. Tamarod started on April 26, 2013, in Tahrir against a backdrop in which pro-state actors, such as Mohamed Abu Hamed, called for collecting 15 million signatures to oust Morsi. Abu Hamed's rationale was that 15 million signatures would exceed the number of votes (13.2 million votes), or about 52 percent of valid votes) Morsi had received in the runoff. The idea was apparently picked up by some youth and military intelligence interested in undermining Morsi's presidency. The Tamarod campaign itself was founded by Nasserist youth who were ambivalent about loyalty to the state. This leadership also worked with the intelligence apparatus, which had infiltrated the movement, and Mubarakists, who were funding it with money channeled through the military from the United Arab Emirates. Thus, the growing momentum on the ground was tainted by infiltration from the military and the old regime, foreign funding, and collaboration between the leadership and the deep state (see Ketchley 2017a, chap. 5).

Like many other ordinary citizens, some of my interviewees joined. A few months after the coup, they would tell me, "We joined because we saw many citizens do so." One interviewee asked quizzically, "How can you have doubts when you see so many people joining, and when we were taking the momentum back to the streets, after it was lost in sectarian and procedural battles?"[31] On June 20, 2013, a leftist writer stated, "The state and authorities in Egypt are scared [due to the Tamarod campaign]. The most impressive thing about the campaign is its momentum. The Tamarod statement is being signed in streets and in factories. People are hastening not only to sign but to take pictures of themselves signing the statement. Groups of Tamarod are forming in neighborhoods and in workspaces to discuss the statement. Discussions are happening, about the performance of the MB, and their goals. Discussions about why the first elected president should be removed from office" (Wagdy 2013).

Even as I fretted that the military was hijacking the process, I, too, personally participated in collecting signatures among Egyptians residing in the United States. Among the activists I talked to who did not participate, some wondered, "How can I participate in a campaign and in protests that include police officers and Mubarakists?" I realize now that they were the wiser.

It is naive to suggest that the movement was entirely state made (the MB narrative) or genuinely organic (the military and state narrative). More important, the core of the group's mobilization was the gathering of signatures on a petition undermining Morsi's victory and proposing a new presidential election.[32] From April to June, the campaign regularly announced the collection of millions of names, and by June 30, the day of a nationwide protest that would pave the way for the coup, the movement claimed 22 million signatures. There is no evidence to verify this number, nor can one disentangle the complexity of the coup and reduce it to the Tamarod campaign.[33] Many actors were involved in the campaign, not all of whom were seriously interested in an early election. Those who were genuinely interested in an early election, but not necessarily in a coup, naively believed that Morsi would make the concessions necessary to avoid a crisis. They hoped that popular pressure could tame the military's ambitious intervention in the process.

The June 30 protests were filmed by the national and international media. The military ordered its own helicopters out and hired a filmmaker to record the events.[34] The goal was clear: to show the mass protests to the world. The stage was set for the coup.

It would happen quickly. On the infamous day of July 3, 2013, Abdel Fattah el-Sisi, the defense minister, announced the ouster of President Morsi in synchrony with the June 2013 protests. Sisi also announced the appointment of Adly Mansour, the chief justice of the SCC at the time, as interim president. The Egyptian people quickly realized that this meant the military was their de facto ruler.

In short, while we should not reduce the Tamarod campaign to the infiltration of the deep state, we also should not reduce a complex process such as the military coup to this campaign. The coup was a complex contingent process. It was possible only due to a combination of many factors. These include the fragmentation and the idealism of the revolutionary left; the weakness and the hypocrisy of the liberal elites; the MB's complicity with the military, which made them an easy target for the military's revenge; the constant repression by the SCAF and the security apparatus, which exhausted the revolutionaries; the role of regional counterrevolutionary forces; and, finally, the role of the military and deep state as well as the Mubarak restorationists in mobilizing against the MB.

In 2013 many scholars and activists focused on one element or another within this complex process. Meanwhile, also in 2013, many revolutionaries were confused, while Egypt was acutely polarized. The debate was constructed as a simple binary: it should be seen as a coup or—as some, especially those supporting the military and the state, argued—as a revolution. If there is one main lesson I have learned from writing this book, however, it is the significance of time and its ability to destabilize meaning. On June 30, 2014, the first anniversary of the June 30, 2013, protests, Big Pharaoh, an Egyptian blogger, wrote on his Twitter account that June 30 was not a revolution, and it was not *just* a coup: "June 30 + July 3 = a coup with popular support."[35] Similarly, Amr Khalifa, a journalist and political commentator, tweeted on the same day, "I termed what occured [*sic*] as a #RevolutionaryCoup. I was wrong. It was a #Coup but [only a] few of us had the right glasses."[36]

I am inspired by the practice of collective reflection of many Egyptian writers and revolutionaries. This practice requires admitting mistakes and previous misjudgments. In one of the most notable reflections, which I cite at length here, leftist writer Hani Shukrallah weighs in and admits misjudgments and miscalculations of revolutionaries' power and the revolutionary momentum during the June 30 mobilization that led to the coup on July 3, 2013. Shukrallah writes,

> I think that my main mistake in reading June 30 at the time was conceiving it as merely a third wave of the Egyptian Revolution. My misconception was not because I was unaware of the counterrevolutionary tricks. The counterrevolution had never ceased these tricks since January 25, 2011. I exaggerated in thinking that the revolutionary momentum was able to overcome the counterrevolutionary games. I did not consider the magnitude of the exhaustion of revolutionary forces after two and a half years of enormous sacrifice and no real gains. Not only enormous sacrifice and no real gains, but also every little gain was accompanied by a new maneuver followed by another backlash. I also did not consider the size of the massive and surreptitious mobilization that the Egyptian bourgeoisie was doing in the countryside and the city to restore "stability" at any price. I did not consider the great complexity in the same phenomenon [June 30 mobilizations] in combining both the revolution and the counterrevolution. In the same phenomenon, the revolutionary momentum was releasing its final and last push, while the counterrevolution was recovering its vitality and taking advantage of the opportunity, moving from retreat and manipulation to do its massive attack. Only with the massacre of Rabaa did I realize that the counterrevolution, not the revolution, had the upper hand.[37] The counterrevolution started with an alliance between the security forces and the Muslim Brotherhood. It was supported and sponsored by the US, European powers, and regimes from the Gulf. But it concluded with the division of the alliance and the slaughter of the Muslim Brotherhood and then the revolution.[38]

Shukrallah here not only touches on the significance of revolutionary momentum and its waning but also provides an example of critical rumination, which has guided my analysis through these pages.

To return to what happened after the coup, among the first actions taken by the coup administration were the dissolution of the 2012 constitution—

approved under the MB—and a major crackdown against the brotherhood. The coup itself was one of the most foundational moments in Egyptian history-shaping politics after 2013.[39] It was followed closely by July 2013 mobilizations outside and against "institutionalist" politics and politics at large in Egypt.[40] This mobilization began on July 24, 2013, less than three weeks after the military coup, as General Sisi delivered a speech during a public meeting with officers of the Navy Academy. He thundered, "I ask Egyptians next Friday [July 26] to rally, to confirm the will of the people to give a *mandate* to the military and the police to confront violence and terrorism. The military and the police will be securing these rallies." The reference to violence and terrorism was meant to exploit the political polarization of Egypt, such that citizens would expect the MB to engage in mass violence. The media, now almost entirely controlled by the intelligence apparatus, initiated broad campaigns demonizing the MB, supported by army propaganda and claiming latent MB and Islamist plans to launch terrorist attacks as a response to the coup. Millions of citizens answered Sisi's invitation and rallied on July 26.

Elections did not take place until a year later, but according to several critical analysts (see, for example, Abd Rabu 2015), Sisi was ruling Egypt and the military via this mandate rather than through elections. Speaking of the rallies on June 30 before the coup, one interviewee told me, "For a while, I heard no slogans and no chants. I only heard vuvuzelas making noise. This signaled the end of politics for me." The same was true of the July 26 rallies, in which I argue that the people surrendered their sovereignty to Sisi and the military. It was counterrevolutionary mobilization par excellence and gave a mandate to the military to later massacre MB protesters. That is, these rallies provide the context for the military's excessive use of violence in 2013 and beyond. To use Charles Tilly's terminology, the July 26 rallies were an ideal case of a prescribed mobilization. Coming at a critical juncture in Egyptian politics, they provided the military and police apparatus with carte blanche to combat terrorism (whatever that meant and however long it might last).

While the legitimacy of the mandate and the de facto rule of the military were the real issues at stake, the interim president, Mansour, issued decrees to safeguard the counterrevolutionary agenda. On November 24, 2013, Mansour signed a new law ostensibly regulating protests. It banned all unsanctioned gatherings, public or private, of ten or more people and gave the authorities the right to attend private meetings. Rights groups described it as an antiprotest law, due to its repressive and undemocratic nature, and scholars called it a law to legalize authoritarianism. Mass arrests followed, for months. Even random citizens from downtown cafés near Tahrir would be swept up.

On January 18, 2014, a new constitution was passed. It retained the military's privileges in Egypt, which was first embraced by the MB constitution. It also retained aspects of the religious foundations of the state, as had the MB-sponsored constitution in 2012. Nine days later, the SCAF threw its might behind Sisi in the presidential election. Here I agree with Mona El-Ghobashy's (2021) thoughtful intervention that Egypt's struggle for sovereignty continued to be uncertain, even beyond the events of the military coup in 2013, until the military announced its backing of Sisi's bid for the presidency on January 2014. Then, between May 26 and 28, a new presidential election took place. In it, the key agent in the coup, Sisi, earned 96.9 percent of the votes. The parliamentary election was subsequently delayed several times, because Sisi insisted on a unified list to represent the state and the nation in the election. Well over two years after the coup, a new parliament was elected at last in late 2015. Technically, the electoral law was structured to minimize party candidates and maximize individual seats (one-third for the former, two-thirds for the latter). But in practice, the majority of seats were taken by a pro-Sisi list called For the Love of Egypt (FLE). Most of the candidates on that list were former military and police generals. Out of the seven coalitions running for the parliament, six were formed by and in coordination with Egypt's General Intelligence Directorate and the Military Intelligence and Reconnaissance Administration. Activists and critics in Egypt described the new parliament as "the generals' parliament" and "the intelligence parliament." Some politicians revealed details about how the intelligence apparatuses and security forces had intervened in and planned the electoral process (see Bahgat 2016). This new parliament held its first session in January 2016.

The Egyptian people had revolted against the "businessmen's parliament" of 2010, but with the ultimate victory of the counterrevolution, they got the "intelligence parliament" of 2015.

Conclusion: Possibilities Halted, and Bitter Lessons

When I went to cast my ballot during the March referendum of 2011, I observed the heavy presence of the military outside the ballot stations. Among the major changes that took place in the aftermath of the uprising, one that has stood out all along is that Egypt's general elections and referendums are now guarded by the army. The juxtaposition of the army erecting barriers, blocking protests, and attacking protesters with the army guarding the polls crystallized what kind of "democracy" had been produced under the military. Nevertheless, there was a huge difference between the elections held before the coup and those that came after. I argued earlier in this chapter that Egypt after Mubarak had elections without democratization. More accurately, Egypt shifted from holding "free elections" without democratization after the 2011 uprising to holding farcical elections under near-totalitarian military rule after the 2013 coup.

It is not true that protests in the postrevolutionary era were led by unrealistic youth who were not interested in democracy or in expanding procedural democracy. A significant part of these protests focused on demanding elections free from the military's control. Yet the SCAF and the military regime deployed legalistic and reformist methods to counter and contain tendencies that called for substantive forms of democracy. First, the SCAF appointed a committee to draft constitutional amendments to Egypt's *old constitution*, thus ensuring that change would be *as limited as possible*. Second, on February 11, 2011, the military promised not to transfer power except to a democratically elected government. But the elections took place under the military's supervision, the electoral laws were designed by military and state legal experts, and they were full of loopholes to obstruct elections and their outcomes. Third, due to the short terms of the various elected bodies between 2011 and 2015, the SCAF effectively ruled Egypt during that time. Fourth, the SCAF resisted announcing a timeline for the presidential election, only finally doing so prior to the parliamentary election and after the Mohamed Mahmoud protests and battles, which mainly sought to end SCAF rule in Egypt. Fifth, the SCAF used its constitutional and legal power to issue constitutional decrees and laws, most of which aimed at criminalizing protest and all forms of revolutionary mobilization, in addition to reducing reform to the most minimalist, proceduralist components possible.

The MB unfortunately participated in endorsing the use of legalistic methods to end or deflate the revolutionary temper in the streets. It fell victim to the same methods, used to dissolve the parliament controlled by the MB and then the Shura Council. With its exclusionary and sectarian policies, the MB also contributed to fueling the public hatred of the MB and Islamists. The military and the MB disagreed on a number of issues, such as the configuration of the constitutional assembly and electoral laws, which reflected a tension around sharing power.[41] Yet they agreed on three key issues: keeping the military's economic privileges and expanding its political privileges, empowering the security apparatus, and opposing social demands and social protests (both were committed to continue working with the International Monetary Fund

[IMF] and World Bank).[42] Even with respect to the civil/secular versus religious divide, the military and the MB agreed on expanding the role of religion in the state. Political scientist Ashraf El-Sherif (2014) states, "Politically, the Brotherhood misread the situation. It moved toward political domination too quickly, making a series of tactical mistakes in the process. It failed to either appease or successfully confront institutional power bases, and, believing its electoral victory to be an irreversible popular mandate, it was reluctant to make the concessions necessary to avoid alienating crucial secular elites. The Brotherhood waged an unwinnable battle, driven more by ideological zeal and delusions of grandeur than by a realistic assessment of the political environment."

The coup was represented by the military as an effort to save the Egyptian state from an extremist group. Most analyses focus on the secular-religious divide and the democratic procedural battles as reasons for the failure of the democratization process. But as Raymond Hinnebusch suggested, most approaches to democratization theory and postdemocratization theory in the Arab world neglected "the underlying political economy motors of politics and the importance of the balance of class power in giving social content to various institutional forms" (2014, 49). If we look only at institutions and procedures, we will fail to see some key economic issues and "who gets what," as Hinnebusch (49) rightly suggested. In practical terms, for example, the military's political and economic privileges were expanded in the MB-sponsored constitution, and then this was maintained under the 2014 constitution after the coup.

As I have been arguing throughout the book, social struggles were never absent, before, during, and in the aftermath of the uprising in 2011. I have charted the trajectory of the intersection of revolutionary mobilization and the project of procedural democracy from 2011 to 2015. Yet workers continued to protest all the way until 2013 and beyond (Bassiouny 2013). Without exaggeration, some who voted for Morsi in 2012 did so because he was not a figure from the old regime and thus could be genuinely interested in combating state corruption. When Morsi's government continued to work with the IMF, public protests took place.[43] It is also a fact that the Tamarod petition campaign template to withdraw confidence from Morsi was almost entirely based on economic and social demands. Some experts (Al-Anani 2020; Gamal 2019; Hinnebusch 2014, 49) noted how critical the neoliberal agenda and the ties to international capital were to the MB's economic performance while in power.[44] Egyptian politics was often misread as a case of a mismatch between protest and election or as a betrayal of democracy. Yet, as this chapter has shown, Egyptians were contesting the meaning of democracy, never separate from economic issues, throughout these eventful times.

I would like to note here that the Project on Middle East Democracy interviewed a group of respected experts and colleagues concerning the failure of democratization in Egypt (Hawthorne and Miller 2020). Looking back nine years (at the time of publication), they emphasized many important factors that contributed to this failure, such as the fact that secular, liberal, Islamist, and leftist forces all failed in making necessary compromises, vulnerability to regional forces of counterrevolution, failure to enforce a plan for transitional justice, the lack of trust in the MB when they took part in power, the failure of civilian forces to neutralize the military's power, the exclusionary politics of the MB, and the United States' blessing of the military coup in 2013, along with the structural challenges, internal economic and social factors, and external support for stability at any cost. Each of these is an accurate diagnosis of one piece or more in the story of the failed transition in Egypt. As Michael Hanna stated, "Failure was not inevitable. Contingency and choice should be seen as central factors" (in Hawthorne and Miller 2020, 6). However, the main difference between my analysis and these respected views is my emphasis on contingency, possibilities, and the relevance and significance of revolutionary mobilization and the revolutionary street and the uncertainties throughout this period.[45]

6 | square zero

The Pharaohs had a monkey god, and an alligator god too
Each god had its own clergy and armed soldiers
And iron safes, bolted tight with lock and key
And a palace, huge like the modern palaces of the republic
Poor god—now he's become a tourist entertainment
Pay heed, ye haughty, contented one, with epaulets on your
    shoulders!
—TAMIM AL-BARGHOUTI, EGYPTIAN PALESTINIAN POET

Violation of "public modesty." That's what Ahmed Naji, author of *The Use of Life*, was sentenced to two years in prison for. In response, Egyptian writers and intellectuals issued a statement, "Open the Political Space," on February 23, 2016. They wrote:

> Our defense of Naji—and other targeted writers—is a call to protect the freedom of expression of writers and artists, in all forms of creativity. Such expression should be protected without any censorship or retaliation. In our statement, we emphasize that we want to expand the protection of

freedom of opinion and expression beyond the intellectual and writers community, to society at large. In fact, we issue this statement as a warning bell to stop the frightening path that the current political regime has chosen. At the core of this path is the annihilation of freedom of opinion and expression in Egypt and the *complete seizure of the political space.* (El-Shamy 2016, emphasis mine)

The Egyptian state had long penalized creative writers for their writing, but this level of repression and silencing struck the public as ironic, so soon on the heels of revolution. As one Egyptian writer put it, in an op-ed on the fifth anniversary of the revolution, "We can see the state battling the ghost of the revolution in the same way [as someone who has a nightmare that might recur at any time, to be averted at all costs]—with increasing panic as the fifth anniversary draws closer. This is reflected in an unprecedented restriction of civil liberties. Almost every day there is news of fresh reprisals" (Ez-Eldin 2016). Citing multiple examples of expanding censorship; closures of publishing houses, small theaters, and galleries; book confiscations; and the arrest and sentencing of dissenting authors, the writer suggested that the regime was attacking all forms of expression and concluded that citizens have "an acute lack of oxygen" (Ez-Eldin 2016).

Indeed, human rights advocates, revolutionary youth, and Egyptian writers alike have commented on the closure of political space after the military coup of 2013. As the military and security apparatus expanded their control over most mediums of expression, they charge, writers and activists have been targeted, even for the content of their social media posts.

As shown throughout this book, the Egyptian Revolution expanded political possibilities and unleashed projects of containment, in which dissenters had to constantly navigate the unsettled political spaces. As street protests unfolded in and outside of formal political spaces, social media spread the uprising into new virtual spaces and new global conversations. Even so, as early as 2011 and 2012, writers and revolutionary youth were emphasizing that the only real gain for the revolution was the opening up of political space. By 2013, however, we could see an emergent discourse about the closure of that space. Known activists and ordinary citizens are arrested for transgressions as minor as singing songs critical of the regime, drawing graffiti or publishing cartoons, posting on social media, and even walking down the street in T-shirts obliquely critical of the government through slogans like "For a homeland without torture." Writers and activists allege the military regime of Abdel Fattah el-Sisi "has no rationality" and bemoan how "even [Hosni] Mubarak's regime never reached this degree of repression."

As I returned to Egypt in late 2015, I was able to witness firsthand the unprecedented political paranoia. Cafés near Tahrir, which had been filled with revolutionary youth during the uprising in 2011, were closed. Many of the bloggers and activists I interviewed during the uprising and its aftermath had been arrested and detained without trial for their online critiques of the military regime's crackdown on democracy. Key leaders of the parties associated with the revolution—such as the Social Democratic Party, the Constitution Party, the Popular Socialist Alliance, Strong Egypt, and the recently formed Bread and Freedom Party—remained in prison by the end of 2019, charged with working to destabilize the state or allegedly being affiliated with the Muslim Brotherhood (MB) and terrorism. The MB and its party, the Freedom and Justice Party, have been banned.

Without necessarily comparing the current military regime with Mubarak's regime, it is fair to say that the new authoritarianism in Egypt is qualitatively and quantitively different from that of Mubarak.[1] Qualitatively, it came through a coup, and it was driven by unequivocal counterrevolutionary goals, a phobia of revolution, and an expansion of the intelligence apparatus. Quantitively, it represented a big shift from Mubarak's calculated or controlled repression to the limitless repression imposed by the Sisi regime. The editors of *World Politics Review* summed it up neatly: "'Simply Put, There's No Freedom of the Press' in Sisi's Egypt" (*World Politics Review* 2019). Egypt saw twenty thousand to thirty thousand citizens detained arbitrarily in the three decades of Mubarak's power, but in the first four years of Sisi's rule, nearly sixty thousand were detained. Rights groups and political observers consistently decry Sisi's human rights record and charge that things are dramatically worse than under Mubarak (see Cook 2017). Since the 2013 coup, the government has allowed no political space, whether on formal political terrain, in the streets, on social media, or in most conventional media forms. It has shown zero tolerance for any form of opposition. Parliamentarians who dare to question the government—even in formal parliamentary sessions—have been targeted. After a radical opening of political space in 2011, it took only two years to see an abrupt and total about-face.

In what follows, I outline three causes of closure. First, I propose a historically sensitive and disaggregated account of the concept of counterrevolution and how it is applied in Egypt. Second, while interrogating Sisi's rise to power and theories such as Bonapartism and Caesarism that have been leveraged to explain it, I propose the notion of the paranoid regime.[2]

In this way, I seek to explain the disproportionate use of violence and the counterrevolution's obsessive focus on seizing political space in Egypt. For the military regime, nothing short of complete political desertification is acceptable. Third, I argue against the idea that the military counterrevolutionary regime has been solely capable of restoring fear, thus forcing revolutionaries to withdraw from political space. Instead, using interviews with Egyptian revolutionaries, I argue that many also *chose* to withdraw. Amid widespread repression, even those who were not actively terrorized so yearned for stability that they were willing to tolerate the dramatic closure of political space.

This chapter is divided into four sections. In the first, I provide examples of the wide, dramatic closure of political space, focusing on the phenomenon of digital repression. In the second, I discuss the transformation of Tahrir into militarized space. The third and the fourth sections are devoted to making sense of the dramatic closure of political space, from the point of view of the regime and revolutionary actors. I analyze the dominance of the paranoid regime and the ways in which activists consciously decided to withdraw from contentious politics as they made sense of defeat.

The data in this chapter come from documentary research and social media analysis, human rights reports, and civil discourse, as well as interviews with thirty-two self-proclaimed activists belonging to the January Revolution (the *yanayergiyaa* in Arabic, or Januarists, as some called themselves), ranging in age from seventeen to forty-five (see appendix 3 for interviewees' demographics).

Before proceeding, I must clarify: I am using the terminology of the opening and closing of political space because actors in Egypt use this terminology. Still, openings and closures are never total, nor are they imposed solely by one group on another; in the Egyptian context, these terms refer to political struggle and contestation between different regimes and actors. Thus, in the decade before the revolution, Mubarak was forced to open some margins of the political space in response to protests in the streets, the rise of social media activism, and some world pressure. As we saw in chapter 1, political space opened gradually through the accumulation of struggles and contestations that took years before the revolution in 2011. The "dramatic closure" of political space in the aftermath of the military coup of 2013 could be explained by the vicious grip of the military counterrevolutionary regime and its paranoia and "Januaryphobia," the fear of a repetition of the revolution. I do not imply that pro-democracy actors had no part in this closure. Throughout this analysis I argue against reductionist narratives about the success of both revolution and counterrevolution and their respective capabilities when it comes to controlling and curtailing political space.

The Copious Seizure of Political Space

Let us look at some specific examples of what happened in the political space in the aftermath of the coup, especially considering the intensification and wide scope of the attack on this space. To deter *street politics*, a new law was enacted on November 24, 2013, presumably to regulate protests. The law was viewed as draconian, as it practically criminalized all protests. Thousands of youth were arrested on charges of violating it. Moreover, since July 2013 cafés in downtown Cairo have become constant targets of security attacks. Especially during political occasions, such as the anniversary of the revolution, youth are arrested randomly at these cafés, whose owners are also randomly ordered to close down their shops. Many of these cafés—thirty-five in one day in Cairo's el-Borsa café district alone—have been completely shut down on the pretext that they were not authorized by the Cairo Governorate (see Rios 2015). El-Borsa is within walking distance of Tahrir Square and famously hosted meetings of revolutionary youth during the uprising in 2011. Also, main streets leading to Tahrir have been constantly blocked by metal gates and or huge blocks from the end of 2011 until 2016 and beyond.

Even symbolic and artistic forms of dissent have not been allowed in the aftermath of the coup of July 2013. Huge resources were spent on whitewashing graffiti. For example, on November 1, 2015, Sisi had complained about social media criticism of his rule, stating, "This is not acceptable" (in slang Egyptian Arabic, ما يصحش كده [mā yiṣiḥḥish kida]). Graffiti was drawn with the statement to mock Sisi in Qasr El Nile Street downtown and remained there for about two weeks before it was washed off. Many interlocutors were surprised that the graffiti was left for two weeks, as graffiti would normally be washed off right away. The famous wall of the American University in Cairo's old campus in Mohamed Mahmoud Street, which once hosted prominent revolutionary graffiti, was demolished.

The military regime has taken many steps to combat dissent in digital spaces. For example, the 2014 constitution—written under the military's oversight—instructed the legislatures to criminalize what it described as violations of cybersecurity, and in August 2018 a new law was enacted to criminalize many activities on social media. The law treated the accounts of individuals with more than five thousand followers as media platforms, subjecting them to "crimes of false news." Most of these popular accounts belong to activists in the January Revolution. Many of them were detained merely because of Facebook posts where they criticize Sisi and military rule in Egypt. The law authorized a pseudogovernmental entity, the Supreme Council of Media (composed of pro-government journalists and media persons close to the security apparatus), to file criminal complaints against digital media platforms such as Twitter, Facebook, and personal blogs because of what was written there (for the text of the law and comments on it, see Tahrir Institute for Middle East Policy 2019).

The Supreme Council of Media set to work, and writers, journalists, bloggers, and ordinary citizens alike were accused of spreading false news, "inciting people to violate laws," or engaging in "defamation against individuals and state institutions." Even before the enactment of this law, the regime had targeted the administrators of Facebook pages critical of the military, or sympathetic with the MB after the coup, as well as of pages that called for any kind of mobilization. The security apparatuses invested billions of dollars in technology for surveillance, hacking, and censorship; blocked no fewer than five hundred websites in Egypt by early 2019 (Tahrir Institute for Middle East Policy 2019); and arrested and even killed some administrators of these pages, based on charges that they had ties to the MB and terrorism.

In December 2015, during a research trip to Egypt, I realized that the internet cafés near Tahrir were highly securitized: the National Security Agency (the State Security Intelligence's new name since March 15, 2011) had instructed the owners of these cafés to record the names of users, their national IDs, and the times of their usage in a registry they kept for the security purposes. I myself had to provide details about my visit and stay to an internet provider when I requested ADSL service for a month. An employee at the company indicated that these details would be provided to the National Security Agency.

Conventional media and even TV channels were also targeted: especially in the aftermath of the coup in 2013, the Military Intelligence and Reconnaissance Administration, the General Intelligence Directorate, and the National Security Agency made huge expenditures to purchase TV channels and media outlets. Consequently, the ownership structure of media outlets in Egypt changed dramatically, with at least 90 percent of these spaces currently controlled by either the intelligence apparatuses or their proxy companies. Almost all TV anchors and writers who were once sympathetic with the uprising were threatened and harassed, ending their appearances on TV. Today most anchors work with the security apparatuses, receiving their instructions from them. Critical media scholar Adel Iskandar (2021) thoroughly demonstrates the nuances of how the post–Arab Spring regimes treat media as a matter of existential importance and have adopted complex ways to control the media that reflect a neoliberal authoritarian logic.

Even TV soap operas and the movie industry were infiltrated by the security apparatus. The goal was clear: to ban any positive references to the January uprising and to launch propaganda campaigns for the military (see Bahgat 2017; Walsh 2019). A central refrain in these shows is that the January uprising was damaging to Egypt: the 25th of January revolution is consistently referred to as "the 25th of Damages" (*khasayer*, Arabic for "damages," rhymes with *'Yanayer*, Arabic for "January"). Military and intelligence apparatuses even expanded their "investments" to soccer clubs, launching their own clubs to compete in the Egyptian Soccer League, even as soccer games took place without any fans in attendance from roughly 2012 to 2018, allegedly for security reasons. In 2018 the regime introduced a system allotting seats to about five thousand fans, after conducting security checks on them.

Formal political space was no less constrained. As discussed in chapter 5, Egypt had no parliament for almost a year and half in the aftermath of the 2013 coup. A parliamentary election was held on December 2014, and the first session started on January 2015.[3] This parliament was almost completely controlled by both the military and public intelligence apparatuses. In a context of very low voter participation and mass arrests of youth, Sisi received 96.9 percent of the votes in the 2014 presidential election. The 2018 presidential election also saw the arrests of all potentially serious opposition candidates, such as the former military chief of staff, Sami Anan. Former military general Ahmed Shafik, who had served as prime minister under Mubarak during the uprising, was placed under house arrest. To give credibility to the election, Sisi and the security apparatus found an "opposition candidate," Moustafa Moussa, who has close ties with the security apparatus and was seen as Sisi's puppet. Sisi won with 98 percent of the votes.

These episodes all entail crackdowns by counterrevolutionary forces on the political space that had been opened by the revolution. The burst of politicization in Egypt from 2011 until the coup was interpreted as a society dangerously "out of control" for the military's totalitarian mindset. The regime and its propaganda machines deployed the terminology of *national alignment* (*istefaf watany* in Arabic), a term drawn from military culture. The logic is that the whole nation should come together to support military leaders against a common enemy—but that enemy remained unclear and was defined variously over time as terrorists, opposition politicians, or the January revolutionaries.

It is useful to return to the ways the political space changed in the decade before 2011, to identify a pattern whereby Egyptian activists turned to social media space and street politics when formal political space was virtually closed. Thus, the aim of social media and street politics was to expand the formal political space and pave a road to democracy in Egypt. The gradual and contested nature of the opening of formal political space resulted in a margin of freedom in street politics. The story goes that the revolution in 2011 disrupted this formula, leading to a collapse of the undemocratic formal political system and a dramatic opening of social media/internet spaces and revolutionary street politics.

Since the coup, in the context of the complete closure of political spaces, the formula has lost relevance. All three political spaces are closed and almost equally targeted by the Sisi regime. Street protest is forbidden. The formal political space is almost entirely controlled by the military and intelligence apparatuses. And the digital space, once immune to the kinds of repression imposed elsewhere, has been transformed into a polarized, fragmented space policed by the regime. Activists and ordinary citizens have been arrested for mere Facebook posts. Mohamed El-Taher (2017), a researcher on freedom of expression and the internet in Egypt, suggests that as Sisi's regime imposed a draconian antiprotest law and shut down all forms of student activism on campuses, "the internet became the only space available for citizens to express their voice." That's when the regime turned its attention to this last refuge of dissent.

Counterrevolution and Digital Repression

Social media contributed to the initial mobilization of the uprising, assisted in the acceleration and dissemination of information and tips about protesting, and even drew bystanders into protest when the internet blackout occurred, as it brought curious information seekers to Tahrir. It helped in the globalizing and iconizing of Tahrir. During the so-called transitional period, digital space also became a site for misinformation, polarization, and fragmentation. For example, at the end of 2012, I had documented nearly thirty Facebook pages invoking phrases like "a new revolution" or "the return of the revolution." Several had variations of the name "the second Rage Revolution" (a reference to the Friday of Rage on January 28, 2011). In late 2013 I was looking for some information on the We Are All Khaled Said (WAAKS) Facebook page when I noticed a new Facebook page with that name. It was titled

WAAKS for All Egyptians—implying that the original WAAKS was *no longer for all Egyptians*. The new page had been founded by the MB, claiming that the older WAAKS page had been involved in promoting mobilization before the coup and was no longer representative of the people's will. An overwhelming number of pages were named after the martyrs of the revolution. Compared to the centrality of WAAKS and the revolutionary cause during the uprising, what I was seeing online was a changing, and polarized, use of digital space.

After the coup the fragmentation continued, but the digital space became marked by *digital repression*. This radical shift in digital space's role—from enabling the revolution in 2011 to becoming a main site of political polarization and a core target of the counterrevolution's war on dissent—was puzzling. How did it happen? First, since the Supreme Council of Armed Forces (SCAF) rose to power after Mubarak's ouster, and more intensely after the 2013 military coup, Egypt has poured effort and money into digital repression. Second, the regime developed a discourse about cybersecurity and cyberwarfare, where digital spaces have been constructed as the central platforms to destroy the state and the nation.

The digital repression I saw in Egypt used all the methods available to control the use and freedom of information through the internet, including blocking access to the entire internet or particular websites; using technological tools to target cyberactivism through hacking, phishing, and doxing; countermobilizing by deploying trolls to contribute pro-regime propaganda and defamatory content about cyberactivists; and establishing legal and penal consequences for cyberactivism. Especially after the coup, the regime's obsession with cybersecurity and cyberwarfare, as well as its use of these to silence and attack pro-democracy activism, became a central political dynamic in Egypt. The examples are innumerable. For instance, the regime claimed that many Facebook pages were affiliated with the MB or opposed the coup and used that as a pretext to arrest their administrators. According to *Youm7* news (Abdel Rady 2016), one source at the Ministry of the Interior announced that the regime had shut down 3,343 Facebook pages associated with terrorist groups and the MB and had ordered the detention of 254 citizens involved with these pages. Four months later, *Al-Watan News* reported the arrest of forty-seven Facebook page administrators associated with anticoup sentiments (Al-Sheikh 2016). Extrajudicial killings of administrators include the murder of Ahmed Abdallah, an activist in Sinai who administrated a Facebook page called Sinai's Dignity (Abu Yazid 2015).

The government also poured money and technological development into its efforts toward digital repression. *BuzzFeed News* reports, for example, that the Egyptian government signed a contract with a California-based surveillance and cybersecurity company, Blue Coat, to help Systems Engineering of Egypt (SEE Egypt) perform government surveillance on Facebook, Twitter, YouTube, and other media (Frenkel and Atef 2014). The CEO of SEE Egypt suggested that his company's job was to train government employees to use the security programs. Separately, *Al Watan* newspaper published what appeared to be a booklet of conditions prepared by the Egyptian Ministry of the Interior pursuant to a request for proposals from companies that might provide internet censorship services (see also *Egypt Watch* 2021). Not only did such practices target activism, but they also revealed, in their overblown targeting of internet activism and dissent, that even the mighty power of state control through legalistic, coercive, and technological means was tinged with paranoia about the power of activists' reach on the internet.

Cybertactics are coupled with on-the-ground practices. Random stops of citizens, especially downtown and at security checkpoints, now frequently involve forcing them to open their social media profiles and show these to security officers. Any criticism of Sisi and the military can lead to arrest, as can a refusal to show officers the apps. By the end of 2019, this form of policing had become systemic in downtown Cairo.

Military and intelligence services have been especially involved in deploying trolls. They assemble armies of informants, citizens, and even soldiers to administer Facebook pages and social media accounts to spread regime propaganda and to chase and defame activists (see Abbas 2014; *Arab 48* 2017). In most cases, the trolls' main task is to follow and repost hashtags and positive statements about the state. For example, on November 6, 2016, a story was published about pro-military journalist Ibrahim Al-Garhy, revealing that he gave specific instructions to members of pro-state Facebook pages to defend Sisi's economic decisions and refrain from mentioning any criticism of the state. Members of the pages receive instructions from these page administrators, and pages are not accessible to nonmembers. Among these pages are "*Union of the lovers of the state*" and "*statist/lovers of the state*" (Amer 2016). Sisi himself has revealed an awareness of these pro-state electronic armies. In the context of defending the state, Sisi warned an audience against social media rumors, especially those tying the regime to the death of an Italian researcher who was studying labor unions in Egypt. Sisi alleged, "I can instruct two military battalions to work on the internet, and make the internet and news work like a closed circuit [echo chamber]."[4] A 2018 Freedom House report gave Egypt a score of 28/100 on its freedom of the internet measure. The report is based on three criteria: obstacles to access, limits on content, and violations of users' rights (see Freedom House 2018).

This radical transformation from a revolution made possible by the internet to an internet targeted by the counterrevolution is not baffling when we consider the changing political and economic context, as well as the military's perceptions of the internet as a space of warfare. Further, the loss of revolutionary momentum, which we can trace to activists' exhaustion, fragmentation among revolutionaries, and the imposition of state violence, has meant that the once-tight link between street mobilization and the internet has frayed, diminishing the power of each.

As for the first factor, let us recall that Mubarak's regime, under an initiative championed by Prime Minister Ahmed Nazeef, promoted the internet as a way to motivate foreign investment in the 1990s. According to Mohamed Gad (2018), that Egyptian regime, which welcomed Bill Gates and promoted the development of an Egyptian Silicon Valley (known as the Smart Village in the late 1990s), became very hostile to social media in the aftermath of the uprising. Today the military regime is making huge investments toward expanding government control of the ownership and regulation of the internet.

The coup also instigated an enormous expansion of the military's bailiwick. As scholar Shana Marshall (2015, 14) suggests, the military both consolidated and expanded after Mohamed Morsi. The work of the Armed Forces Engineering Authority in civilian-related projects expanded dramatically: according to the authority's director, Sisi authorized them to work on 1,737 projects from the moment he came to power in mid-2014 until early May 2016, all in the civilian domain (Ali 2016; Reuters 2018). Part of the military's economic expansion includes the information and communication technologies market. The military and intelligence agencies started WE, a new company providing internet and mobile service in Egypt. The military and security apparatus also seem to work closely with internet service providers with regard to phones, ADSL, and blocking and disrupting of VoIP services that allow for the use of communications apps including WhatsApp, Apple's FaceTime, Viber, Skype, and Facebook Messenger. According to the Speedtest market report in 2017, Egypt's internet service is one of the slowest and most expensive in the world (Noureldin 2017).

These important changes remind us of the significance of regulation of the internet. In an email interview conducted on April 11, 2019, Ahmed Gharbia, a leading blogger and activist in internet freedom in Egypt, asserted, "In understanding the shifting role of social media and internet in Egypt and in general, we cannot forget who owns the internet business and who has the power to regulate this business." Thus, the internet has become a special target for the regime, both economically and in terms of security, even as revolutionary actors are exhausted from polarization and fragmentation.

Many of the revolutionary actors I recently talked to affirmed that they now find the internet and social media to be depressing spaces. Using the internet feels like a confirmation that the counterrevolution has won. They face retaliation if they post anything related to protest and the revolution. Their personal social media pages are treated as websites, making them a reason for criminal liability according to Egypt's new internet laws. These activists feel driven away from the internet—a key organizing tool—by the curtailment of their freedoms of speech, the threat of military reprisals and arrest (or worse), and the depression caused by the inundation of pro-government propaganda. In a separate interview with Ahmed's brother, Amr Gharbia, who is also a leading blogger and expert in internet activism in Egypt, Amr returned to the idea that the internet wasn't necessary for revolutionary action—instead, he affirmed, mobilization on the ground was the most critical component of revolutionary mobilization. He suggested that during the revolution in 2011, "the most reliable technologies were sticks, stones, and blankets." He stated,

> Whatever appears on Twitter is secondhand, either a secondhand reflection by the people who were in the experience a few hours or a few days earlier, or literally a secondhand experience by someone else. Most of the internet presence during the critical days of the January 2011 sit-in (between January 28 and April 4, for example, when the square became a proper camp with electricity, and telecom was restored) was done by half of the then blogsphere. Half of us stayed in the square for most of the time, while the other half came to visit a few hours a day, then went back to their camp at Sarah Carr's residence across the Nile in Dokki, where she never lost her internet connection because she was on a small ISP called Nour. (April 1, 2019)

The global tolerance for limiting internet freedom enables the actions of the Egyptian regime. Shutting down the internet has been a tactic for governments in China, Turkey, Iran, Iraq, and other countries in recent years. True, there was a global outcry when the Egyptian regime shut down the internet in Egypt for four days during the uprising, but Egypt has now been systematically shutting down and controlling and limiting access and continually censoring websites since 2013, without a strong response. In other words, digital repression has become an accepted global practice. As El-Taher (2017) suggests, "The state has considered the internet, the media and NGOs as part of the fundamental reasons that led to the failure of the old regime in the aftermath of the revolution in 2011. As a result, it has become a goal of security apparatuses to control these [platforms] or annihilate them if possible."

Tahrir: A Militarized Space

After the 2013 coup, Tahrir and downtown Cairo were transformed into a militarized zone.[5] Authorities used excessive force to crush protests and installed more metal fences to control pedestrians and crowds. Symbolic violence was rampant. Earlier, we saw how Tahrir Square had become an emblem of the Egyptian Revolution. Mobilization in and around the square became the central mode of action and the defining image of the revolution. This did not happen without contestation.

Two important dynamics took place in 2011 and 2012 and through the coup in 2013. The first is the rise of battles over Tahrir, based on its symbolic power. That power peaked during the revolution but continued into the transitional period. Protesters and commentators were quick to proclaim the resurgence of the revolution whenever protesters returned to the square (see, for example, *60 Minutes* 2011). It was natural that various groups continued to rally there in the transitional period. Disputes quickly emerged, however, as groups debated who was entitled to claim the space, as doing so meant representing themselves as embodying the spirit of Tahrir and the revolution.[6] Secular and leftist groups and young people continued to attempt sit-ins in the square; meanwhile, MB members and Islamists developed a closer relationship with the SCAF. Supporters of the MB rarely attempted sit-ins, with the notable exception of a one-day occupation of Tahrir to protest the delay in announcing the presidential election results, which ended with the victory of their candidate, Mohamed Morsi.

The meanings of the square transformed over time, especially among the public. As I remained in Egypt for fieldwork after the uprising, I was able to visit camps in Tahrir in March and April 2011. I documented ten sit-ins from February 12, 2011, the day after the ousting of Mubarak, to December 5, 2012 (for more details, see A. Said 2022). Compared to the revolution's huge banners declaring "We are the revolution," the smaller signs at these sit-ins carried both the broad demands and slogans of the revolution and new demands, such as ending SCAF rule or ensuring justice for the martyrs of the revolution and their families. Other slogans included "The revolution continues." Activists themselves reframed the revolution, acknowledging that it had encountered challenges and needed to be continued. The camp itself was now named by many revolutionaries as "the Tahrir sit-in," not "the revolution's camp." Throughout, the state-run media portrayed the protesters as thugs and the camps as dangerous and disruptive, rather than representative of the public. In my field notes during this period, I wrote that many protesters' main concern was simply trying to convince a skeptical public that the revolution was not being "stolen" and redirected toward destructive ends.

2011–2013: Parallel Squares and Violence

Competing squares also emerged after Mubarak's ouster. Supporters of the SCAF, for instance, gathered in Abbāsīyah Square and near the Unknown Soldier Memorial in the Nasr City neighborhood of Cairo in April and May 2012. Thus, while the January revolutionaries were mobilizing in Tahrir, pro-regime supporters rallied in these other places. Supporters of the MB encamped in Rabaa Al-Adawiya Square in Nasr City and Nahda Square near Cairo University after Morsi's ouster on July 3, 2013. The MB also occupied the area in front of the Supreme Constitutional Court in January 2013. The Salafi group Hazemoon, for its part, occupied the entrance area of the media complex center in 6th of October City in Southwest Cairo in December 2012.

In almost all these documented cases, attempts at encampment ended with authoritarian violence. As early as July 2011, for example, protesters established a camp in Tahrir Square that lasted almost an entire month, significantly longer than the camps in January and February of that same year. But when police and military forces evacuated the camp on August 1, over one hundred people in the square were arrested and tortured (see Khalifa 2011). According to one of these protesters, "We were beaten and electrocuted. We were kicked with military boots, targeting our private parts." Another person described beatings and degradation by military soldiers who yelled that the protesters were "infidels . . . destroying the nation" (Khalifa 2011).

Morsi's supporters were evacuated from Rabaa and Nahda squares by force too. Rabaa camp witnessed a massacre by the military regime in Egypt on August 14, 2013. Different human rights groups estimate that more than a thousand people were killed in these raids. Human Rights Watch (2013) described the forced evacuations as the "most serious mass unlawful killing in modern Egypt." It is fair to say that the occupation of Tahrir Square symbolized the revolution, while the Rabaa Massacre symbolized the triumph of the leading counterrevolutionary force: the military.

The tragic events of 2013, especially the coup and the Rabaa Massacre, marked the transformation of Tahrir into a hypermilitarized zone. Authorities imposed random security checkpoints throughout downtown Cairo as they removed opposition protesters from Tahrir. The military junta launched frequent attacks on downtown cafés and ordered many of these to close, under the pretext that they violated Cairo and downtown municipal regulations. These had been, of course, important spaces for intellectuals, activists, and writers to meet.

The military regime also deployed several strategies to change the meaning of the space. This included the systemic erasure of revolutionary graffiti, a process that resulted in the demolition of a wall in Mohamed Mahmoud Street. The most noteworthy example of symbolic violence and the military regime's effort to "erase" the radical meanings of Tahrir came when it built a memorial in Tahrir on November 19, 2013. The date was presumably chosen to commemorate the violent clashes in Mohamed Mahmoud Street, with the memorial unveiled in the center of Tahrir Square only four months after the military coup. By the time it went up, it had been two and a half years since the revolution, and most considered the revolution lost. Egyptians had not achieved a working democracy or even stability. While systemic violence never stopped against the opposition and revolutionary youth, many of whom were subjected to military tribunals in 2011 and 2012, the memorial was nothing but "a hypocritical and crude insult" to the revolution and revolutionary aspirations, according to one of my informants. It was also a case of symbolic violence, because the families of the martyrs supposedly commemorated by the memorial—both the martyrs of the January 2011 revolution and the "June 30 revolution"—never received justice.

Egyptian activists I talked to in the summer of 2015 recalled their anger about the memorial. They spoke of the irony that the military regime, the main party responsible for obstructing the democratic transition and involved in killing protesters in the aftermath of the uprising, wanted to commemorate the martyrs of the revolution. The day the memorial was unveiled, no spectators were allowed into the space. Activists suggested that the memorial was built to silence discussions about justice for martyrs, a military token to officially claim control over the narratives of the revolution. Protesters vandalized the memorial in November 2013, and Cairo's governorate administration renovated it. The memorial was unveiled again on December 4, 2013, and again the vandals returned (*Almasry Alyoum* 2013). The regime seemed to accede, and the memorial was finally demolished by the state in later renovations of Tahrir Square. In short, one can describe the regime's political project as complete seizure of political space, practicing military control and both physical and symbolic violence concerning Tahrir and its legacies.

Counterrevolution as a Paranoid Regime

We cannot make sense of Tahrir Square's closure without situating it within the context of the counterrevolution in Egypt. Paranoia marked the counterrevolution, and military and security leaders feared losing control should any sign of revolutionary mobilization come back, resulting in what I call a paranoid regime.

Counterrevolution as a Sociological Category

Despite the existence of important analyses of the concept (Marx [1851] 2008; Tilly 1964), counterrevolution is loaded with misapprehensions. The first is reducing its actors to the forces of the old regime, rather than recognizing that those forces are an anchor but an incoherent one full of actors whose positions are never fixed. The second is assuming that counterrevolution waits to launch its attack after a given uprising. Conservative, counterrevolutionary forces do not come out of nowhere; they predate, and coexist alongside, the revolution. A third misapprehension involves confusing the definitions of countering actions. For example, are the countering actions about restoring order to *the state* prior to revolution, undoing the revolution, making some corrections to keep the status quo, or creating a new status quo? These are not synonymous. In Egypt the counterrevolution was not invested in bringing back the Mubarak regime but in expanding military rule and taking revenge against actual or suspected revolutionary actors.

In the same way that we discursively and dialectically examine mobilization and demobilization, democratization and de-democratization, and other concepts of contentious politics, we must consider revolution and counterrevolution in relation to one another. When we consider counterrevolutionary actors, we should not limit our attention to a narrow definition (for example, the members of the ruling party). Counterrevolutionaries may include most, if not all, segments of the ruling class, including political, economic, and security elites. Even some revolutionary actors may become counterrevolutionary over time. Additionally, counterrevolution is not bounded by the nation-state but can include the support of regional and international forces. In terms of actions, counterrevolutions use many methods, ranging from physical force to propaganda and coercion. In short, we should consider and analyze the shifts in the composition of counterrevolutionary forces as well as their methods temporally and spatially.

Some critical scholarship on the Egyptian Revolution provides us with compelling insights to attend to the contradictory dynamics of counterrevolution. Leading sociologist Asef Bayat has not discussed the counterrevolution in depth, but he presented one important insight: "All revolutions carry within themselves the germs of counterrevolutionary intrigues" (2017, 16). In this sense, to do a better analysis of revolution, we should attend to how revolutions and counterrevolutions are entangled. Similarly, Gilbert Achcar has suggested we include, in our counts of counterrevolutionary forces, "the reactionary alternative to the reactionary order" (2016b, 8). More important, Achcar has proposed a novel formulation for understanding what happened in the region: one revolution versus two counterrevolutions. So besides the revolution and the military, another important anchor of the counterrevolution was regional forces, especially political Islamist forces. Achcar specifically noted the role of the Kingdom of Saudi Arabia, the State of Qatar, and the Islamic Republic of Iran, which, he wrote, "all compete in supporting various brands of movements covering the full spectrum of Islamic fundamentalism, from conservative Salafism and the Muslim Brotherhood to Khomeinism and fanatical 'Jihadism'" (2016b, 8). Achcar's formulation is very useful because it reminds us that the mobilization of the reactionary alternative to social order is a dynamic process. We must see the counterrevolution as a nearly automatic response by the elite after an uprising.

Both Bayat and Achcar provide illuminating and useful insights. But they seem to disagree on one issue: Bayat is ambivalent about whether or not the MB was part of the counterrevolution (as part of his argument about post-Islamic politics in the Arab Spring), while Achcar argues that that the group was counterrevolutionary *all along*. My analysis is indebted to their insights but goes further to entail a disaggregated and temporally sensitive analysis of groups such as the MB, demonstrating how this political group was contradictory (playing revolutionary and counterrevolutionary roles) at certain moments during the uprising itself, then played a counterrevolutionary role throughout most of the transitional period.[7]

Specifically, I show that the MB's position in relation to the revolution fluctuated over time. During the uprising, for example, the MB played both sides. It was "revolutionary" in the sense of participating in the protest (albeit three days after the beginning of the protest). But it also played a counterrevolutionary role in negotiating with Mubarak's vice president, Omar Suleiman, with the goal of finding a compromise that would end the protest without Mubarak's ouster. Further, MB leaders ordered their youth to leave the square during the Camel Battle on February 2, 2011, though the MB youth remained to protect Tahrir for the revolution.

After the revolution succeeded in ousting Mubarak, the MB's relation to the SCAF proved critical. The MB came to play a counterrevolutionary role, participating in containing the revolution and minimizing its implications to the narrowest possible electoral reform. During that period the MB fueled sectarian tensions for electoral gains and justified and cooperated with the SCAF in targeting and crushing revolutionary youth. In sum, we see that the MB first participated in the revolution with restraint, then worked closely with and coordinated with the SCAF (though not without tension), and then shared power with the SCAF as Morsi came to power and the MB majority controlled the first parliament after the uprising. After the military coup in 2013, the MB became a target of persecution again. The story of its participation in the revolution is one of shifts, changes, and constant contradictions. The military, however, was consistently counterrevolutionary throughout the revolution and its trajectory, albeit using different strategies that shifted in accordance with the shifting momentum of the revolution. Of course, despite the tension in their short-lived alliance, the SCAF-MB partnership would not have been possible without the blessing of the US administration (Selim 2015).

Businesspeople had a similarly transient relationship with the revolution and its trajectory. Many supported the uprising due to their competition with Gamal Mubarak but joined the SCAF in counterrevolutionary politics after Mubarak was pushed from office. The same can be said of the Egyptian middle class, who participated in the uprising but soon yearned for a return to the status quo and called for the repression of revolutionary youth. Table 6.1 summarizes how counterrevolutionary actors and actions shifted over time.

Table 6.1. Shifting Counterrevolutionary Actors and Actions in Egypt (2011–Present)

Period	Phase	Counterrevolution's Key Actors	Counterrevolution's Main Actions	Type of Action
Revolutionary crisis (Jan. 25–Feb. 11, 2011)	Counterrevolution instigated	Mubarak regime (Hosni Mubarak, ruling party, security apparatus)	Propaganda, unsuccessful repression	Defense
Transitional period (Feb. 12, 2011–June 30, 2013)	Counterrevolution gaining power	The military and its intelligence apparatus in collaboration with the Muslim Brotherhood and other political forces	Containment of the revolution and escalated repression	Manipulation and war of attrition
Military coup and its aftermath (July 3, 2013–present)	Counterrevolution's victory	The military and its intelligence and other security apparatuses	Unlimited repression, revenge, and expanded military rule	Offense

Source: Adapted from A. Said (2021, 11).

Sisi's Bonapartist/Caesarist Moment

One of the unique features of the counterrevolutionary dynamics in Egypt was Sisi's rise to power during and in the aftermath of the July 2013 coup. At the peak of his popularity in 2013 and 2014, critical scholarship invoked the notions of Bonapartism (Achcar 2016b; Younis 2015) and Caesarism (De Smet 2016). The first is based on Karl Marx's classic *The Eighteenth Brumaire of Louis Bonaparte* ([1851] 2008), which analyzed the French counterrevolution and coup led by Louis-Napoléon Bonaparte (Napoleon III) to reestablish the monarchy in 1851. Louis Bonaparte was the nephew of Napoleon, who was a consul of the French Republic from 1799 to 1804, then emperor of the

French from 1804 until 1814 and again in 1815. Similar to his uncle, Napoleon III was president and then led a coup, in 1851. After the coup, Napoleon III consolidated his power by ending the republic and proclaiming himself emperor. Caesarism is explained by Antonio Gramsci in his *Prison Notebooks* ([1971] 1992, 219–23) and refers to an opportunistic exploitation of a moment of political conflict in which progressive and reactionary forces seem locked in a stalemate. In this moment of weakness, a Caesar may arise, promising a compromise (in the form of his own leadership) that will resolve the crisis, preventing the bloodshed that might occur if the crisis continued.

Applying these notions to Sisi's rise allows scholars to highlight how political space is closed by charismatic figureheads. One divergent argument was made by Egyptian historian Sharif Younis, who proposed that Egypt's Bonapartist moment was important and necessary. He wrote that rallies in the streets on July 26, 2013, aimed at "sav[ing] the state, and stop[ping] the fascist rule of the Muslim Brotherhood" (2015, 19), gave Sisi a mandate that superseded the military mandate to lead the transition after the 2011 uprising. At this moment, Sisi continued to be part of the state and the military but rose above the military to become a mediator and savior of the state.[8] Respectfully, I disagree. One cannot miss the fact that Sisi was the military's candidate in the election and that his rule brought an expansion of military power. He did not rise above the military; he elevated it.

Other critical scholars—as well as Sisi's supporters and nationalist propaganda peddled by the state-controlled media during and following the coup—have compared the rise of Sisi to Gamal Abdel Nasser's popular rule in the 1950s and 1960s. The 1952 coup that brought Nasser to power occurred on July 23, with the Free Officers overthrowing Egypt's monarchy. When, on July 3, 2013, Abdel Fattah el-Sisi led the coup toppling Mohamed Morsi, he ended the short-lived Egyptian Second Republic (2011–13). Achcar insists we cannot ignore the specificities of these cases, while urging that Sisi's coup was a counterrevolutionary coup par excellence and continues to bear more resemblance to Bonaparte's coup than Nasser's:

> Without any fear of ridicule, Sisi's coup was travestied ad nauseam by its enthusiasts as a second iteration of what, in Egypt, is referred to as the "23 July Revolution." The truth, however, is that Louis Napoleon Bonaparte's coup had much more in common with his uncle's—they were both essentially reformist coups, ending a phase of revolutionary turmoil in order to carry through a major stage of France's bourgeois transformation—than Abdul-Fattah al-Sisi's coup has with the one led by Nasser. The latter was

a textbook case of a *revolutionary* coup d'état, whereas the coup executed on 3 July 2013 was definitely a *reactionary* one that restored Egypt's old regime—indeed, with a vengeance. (2016b, 65–66)

Regardless of the terminology of a *reactionary* or *progressive coup*, Nasser and Sisi shared a method: ruling through an inflated security apparatus, despite the differences in the composition of that apparatus in the two eras. The big difference was that Nasser was no friend to the Egyptian bourgeoisie. Nasser flirted with workers and peasants, and his rule was based on social reforms. Scholar Brecht De Smet maintains that, in contrast, Sisi resorted to courting the bourgeoisie. He appeared in a moment of weakness, both social and political, and at a time when security apparatuses had a sort of carte blanche to do what they must to achieve state stability. De Smet suggests, then, that the uprising and the turmoil that followed created a social base yearning for security and stability. Indeed, Sisi mobilized the most reactionary sentiments in society, in the context of unifying the military and security forces behind him, and all of these elements contributed to consolidating Sisi's hegemony over the moment (De Smet 2016, 217–18).

Alongside the deep desire for stability, especially among the middle and upper classes, this moment in Egyptian history was marked by an enduring alliance between the military and the bourgeoisie. This partnership has been a crucial element in previous historical examples. In his study of military regimes in Latin American countries in the 1970s and 1980s, Alfred Stepan suggests that in the classic equation of the *Brumairean moment* (a term he coined to analyze this unique configuration of power), the bourgeois class becomes so weak and afraid to govern that it will accept military rule "in exchange for protection, by the ensuing of a strong state" (Stepan 1988, 11). Stepan contends that these "brutal moments" can be transformed into decades of military rule and brutal repression of the lower classes, as we have seen in a number of cases from Latin America (Stepan 1988, 128) and, indeed, throughout the world.

Whether we call Sisi's rise a Bonapartist or Caesarist moment, in both cases we are referring to counterrevolutionary dynamics par excellence. His rise came in a context that included a crisis of power and hegemony, weak parties, and scared social classes. A strong man arose from the ranks of the military with a mandate to create stability for the upper and middle classes. With the extraordinary powers granted to this man, political space was closed through the suppression of popular uprisings and agitators and the imposition of martial law.

Paranoia is an irrational state of mind, a key feature of which is unreasonable suspicion of others, who are believed to be after the paranoid person. Paranoia is generally a characteristic of individuals, not institutions or governments, but interdisciplinary critical scholarship has recently adopted the term to describe states, governments, and regimes.[9] Scholars of post-Soviet nations, for instance, propose that conspiracy theories shape electoral politics in these nations (Ortmann and Heathershaw 2012; Radnitz 2016). One political scientist notes that studying paranoid regimes can make scholars themselves paranoid—such regimes constantly target critics and scholars; therefore, the analyst's fear may reflect the fear hovering around their topic (Malekzadeh 2016). Not only do many nationalist narratives involve conspiracy theories, but world politics can also be seen as "a paradigm of planetary paranoia marked by cybersurveillance, cartographies of cartels, and webs of international relationality within and outside the nation, and on the edges of legality" (Apter 2006, 365).

As evidence of the paranoia I see in the Egyptian counterrevolutionary regime, I can start with three points: first, the Sisi regime regards all civilians as untrustworthy, and it deploys propaganda, significant parts of which are conspiracy theories; second, the regime does not distinguish between real threats and delusional threats, functioning in constant fear of losing control; and, third, the January Revolution of 2011 is easily seen as the trigger of this paranoia. Indeed, Egyptian revolutionaries experienced an obvious trauma of defeat, especially in the aftermath of the 2013 coup.[10] But for an inflated security apparatus, and from the perspective of an undemocratic body like the military that is based entirely on obedience and their superiority over civilians in Egypt, losing control during the uprising, especially on January 28, 2011, was a nightmare, which they deem should be unrepeatable. Although the military used violence in 2011 and 2012, they did not have total control of the revolutionary street, nor could they use excessive violence to the degree that it was used in the aftermath of the coup. At that later moment, as Sisi took power and expanded the mandate of the military and security services, they found an unparalleled opportunity to avenge the defeat they had endured two years prior. That is, they were able to act on their paranoia.

The regime's ongoing obsession with the January Revolution evidences the extent to which it has remained paranoid. Military and intelligence leaders—especially Sisi—made and continue to make relentless references to the revolution. In a speech delivered on December 22, 2015, on the occasion of the Prophet Muhammad's birthday, Sisi warned, for instance, against calls for protest on the anniversary of January Revolution, warning that "a call for a new revolution means a call to destroy Egypt" (Al Jazeera 2015; R. Ghoniem 2015). And on January 31, 2018, during an event to launch a new gas line project, Sisi told the audience, "What happened seven years ago will not happen again" (BBC Arabic 2018). The revolution continues to be constructed as the most dangerous event in modern Egyptian history.

Since the military coup, revolutionary youth have been persistently targeted. Ahmed Maher, Alaa Adel Fatah, Mahienour El-Masry, Mohamed Al-Qasas, Israa Abdel Fatah, Ahmed Douma, Haitham Mohamadain, Mohamed Adel, and Shady al-Ghazaly Harb, for example, have frequently been detained.[11] Some of them participated in the mobilization against the exclusionary politics of the MB that paved the way for the coup, and they were targeted after the coup with arbitrary detention—often marked by solitary confinement—and repeated lawsuits alleging that they were plotting against the state or had criticized the leadership of the nation. Human rights groups describe such charges as "recycled lawsuits" or "revolv[ing] door charges," meaning that if the subject is released after detention and/or trial, they will surely be charged and returned to jail again (Sorour 2019; see also Aspden 2016). Egyptian activists and writers have continually suggested that the state has become more obsessed with the January Revolution than the revolutionaries themselves and is fixated on fighting January's ghosts.

Targeting dissidents, silencing criticism, and spreading fear are all characteristic of the leadership's discourse. For example, in a speech launching the gas line project, Sisi declared, "I have spent fifty years of my life learning the meaning of the state. I swear to God. I swear to God I have spent fifty years getting educated [perhaps referring to military education] and teaching myself about the meaning of the state. Now I hear illiterate people who want to have a say about the state. This is not acceptable" (CNN Arabic 2018). Sisi insists that only he and the military know the state and can protect the state. They act as one. Sisi went on to state, "Egypt's security is guaranteed by my life and the life of the military" (CNN Arabic 2018).

Part of the state's paranoia is the sense that it is misunderstood, that citizens do not listen to or understand it. In a February 24, 2016, speech, Sisi stated, "I know Egypt very well. I know Egypt's problems and solutions. I am telling this to everyone everywhere: do not listen to anybody else, only listen to me" (*Mehwar TV* 2016). Sisi constantly exhorts the media to teach society about these issues. During an international youth convention on July 25, 2017,

Sisi stated, "We worked [in the aftermath of the coup] to mobilize the state against all efforts to destroy it. We worked to combat all reasons that can lead to demolishing the state. I ask the media to create phobia [for all Egyptians] of the idea of the collapse of the state" (quoted in S. Hussein 2017).[12] Here the leading regime figure openly talks about the need to promote propagandistic education and spread fear about the risks of demolishing the state. Of course, implicit in this discourse is that citizens must obey the military and Sisi and that "civilian politicians, supporters of populism and civilian institutions are incapable of providing national security" (Hamzawy 2018, 495). Sisi personally, and his role in the coup and the massacres that happened afterward, is perhaps a central piece in the making of the paranoid state. As put by Egyptian writer Yehia Mostafa Kamel, "Sisi sees the Egyptian people as a burden or unescapable plight; a hurdle in the way of his vision and the state; a nation of fools, who have mutinied and risen, and by doing so have impeded and ravaged" (2022). And as another analyst put it, "Sisi's Catch 22 goes something like this: 'I have to arrest more and more of the people around me, because if I don't, one of them will get me. After all, I did the same to my president'" (Hearst 2018).

Conspiracy theories are central to this regime's discourse but can be traced as far back as January 2011. For example, the state security intelligence report about the revolution, mentioned in chapter 2, agreed that the revolution started with a popular protest, yet emphasized the idea that foreign elements and infiltrators had participated in the uprising. The report suggested that elements from Hamas and Hezbollah, among other groups, had spirited into Egypt during the uprising and that at least twenty-nine foreign nationalities were present in Tahrir Square in those days (Mohie 2015). Since the 2013 coup, conspiracy theories have become central themes in public media and military leaders' narratives—even in state and military training. On April 9, 2013, for example, army leaders, including the minister of defense, Abdel Fattah el-Sisi, attended a lecture by Colonel Usama Al-Gamal titled "Egypt's Position and Status." The colonel emphasized that the army should not be separated from the state and that the army belongs to the people and vice versa. But he also repeatedly referenced dangerous plots against the state and the army, citing the book *Pawns in the Game*, by William Guy Carr ([1955] 2013). According to the colonel, *Pawns* explains how "secret international organizations" instigate wars and revolutions to control and eliminate countries seen as threats to the world order.[13] In conjunction with the state-run media's incessant references to international powers and their plots against Egypt, the lineage of conspiracy theorizing from Mubarak through Sisi is clear. But where Mubarak mentioned what his regime conceived as specific terrorist threats, including imperialist, Zionist, communist, or Shiite plots, Sisi's regime uses broader, vaguer terms, referring to worldwide "evil" and "dark powers."[14] The constant references to international plots against the state is combined with a narrative that the Sisi regime's goal and main accomplishment was saving the state, after what happened in the revolution, which was simply a plot against the state. According to Sisi and the regime, the state is an end in itself. As Mona El-Ghobashy put it, "State prestige is the apogee of revolution-as-turmoil, and the bedrock ideology of the counterrevolutionary regime of Abdel Fattah al-Sisi" (2021, 37). In short, a constant impromptu statism, meaning a persistent deployment of discourse about saving and defending the state, regardless of what the state is doing, is part of the mindset of the paranoid regime.

The excessive and disproportionate use of violence and the flaunting of the state's coercive apparatus through military parades is more evidence of the paranoid state. According to a July 3, 2019, report by the Arab Organization for Human Rights, some 3,185 civilians were killed extrajudicially by Egyptian security forces in the six years following the coup (see *Middle East Monitor* 2019). Yehia Mostafa Kamel (2019) suggests that the inflated security and intelligence apparatuses are a response to their earlier loss of control: "The only ideal solution that is acceptable to Sisi and the supporting class is to get revenge for January. Their main goal is the untiring work to prevent its repetition, *through disproportionate and unlimited violence*" (emphasis mine). Simple fear of another uprising is not demonstrative of paranoia, but the overblown reactions and disproportionate violence are—as is the obsession with shows of force. In the aftermath of the coup, military planes have made a habit of flying low in the skies of Cairo and other major cities. On October 5, 2013, two months after the coup and on the fortieth anniversary of the 1973 October War, military planes flew in the formation of the Egyptian flag, as well as Sisi's name (see *Almasry Alyoum* 2015; A. Ghoniem 2013; *Al-Watan News* 2013). The military has also increased its purchase of heavy weaponry to the degree that scholars note "significant capacity upgrades," though they caution that it is "less clear . . . whether or not these changes are being accompanied by improvements in training, maintenance, and overall readiness" (Springborg and Williams 2019). Several activists I talked to in 2015 and 2016 made similar comments, wondering how they should "make sense of this absurd expansion of military power if the country is not using this, except to show off power."

The paranoia has led to the complete silencing and closure of political space, or what can be described as *political desertification*. In analyzing the dominance of Sisi in the Egyptian political landscape and the counterrevolutionary space, political writer Hazem Saghieh (2018) suggests, "The man confronted the mission without having the experience of Abdel Nasser and Sadat in secret organizations, and Mubarak's experience as a vice president which lasted for six years. He came to power from zero. His power was required to come from zero. This is because the political surplus [read, of hope and change] created by the January 2011 Revolution necessitated a surplus of void to which it should respond [from the point of view of the military regime]."

In this sense, counterrevolution is the making of a surplus of political emptiness. This was true under Mubarak, of course, but there was still room for limited political protest and some margin of freedom. That resulted in a gradual opening of political space in the decade prior to the uprising, as discussed in chapter 1. Under Sisi, the state's *main political project* has become this political desertification.

Revolutionary Withdrawal, Complicity, and Fear

Demobilization is an important term in the social movements literature, which remains undertheorized (Fillieule 2013). This is mainly because scholars tend to prefer studying the rise of movements over examining their decline. As Olivier Fillieule (2013) suggests, we can think of demobilization in two senses: both collective demobilization and individual disengagement.

In my email interviews with Egyptian revolutionaries in the summer of 2015, I identified three recurring themes related to making sense of political space under the counterrevolution. The first was the idea that withdrawal from political space was necessary for the revolutionaries' own safety. Second, it was clear to me that the regime had been highly successful in restoring fear among revolutionary actors. And, third, I noted that one cannot make sense of the dramatic closure of space without taking into account the complicity of many groups that provided carte blanche support to the counterrevolution. Without public tolerance, much of it from the middle and upper classes, the counterrevolution would not have been able to viciously close political space.

Collective Withdrawal

On February 25, 2015, an influential Egyptian blogger and writer published a Facebook post that was widely circulated among activists. He urged revolutionary youth to evacuate Egypt's public spaces:

Please leave public spaces as much as possible when danger is detected or especially when you see official armed creatures around. Avoid interacting with the state, and don't approach the state at all unless you have to deal with it. Do not deal with the military, the police, or even the judiciary. Any noncalculated move on your part may lead to your death or a charge and detention for unlimited and many years to come.[15]

In the same post, the writer suggested that the regime was paranoid about a global conspiracy against protesters and that the regime's agents were walking the streets and squares with guns. Public space was now totally reserved for violence between the regime and Islamists. The writer ended the post with a call to "please protect your lives and your safety. No dissent is acceptable in Egypt for a while."

Such collective, conscious withdrawal has become a big theme in Egypt in recent years. Nael El-Toukhy (2016), an Egyptian novelist and writer, wrote, "Despite evidence that the objective conditions of the revolution are still existing, Egyptian revolutionaries made this mass withdrawal to protect themselves."

Activists told me much the same story. Many even suggested that withdrawal was a reality, not just a decision. One told me, "Millions of people are already antipolitics and have become antirevolution, because they are tired." In other words, *withdrawal* was just activist terminology for the critical mass who had already left the revolution and boycotted revolutionary activities due to the troubled transition, or in the aftermath of the coup.

Activists also invoked immense despair and a sense of loss related to this withdrawal. One said, "Even with this great sadness and loss, I have hope. At least I saw this dream happening, and it is still there in our memory." But for now, they added, "I am staying away." Another activist referred to 2015 as a "moment of anger, bitterness, and great disappointment," while another lamented, "I have no doubt people will fight back [in the near future], but for now, I am only re-collecting myself." One mentioned, "If all revolutionary figures are now either forced to leave the country or are in jail or marginalized, I would rather be marginalized."

Along with bitterness, anger, sadness, and great disappointment, some of my respondents also articulated blame—for themselves and others. Some blamed the revolutionary youth coalition for being reformist, or blamed the MB for partnering with the SCAF and thus contributing to the conditions that led to the coup. A few suggested that the regime was capable of maintaining some stability, and as stability was the driving force behind their support for the coup, they had resigned themselves to withdrawal. Demands for liberty and social justice were no longer main priorities; now safety and personal security were paramount. One person asked despondently, "Why antagonize the regime, if many citizens believe that order and security are main priorities, which the regime seems to be delivering?" Indeed, the regime had succeeded in installing stability after the coup, but this came without any improvements in the economic and social lives of everyday Egyptians.

Complicity

Several of my informants emphasized the idea of complicity and the way it had enabled the counterrevolution's grip on political space. One told me, "There are multiple factors behind people's acceptance of repression. But I would suggest that it is mostly because of exhaustion. So many people participated in the uprising. They believe that the political elite betrayed them and betrayed the uprising. They grew to resent the uprising and its troubles. In short, many people stopped believing that protest and the revolution can bring change and gave up, for now." Another suggested, "The media have become viciously against the revolution. Nothing positive is mentioned anywhere about the uprising. An important outcome is the revival of selfishness and the deserting of solidarity and organizing talk. While the revolution brought the idea of solidarity and collective work upfront, the dominant idea now is to live. This is the reason for complicity." And a third stated:

> People accepted the severe repression after seeing what happened in Rabaa. That massacre had a message: "Do not dare to protest or organize a sit-in anymore. Rabaa is your fate." The regime's only message now is "We control violence, and you are at our mercy." The outcome was not just that people stopped protesting; they also gave up on politics again, with low participation in elections. I don't blame people who lost hope. The reasoning of millions today is that they need to stay alive. Just stay alive. Under repression or freedom, it does not matter. They just need to live.

Additionally, some intellectuals who were supportive of the revolution in 2011 seemed to change their positions radically in the aftermath of 2013. The term used to describe this group is often *dawlagiya* (statist, or pro-state), while activists describe public figures, TV anchors, and pro-state intellectuals as *motableen* (drummers, meaning their only job is to drum up support for the regime) or *mo'araseen* (procurers or ass lickers). Most of the pro-state intellectuals are liberals and nationalists, or others who have been tied to the state throughout their career.

The most common justification for accepting the closure of political space is siding with the state in combating terrorism. In a meeting with prominent intellectuals on March 22, 2016, Sisi was patrimonial: "You should stop theorizing and talking about abstract things and be in touch with reality," he told them (quoted in Basal 2016; see also *Economist* 2015).

Similarly, a phenomenon of what is described as "honorable citizens" is on the rise since Mubarak's ouster and the rule of the SCAF. These include ordinary citizen volunteers, a large army of paid poor citizens, and an array of informants, all collaborating with the police. They are known to attack potential protest organizers, attack protesters, and/or assist the security apparatus by providing information about activists. They also appear at pro-military and Sisi rallies (the only rallies permitted by the security apparatus in the aftermath of the coup). Without proper research, it is difficult to distinguish between those who are volunteering and those who are paid for this collaboration. In fact, many of the "honorable citizens" come from very poor areas. Others are ex-convicts forced into working as spies.

Fear

As discussed earlier, the regime is talking openly about the need to reinstall fear, especially fear that revolutionaries will demolish the state. Many of my informants agreed that the regime has been successful in promoting this "phobia." One young lawyer working for an NGO told me, "Anyone who denies that the current regime was capable of regaining control through intimidating and spreading fear among citizens does not read the political scene well." Another noted some of the ways the regime deployed fear: "scaring all citizens about any future revolution, scaring upper-class people about poor people's revolt, scaring all citizens about terrorism, scaring activists about the fate of Islamists who have been massacred in Rabaa in August 2013." Civil wars of the kind that took place in Syria after its uprising and in Iraq after sectarian violence and war became bogeymen central to counterrevolutionary propaganda such that a key media slogan is now "We are better [safer] than Syria and Iraq." Fear, I was told, is a natural response when "ordinary citizens see the excessive retaliation against revolutionary figures and prominent politicians. The logic goes, if this can happen to famous people, what about ordinary citizens?"

Still, many respondents explicitly argued against crediting the regime for sustaining repression and fear. One of the informants said, "Yes, it is true that the unlimited and unprecedented repression is reason for fear, but people are also wary of the unknown and also worry when they look at what happened in the aftermath of Arab uprisings in many countries in the region." In this vein, one respondent suggested, "We should not think of fear as only a personal thing. But people worry about their loved ones and family. They may not be scared for themselves, but they are scared about the safety of their loved ones." Fear, that is, was a reasonable response to the current political climate. A trade unionist told me, "All the talk about breaking the fear barrier during the uprising is exaggeration. I have always feared the security forces; they have never been held accountable." They continued:

> I do not agree at all about losing the fear barrier during the uprising. In fact, the same folks who had been resisting the regime before the uprising are almost the same group who continue to resist after the coup. The only significant difference was the fact that a huge army of poor people joined the uprising. At the time, because of that critical mass, many people had high hopes for change. I would suggest that only poor people lost the fear barrier, and they had hope in the revolution. We betrayed them. On February 12, 2012, when I went back to work, I realized that everybody is the same: their main worry/fear is how soon they can get their bread.

Class, it seemed, influenced the variations I saw in different groups' legitimate fears. I was told that "the fear barrier issue was an elitist phrase by revolutionaries" and that "what matters is the existence of fear or not among the public other than activists." Other informants also problematized the idea of restoring fear temporarily (and discussed how this varied from moment to another). Time mattered in this man's experience with fear: "I was over the moon on February 11, 2011, at night [the day of ousting Mubarak]. I felt I had great powers. The only worries I had at the time were about the revolution's trajectory and its fate. I had no personal worries. But after only one week, when I realized that the military seemed to have bad intentions toward the uprising, the fear was back. I learned that the military and the intelligence are spying on Facebook and main social media platforms. I stopped writing about the revolution explicitly and decided to be more careful." The temporal shifts in fear and different sources of fear show that this is complex. Again, one cannot simply credit the regime for reinstalling popular fear. In an interview historian Khaled Fahmy (2016) pointed to the idea of fear's centrality to the regime's counterrevolutionary tactics: "Sisi offers a security solution, and this provides no hope or any future. Fear is a very strong feeling that should never be underestimated. Fear can mobilize people and paralyze others. The discourse of fear is central to this regime. Not only that, but it has become central in the region in recent years." Even when debating and questioning the sources of fear, revolutionary actors have agency.[16] The return of fear is coupled with activists' withdrawal and complicity in tolerating repression and the dramatic closure of political space. The regime would not be able to get away with its escalated repression without the complicity and acceptance of large segments of the population who yearn for stability.

Conclusion: The Shaky Future of Counterrevolution

Throughout this chapter I have interrogated the dramatic closure of political space that has been such a central dynamic of the military counterrevolution in Egypt. But that complete closure is not a sustainable political project, as it would allow more extremism. Complete closure means shutting down venues of political representation and expression. It means the absence of venues to discuss and resolve societal problems. On the other hand, if the reader follows my argument about the interconnectedness of key spaces (formal political space, digital space, and street protest), guaranteeing free elections or allowing more freedom and representation in the formal political space alone cannot be sufficient to create a healthy, democratic Egyptian society anytime soon.

I focused mostly on the period from 2013 to 2018 in this chapter. But despite the seemingly strong grip of Sisi and the military regime throughout this period, one could still argue that Sisi's popularity has been declining (it peaked during the coup and conceivably the year after). Public support without regime accountability has always been important to this regime, tied to a hatred of politics. The regime shifted strategies to gain public support from 2013 onward. Shifting strategies with a continuous goal of rallying society behind the state indicates uncertainties. For example, from 2013 to 2015 the regime roughly focused on the war on terror, where Sisi presented himself and the military as the savior of the state, implying and sometimes stating clearly that no economic or social accomplishment should be expected from his regime because the state is busy combating terrorism. From 2015 to 2021, the Sisi regime focused on fast, large-scale achievements (megaprojects, such as opening a new waterway in the Suez Canal, which his regime called the New Suez Canal) to regain public support (see S. Carr 2015). During this window, and on November 11, 2016, Sisi's regime signed two agreements with the International Monetary Fund (IMF), borrowing over US$17 billion. Thus, the military has been constructed as the main anchor of security and the leading investor in massive new projects. In 2021 the Sisi regime announced their plan to build a new administrative capital that will symbolize what he described as the New Republic in Egypt. In all these phases, whether or not these projects are done as a performance, or for the sake of a fruitful outcome for the public, it is a fact that the regime is constantly deploying impromptu and hollow statism, constantly seeking public support, despite alienating the public further and further. It is fair to say that the Sisi regime is far from stable, not only because it has failed to deliver economic improvements to the alienated Egyptian majority, focusing instead on protecting itself and its megaprojects, but also because the regime has to constantly navigate contradictory goals, such as continuing its unlimited repression, containing the military and bribing its ranks, preventing a coup, preventing another revolt, dealing with unlimited foreign debt, and confronting the near bankruptcy of the state.

It is useful to note here that Mubarak was described as a modern-day pharaoh. Sisi's unlimited power has made him a new pharaoh with godlike power. But even with this power, Egyptian artists and writers have written poetry and songs to ridicule military rule. The poem mentioned in this chapter's epigraph was written in 2012 during the SCAF's rule, by revolutionary poet Tamim al-Barghouti. Finally, since paranoia has been a driving force of the military regime's action, and nothing has been acceptable to this regime but complete political desertification, uncertainties and instability are also defining features of governing in Egypt, even if the regime seems to enjoy a total grip on power.

conclusion

Revolution as Experience

Revolution is an act of love
               Revolution is selfish,
        As is love
               Revolution is sacrifice,
        As is love
               Revolution is madness,
        As is love
             Revolution is pain without limit,
        As is love
Love's sweat is the blood of life,
Love's tears cleanse the soul.
So too the revolution
               I went to bury the revolution,
         With my two hands, I poured dirt over my love
               Alone, no one consoled me
             They were too busy burying their own
          Will the revolution forgive me for burying her?
        Do lovers forgive?

—THE AUTHOR

On June 29, 2013, one day before the planned June 30 protests against Mo-hamed Morsi, Egypt's *Socialist Papers* magazine published "The Revolution Should Not Be Fooled Twice: The Army and the Revolution in Egypt," an essay I had written for them (A. Shahat Said 2013).[1] In this piece I stated, "If we were to embrace the revolution's logic, then we ought to be, by defini-tion, against coups. The revolution's logic reflects the will and the action of the masses. But a coup is the work of the ruling elite. The goal of the coup is to conspire against the will of the people, or end people's actions. The administration of Egypt's affairs by the military is the opposite of the revolution." I also stated, "Let us recall what the January Revolution was all about. It was a revolution against Mubarak's despotism and exploitation as much as it was a revolution against the state and the party of the old guard, and against dependency on US imperialism, and neoliberal policies. The military institution in Egypt represents and embodies all these features. An acceptance of the leadership of the military in Egypt means betrayal of the revolution. This represents simply the defeat of the revolution."

Four days after these words were published, a military coup took place, following which many Egyptian revolutionaries began to acknowledge the revolution's decisive defeat. My words may have been little more than polemi-cal talk at the time, and I am not sure how widely read they were, nor whether they had any vital impact or none whatsoever. By referencing these words here, my intention is not to claim any exceptional capabilities of critical perception or foresight. On the contrary, my goal is to bolster an argument I have developed throughout this book, about the notion of lived contingency. In chapter 5 I mentioned that I had collected signatures for the Tamarod campaign in the United States. I gathered fewer than ten signatures, which I did not send anywhere, as I could not identify any mechanism for submitting them. Was I naive and blindly optimistic in both actions: collecting signa-tures to force a democratically elected president to accept an early election, in a context where things were extremely muddled and unclear and fraught with the danger of a military coup, while at the same time writing a piece warning revolutionaries and comrades about this military coup?[2] Was I more or less revolutionary in any of these actions? Around the time of the coup and shortly afterward, many were speaking with full certitude about their abilities to see clearly, especially among the pro-military and the pro–Muslim Brotherhood camps—ironically the two parties that played the most critical counterrevolutionary roles.

The Meaning of *Revolutionary*

Here we have a case of a participant-observer in this revolution, albeit with complex positionality in relation to the revolution, with a degree of organizational experience, who was nonetheless blind to possible negative outcomes. In the introduction to this book, I presented the notion of lived contingency and suggested that many revolutionary actors I talked to spoke of joining the revolutionary mobilization as a calling. They viewed the revolution as a siren or a case of enchantment and were determined to engage in certain actions, believing that no outcome could possibly be worse than what they were experiencing at the time. I was one of these folks. My ingenuousness or confusion about the practice of power, as distinct from taking serious action about power during the uprising and participating in the revolutionary trajectory in different ways, is paralleled by that of numerous comrades, with many of us exemplifying being part of the revolution as a lived contingency. As I have argued and demonstrated throughout this book, *lived contingency* refers to how revolutionary actors practice and experience the revolution, particularly in terms of the actions they do or do not take in relation to the possibilities, unpredictabilities, and practices of power during the course of a revolution. I demonstrated that the Egyptian Revolution not only was not doomed to defeat but incessantly involved multiple revolutionary trajectories laden with contingency.[3] As also mentioned in the introduction of this book, revolutionary enchantment and the navigation of possibilities, unpredictabilities, and practices of power partially imply the ideas of love and the blindness in love, as the epigraph above reflects as well.

In 2003 Jeffery Paige, one of my graduate school professors and a leading scholar of revolutions, suggested that conventional definitions of revolution in both the social sciences and revolutionary Marxism-Leninism have become inadequate and that we need to broaden our understanding of how revolutions are conventionally understood in both the social sciences and revolutionary Marxism-Leninism to include more focus on revolution as a utopian vision and source of power transformation (19). Paige emphasized that, in his view, revolutions entail "rapid and fundamental transformation in the categories of social life and consciousness, the metaphysical assumptions on which these categories are based, and the power relations in which they are expressed as a result of widespread popular acceptance of a utopian alternative to the current social order" (24). But he also suggested that revolutions, or fundamental change, can occur "without violence, class conflict, seizures of state power or other of the traditional elements of revolution" (25). I would argue that it is almost impossible to separate the utopic vision, the transformative power of revolutions, and their capabilities of changing power relations, from the necessity of seizing state power. In my analysis of the Egyptian case, one could argue that the military's earlier grip on the state apparatus and revolutionary actors' incognizance of the significance of seizing power were key determinants of the revolutionary trajectory. Thus, conceivably, seizing state power cannot be a minor element in revolutionary change. In my opinion, Paige went too far in centering revolutions as a case of popular acceptance of a utopian alternative to the standing social order, while giving up the organizing piece in revolutions altogether. But he was on point in suggesting that "current concepts of revolution may well be obsolete, but this does not necessarily imply that revolution properly understood has no future" (19). Since he wrote this in 2003, numerous revolts have taken place across the globe. Even when these did not meet the classical criteria of success, many presented serious challenges to existing regimes, and some changed the political order, or some aspects of the social order.

These reflections and Paige's conviction are an invitation for us to think deeply about the meaning of *revolutionary* in general and revolutionary actors in particular. Elsewhere, Pete Moore and I suggested that a proper understanding of revolutionary trajectories requires thinking of the full scope of the revolutionary subject's participation in and experience of revolutions (A. Said and Moore 2021). We proposed that Henri Lefebvre's tripartite model of the production of social space (Lefebvre [1974] 1991, 33, 38) can be a useful framework to identify three kinds of revolutionary actors, although individuals may fall into more than one of these categories and will have different ideas about the kind of change they are working toward. The first are actors who lived and experienced the revolution, meaning the revolutionary in an ethnographic and sociological sense. The second type are revolutionaries in the political sense, defined here as those who engage with and manage the political struggles while the revolution is ongoing. The third are those who perceived the revolution in a philosophical and historical way, or in the larger social sense. Only this last type of revolutionary subject makes the outcome of revolution their primary concern. This speaks to the classical meaning of the term: the vanguard revolutionaries who are devoting their energy to organizing and seizing power. We suggested that when some scholars define revolutionary actors exclusively as those who are primarily concerned with the outcome, they are displaying a narrow understanding that "not only presumes a universal objective consensus around the meaning of the revolutionary subject [but also] strips Arab revolutionaries of their experience of the revolution" (A. Said and Moore 2021). It is important not to collapse these types, not least because revolutionaries in a given revolution disagree and experience it and act differently in relation to power and change. We would be overlooking these differences if we conflate these experiences into one single category.

As Antonio Negri (2007, 253) suggested, any discussion of twenty-first-century revolutions must include an expansive analysis of how subjectivities have been transformed in the neoliberal age. Here it is important to acknowledge that neoliberalism has contradictory impacts on the possibilities and the idea of revolutions. On the one hand, it continues to deepen poverty, misery, and inequality and damages all substantive meanings of democracy. Thus, it creates the conditions that make revolutions possible. On the other hand, it also flattens, appropriates, and perhaps damages all radical meanings of revolutions. Attending to only one set of impacts is a serious mistake. I argue that analyses that focus only on neoliberal globalization's damaging effect on the idea of revolutions do not merely reflect simple pessimism, or imply end-of-history arguments, but are also reductionist. It is critical to see the contradictory ways neoliberalism played out in the Egyptian Revolution: the latter was a revolt against neoliberalism, even as it was shaped by neoliberalism (Armbrust 2018). It was a revolt against brutal policing, the lack of economic justice, and a life deprived of dignity, all imposed by neoliberal policies. But these policies also changed subjectivities, whose imaginations became deradicalized under the vicious precarious life of neoliberalism (Armbrust 2018). I echo Walter Armbrust, while arguing that it is almost empirically impossible to draw any definite conclusions about the impact of neoliberal conditions as conducive to revolutions, compared to their damaging and appropriating impact (see my four theses on defining revolution in the introduction of this book).

The idea that Arab revolutionaries were not revolutionary enough assumes a singular meaning to *revolutionary*. Obviously, in order for revolution to succeed, revolutionaries cannot afford to give up the question of organization to center the question of seizing power in their work. I am not suggesting that giving up on seizing power is possible, especially as, at least in the scholarly definitions, we still deem revolutions successful only when they do seize power. But as I argued in the introduction of this book, it is really important to acknowledge the full scope of the practice and experience of revolutionary actors, not all of whom are leaders, and not all of whom are concerned with a predetermined outcome.

Throughout this manuscript the conventional wisdom about being revolutionary holds true: we still need professional revolutionary organizers and cadres, despite the counterrevolutionary global context. Yet, much as we have focused on revolutionary leaders, we have also erred in not paying adequate attention to the masses in revolutions. Focusing on leadership and leaders is understandable. But revolutions on the ground are a blend of the ordinary and the extraordinary. If observers look only for a new Vladimir Lenin or Leon Trotsky or Ruhollah Khomeini or Fidel Castro and limit their search to earlier decades and centuries, they not only are thinking in an ahistorical way, and assuming that leadership patterns are repeatable, but will also lose sight of the full spectrum of actors. More attention must be paid to the revolutionary armies and ordinary citizens who participated in a given revolt, so as to understand the complexities of its trajectory (A. Said and Moore 2021). An adequate analysis of revolutionary and counterrevolutionary actors ought to take into account that actors change their positions all the time. Some of the revolutionaries in 2011 stopped being so and wooed the military throughout 2011 and 2012. Others became some of the main supporters of the coup in 2013. The Muslim Brotherhood, a key player in Egypt's revolutions and its troubles, played a contradictory role during the uprising itself, only allowing their members to participate at a late stage, yet they were also negotiating with Hosni Mubarak's regime at the very same time. They were relentlessly counterrevolutionary for most, if not all, of the time after ousting Mubarak, until they themselves became victims of the main counterrevolutionary force: the military in the aftermath of the coup in 2013. The point is that neither revolutionaries nor counterrevolutionaries are consistent or homogeneous camps. I argue that analysts who prefer easy convictions and generalizations about revolutionary failure and success are no less mistaken than Egyptian actors who fall into the politics of mutual blame—about which political faction made more mistakes than the other in the revolutions—in the context of hostile and extremely polarized political spaces. Many actors prefer reflections to blame. I align with them, as I hope has become clear in this book.

Another piece of established wisdom in the scholarship of revolution is also confirmed here: the fate of the coercive apparatus (who controls it and in what ways a transformation or reform can or cannot take place) shapes to a great extent the outcome of an uprising (Foran and Goodwin 1993). After the defeat (not collapse) of the Egyptian police apparatus by protesters on January 28, 2011, the military intervened. During the 2011 uprising and beyond, the military, a significant component of the repressive apparatus of the state, retained this power, although it acted as if it was siding with the revolution initially. The military was not able to shoot at protesters during the revolution, for complex reasons discussed earlier, especially in chapter 2. But it was able to do so and even kill protesters later in the context of the decline of revolutionary momentum. While this conventional wisdom is true—the revolutionary trajectory and outcome are significantly affected by who has an upper hand in the coercive apparatus—my research demonstrates that we need to take into serious consideration the nuances of power on the ground. Policing during uprisings is a very important piece that we ought to study closely. For example, as this research demonstrates, it is one thing to highlight the significance of protesters establishing a liberated zone in ordinary times and another to examine how significant this process is during a revolution. During revolutionary situations, I argue, a liberated zone is a site where revolutionaries establish an alternative state with actual sovereign power, or at least some degree of it. Besides, the idea of establishing some degree of organization or coordination between the popular committees and Tahrir protesters seems a hypothetical past possibility now. But this was a possibility, even if we cannot reach a final verdict about it empirically now. It was a possibility if the military had delayed distancing itself from Mubarak further (it did so only on February 10, 2011, one day before Mubarak's ouster). Had there been any further delay in the military's decision to distance itself from Mubarak and had its leaders decided to escalate its initial efforts to suffocate, impede, or attack protesters, military defections would have been very likely. Indeed, a very few low-ranking officers announced their defection from the military in the initial days of the uprising, and this defection could have expanded.[4] This is only a hypothetical possibility now. But if it had happened, it could have changed the course of the revolution, especially because low-ranking officers are closer in class status to the majority of Egyptians, especially in the context of the triangle of power discussed in chapter 3 (the military, the popular committees, and Tahrir revolutionaries). All three groups had some power of policing, with huge differences, indeed, since the military still had the upper hand in terms of controlling a heavy coercive apparatus. I described this triangle of power as an embryonic case of Trotsky's dual power. But had there been an expansion of military defection, along with coordination among Egyptians who held police power at the time, this embryonic case of Trotsky's dual power formula could have become a real dual sovereignty in Trotsky's sense, especially if we take the class of low-ranking officers into consideration and if more revolutionaries' degree of sovereignty had corresponded to a share of the coercive power. Even if we cannot prove this possibility now, it remains very important to study closely policing on the ground during revolutionary situations.

Revolutionaries' Biggest Mistake

It remains to discuss the implications of this book's arguments for revolutions in general, and empirical issues pertaining to the Egyptian Revolution in particular. Before doing so, however, it is critical to address one simple question about the biggest mistakes that Egyptian revolutionary actors made. According to the discussion throughout this book, which placed contingency and the role of revolutionary actors at the center of the analysis, one could argue that the biggest mistake made by the revolutionary actors in Egypt was not simply that they left Tahrir Square on February 11, 2011 (they went back to it, but the momentum was gone) or that they trusted the military in 2011 (it was one thing to trust or be ambivalent about the military and another to ask the military explicitly to intervene). Instead, their mistake was that they did not believe in the immenseness of their own power. Indeed, overlooking the question of seizing power was a grave mistake. As my analysis has demonstrated, Egyptian revolutionary actors practiced some power, in terms of policing, while lacking a vision and revolutionary articulation to take the revolution a step further. They did not think of themselves as capable of reclaiming and seizing power. This was a huge mistake.

As demonstrated in chapters 2 and 3, during the uprising the military guarded the state, but it was Egyptian revolutionary actors who policed almost all of Egypt, as well as the revolution in Tahrir. Why these revolutionaries were not interested in seizing power is a big question that I believe this manuscript or many others cannot do justice to. But briefly, as I discussed in this book, three major factors were at play. First, the revolutionaries were ambivalent toward the military and the state, which they historically thought of as sacred, due to the military's role in the making of the postcolonial state, while at the same time they had a narrow understanding of the regime, which they saw only as revolving around Hosni Mubarak and the ruling party. Second, the cross-class coalition that existed during the revolution was critical in toppling Mubarak but created ambiguities about the steps beyond that, in light of the conflict between these different classes. Third, there was a lack of unifying political revolutionary organization that could link the practice of power on the ground with developing a centralized articulation and intention about seizing power. In my analysis, pondering why Egyptian revolutionaries did not seize power is an important matter, but a more refined question would be, Why and how did Egyptian revolutionaries practice aspects of power in the revolution, without either realizing or articulating this in relation to revolutionary change? I demonstrated in chapter 3 that what I described as performative unity, in light of the three factors just described, is part of the answer. I hope that new research will advance, or challenge, the analysis presented here and provide better answers.

Research Implications

Overall, this research confirms what notable scholars of revolutions (Beck et al. 2022) have recently suggested concerning questioning the existing dichotomy between violence and nonviolence (as I discussed in chapter 2), the dichotomy between social revolutions and political revolutions (as I demonstrated in chapter 4), and the dichotomy between successful and failed revolutions (as I have demonstrated throughout the book with regard to the existence of minisuccesses and failures in the Egyptian Revolution).[5] Thus, I move now to three sets of interrelated conclusions and implications based on the analyses presented in this book. The first relates to developments in Egypt since I finished research in 2018. Overall, it seems that the picture is even gloomier than what I presented in chapter 6. Nevertheless, one important development is worth mentioning here: the new military regime in Egypt, headed by Abdel Fattah el-Sisi, has announced a plan to establish what they describe as a new administrative capital (NAC) of Egypt. Launched in 2015, the projected NAC is located approximately forty-five kilometers (twenty-eight miles) to the east of Cairo, on a "swath of desert equal to the size of Singapore" (Menshawy 2021). Additionally, the regime has invested in a series of megaprojects, used for propaganda purposes as well as for economic benefit, with the army's engineering authorities being both key executors and beneficiaries of the majority of these projects. I argue, however, that some of these projects are grounded in security-related concerns. The NAC itself is a perfect example of the latter. The plan is to move the headquarters of the government, including all ministries, the parliament, and so on, along with upper-class Egyptians who can afford to purchase homes in that area, away from the highly populated and currently poorly developed old historical Cairo. Some scholars suggest that we cannot disentangle how the regime thinks of the NAC, believing it would simply be a "reproduction of clone structures of western models," from the fact that the old capital has become underdeveloped in terms of its livability, with respect to its sociospatial structures and everyday urban reality (Abdelmonem 2016). One observer suggested that we cannot overlook how the pharaonic and propaganda ambitions of the new regime's investments in megaprojects are inherently coupled with destroying old Cairo (El Rashidi 2021).

Does this mean that once this project is finalized—assuming, that is, that it can succeed—that protest in old Cairo will vanish or that the regime will be more protected from the expendable populations in the old capital city?[6] I doubt this, not only because of the dubious material viability of this regime's escape to a new capital, but because of what I view as the impossibility of this regime remaining in complete control and because of the political psychology of its counterrevolutionary ethos. As I discussed in chapter 6, downtown Cairo, including Tahrir, became one of the most militarized and policed areas in Egypt. Today the regime seems to be in complete control of the political space, through resorting to levels of violence unparalleled in Egypt's contemporary and modern history. It is also accurate to suggest that revolutionary actors have chosen to withdraw from political space and have been enduring the trauma of defeat. Many of them are in jail, in solitary confinement. Others have fled and are living in exile. Yet I also demonstrated that the Sisi regime remains paranoid about anything associated with the January 2011 revolution. Thus, while the claim that the regime has succeeded in reinstating fear among Egyptians is true, it only tells part of the story. According to many actors and observers, the current regime in Egypt is fighting off the ghosts of January 2011. This means that it itself continually fears a repetition of what happened in 2011. This renders it vulnerable, even though it seems mighty, protected as it is by one of the most repressive apparatuses in modern Egyptian history, along with enjoying regional and international support.

One important note should be mentioned here. The Sisi regime also announced that the NAC will symbolize and embody the creation of a new republic. The idea of a new republic has been invoked several times in recent Egyptian history, especially in the aftermath of the January Revolution. And as mentioned in chapter 1, the July Republic was announced through a constitutional declaration on June 18, 1953. Several Egyptian intellectuals have emphasized that the July Republic was born deformed because it never achieved democracy. As political writer Mohamed Naeem suggests (2021), the January Revolution of 2011 was the real first attempt by Egyptians to create a republic and establish democracy. But this attempt was aborted by the military counterrevolutionary regime. In this context, the Sisi regime's claim that Egypt is moving toward a new republic is incongruous since the first republic was never completed. As Naeem rightly puts it,

Unfortunately, modern nation-states cannot be formed based on rhetorical and ostentatious visions, regardless of how popular or emotional they are. I am a firm believer that the Egyptian republic that was founded after the July 23, 1952, revolution was a deferred and deformed experience since its foundation. The 18th of June, 1953, the date of declaring the foundation of the Egyptian republic, is not an important date in the Egyptian public's consciousness or Egyptian intellectuals' consciousness and memory. This deformation and the deference of the key bases of the Egyptian republic's creation was—and has been—the deep root of all legitimacy crises and the root cause of the prevalence of tyranny that has been shattering us one generation after another. (2021, 198)

Naeem adds, "The proclamation of the republic was not a real republic, the most important aspect of which is achieving true citizenship and equality before the law, and when people become truly sovereign. The crisis of the Egyptian republic stems from the consciousness of those who made this proclamation after July 1952: a few military officers who believe that they are still looking for the meaning, the conscience, the material existence of the people. The proclamation was made on behalf of the people (without their presence)" (198).

The second set of conclusions relates to the theoretical and empirical implications of this study concerning research on revolutions. To begin with, this book is partially inspired by recent debates in the scholarship on revolution, specifically the calls that the so-called fourth generation of this scholarship needs to advance thinking about the revolutionary process, along with criticism that, despite that generation's focus on processes and trajectories, their analysis was not processual enough. Briefly, for nonexperts on the topic, there seems to be a consensus among scholars of revolutions that the literature in this field has gone through four generations of scholarship (Beck 2014; Foran 1993; Goldstone 2001; Lawson 2016). These are the natural history approach; the modernization and the social-psychological models; the state-centered and structural frameworks; and, last, cultural, agency-based, ideology-based, and/or process-based analyses. Recently, George Lawson suggested that "the realization of the processual ontology [is] favored but not actualized by fourth-generation revolutionary theory" (2016, 113–14).[7]

I see this study as advancing processual analyses of revolutions in two ways. First, in presenting and deploying the concept of lived contingency, and demonstrating how we should think of revolutions on the ground as a series of unpredictabilities and uncertainties combined with open possibilities, I hope that scholars can advance this idea further in analyzing the trajectories of any given revolts. Scholars of revolutions have been fixated for many years now on the question of the predictability or unpredictability of revolutions. What they perhaps omit is that the course of revolutions itself is loaded with numerous series of unpredictabilities and uncertainties. If we really want to advance the analysis of revolutions as a process, we need to attend to how these issues happen on the meso- and microlevels, and to how revolutionary actors struggle to make sense of them, and make or fail to make decisions about these issues.

Second, while centering the role of revolutionary actors in relation to lived contingency, I hope that I have also contributed to research on revolutions by highlighting some of the real issues at stake for revolutionary actors on the ground. We cannot do justice to analyzing revolutions, especially challenged or defeated ones, unless we pay adequate attention to revolutionary actors' role in the ethnographic sense: studying their bravery, their determination, their fear, their hopes, their contradictions and confusions. Only through this fine-grained work will we obtain a better analysis of how actors made decisions, or failed to do so, in relation to a revolution's possibilities and counterrevolutionary projects of restoration or containment. Recently, sociologist Isaac Reed (2020) presented a compelling theorization of power in his analysis of the American Revolution and state formation in colonial North America and the early American republic. Reed presented what he termed the triangle of power relations (based on the role of agency), involving three parties: actor, rector, and other (Reed 2020, 9–28). Reed's work is an important contribution in terms of presenting this typology of agency and power in revolutions, and my work complements his by focusing on the notion of lived contingency and the different degrees of practicing power during a revolution. In chapter 3 I provided a ground-up theorization of three instances of how power is practiced on the ground during revolutionary situations: (1) practicing state power, or part of state power; (2) articulating this power, in the sense of developing vocabulary and communicative links or a vision about state power; and (3) actually seizing state power. My three distinctions provide us with more nuance about the wide range of practicing or making sense of sovereignty battles on the ground during revolutionary crises.

One could imagine that we could gain deeper analytical insights on issues and discrepancies of power on the ground if we apply this distinction on historical cases of revolutions, especially more recent revolts where revolutionary actors failed to seize state power at the end of revolutionary situations. These two projects, Reed's and mine, hopefully are promising efforts in presenting theorizations and deep analyses of the role of agency in revolutions.

In addition to advancing the processual analysis of revolutions, this book is a reminder of the significance of barricades in revolutions. Barricades always carry a significant meaning and symbolic political power in the political imaginary and scholarship of revolutions. Even though I didn't offer a comprehensive account of the variations of barricades throughout the Egyptian Revolution, and therefore did not do justice to this phenomenon, I provided a glimpse into it, demonstrating how barricades varied in terms of composition and function, from the presumed center of the revolution, Tahrir Square, to the periphery, the neighborhoods. I showed how some barricades were strongly associated with dividing revolutionary from nonrevolutionary spaces, while others were associated with checkpoints erected by protesters, and yet others were not. I proposed that it is critical to take into account these nuances on the ground when we analyze barricades and their potential use in future revolts.

I also examined the expansion of political space in the decade prior to the revolution and then the dramatic contraction of political space after the revolution, especially in the aftermath of the coup in 2013. I paid special attention to the role of technology and social media in contributing to mobilization prior to and during the revolution. I also examined closely the rise of digital repression in the aftermath of the coup. I provided a historicized analysis of the techno-utopic moment of 2011, up to the seeming techno-dystopia in the aftermath of 2013 and beyond. This is not unique to Egypt. The literature on communication, repression, and digital capitalism and surveillance has been growing. Leading manufacturers of this technology include Russia and China but also the United Kingdom, France, Italy, and the United States. Many of these countries have been integral in supporting the Sisi regime with the technology of digital repression. In short, it is important to develop more historicized analyses of how digital capitalism is changing over time, steering away from simplistic generalizations about the role of technology in promoting democracy or dissent.

I started this book with a series of questions about the when and where of revolutions. Alongside my discussion of barricades and digital spaces, I have examined how the composition of political space in Egypt shifted over time. At the center of these shifts were continual struggles and interactions between pro-democracy actors and successive regimes. Given my conclusions about the continuous shifting dynamic of political spaces (involving an entanglement and struggle over formal political space, street politics, and digital spaces between pro-democracy actors and different regimes), it is fair to say that democratic struggles over political spaces will continue to be complex and are not limited to the ballot box. Most important, especially during the peak of revolutionary crisis, streets will continue to be at the core of battles for sovereignty. The streets are where the battles between repressive coercive apparatuses and protesters take place.

A final set of implications relates to ideas of democracy and revolution together. As I discussed in chapter 5, Egyptians debated the meaning and the limitations of procedural democracy in the aftermath of the revolution. I also discussed how procedural democracy, combined with extreme violence, along with a commitment to free-market politics, was used as a strategy by the counterrevolution in Egypt to smother the demands for more substantive democracy. Elections without democratization, combined with extreme hostility to the social demands of average Egyptians, were at the core of counterrevolutionary actions in Egypt, even in a context where many were exclusively obsessed with the secular or religious and identitarian debates in 2011 and 2012, until the coup of 2013. One conclusion of this study is that it is an egregious mistake to conceive of any viable democratization project that is riddled with or based on extreme categorical social inequalities.[8] A significant part of the mobilization against Morsi in 2012 and 2013 was motivated by his failure to deliver promised solutions to immediate economic and social problems and to meet the aspirations of Egyptians after the revolution, even though his electoral platform was based on these. Indeed, matters got worse, and he was obstructed by the deep state. However, mobilization after the revolution did not revolve simply around sectarian and electoral politics, as many observers and critics insist.

Egypt's experience makes clear that for any democratization project to be sustainable, it needs an international environment that is conducive to the thriving of democracy. Most specifically, when imperial powers or superpowers are involved, they work to contain or limit the radical possibilities of democracy. In this particular instance, Egypt could be described as a client state of the United States. Two important pieces of scholarship have discussed the role of the US administration in relation to the Egyptian Revolution and its troubled trajectory. Daniel Ritter (2015), for example, has suggested that Western-aligned autocrats, in this case the Mubarak regime, eventually find themselves restrained by their strong international allies, which generally operate internationally according to liberal logics. In this case, the US administration, under Barack Obama, realized that the Mubarak regime had become a liability and decided to end their support for this regime after an unarmed revolution took place. In contrast, Jason Brownlee (2012) suggested that the US administration consistently prioritized stability in Egypt and strove to establish and sustain the status quo by whatever means possible. On-the-ground developments seem to validate Brownlee's analysis, especially in the context of US support for the coup in 2013 and for Egypt's regime in the aftermath of the coup. As early as January 30, 2011, then US secretary of state Hillary Clinton firmly stated that Egypt should witness an "orderly transition" (Clinton 2011). This phrase was a central piece in official US discourse at the time and was adopted by many scholars, with some activists and writers also celebrating what happened in Egypt as an orderly transition (see, for example, DeYoung 2011; Hanieh 2011; Landler 2011). Considering that the transition happened under military rule, it is clear that for both the Egyptian army and the country's international allies, the main concern was *managing* the process of transition, rather than ensuring the democratic nature of its content.

One cannot overlook how, in recent decades, the entire globe has witnessed a constant backlash to democratization and the substantive meanings of democracy, even in the most established Western so-called democracies, which have been experiencing the plutocratic role of financial capital, lobbies, and militarist, nativist, and right-wing politics. In many cases, "democracy" in these countries has been reduced to a form of electoral authoritarianism. Thus, one may wonder what *liberal democracy* even means. And should we revisit the established wisdom in the scholarship of revolutions that democracies are immune from revolutions? Where the social and the political are highly intertwined, what does this mean for the taken-for-granted dichotomy of social/classical revolutions, on the one hand, and political revolutions, on the other? I cannot resolve these big questions here. But I would like to argue that significant segments of the scholarship of social movements and revolutions went too far in their rejection of a structural analysis of movements and revolutions, presuming that structural analysis is simply or always a form of economic determinism. Indeed, it is a good corrective move to study agency, ideology, and other important elements in revolutions and movements. Still, I suggest that by going too far in their rejection of structural analysis, some scholars resist examining the relevance of social grievances and underpinning issues in movements and revolutions. Resisting mechanistic structural thinking is one thing, but refusing to acknowledge social grievances or the relevance of class altogether is another. In short, whether because of the obsession with the dichotomy between social and political revolutions, or because of adhering to certain anti-Marxist genealogies and analyses, or the fixation on postideological argumentations, or the fetishization of deploying revolutionary scholarship jargon while undermining the interest in analyzing revolutions as complex processes, it is my conviction that much scholarship of revolutions is exhibiting a strong tendency to downplay the social components of revolutions or is even embracing a high degree of hostility toward the social question altogether. The analysis presented here is a call for a corrective balance. Any analysis of movements and revolutions that ignores social grievances is inadequate, especially in a global context where the possibility of democracy cannot be separated from social justice issues.

Revolution, as much as it is a utopic and romanticized project, is not easy. Revolutions require hard work and plentiful sacrifices to succeed. Calling for a revolution is one thing, making it succeed quite another. As a scholar, I learned that it is critical to observe what happens on the ground and think of the nuances of power in concrete sociological, ethnographic, and historical terms. As revolutions have become global spectacles, and counterrevolutions are more globalized than ever, it is important to understand these nuances of power and the challenges of revolutionary success on the ground, not just as these are represented in the spectacle world. As a participant in a revolution, I learned that revolutionaries should devote more energy to organizing in relation to power and should be brave in seizing power while remaining skeptical about the baggage of history, such as illusions about the sacred nature of the nation-state in a postcolonial or late capitalist world. "Another world is possible" has become an outdated cliché. In Egypt, as across the globe, dreams of true freedom and justice hover over our tragic and uncertain despotic realities. A better world is a must.

appendix one

Brief Timeline of the Egyptian Revolution, 2011–2018

DECEMBER 2010. Activists call for protests against police brutality and against poverty. One of the main sites of mobilization is the We Are All Khaled Said Facebook page. Khaled Said was an Egyptian blogger who was tortured to death in June 2010. The page was first started to mobilize youth to organize and call for justice for Said's death.

JANUARY 25, 2011. Activists and youth take to the streets in Cairo during National Police Day. A few thousand protesters gather in Tahrir Square and chant, "The people want the downfall of the regime." At night, the police evacuate the square by force.

JANUARY 26/27, 2011. Scattered protests continue in Cairo. Activists call for a Friday of Rage on January 28. Protests also continue in several other cities, especially in the Suez Canal city of Suez. Police use violence in Suez, and the first few protesters are killed. The deaths of fellow citizens in Suez increase anger. In anticipation of more protests, Egypt's minister of the interior shuts down the internet and cell phone communication. This decision also angers protesters and galvanizes mobilization and protests on January 28.

JANUARY 28, 2011. Hundreds of thousands rally in Cairo and in all main urban centers in Egypt. Battles with police take place in the streets. The police use live ammunition as well as tear gas to disperse protesters. Protests continue throughout the day, and police forces are exhausted and defeated. Protesters occupy Tahrir Square. At the end of the day, Hosni Mubarak refuses to make any concessions and orders the military to restore order. The army orders a curfew in Egypt from 6:00 p.m. to 6:00 a.m. (in Suez, from 4:00 p.m. to 6:00 a.m.). The military closes roads in Egypt.

JANUARY 30, 2011. Mubarak delivers a speech announcing that he refuses to step down and that he has shuffled the cabinet and appointed General Omar Suleiman, the country's spy chief, as vice president. Protesters continue to rally in Tahrir Square and violate the curfew. The military and Mubarak send F-16 fighter jets streaking over downtown and Tahrir to scare protesters. The protesters refuse to leave and chant, "We will not leave, he [Mubarak] should leave."

JANUARY 31, 2011. Protesters continue to rally in Tahrir and elsewhere. Omar Suleiman announces an initiative for dialogue with the opposition. Protesters refuse to dialogue, and only formal parties join the meeting with Suleiman. Egypt continues to be without internet and cell phone service, and protests continue. The protesters call for a "million-person march" and a general strike on the next day to commemorate one week since the protests began.

FEBRUARY 1, 2011. The first million-person march takes place. And protests grow in Egypt. At night, Mubarak delivers a speech announcing he will not run for another term but vowing to continue his term. Mubarak's emotional speech makes many segments of the public sympathetic with him.

FEBRUARY 2, 2011. In the early morning, pro-Mubarak militia and supporters attack protesters in Tahrir with stones and Molotov cocktails. The army does not intervene to protect the protesters, a move that embarrasses the army. The public becomes more sympathetic toward the Tahrir protesters after the regime's constant attacks on peaceful protesters. Internet access is restored in the morning. One of the first globally circulated images of the regime's response to the revolution, after internet has been restored, is that of Mubarak's militia attacking the Tahrir protesters. The hashtags #tweetsfromtahrir and #tahrir and global attention contribute to iconizing the Tahrir image.

FEBRUARY 3, 2011. Pro-Mubarak supporters continue to attack Tahrir. The Tahrir protesters become more organized, erecting their own checkpoints and protecting themselves.

FEBRUARY 4, 2011. The second million-person march takes place.

FEBRUARY 5, 2011. Army forces attempt to evacuate Tahrir, without success. The leadership of Egypt's ruling National Democratic Party resigns, including Gamal Mubarak, the son of Hosni Mubarak.

FEBRUARY 6, 2011. Banks, which had closed on January 28, reopen, and workers are told to go back to work, a move that facilitates workers' strikes. Suleiman continues to dialogue with the opposition. The Muslim Brotherhood announces it will participate in the dialogue; some of its members are protesters in Tahrir Square.

FEBRUARY 7–11, 2011. Many labor strikes take place in Egypt, and these intensify the regime crisis.

FEBRUARY 11, 2011. Mubarak resigns after almost two weeks of intense protest, handing over power to the army.

FEBRUARY 14, 2011. The military announces a plan to draft a new constitution and hand over power to elected officials in six months. The military also calls for national solidarity and criticizes strikes. It urges workers to play their role in reviving the economy.

FEBRUARY 25 AND MARCH 9, 2011. When protesters return to the square to demand a quicker transition to a democratic government, military and police forces beat and arrest them, in a pattern that will continue throughout the transitional period.

OCTOBER 9, 2011. As sectarian attacks against Copts in Egypt continue to escalate, the Copts protest. The military attacks a peaceful protest of mostly Christian protesters and runs them over with armored vehicles.

NOVEMBER 28, 2011. The first parliamentary election takes place, and the Muslim Brotherhood and Islamic parties win the majority.

MAY 23, 2012. Presidential elections begin. Mohamed Morsi, the Muslim Brotherhood's candidate, wins the election.

JUNE 15, 2012. The military dissolves the parliament based on a ruling by the Supreme Court and grabs power, in anticipation of Morsi's becoming president, so that the Muslim Brotherhood will not control both the legislative power and the presidency.

JUNE 30, 2012. Morsi is sworn in as president.

NOVEMBER 21, 2012. Morsi grants himself more power by issuing a constitutional decree that expands presidential powers and places his decisions above judicial oversight.

NOVEMBER 29, 2012. Islamists finish a draft constitution.

DECEMBER 4, 2012. Egyptians march to the presidential palace to protest Morsi's attempt to expand his power.

FEBRUARY–MARCH 2013. Protests rage in cities across Egypt following a massive fuel shortage and widespread electricity blackouts.

APRIL 2013. A new protest movement emerges, including the Tamarod ("rebel") campaign, calling for new elections.

JUNE 21, 2013. Abdel Fattah el-Sisi, the minister of defense, issues a public statement warning that the growing "split in society" between Morsi's supporters and their opponents might compel the army to intervene and demands concessions from Morsi.

JUNE 30 / JULY 1, 2013. Nationwide protests call for Morsi to step down, and the military gives an ultimatum to Morsi.

JULY 3, 2013. The military arrests Morsi and removes him from office.

JULY 4, 2013. Sisi chooses Adly Mansour, the chief justice of the Supreme Court, as an interim president.

JULY 26, 2013. Sisi calls for a nationwide mandate to "fight terrorism." Many Egyptians rally for Sisi.

AUGUST 14, 2013. The military commits a massacre and kills no fewer than one thousand protesters—supporters of Morsi—in Rabaa Al-Adawiya Square.

AUGUST 15, 2013. The United States condemns the massacre but continues aid to Egypt's military.

AUGUST 22, 2013. Mubarak is released from prison.

MAY 26–28, 2014. Sisi sweeps to a landslide victory after an election.

APRIL 2, 2018. Sisi is reelected for another term.

appendix two

A Note on Positionality

When I arrived in Egypt on February 4, 2011, I embodied five interwoven layers that shaped my positionality. I was

1. an outsider coming from the United States;
2. an insider returning to a familiar context (I grew up and lived in Egypt until 2004 and still maintain my Egyptian citizenship);[1]
3. a scholar conducting research in pursuit of a degree at a US institution;
4. a former human rights and leftist pro-democracy activist in Egypt who still maintained connections with key activists and activist networks there; and
5. simultaneously a participant in and an observer of the revolution.

My research is informed by these layers. They pulled me in opposing directions, and the way they affected me shifted through the various stages of research, from conducting the research to analyzing the data and then writing, in different iterations. One illustration of these complex dynamics is that during the uprising itself, events were happening at lightning speed, so that I got to witness multiple events in one day, sometimes within just a few hours. In addition, because I have contacts within key organizations, such as some founders of the Revolution Youth Coalition, I had access to many critical insights about important events while they were happening. My friendship with key bloggers and organizers also gave me access to important meetings and spaces. This included attending meetings where new parties were founded or where a new trade union or a new trade union coalition was formed. I attended meetings where actors engaged in key debates, for example, about the nature of the revolution and the need for organizing, or about what type of new leftist party Egypt needed at the time. My revolutionary friends asked me to write and translate statements for them, and I did. For example, a few months after the uprising, I wrote a short piece in a magazine titled the *Voice of the Revolution* that was hand distributed in Tahrir.

Yet despite this great and unparalleled access, because of my special ties to the place, and the people, as a native Egyptian and as a former activist, the events were emotionally overwhelming. At the time of the uprising, I thought that deep emotional attachment was a burden. I was overwhelmed with the developments and the need to make decisions at a moment's notice, moving around and deciding which events to observe and what to do in the breathtaking space of Tahrir Square. In many instances I felt immobilized by the intensity of events. All I wanted to do was open my eyes and witness history. I could not think clearly. I was perhaps particularly prone to anxiety because I had come from the United States. I had to hide all my American IDs, such as my driver's license and university card, and make sure I was not carrying any American currency on me. At the time, the regime was spreading rumors about foreign spies and agents paying the protesters to destabilize the nation. When I commented to my friends a few months later about how overwhelmed I had been, they told me they all were.

Precisely because I knew many activists and leading bloggers personally, I was reluctant to impose on their time or appear to be exploiting our relationship. I understood at a very deep level how intense and tragic some of the events were, and I could not bear to disrespect anyone enduring these horrors by asking them to take time away from their struggle in order to sit down with me for an interview. Some of them were being interviewed constantly, especially by Western researchers, and Egyptians were already growing critical of the ways Western researchers were entering and exiting Egypt simply to collect people's stories, only to disappear from the scene and publish their work elsewhere.[2] I was deeply conscious of this dynamic and sometimes found it difficult to request interviews for fear of being perceived as a selfish researcher. In sum, while my deep ties granted me great access, they also formed an emotional burden.

But on my second research trip, I was more prepared to do interviews and less anxious. All of my trips to three cities outside Cairo (Alexandria, Mahalla, and Suez) occurred with the help of activists. During this period my insider positionality was no burden whatsoever. It enabled me to meet and interview key people, such as the founders of the Revolution Youth Coalition, one of the administrators of the We Are All Khaled Said Facebook page, some of the founders of the Egyptian Movement for Change (Kefaya) and the National Association for Change, some of the workers who were crucial organizers of the Mahalla strikes in 2007 and the attempted strike of 2008, and some of the founders of the blogging movements in 2005 and beyond.

Analyzing the data, and writing, proved exceedingly difficult given the massive, unpredictable changes that have continuously taken place since 2011. My attachment to some of the individuals targeted after the revolution led me to feel a constant sense of responsibility to keep the research up to date. It was difficult to feign any level of detachment from either the events themselves or my informants. The period from 2011 until 2013 was also radically different from its aftermath. Neither I nor the field and my subjects were the same.[3] As I am writing, many of my informants are serving jail sentences or have been arbitrarily detained by the military regime in Egypt. Many of them are icons of the revolutionary youth movement and are people I know personally, people whose families and close communities or loved ones I have known for over two decades. A very close friend is also detained merely because of Facebook posts in which he criticized the military junta in Egypt. I have shed many burning tears as I quote informants now languishing in the jails of the counterrevolution. Some of them have been in solitary confinement for the past few years. They have been punished for their role in the uprising. Years earlier, during the uprising, I also cried, but those were tears of excitement.

Some parts of this book were especially difficult to write. There were passages when I was thinking critically about Tahrir and wondering how I dared write critically about mistakes the Egyptian revolutionaries made, when so many of them are experiencing the bitterness of defeat and living under constant attacks by the military regime. Many of the revolutionaries I know are struggling through their PTSD (post-traumatic stress disorder). I also had another overall challenge during writing. On the one hand, I wanted to write a book for myself, for my friends, to preserve our memories of the revolution. Thus, I wanted to demonstrate the participant's voice and perception of events throughout the book. On the other, I was writing this book to obtain tenure. Consequently, I wanted to demonstrate my scholarly precision and rigor more than anything. I decided that I could meet both goals with self-reflexivity, as I show in the following.

Within the general agreement that every researcher comes with a "position," one methodological strand questions the relationships between researchers who are "outsiders" and those who are "insiders" to the communities they study (Abu-Lughod 2006). Such analyses illustrate that there is no simple binary between the "outsider" and the "insider" and that insiders are also, to some extent, outsiders, while outsiders often become insiders in one way or another. Thus, many scholars have critiqued the concept of the "native researcher," as it reduces people conducting research in their own communities to a one-to-one relationship with their research subjects. Anthropologist Kath Weston (2000) replaces the insider-outsider binary, or the idea of native versus nonnative researchers, with the idea of the "hybrid researcher," which I think more accurately captures the multiple kinds of relationships and power dynamics between any researcher and their research subjects.

In navigating these layers of positionality and the constant and dramatic shifts in Egypt, having read critical feminist and anthropological and sociological scholarship on positionality, I was reminded that there is *no such thing as objectivity*, and every researcher approaches their research with their own set of biases, experiences, and identities. I am influenced by this critical scholarship, and I have become aware of the need for self-reflexivity through all stages of research. I am aware that the kinds of questions I ask and the knowledge I produce are shaped by my positions. In this book I follow critical qualitative sociologists and anthropologists who emphasize that self-reflexivity is a must, especially in contexts where questions of power are relevant to the research (see Bourdieu 2003; Bourdieu and Wacquant 1992). These authors do not reject objectivity, but they argue against mendacious objectivity, and they argue for a need to objectivize the researcher's own position.[4] Self-reflection helped me to write this book despite all these difficulties. For example, in many instances in the book, I have sought to demonstrate how I thought about a specific event as a scholar compared to how I thought about it as an engaged actor. Besides, I was committed to presenting an accurate account of my (and the actors') sentiments at given moments, with the emotions and awareness that are attached to these moments. Then I also demonstrate how I thought about this moment and action a few months or few years afterward, highlighting how I was critically perceptive or mistaken or naive in my judgment earlier.

Certainly, I wrote this book against forgetting and against the systemic erasure of documents and the censorship about the revolution that are taking place in Egypt today. I also wrote it to the best of my ability as a scholar. I am not sure if I succeeded in meeting my goals. Speaking from self-reflection, I am certain that I am pleased with the outcome. But readers will have the final say.

appendix three

Notes on Methods, or How I Conducted Historical

Ethnography of a Revolution

As mentioned in the introduction of this book, I have deployed an interdisciplinary approach, at the center of which was historical ethnography. To use the conventional disciplinary terms in the social sciences, I conducted firsthand ethnography, I conducted eighty-four interviews, and I engaged in documentary/historical research over three research trips. But as I explain in the following, all these approaches worked together in my historical ethnographic research and analysis of the revolution. My first research trip took place from February 4 to April 16, 2011, overlapping with the revolution itself; the second was from July 16, 2012, to January 5, 2013; and the third was from mid-December 2015 through January 7, 2016. Most of my research during the first trip was based on firsthand ethnography. In the second trip, I combined ethnography, interviews, and documentary research. The third trip was primarily devoted to historical and documentary research, but I conducted many interviews via email, as I explain below. I also continued to do intensive documentary work well into late 2018. In this appendix I (1) discuss how I defined and deployed historical ethnography; (2) present basic information on conducting interviews, as well as the demographic distribution of my interviewees; and (3) provide information on specific documentary research with regard to battles during the revolution and with regard to the popular committees, as well as some demographic information about the martyrs and the injured during the revolution.

I start this note with a simple fact about my training. I am a historical sociologist by training who ended up doing ethnography of a revolution. While conducting my research, I could not help but think intensely about history and temporality and their relevance to my work. In graduate school I was also trained in using qualitative methods and conducting interviews. I have not received sufficient training in ethnography in the discipline of anthropology. Besides, even though the expression *historical ethnography* may seem redundant, since all ethnographic research should be historical, as I explain in the following, I realized over the course of writing this that I should be using the term intentionally to demonstrate the need to integrate historical and temporal sensitivity in research, and as a position against *presentist* analyses in the social sciences of revolution and social movements. Additionally, as I started to read some work by historical anthropologists on how they define this practice (e.g., Coronil 1997; Middleton 2003; Stoler 2010), I realized we historical sociologists and historical anthropologists have much in common. Recently, historical sociologists and qualitative sociologists seem to be coming to the same conclusion I reached when I was conducting this research (Benzecry, Deener, and Lara-Millán 2020).

What is historical ethnography? In simple terms, historical ethnography is a systemic practice of research in which the field should be in conversation with the archive/document. Some of the advocates of this type of research insist that anthropologists and historians have much in common. For example, as put by Charles Tilly, "ethnographic field work resembles the historian's archival research more than it does the sociologist's survey design or the economist's national income accounting" (1978, 207). With that said, *historical ethnography* is an umbrella term that includes numerous approaches. Here I present the two that I used in my research and give examples of how I have done so.

Retrospective Ethnography

To my knowledge, the term *retrospective ethnography* was coined by Charles Tilly, who has advocated this as a form of historical sociology. Tilly describes retrospective ethnography as work that involves "empathetic reconstruction of alien times and people and uses current understandings of social processes to show how those instances fit into a known range of variations" (2007b, 327). Simply put, retrospective ethnography means to "reconstruct actors' dispositions from the historical record" (326). In another piece Tilly discusses the specificity of retrospective ethnography in studying collective action and defines it as "the effort to reconstitute a round of life from the best historical equivalents of the ethnographer's observations, then to use the reconstituted round of life as a context for the explanation of collective action" (1978, 210). Tilly here seems to focus on one direction of research (starting from the archive / the document and thinking of it as an ethnographer, to make sense of collective action in the past). But I also think that one can imagine the reverse, starting from an ethnographic observation, in the present, and striving to look for archives/documents to provide a satisfactory historical context of collective action in the present.

Here are two examples of how I have conducted retrospective ethnography (or dialectical retrospective ethnography, if we may) in this research. The first example relates to an important student protest in Egyptian history that took place in Tahrir Square in January 1972. The protest ended up forming a camp that has become quite famous in Egypt's history of protests. The camp lasted for just about one day. I have read about it in books and poems. Revolutionaries in 2011 kept bringing it up. It was an inspiration to them. In short, the 1972 camp shaped how revolutionaries thought of Tahrir Square in 2011. Thus, when I started from my observations in Tahrir during the revolution and realized that many revolutionaries kept mentioning the 1972 protest, I decided to study its relevance. To do so, I asked my interlocutors and interviewees in 2012 about their thoughts about the relevance of the 1972 event. I was very fortunate in that one or two of my interviewees were key leaders of the protest in 1972, and they offered me helpful insights as they provided me with their recollections about that event. When I did archival/documentary research in 2012 and beyond, I looked for and consulted some documents (accounts written by some key actors of the event, or autobiographies). Many analyses existed about this event. I did not approach it as a historian but mostly focused on this event's relevance to the revolution in 2011. I noticed many interesting aspects of the connection between 1972 and 2011. Even though I discuss this connection only briefly in chapter 1, there was a lot of back and forth—between present and past, between observations and interviews and documents—in my research about it. Perhaps this is why I call it (dialectical) retrospective ethnography.

The second example is less complicated. Because of my positionality, I was fortunate that I participated in many protests in Egypt in 2000–2004 (in 2004 I immigrated to the United States). Most of these protests were spontaneous, in the context of Egyptians' solidarity with the second Palestinian Intifada (also known as the Al-Aqsa Intifada). But some were planned by a coalition known as the Egyptian Popular Committee in Solidarity with the Palestinian Intifada (EPCSPI). I also joined protests in the context of the antiwar movement in Egypt (against the Anglo-American war on Iraq in 2003). I did not have a chance to participate in the Egyptian Movement for Change (Kefaya) movement, a pro-democracy movement that started in late 2004 in Egypt, (even though I was fortunate and perhaps brave enough to sign its founding document in late 2004, a few months after immigrating to the United States). When I started to study the decade of dissent prior to the revolution, I relied on some of my memories and scattered journaling about places and locations of protest, and generally the street politics that I experienced in this window (2000–2004). When I started to think and read about protest practices by Kefaya movement organizers, I relied on interviews and documents. I realized that my observations about protests in 2000–2004 and the data shared by interviewees—some of whom were leaders of Kefaya—as well as the documents had significant resonance with some of the familiar places of protest and emphasis on lessons and mistakes from the period from 2000 to 2004. These issues of resonance related to the shifting dynamics and sizes of protests, their locations, and spatial practices. I realized that my recollections, my journaling, and the way actors related their experience to me complemented each other. This was another example of retrospective ethnography.

Kairós as a Research and Analytic Strategy

This approach is an invention of mine, as it is not known in the social sciences at all, to my knowledge. In fact, it is a philosophical notion about time and is also known in English and comparative literature. Thus, I discuss it in more depth here. Let us start from an assumption that scholars of revolution cannot help but be attentive to the exceptional richness of meanings, the profound temporal weight, and the overwhelming multiplicity of spaces in revolution—not only the richness of meaning of places but also actually the ways we can think of time. Here one of the main challenges is finding balance between studying the *chronology* of events and examining important *spatial and temporal markers* in this chronology. Instead of considering this balance as a theoretical or methodological burden, it is best to find a solution to use this tension and richness analytically. To attend to this problem, I found help in an old Greek notion of time: *kairós*. Whereas *chronos* refers to chronological, sequential, or ordinary time, *kairós* refers to a proper or opportune time for action. As one scholar puts it,

> *Kairós* [is] the brief decisive moment which makes a turning-point in the life of human beings or in the development of the universe. This concept was illustrated by the figure vulgarly known as the Opportunity . . . a man (originally nude) in fleeting movement, unusually young . . . equipped with wings both at the shoulder and at the heels. His attributes were a pair of scales, originally balanced on the edge of a shaving knife, and, in a somewhat later period, one or two wheels. Moreover, his head often showed the proverbial forelock by which bald-headed Opportunity can be seized. (Pankofsky 1939, 71–72, quoted in Miller 2002, xii)

Overlooking its more philosophical subtleties, I emphasize that the term is associated with notions of praxis and finding the moment when the time is "right" (Smith 1969). *Kairós* is not only defined as an opportune and right time but also can be seen as a "rare convergence of opportunities" (K. Marshall 2015). This has led several scholars to explicitly connect *kairós* to revolutions (see Miller 2002; Boer 2013; Murchadha 2013). As philosopher Roland Boer argues, the "concept is arguably one of the great organizing categories for a spate of recent and not so recent efforts to rethink revolution" (2013, 116). Boer states that despite some differences, "with the agreed sense of the critical time, the opportune and revolutionary moment that must be seized, the term enables us to identify the common ground of various proposals by some leading Western Marxists: Walter Benjamin, Giorgio Agamben, Antonio Negri, Slavoj Zizek, Fredric Jameson, Alain Badiou, and Ernst Bloch. However, on closer examination, a number of problems emerge in relation to their efforts" (116). I have used *kairós* as a research and analytic strategy in this project. I have followed my ethnographic observations—a rare historical opportunity to be present and do ethnographic research during a revolution—and I have followed what my interlocutors suggested as key sites/spaces and key moments in the Egyptian Revolution.[1] I interrogated how actors defined the times and spaces of the revolution and followed how these notions changed over time. I also studied how these notions relate to one another over time. Even so, I argue that we cannot give up the significance of chronology, defined here in the two senses of the ancient Greek *chronos*, as sequential time and as ordinary time. We cannot make sense of the exceptionality of some of the revolutionary moments and spaces without situating them in chronology and mapping out how these spaces mattered in contention before the revolution, as well as doing a proper chronology of events during the revolution.

What are spatial markers and temporal markers? I build on critical scholars of contention and the Egyptian Revolution to highlight the significance of mapping these markers in the revolution (McAdam and Sewell 2001; Sabea 2013; Schwedler 2016; W. Sewell 1996). Analyzing Tahrir Square during the revolution, anthropologist Hanan Sabea (2013), for example, states that the everydayness "was spatially marked by the carving out of the space of the 'midan' (the square) and the regulation of entry at its multiple check-points." Mapping out temporal and spatial markers in a given revolution in this way is useful to understanding its temporal and spatial composition and eventual trajectory. In interrogating spatial markers, it is critical to take into account how claim making is spatial, especially interrogating the ways in which contention can be contained, transgressive (Tilly 2000, 138), or both.

In this research I mapped spatial and temporal markers in relation to Tahrir, as well as in relation to the larger revolutionary repertoire. This mapping, for example, demonstrates the radical changes in and the transformation of the effectiveness and meaning of the refrain "Occupy Tahrir" in different moments. This also demonstrates how the meaning of Tahrir changed over time. On January 28, 2011, when protesters defeated the police apparatus and Hosni Mubarak ordered the military to intervene, it was the culmination, or peak, of the revolution. So, too, was July 26, 2013, when rallies in Tahrir and throughout Egypt supported Minister of Defense Abdel Fattah el-Sisi just three weeks after the military coup. The rallies presumably gave the military commander a mandate to fight terrorism but later proved to be a moment in which the public seemed to give Sisi a carte blanche. July 26, 2013, then, marks the defeat of the idea of rallies, making it the most important moment in the counterrevolution.

As for spatial markers, we can return to January 28, 2011, when protesters succeeded in liberating Tahrir Square, as the moment when the revolution was spatially embodied in Tahrir. On August 16, 2013, when the military regime attacked protesters (mainly organized by protesters who supported the Muslim Brotherhood and Mohamed Morsi) camped in Rabaa Al-Adawiya Square, a massacre in which the regime killed no fewer than 1,200 protesters, this embodied the counterrevolution. Taken together, I consider the revolution's unique and complex spatiotemporal configurations, taking into account both revolutionary possibilities and the projects of containment, and use *kairós* as a research and analytic strategy throughout.

FIRSTHAND ETHNOGRAPHY

Before discussing interviews and documentary research, let us look closely at what conventional sociologists and anthropologists might describe as *firsthand ethnography*. During the first and second phases of my research, I participated in many events, including walking in rallies, gathering in Tahrir, talking to people, attending events such as the formation of new parties and new trade unions, and attending many press conferences related to the revolution. These activities were in various locations in Cairo, not only Tahrir. Ethnography was especially important in the first phase of my research, as I was in Tahrir every day from February 4, 2011, to February 11, which saw the ousting of Mubarak. My ethnographic work continued beyond Tahrir after that date, until I ended the first phase of research and left Egypt on April 16, 2011.

During the time in Tahrir, my presence and participation there enabled me to talk to people in tents and behind the stages. I talked to artists, doctors, and journalists. I talked to seasoned activists and people who had never participated in a protest before but were drawn to see what was going on in Tahrir. I sometimes saw the aftermath of violent events. I witnessed police and pro-Mubarak thugs attacking the square, and I saw many injured people in Tahrir. I experienced the process of going in and out of checkpoints around and outside of Tahrir. Being in Cairo during that time, I was also able to participate in one of the popular committees at night (discussed in chapter 3). I participated in many unplanned conversations, as well as organized meetings. Some friends asked me to help with translating or editing or contributing to magazines distributed around Tahrir after Mubarak's ousting. One of the magazines I contributed to was called the *Voice of the Revolution*. In the second phase, I also participated in many rallies and attended many events protesting against the Supreme Council of Armed Forces and against the elected president at the time, Mohamed Morsi, though these latter activities are less relevant to this research. For the most part, I did not plan what I was going to do on any given day but rather sought to adapt my research to the unfolding events—events that were often profoundly overwhelming. Seeing a million people protesting and seeing military tanks in the streets of Cairo were experiences I had never had before and could hardly have planned around. Some days, I went directly to Tahrir; other days, I met friends first, and we went there together. In some instances, I planned to participate in specific rallies when I heard in advance about their route and if it was not too far from where I was staying. Other times, I simply found myself participating in a rally almost before I realized what was happening. On February 6, 2011, for example, I was visiting friends at an NGO that was helping to collect aid and organize legal aid for the protesters in Tahrir. After the meeting, but while I was still downtown on my way to Tahrir, I saw a rally of lawyers heading from the Egyptian Bar Association headquarters in Ramses Street / Abd El-Khalik Tharwat to Abdeen Square. Abdeen Square houses one of the presidential palaces. I spontaneously decided to join the rally, as many of my lawyer friends were also participating. In these rapidly changing and often unpredictable circumstances, it was difficult to keep up with writing ethnographic notes every day. Another complicating factor was the security situation. During the time I was able to participate in events, from February 4 to February 11, efforts to intimidate and attack protesters were still intense. I made an effort to walk away from all events empty-handed and to keep my minimal notes at home.

During this time pro-government media targeted Tahrir and protesters in Tahrir, labeling them as infiltrators and also emphasizing that many foreigners were in Tahrir. Mubarak's thugs arrested many journalists, especially foreigners, particularly in the first week before my arrival. I had to ensure that my wallet contained only an Egyptian ID and Egyptian money; I hid all my American IDs, such as my student ID and my driver's license, as well as any American money in a secured place in my parents' home (see also appendix 2 on my positionality).

Because of the security situation and because the events were so overwhelming and physically exhausting, I wrote only scattered notes, when it was possible. I was able to sit and revisit some of these short notes and expand them from memory in the few weeks after Mubarak's ousting. Some of these events were so memorable that I could not forget them, even when I wrote my notes in 2019.

Another critical methodological note is needed here specifically in relation to using *autoethnography*. As shown in the pages of this book, there were many instances in this research when I found it necessary to do autoethnography. Autoethnography is a specific methodological approach in anthropology whereby the researcher systematically analyzes their experience or biography and situates it in the larger cultural and political context in order to understand the latter (Bochner and Ellis 2006; Chang 2008; Denzin 2006; Ellis, Adams, and Bochner 2011; Ellis and Bochner 2000; Hayano 1979; Reed-Danahay 1997). As some proponents of autoethnography suggest, the method is a combination of autobiography and ethnography, and it is both a process and a product (Ellis, Adams, and Bochner 2011). Unlike traditional positivist anthropology, autoethnography is based on the assumption that the subject of the researcher is strongly present and should be acknowledged and examined. Not only that, but if an analysis of the researcher's experience is relevant to the research, why not study it as well? In simple terms, in autoethnography researchers are self-reflexive and constantly study themselves in addition to their subject matter, especially when they are part of the context they are studying. And this is not about the researcher's emotions but rather about locating their experience and biography within the relevant social and cultural context.

Because I was fortunate enough to be present for and participate in many of the crucial events of the revolution, I decided that it would enrich the research to draw on my own insights and experience of those events. For example, given my prior experiences in the field as a pro-democracy activist and human rights attorney in Egypt, it was impossible for this personal history not to shape my own experience and observations about how antiriot police in Tahrir developed strategies against protesters, as well as how the latter developed their own strategies in response. Also, before conducting this research, from 2000 to 2004, I worked in a human rights NGO that was hosting many antiwar and pro-democracy groups and coalitions, for whom it was difficult to meet elsewhere. My own experience of the place and these meetings was a crucial part of the story of place and space and coalition work under Mubarak. I was fortunate to be in these important places and undergo these important experiences. I thought it would be a big error to simply suppress these insights.[2]

Still, despite the richness of my observations, due to the overwhelming conditions while doing this research, I decided that I needed to conduct interviews to gather a more complete picture of Tahrir and the revolution, as I discuss in the following section.

INTERVIEWS

I conducted a total of eighty-two interviews for this research. Fifty interviews were conducted during my second research trip in 2012, and thirty-two were conducted in 2015.[3] In this section I present details about these two rounds of interviews, followed by a table that summarizes the demographics of my subjects.

Interviews in 2012

My 2012 interviews were based on snowball sampling. While I started with one or two identified activists, they simply introduced me to others and so on. I had only two criteria: I would (1) recruit interviewees using snowball sampling but also (2) try to include a diverse group of people in terms of gender, political experience, and class. All the interviews took place downtown in cafés, in the offices of political organizations or parties, or at activists' homes. Several young activists and researchers helped me with recruitment and were provided with an honorarium. Others volunteered to help without any honorarium. Although all interviews were structured, I was open and flexible to hear whatever information subjects wanted to share about Tahrir and their participation in and experience of the revolution. A complete list of the interview questions follows.

FIRST: GENERAL DEMOGRAPHIC INFORMATION

1. What is your name?
2. What is your age?
3. What gender do you identify as?
4. What is your occupation?
5. How do you see yourself in terms of class? Choose one of the following: working class, middle class, upper middle class, capitalist class. And tell me why you chose that.
6. Or, if you do not feel comfortable or have difficulty choosing among the above categories, please choose from the following options: You are economically barely surviving, you have a little extra income beyond surviving, or you have a lot of money beyond surviving.

SECOND: GENERAL QUESTIONS ABOUT ACTIVISM AND
PARTICIPATION IN THE REVOLUTION

1. Did you participate in any protest before the January 25, 2011, revolution? If so, which ones?
2. Did you consider yourself a political activist before the revolution? Why?
3. Describe to me what you generally did in the days from January 25 to February 11, 2011.
4. Do you have important stories that you do not mind sharing about these days? What are these?

THIRD: QUESTIONS ABOUT CLASSES IN THE REVOLUTION

1. Most analysts and media circles portray the revolution as initiated and led mainly by middle-class Egyptian youth (those who have iPhones and activists on social media). Do you think that this portrayal is accurate? Why or why not?
2. Do you remember the presence of trade unions and working-class protesters in Tahrir? Tell me more about that, if yes.

3. Did you learn that many workers' strikes took place in the last days of the revolution? Do you think these were important? Why or why not?
4. Many activists I talked to, including when I was in Tahrir, told me that many owners of small businesses and white-collar workers were in Tahrir and participated in the revolution. How do you explain that?
5. If all of these stories are true, how do you explain that blue-collar, white-collar, and small business owners / middle-class people all participated in the revolution?

FOURTH: QUESTIONS ABOUT TAHRIR

1. Did you participate in the famous sit-in in Tahrir Square from January 25 to February 11, 2011? (This section in the questions may be skipped if the subject did not participate, and they can answer only questions relevant to their experiences.)
2. If yes, describe to me your participation in these days.
3. In your opinion, why did protesters decide to hold a sit-in in Tahrir in the first place?
4. Describe the sit-in in terms of the organization of space.
5. Describe the sit-in in terms of social life and day and night activities and so on.
6. Did particular political movements and coalitions organize the sit-in? If yes, which ones?
7. From your observations and experience in the sit-in, how was the diversity of opinions managed in the sit-in?
8. In the media and according to many analysts, the Egyptian Revolution was referred to as the Tahrir revolution. Why is that, in your opinion?
9. Are there any specific reasons why Tahrir Square was geographically important?
10. After the revolution, activists kept coming back to Tahrir. Why is that?

FIFTH: QUESTIONS ABOUT THE REVOLUTION/DEMANDS AND VISION FOR THE STATE

1. In the revolution protesters raised a general slogan: "The people want the downfall of the regime." Do you remember the first time this slogan was raised?
2. Protesters tried to translate their general demands into another slogan: "Bread, freedom, and social justice." What does this mean?

3. Protesters also made a list of demands during the revolution. Do you remember these demands? Tell me some of them.
4. One of the key demands was to establish a democratic state, which is based on parliamentary democracy. Why is that?
5. Do you think that this demand is sufficient or may be seen as the cornerstone of the list of demands? Why or why not?
6. Do you remember any discussions in Tahrir and/or during the time of the revolution about the experience with or the failure of parliamentary democracy in Europe, arguing that it is not enough to raise this demand in the Egyptian Revolution? If this happened, tell us about these discussions.
7. Were you and/or others worried about the role of the Supreme Council of Armed Forces leading the transitional period in Egypt? Why?

LAST: FURTHER THOUGHTS ON WHAT HAPPENED DURING
THE REVOLUTION AFTER MUBARAK'S OUSTING

1. In your opinion, what has happened in the transitional period so far, in terms of factors that make you worry or feel assured about the future of democracy in Egypt?
2. Do you have any general comments you want to add about the revolution?

Interviews in 2015

By the time I started to think of these interviews, so much change had happened in Egypt, including the tragic events of the coup in 2013. I realized that I needed to include some reflections about these changes from actors, especially in relation to changes that took place after 2013 and how activists made sense of these changes. The interviews this time were semistructured. All the interviews in this phase were conducted by a research assistant in Egypt. All of them were conducted via email. My research assistant sent emails to many revolutionaries who participated in the January events, and only some responded. He sent reminders, and then others responded. The thirty-two activists interviewed in this phase varied in terms of class and gender. Unlike the interviews in 2012, these were all in a written format. A list of questions was sent, and interviewees were instructed to say whatever they wanted in response. There was only one criterion in the selection process: the respondent identified as a Januarist. This is a term many Egyptian activists use to refer to the revolution of January 25, 2011. But it may refer specifically not only to someone who participated in the January 25, 2011, revolution but also to someone who probably still upholds its ideals. The following is the list of questions sent to these Januarists.

1. How do you remember the January Revolution now?
2. How and what do you think about the idea of "the revolution's defeat"? Do you acknowledge the defeat in the first place? If yes, when exactly / what events did you acknowledge as the moment of defeat?
3. Which of these reflect your emotions the most now: bitterness, anger, sadness, disappointment, despair, some hope, or other emotions? Please name them.
4. What is the main impact of the January Revolution on your life/personality generally?
5. Do you see any changes, specifically in recent years, that make you think there is hope in reclaiming the revolution and/or hope for better social change? If so, why, and what are these?

Table App3.1 summarizes the demographics of the interviewees in the two rounds.

Table App3.1. Interviewee Demographics

Gender	Class*	Place	Age	Previous Political Experience	Participated in Tahrir?
ROUND 1 (JULY 12, 2012–JANUARY 8, 2013); N = 50					
23 women 27 men	10 WC 40 MC	29 in Cairo 4 in Giza 6 in Alexandria 6 in Mahalla 5 in Suez	11 aged 20–30 28 aged 31–40 7 aged 41–50 3 aged 51–60 1 aged 61–70	32 had prior protest experience; 18 had not protested before the revolution	33 participated; 17 did not participate
ROUND 2 (DECEMBER 16, 2015–JANUARY 7, 2016); N = 32					
15 women 17 men	12 WC 20 MC	28 in Cairo 3 in Alexandria 1 in Port Said	19 aged 20–30 13 aged 31–40	32 participated in the Egyptian Revolution in 2011	29 were in Tahrir in 2011; 3 did not participate in Tahrir but define themselves as Januarists

* Self-identified class of interviewee; WC = working class, MC = middle class.

I have conducted different types of documentary research for this book. Most of this research relates to protest history. The documents were newspapers, as well as leaflets, magazines, and the newsletters of political groups such as Kefaya. This included activists' diaries of activists. During my first research trip, I saved many newspapers with daily details about the uprising, and I collected leaflets distributed in Tahrir. I asked activist friends to share documents with me, especially PDFs of newsletters and magazines distributed in the few weeks after the uprising.

In addition to my own documentary work, I have relied on the work of others, especially the organized work of teams of researchers in Egypt on three specific issues: information about battles during the revolution, the popular committees, and demographic information about the martyrs and the injured during the revolution. For these issues, I have relied on the work of Daftar Ahwal, a data service center and research institute in Cairo.[4] I have used the data compiled by Daftar Ahwal, specifically demographic information about the martyrs and the injured during the revolution, and information about the battles and clashes during the uprising, especially on January 28, 2011. I have asked Daftar Ahwal to document news about the popular committees for me. As this documentation was conducted by the Daftar Ahwal center, I asked them to provide me with details about how the documentation was done. The following are three notes on the data collection with regard to the battles on January 28, 2011; the popular committees; and demographic information about the martyrs and the injured during the revolution.

Notes on Methodology and Information Evaluation for Battles Data Set

During this research project, we worked on producing a data set on battles and rallies in Cairo, Giza, and Alexandria during Gomaet al-Qhadab (Friday of Rage) on January 28, 2011. It includes very specific and accurate details on the events' location, time, path, participation, type of protest action, weapons and tools used, repression, human casualties, and damage. It includes 115 protest actions/events in the three centralized governorates, while one hundred acts of repression by the authorities were recorded.

The data sets mostly relied on sources from official documents and local human rights organizations for verification. Additionally, we used reports from widely spread local newspapers published by their own correspondents or through official statements. We could get a specific official number from judicial records for thirty-two events.

The data set was generated through the methodology of triangulation and data verification, as we depended on several sources for the same piece of information, and during this process we evaluated all information based on the following factors.

FACTORS OF INFORMATION EVALUATION

1. What type of incident was it, and when and where did it take place?
2. Which elements/parties intervened in the event?
3. How many details does the source contain?
4. To what extent does the main frame of the source's narrative match the truth (where *truth* means as verified by two other sources)?
5. How many contradictions and inaccuracies (compared to other documents) are present in the source?
6. How rational and logical is the source?
7. Is any or all of the information obsolete?

Regarding the spatial variable in Cairo, there were clashes and protests everywhere downtown around Tahrir Square. We merged the linked districts of Azbakiyya, Abdeen, Qasr El Nile, and Boulaq Abo al-Ela into one single region called "downtown districts." As a unit of analysis in this region, a new event represents a specific protest or violent action that had a particular governmental target or that happened through the varying participation of protesters or authorities. Therefore, we marked the attacks against the Egyptian Museum and the National Democratic Party headquarters, and also clashes in front of the headquarters of the Egyptian Radio and Television Union (Maspero) and the Ministry of Foreign Affairs, as separate events in multiple rows. On the other hand, all clashes around Abdel Moneim Riad Square, Qasr El Nile Bridge, Al Galaa Square, and Tahrir Square on this day were recorded as one single event because of their consistency.

Notes on Methodology and Information Evaluation
for Popular Committee Data Set

During this research project, we worked on producing a data set on popular committees during the eighteen days of the January Revolution. It includes around 152 Popular Committee Units with accurate details on their places, their formation, and associated instances of violence, as mentioned in the local daily newspapers.

Because of lack to access to systematic information on popular committees from official records or NGO documents, as they were informal entities established by local residents of neighborhoods in a decentralized way during a critical period of Egypt, we mainly used source material from three daily newspapers (one government-run and two independent): *Al-Ahram*, *Almasry Alyoum*, and *Shorouk News*. These widely circulated newspapers have their own active correspondents all over Egypt reporting on events everywhere. However, we cannot say this represents all popular committees in Egypt but only media reporting on popular committees. For example, it covers around 80 percent of all districts in Cairo but lower percentages in other governorates due to the centralization of information.

The data set was generated through the methodology of triangulation and data verification, as we depended on several sources for the same piece of information, and during this process we evaluated all information according to different factors.

FACTORS OF INFORMATION EVALUATION

1. What type of incident was it, and when and where did it take place?
2. Which elements/parties intervened in the event?
3. How many details does the source contain?
4. To what extent does the main frame of the source's narrative match the truth (where *truth* means as verified by two other sources)?
5. How many contradictions and inaccuracies (compared to other documents) are present in the source?
6. How rational and logical is the source?
7. Is any or all of the information obsolete?

As a unit of analysis, each row in the data set "Popular Committee Unit" represents a specific popular committee in a "consistent region" inside a governorate during the eighteen days. This "consistent region" can be a geographic region of one district, one subdistrict, or several subdistricts connected with the same demographic and local features. In Cairo city, most districts can be presented individually, and in some areas there are different "consistent regions" within the same district. In other governorates of the Nile delta and Upper Egypt, most cities or Marakez ("centers" that, in addition to villages, are governmental administrative units in Egypt's countryside, compared to police stations and districts in urban areas) can be presented only as one single unit because of their homogeneity.

Regarding the time variable, it represents the day of media reporting on a committee in the newspaper. It does not indicate the day when a specific popular committee was established. As understood from the context, in general, most committees were initially established between January 29 and 31 after prisons were broken into and police stations were burned.

Notes on Methodology and Information Evaluation
for Killings and Injuries Data Sets

During this research project, we worked on editing and producing two data sets of casualties (Killings and Injuries) during the eighteen days of the January Revolution. It includes very specific and accurate personal information with full names, date of birth, residency, and job. Using a first version of the data set of killings issued by Daftar Ahwal Data Research Center, we managed to adapt it to our perspective. However, we built a data set of injuries from scratch. The killings totaled 1,084 persons, while 1,072 injuries were collected and validated.

Both data sets—Killings and Injuries—mostly relied on documents from official authorities as a main source of verification. Of the total killings, 19.3 percent were authenticated by official documents, and 37.6 percent by official statements; the remainder were verified by NGOs. (In this case, "documents" refer to government and court documents, while "statements" refer to statements made by officials.) The injuries data set depended almost entirely (96.2 percent) on official documents from judicial cases, while the few remaining cases were verified by NGOs.

Both data sets were generated through the methodology of triangulation, as we depended on several sources for the same piece of information, and during this process we evaluated all information according to different factors.

FACTORS OF INFORMATION EVALUATION

1. What type of incident was it, and when and where did it take place?
2. Which elements/parties intervened in the event?
3. How many details does the source contain?
4. To what extent does the main frame of the source's narrative match the truth (where *truth* means as verified by two other sources)?
5. How many contradictions and inaccuracies (compared to other documents) are present in the source?
6. How rational and logical is the source?
7. Is any or all of the information obsolete?

Regarding the spatial variable, there was an information gap in the data set of injuries. We mainly used official documents of court cases in Cairo and Giza, such as the big case over the killing of protesters in which Mubarak and Habib El-Adly were involved; the cases with regard to the killing of protesters in front of police stations; and the Camel Battle case. So, we preferred to use descriptive statistics on Greater Cairo to pick up findings as this is more representative for the demographic and personal information of human casualties in the revolution. On the other hand, data from the killings data set covers all geographic regions in Egypt because we could access information without any limitations.

appendix four

Major Political Coalitions in Egypt, 2000–2010

In this appendix, I list all major political coalitions that existed in Egypt from 2000 to 2010. Most observers of Egypt know only a few of these coalitions, especially Kefaya and the National Association for Change, two important groups that led the pro-democracy movements in the few years prior to the revolution. But as shown in this book, especially in chapters 1 and 4, several political coalitions in Egypt provided inspiration and lessons to one another, and these coalitions contributed to creating consensus around political reform, a dominant vision that existed during the revolution. Understanding how these coalitions worked gives us a better sense of the many forms of collective actions that occurred in Egypt during the 2011 uprising.

Major Political Coalitions in Egypt, 2000–2010

Date of Formation (approx.)	Name of Coalition	Component Groups/Forces	Main Objectives	Status
2000	The Egyptian Committee for Defending the Prisoners of Conscience	Formed by leftists and Islamist lawyers and hosted by the Egyptian Bar Association and the Egyptian Press Syndicate	To defend prisoners of conscience in Egypt	Continues today, mainly hosted by the Egyptian Press Syndicate
September 2000	Egyptian Popular Committee in Solidarity with the Palestinian Intifada	Formed mainly by activists from the 1970s generation; also included members of these groups: Al-Karama Party (new Nasserist group), Egyptian Communist Party, Al Tagamoa Party (leftist), the Revolutionary Socialists, and the Muslim Brotherhood (MB)	To collect donations, food, and medical aid for Palestinians, as well as to protest against the Mubarak regime's complicity/biased role in the peace process	Divisions developed between reformist and more radical members; reemerged in April 2002 for a short period and again in 2009 after the siege of Gaza. No longer exists in practice.
August 2001	Coordinating Committee for Workers and Trade Union Rights	Started as an initiative by unionists and human rights NGOs working on labor issues; later joined by many parties and groups and other additional unionists	To assist trade unions and workers with labor rights/organizing issues; provides legal aid and awareness campaigns	Continues today

September 2001; first formal founding meeting on June 28, 2002	The Anti-Globalization Egyptian Group (AGEG)	Leftist and socialist organizations but also open to individual members	To mobilize against globalization and neoliberal policies in Egypt, particularly those negatively affecting workers, peasants, and the poor in Egypt. Organized a public conference opposing the visit of the World Bank president to Egypt on October 12, 2003,	Defunct
September 2001	Coalition against the War on Afghanistan	Impromptu coalition that included socialists, Nasserists, and other independent members	To mobilize people in the streets in opposition to the US war on Afghanistan	Defunct
December 2002	Egyptian Popular Campaign against the War, Imperialism, and Zionism	Founded by the Nasserist Party and also the Al-Karama Party, as well as socialists, mainly the Revolutionary Socialists, as well as the Muslim Brotherhood and the Egyptian Communist Party	To coordinate and organize efforts to support anticolonial and antiwar movements in the region. Organized an annual international conference in Cairo against the war for six years (2002–8).	Ended in 2008

(continued)

Major Political Coalitions in Egypt, 2000–2010 (*continued*)

Date of Formation (approx.)	Name of Coalition	Component Groups/Forces	Main Objectives	Status
January 2003	Campaign against the War on Iraq	Leftists (socialists, Nasserists, and others)	To mobilize people in the streets in opposition to the US war on Iraq. Developed as part of an international campaign (and regular conference in Cairo) against war and imperialism.	Faded after 2005
March 9, 2003	Movement for Independence of Universities (March 9 movement)	Mostly individuals, but many of them belonged to political forces and parties, mostly liberal and leftist	To defend universities against state control and expose corruption on campuses (sparked by Cairo University's administration appropriating a building for Gamal Mubarak's association, Al-Mostaqbal)	Continues today
January 4, 2004	Committee to Defend Pension Rights for the Retired	Mostly leftist lawyers and unionists but joined with workers, unions, and other groups	To save pensions and pension rights (due to the fact that the government under Mubarak had wasted most pension funds)	Now defunct but gave birth to a union of the retired, which was founded after the revolution

Founding meeting on March 13, 2004	20 March Movement for Change (named after the protest held the year before against the war on Iraq)	Mostly socialists from different groups but also open to individuals	To mobilize against despotism, dictatorship, poverty, and imperialism	Defunct
September 4, 2004	Kefaya (Enough), the Egyptian Movement for Change	Nasserists, socialists, and members in different political parties; also NGOs, with individuals from the Muslim Brotherhood	To mobilize around amending the constitution to allow free, multicandidate presidential elections, among other things	Active until the revolution (but became less visible after the formation of the National Association for Change in 2010)
September 2004	National Coalition for Change	Muslim Brotherhood and Revolutionary Socialists (RS), as well as members in the 20 March Movement for Change	To mobilize for democracy in Egypt, specifically, to end succession and amend the constitution. Organized some press conferences and protests.	Short-lived and generally ineffective; seen as largely dominated by the Muslim Brotherhood members, who outnumbered the Revolutionary Socialists
2005	Leftist Union	Many socialist organizations and parties in Egypt (mostly underground) such as the Egyptian Communist Party, the People's Party, and the Revolutionary Socialists; did *not* include the Al Tagamoa Party	To build a general socialist network (and, hopefully, a Socialist Party in the future); activities were limited to meetings and writing papers	Did not continue beyond 2005

(continued)

Major Political Coalitions in Egypt, 2000–2010 (*continued*)

Date of Formation (approx.)	Name of Coalition	Component Groups/Forces	Main Objectives	Status
2005	Workers for Change	Unionists, NGOs, and individuals	To establish a minimum wage in Egypt; change regulations on bonuses; enact laws about workplace health conditions, and laws related to health and social insurance for workers; criminalize child labor; and change laws related to labor organizing rights to make sure they meet international standards	Defunct
February 2005	Youth for Change	Youth from different parties such as the Nasserist Party, Ghad Party, Al-Karama Party, the Revolutionary Socialists, and also the Wasat Party, the Egyptian Islamic Labour Party, and independent youth	Started as part of Kefaya but split off when youth wanted to be more flexible with organizing activities. Works mostly for the same goals as Kefaya but on campuses and in the streets.	Now defunct but gave birth to many later youth groups such as the April 6 Youth Movement and others

(continued)

June 2005	Journalists for Change	Members of press syndicates from different parties, but mostly members of Kefaya	To end emergency status in Egypt and release political prisoners; also to change press laws in Egypt to make sure journalists are not jailed for their writings	Defunct
June 2005	Writers and Artists for Change	Artists, writers, and public intellectuals, some independent and some belonging to parties	To mobilize for democratic change in Egypt and also to defend the rights of artists who died in Banī Suwayf (a theater that was burned in 2005). Organized a number of protests in downtown Cairo, particularly Talaat Harb Square.	Defunct
2005	Engineers for Change	Engineers, mostly members of Kefaya	To mobilize for the independence of the Engineers Syndicates from the control of the state, and also mobilize for democracy in Egypt	Defunct
June 29, 2005	Lawyers for Change	Lawyers, especially members of Kefaya	To mobilize for democracy and liberties in Egypt, including rights to organize and personal freedoms, and also to end emergency status	Defunct

Major Political Coalitions in Egypt, 2000–2010 (continued)

Date of Formation (approx.)	Name of Coalition	Component Groups/Forces	Main Objectives	Status
July 30, 2005	Students for Change	Student members of Kefaya and political parties	To end Mubarak's rule and stop succession in Egypt, end security control of campuses and expand free education to all, end emergency status, and establish independent universities	Defunct
April 2006	Egyptians against Religious Discrimination	Founded by two hundred Egyptian individuals—mostly public intellectuals, writers, academics, and activists—many of whom are members of various parties, groups, and associations	To defend citizens and citizenship rights, especially those of minorities facing religious discrimination	Continues today
August 2006	Leftist Coalition	Many socialist organizations and parties in Egypt (mostly underground) such as the Egyptian Communist Party, the People's Party and the Revolutionary Socialists; did include Al Tagamoa Party	To build a network of socialist groups in Egypt to work together around issues of poverty and social justice; activities were limited to meetings and writing papers	Did not continue

| December 28, 2006 | Front to Defend Peasants (Peasants Strife Campaign) | Political parties, NGOs, and leaders of farmers movements | To support the struggle of peasants in Egypt, end peasants' debt in Egypt, and combat the negative implication of law number 96 of 1992 (the purpose of this law was to undo the policy of land appropriations and rent laws for poor peasants set since Nasser in 1952, which means more privatization of agriculture, seen as more bias for landlords and old feudalists in Egypt) | Defunct |
| 2007 | Doctors without Rights | Individual doctors and activists, especially in the doctors syndicates, and doctors who are members of political parties | To apply special laws for underpaid doctors who work in the government, increase bonuses related to the conditions of doctors' work, and improve the health care budget in Egypt | Continues today (and gave birth to Doctors of Tahrir, an entity that assisted the injured in Tahrir during the revolution and in the transitional period) |

(continued)

Major Political Coalitions in Egypt, 2000–2010 (*continued*)

Date of Formation (approx.)	Name of Coalition	Component Groups/Forces	Main Objectives	Status
February 19, 2008	Tadamon (Solidarity)	Revolutionary Socialists, unionists, and some members of NGOs	To support social movements in Egypt, especially labor movements and economic and social justice–based movements	Did not continue, but there were some attempts to revive it in 2009
May 2008	National Committee to Defend Egypt's Wealth	Mostly individuals but members of political parties and other groups too	To organize campaigns against exporting gas to Israel, to end and/or limit monopolies in Egypt, and also to organize campaigns against the government wasting natural resources in Egypt	Unclear when it ended but probably gave birth to a similar group after the revolution that aimed to get back money stolen by Mubarak officials
September 21, 2008	Egyptian Movement for Democracy (Shorakaa; Partners)	Individuals and NGOs	To make constitutional amendments to Article 76 (facilitating Gamal Mubarak's succession) and limit presidential terms to two	Defunct
May 22, 2009	Popular Preparatory Commission for Labor	Revolutionary Socialists, unionists, and some members of NGOs	To assist workers in Egypt to unionize, to launch a campaign to enact a minimum wage law in Egypt, to stop privatization, and to end corporate monopolies in Egypt and/or nationalize these	Ended before the revolution

October 2009	Egyptian Campaign against Succession	Members from different political parties and NGOs	To campaign against the succession of Gamal Mubarak to his father's position; involved political, constitutional, media, and legal fronts, as well as raising awareness about the issue	Ended with the revolution
December 8, 2009	Egyptian Campaign to Boycott Gas Companies	Open to individuals and political parties and groups	To boycott the natural gas company in Egypt (through not paying monthly gas bills) to protest overpricing and also to stop gas exports to Israel	Defunct
January 9, 2010	Egyptian Campaign to Combat the Wall of Shame	Individuals and groups from different parties	To protest against the building of an underground steel wall between Egypt and Gaza and to organize campaigns to collect donations for Palestinians	Defunct

(continued)

Major Political Coalitions in Egypt, 2000–2010 (continued)

Date of Formation (approx.)	Name of Coalition	Component Groups/Forces	Main Objectives	Status
March 2, 2010	National Association for Change	Almost all opposition political parties in Egypt, with NGOs and political groups from socialists to Islamic groups. Was the main platform for youth groups and demands in the revolution. Collected over a million signatures to endorse demands. Chaired by Mohamed ElBaradei.	To end emergency status and demand judicial supervision of elections, as well as constitutional amendments	Continues today and played an important role in the revolution
June 2010	Democratic Popular Movement for Change (Hashd)	Mostly leftist individuals and organizations but coordinated mainly by the Revolutionary Socialists	To mobilize the masses for change in Egypt and to build a radical revolutionary alternative in Egypt	Continues today but is largely ineffective

notes

The epigraph to this book is by Sheikh Abd Rabbih al-Ta'ih, a fictional character who appears in two late works (*Echoes of an Autobiography* and the *Final Dreams*) by the Egyptian Nobel laureate in literature Naguib Mahfouz. The character's name can be translated literally as "the Wandering Servant of His Lord," which adds more than a touch of irony to his existentialist aphorisms.

All translations from Arabic sources are my own unless otherwise noted.

INTRODUCTION. REVOLUTION AS LIVED CONTINGENCY

1 Throughout the book I use the terms *popular committees* and *neighborhood committees* interchangeably.
2 Throughout the book I use "Egyptian Revolution" and "January Revolution" interchangeably.
3 Ahdaf Soueif (2012, 10) and Sherine Hafez (2019, 12) prefer to use the Arabic word *midan* rather than *square*. Soueif, for example, states, "I prefer the Arabic word, 'midan,' because, like 'piazza,' it does not tie you down to a shape but describes an open urban space in central position in a city, and the space we call Midan el-Tahrir, the central point of greater Cairo, is not a square or a circle but more like a massive curved rectangle covering about 45,000 square meters and connecting Downtown and older Cairo to the east" (10).
4 See also Youssef El Chazli's important 2016 article, "A Geography of Revolt in Alexandria, Egypt's Second Capital." The names of all interviewees in this book who reside in Egypt have been anonymized to protect their identity. Real names have been used for interviewees who reside outside Egypt. Throughout the book, all published materials by activists and revolutionary actors in Egypt are referenced using their real names.

5 This is according to Egypt's Central Agency for Public Mobilization and Statistics in 2012 (see *Ahram Online* 2012a). Another category Egyptian experts and demographers use is Greater Cairo, which includes all cities in the Cairo Governorate and many key cities in the Qalyubia and Giza Governorates, such as Shubra El Kheima, Obour, 6th of October City, and Sheikh Zayed City, among others. The total population in Greater Cairo is about twenty million.

6 The military position was ambiguous before that date. For example, on the afternoon of February 2, 2011, the spokesperson of the SCAF, General Ismail Othman, asked protesters, among other things, to "go back to their homes, as their demands are heard" (*Shorouk News* 2011a). This statement implied that the SCAF approved of Mubarak's announcement to continue his term and his pledge not to run again. General Othman's request did not mean the SCAF sided with the revolting protesters; it merely halted protesters' demands of ousting Mubarak.

7 Amy Holmes (2012) invoked the phrase in an article title: "There Are Weeks When Decades Happen." That article, I believe, is one of the most important pieces on Egypt's famous eighteen days, alongside Mona El-Ghobashy's (2011) "The Praxis of the Egyptian Revolution."

8 Historian Sherene Seikaly (2019, 1686) suggests that subjectivities are intertwined with temporalities all the time. In a vivid account of her great-grandfather, a Palestinian doctor who lived under both the British Mandate and the Anglo-Egyptian administration of Sudan, Seikaly demonstrates that her grandfather inhabited a complex and contradictory temporality (of deferral and permanent abeyance) due to his entanglement in colonial conditions (1684). This has been very useful in my research, as I argue that revolutionary contingency is complex and invokes the role of subjects in similar ways.

9 See Nadine Naber's (2021) very rich account of the role of mothers during the revolution.

10 I owe this term to Egyptian Canadian sociologist Rachad Antonius in a long thread of Facebook communication with him and others. Many esteemed colleagues across many places in the United States, Europe, and the Middle East participated in the conversation. The list is long, but I am thankful to them as well.

11 The idea of radical and/or uncalculated unbounding resonates with the notion of high-risk activism in social movement literature. See, for example, McAdam (1986); Pichardo Almanzar and Herring (2004); and Taylor and Raeburn (1995). Also, see especially the recent important work of Rachel Einwohner (2022) about resistance activism in three Jewish ghettos in Europe (Warsaw, Vilna, and Łódź) during the Holocaust.

While participating in a revolution certainly could be conceived as high-risk activism, I believe that this is not simply due to the nature of the risk involved. In addition, participation in a revolution is entangled mainly with ideas of regime change, freedom, and/or systematic social justice.

12 The idea of radical or uncalculated unbounding I propose could be misunderstood to mean that actors lose their agency when they follow their mission to win freedom. Indeed, many interlocutors used the notion of the revolution as enchantment, as a mythical mission for freedom, as a siren song, or as Al-Naddaha. Al-Naddaha (the caller) refers to a myth of a beautiful woman who seduces people in Egypt's countryside until they lose their mind or disappear. Actors in a revolutionary situation do confront difficult and risky decisions, which sometimes involve life and death, and in this way the revolution does constitute a dangerous temptation. But in my analysis throughout this book, I argue that Egyptian revolutionary actors do not lose their agency, even when they emphasize that they were enchanted by the revolution's call and had limited and risky choices to make.

13 On the Muslim Brotherhood, see the important work of Khalil Al-Anani (2016) and Abdullah Al-Arian (2014). And on the Egyptian military, see the important work of Zeinab Abul-Maged (2017); Hazem Kandil's (2014) excellent historicization of the makeup of the ruling security regime in Egypt from Nasser to the 2011 revolution (presidential power, the military, and the security apparatus); and Zoltan Barany's (2016, 16–43) valuable analysis of the internal and external factors that affect how armies respond to uprisings.

14 Recently, Bayat (2021, 395) made it clear that his notion of revolutionary movement is not identical to what we know in the literature as a revolutionary situation. While I overall disagree with his assessment about the case of the revolutionary situation in Egypt, I remain indebted to his important analysis, which helped me think through many parts of this research.

15 Holmes also coined an interesting if problematic term (*coup from below*), which I do not agree with. Perhaps it is more accurate to name what happened between June 30 and July 3, 2013, as a popularly supported coup.

16 With the exception of Achcar, who provides a thick analysis of counterrevolution, these respected scholars do not.

17 Ash coined the term *refolution* in two essays about the revolutions in Hungary and Poland, published in the *New York Review of Books* in 1989 (Ash 1989a, 1989b). In the first piece, Ash states, "But what is happening just now is a singular mixture of both reform and revolution: a 'revorm,' if you will, or perhaps a 'refolution.' There is, in both places, a strong and essential element of voluntary, deliberate reform led by an enlightened minority (but only a minority) in the still ruling Communist parties, and, in the Polish case, at the top of the military and the police. Their advance consists of an unprecedented retreat: undertaking to share power, and even—*mirabile dictu*—talk of giving it up altogether if they lose an election."

18 It is important to acknowledge that this outcome is not atypical in many revolutions; even some classic revolutions started with a "moderate" phase when forces of the old regime and the elite came to power.

19 In chapters 5 and 6, I propose that we should problematize the notion of restorations and argue against conflating these terms: seeking to restore the state prior to revolution, seeking to undo the revolution, making adjustments to keep the status quo, or seeking to create a new status quo. I propose a temporally disaggregated account of counterrevolution in Egypt, in which I demonstrate how counterrevolutions had different, shifting goals through the course of the revolution. I also demonstrate that after the coup in 2013, the counterrevolution led by the military in Egypt did not have the goal of bringing back the Mubarak regime but expanding the military rule.

20 Colin Beck rightly suggests that revolution is a complex phenomenon that requires combining many levels of analysis. According to Beck, we need to develop "a meta-framework for revolutionary theory that combines multiple levels of analysis, multiple units of analysis, and their interactions," and this requires a "multidimensional social science of revolution" (2014, 197).

21 I am inspired in this distinction by Rod Aya's (1979) work and their distinction between different modes of revolutions and collective violence.

CHAPTER ONE. PRELUDE TO REVOLUTIONARY POSSIBILITIES

1 I explain this further in chapter 5.

2 In 1977 the Bread Uprising took place, also called the Thieves Uprising by the regime of Anwar Sadat (see Montaser 2013).

3 It was not only the AUC that protested. However, the AUC protest was crucial to the dynamics of protest on Tahrir, because the (now old) AUC campus was located right on Tahrir.

4 Interview with a male activist who was a member of Youth for Change, then of Youth for Justice and Freedom, then a founding member of the Revolution Youth Coalition, November 10, 2012.

5 This is based on my field notes.

6 The campaign name was taken from a song in *Al-asfour* (The sparrow), an important political movie produced in 1972 and directed by Youssef Chahine. The film focuses on a family dominated by a patriarch that ends up being fragmented and subjected to violence and abuse. The story has been interpreted as an allegory of the Egyptian people under Gamal Abdel Nasser, captured like a "sparrow in a cage."

7 While these efforts were focused in urban areas, spatial battles also played out in rural areas. Rural villagers, for example, attempted to block specific roads to protest the fact that many Egyptian villages still lack tunnels or bridges to cross highways, resulting in many road-related deaths every year.

8 For more details about the history of the Egyptian working-class struggle, see Omar Said and Mostafa Bassiouny's 2008 pamphlet *Rāyāt al-iḍrāb fī samāʾ miṣr* [Banners of strikes in the Egyptian sky].

9   I do not discuss labor strikes as a repertoire in detail here. But I aim to show the larger context of the rise of the labor movement at the time. Also, in this context, the labor movement relied heavily on the sit-in as a repertoire, and it was a very common practice in actions near the cabinet and in downtown Cairo, especially in the headquarters of the Egyptian Trade Union Federation.

10   Shukrallah also revealed to me in a long conversation (June 28, 2013) that he was mistaken about his high skepticism toward these small protests that took place in the window from 2002 to 2003. He suggested that these protests provided some symbolic victories for the opposition at the time but also taught important lessons about maneuvering police repression on streets. They also gave activists confidence and boosted their bravery in claiming some control over public space and in some sense assisted in paving the way to the revolution in 2011.

11   The phrase *million-person protest* was virtually unheard of until the Egyptian Revolution in 2011. The phenomena of million-person protests are discussed in chapters 5 and 6 in this book. In many Egyptians' memories, Tahrir and other main squares in Egypt witnessed massive rallies at the funerals of Gamal Abdel Nasser and the singer Umm Kulthum. Umm Kulthum's funeral and the funerals of notable politicians such as Mostafa Al-Nahhas took place in Omar Makram Mosque, which is located in Tahrir.

12   The pedestal at the center of Tahrir Square has a storied history. Originally, it was meant to be the base of a statue of Khedive Ismail, which was never installed. After the 1952 coup d'état that made Egypt a republic and eventually led to Nasser's presidency, there was talk of installing a statue of Nasser on the pedestal. Then Nasser's successor, President Sadat, removed the pedestal.

13   The works of both Sheikh Imam (a composer and singer) and Ahmed Fou'ad Negm (a poet) were very important at the time and have since become significant in Egypt's contemporary protest history. The two artists were present in 1972 and visited student protesters in the square. They were heroes of resistance movements throughout the 1970s and beyond, including the 2011 revolution. Their songs were banned in Egypt throughout the 1970s and 1980s. See also Colla (2020).

14   The song is available on YouTube (see Nota Media 2020). The War of Attrition refers to a period of mutual attacks between Egypt and Israel that took place from 1969 to 1970, between the Six-Day War of 1967 and the 1973 war.

15   In my book published in Arabic in 2001, *Torture in Egypt Is a Judicial Reality*, I analyzed 1,124 civil compensation lawsuits for torture victims in 1981–99. I found that out of the 1,124 cases, 1,117 occurred during arbitrary detention under emergency law. It was during this period that political torture became de rigueur in Egypt, leading several national and international human rights groups to conclude that torture in Egypt was now systematic.

16 The idea that admission to the police academy in Egypt requires paying a bribe to some officials has been pervasive, especially under Mubarak. In 2012 Ministry of the Interior officials implicitly admitted that the practice of offering bribes has existed and urged the public "not to try to pay a bribe" before admission. See the relevant report in *Almasry Alyoum* (H. Hussein 2012). Security surveys before admission have also been an informal rule, whereby nobody would be admitted to the police academy if they had family members who happened to be active in any opposition, or perhaps even any political circles broadly. This was the case under Mubarak. Recently, after the expansion of military rule under Abdel Fattah el-Sisi, it seems that security checks have increased. The goal is not only to reject any political candidates but also to ensure complete loyalty to the regime. This also goes for applicants to the prosecutors' offices (many of whom would be judges in the future).

17 The plainclothes police either are actually from the security state intelligence service or are informants and thugs hired by the police, or even soldiers in the Central Security Forces (Riot Police), but they were instructed to wear civilian clothes and spread among protesters before attacking them or arresting them or helping to disperse the protest by force later. See Baheyya (2005) for a discussion of the use of plainclothes police in 2005. See also the 2005 statement by Joe Stork of Human Rights Watch. Even though the phenomenon is older, I think that it only caught the attention of analysts in 2005 due to the rise of Kefaya activists and protests.

Regarding the rise of patterned sexual violence by the police against female protesters since 2005, see also Amar (2011), Egyptian Center for Women's Rights (2005), and Zaltzman (2012).

18 To my knowledge, very few scholars have paid attention to the role of social media before the revolution (Ghannam 2011; Hirschkind 2011; Lim 2012).

19 I build here on the work of Merlyna Lim, who argues that we should conceive of social media as both a *tool* and a *space* and that the relationship between social media and protest in Egypt should not be seen as only technological but sociopolitical (2012, 234).

20 Of course, activist use of social media during the revolution is a complex topic. The drawbacks of digital activism are not limited to the rise and expanded use of digital repression, which intensified after the revolution (see chapter 6). Many analysts highlighted, correctly, that while social media may have contributed to the revolution in many positive ways, it also created global spectacularity, which entailed racialized and orientalist representations. Several scholars have demonstrated, for example, how Western scholarship emphasized the surprising fact that Arabs used social media (and carried iPhones, etc.) "just like us" and exaggerated the role of Facebook or Twitter in the uprisings (Abul-Magd 2012; Salvatore 2013).

21 Compare this opening to what happened in the aftermath of 2013 and the rise of the phenomenon of digital repression. I discuss this further in chapter 6.

22 Egypt had been on the International Labor Organization blacklist for decades before the January 2011 revolution due to the government's restrictions on labor union freedoms. The listing was lifted briefly after the revolution but was reinstated in 2013 (see El-Fiqi 2013).

CHAPTER TWO. PEAK OF REVOLUTIONARY POSSIBILITIES

1 One important detail is needed here. Tahrir Square, known as Ismailia Square at the time, and many parts of downtown Cairo were designed by Georges-Eugène Haussmann (1809–91). Haussmann was known for his massive urban renewal program in Paris. He was commissioned by Emperor Napoleon III. In a sense, the program can be described as counterrevolutionary, as it was meant to widen Paris's streets; wide boulevards would ensure that soldiers would have easy access to all the corners of the city. Ironically, this "modernized/counterrevolutionary " design of Tahrir worked in protesters' favor during the uprising in 2011, when they surprised Central Security Forces from different directions at around the same time.

2 For the purposes of clarity, I differentiate here between clashes and battles. Clashes are shorter, less intense confrontations, involving less violence. Examples of these are the police blocking roads with troops of Central Security Forces and the use of sticks and batons, and protesters fighting back. Battles, in contrast, involve the police attempting to disperse protesters by using heavier methods, such as water cannons, rubber bullets, and live ammunition, while at the same time the protesters continue to persist and fight back.

3 For the sequence of the confrontations in this battle, see video footage at 003superman 2011 and *Almasry Alyoum* 2011b.

4 Important accounts of the events of January 28 and violence in the Egyptian Revolution appear in Holmes (2012) and El-Ghobashy (2011); see also the compelling analysis of unarmed collective violence in chapter 2 of Ketchley (2017a).

5 It is important not to conflate the following terms regarding the police apparatus during the Egyptian Revolution: *police apparatus defeat, police withdrawal,* and *police apparatus collapse.* It is most accurate to say that the police apparatus was defeated on January 28, 2011, and this defeat was a significant reason for the police withdrawal from the streets and from many police stations. To suggest that the police apparatus collapsed during the revolution is an exaggeration. Indeed, because the police apparatus did not collapse, it was easier for the transitional administrations and the counterrevolutionary regime of the military to reorganize for repression.

6 According to a statement released by Wael Ghoneim (see Fayed 2011), one of the founders of the page, the page had reached 1 million members (or "likes") by March 8, 2011.

7 Notably, books began to appear with the words *Twitter* and *Tahrir* in the title only months after the revolution; the most important of these was *Tweets from Tahrir*, edited by Alex Nunns and Nadia Idle (2011).

8 Egyptian protesters themselves did not use the language of *occupation* (given the term's loaded historical meanings within the region) but described the extended staging of protest in Tahrir using the Arabic word اعتصام. (i'tiṣām) best translated as "sit-in." Throughout this book I use the terms *Tahrir camp* and *Tahrir sit-in* interchangeably.

9 Tahrir Square and Talaat Harb Square are connected.

10 One of the best accounts of the RYC is Latif (2022).

11 The National Association for Change is a group that evolved from Kefaya. Kefaya did not disappear from politics until the revolution and its aftermath. But the National Association for Change was a broader coalition that did not include only leftists (Nasserists and Marxists in the case in Kefaya); it included many liberals and also Islamists.

12 The coalition started with five groups, and then a sixth group joined: Al-Karama (Dignity) Party, a Nasserist political group.

13 In 2013, after the events of the coup, the military regime in Egypt targeted many of these apartments and ordered the implementation of rigid security requirements to prevent activists from renting these places. The regime also closed many cafés in downtown Cairo, near Tahrir, to prevent meetings of activists in these cafés.

14 Here I agree with anthropologist Hanan Sabea (2013), who suggests that one cannot separate the ordinary from the extraordinary in Tahrir during these days.

15 The name does not have any connection to Mubarak's family. It was named after a human rights attorney who died young after launching many human rights initiatives, especially in the field of legal aid for human rights victims.

16 One day before my arrival in Tahrir Square on February 4, 2011, the HMLC was stormed by forces from the Military Intelligence and Reconnaissance Administration and State Security Intelligence, as well as a group of Mubarak supporters. They arrested the executive director of the HMLC and two other researchers who worked for Amnesty International. The authorities confiscated many things in the office, including blankets, medicine, and food, as well as computers and office supplies.

17 This distribution site was a Hardee's fast-food restaurant, at the corner where Mohamed Mahmoud Street reaches Tahrir Square. After the restaurant was burned on January 28, its main space was used by protesters as a key location for food storage, and its bathroom was used by female protesters.

18 The RYC's stage was mainly financed by Mamdouh Hamza, a civil engineer and businessman critical of Mubarak. Some businesspeople, especially those who suffered from the monopoly of Gamal Mubarak's networks, participated in the revolution and contributed donations to assist the organization in Tahrir.

19 For footage of this incident, see Al Jazeera 2011b.

20 Other messengers were Amre Moussa, former secretary-general of the Arab League, and Ahmed Kamal Abu Al-Magd, a former minister from Gamal Abdel Nasser's time. Abu Al-Magd, along with some other intellectuals and elites, formed what is called the "committee of the wise," which sought to act as an arbiter between the regime and the protesters. The committee was not effective.

21 For the negotiations, see *Al-Ahram* 2011a.

22 For Suleiman's talks with the opposition, see Al-Wafd TV 2011. For a statement by Suleiman about his mandate from Mubarak to talk with the opposition, see calltoAllah1 2011.

23 That the regime targeted Tahrir and its youth in an attempt to isolate them and then invited some of the youth to the talks with Suleiman needs an explanation. My guess is that this was simply a tactical move to sow division among the youth. The goal was to present the negotiators as good citizens and those who refused to negotiate as troublemakers. See Abdel Rahman Youssef's (2011, 142–48) account of the meeting and the marginalization.

24 Jeffrey Alexander (2011) created a cultural coding analysis about how the media constructed Tahrir and how Tahrir was seen compared to the regime.

25 For footage, see Mubarak 2011.

26 To my knowledge, few scholars have given much attention to the question of barricades in the Egyptian Revolution, the most notable exception being El-Ghobashy (2011); see also Naguib (2011).

27 Another common confusion in media coverage about Tahrir and the revolution is conflating the rallies/marches with the camp in Tahrir. Although the rallies and the camp were connected, as the rallies fed the camp with sheer numbers, most media coverage failed to distinguish between these two components of the revolutionary repertoire.

28 I use *the Tahrir repertoire* and *the revolutionary repertoire* interchangeably.

CHAPTER THREE. SOVEREIGNTY IN THE STREET

1 This perception took months to change. Eventually, police personnel were able to "restore" their image and resume their work in Egypt. For months after the revolution, there was a discourse in Egypt about the problem of bringing back security and the return of the police. This was connected to the rule of the Supreme Council of Armed Forces (SCAF) and the pseudosecurity

reform in Egypt. The discourse about the need for security was used against pro-democracy protesters during the transitional period. Neither the SCAF nor Mohamed Morsi was interested in real reform of Egypt's security apparatus, only in supporting the restructuring of the apparatus and using this against their opponents.

2 The primary focus is on the strikes and their effects leading up to February 11. Also, in addition to the four other modes of actions just listed, there were some scattered and small protests in southern Egypt.

3 Some revolutionary actors suggest that this was all part of a Ministry of the Interior plan to combat the protests, with the goal being to scare people and make them end the protests and go home. Some police generals confirmed this to be the case (see *Shorouk News* 2011b). For footage of the jails and people escaping, see Hima zamalek 2011.

4 See, for example, the video footage in True Egypt 2011.

5 *Shorouk News* 2011a.

6 *Al-Ahram*, January 31, 2011; and *Shorouk News*, February 2, 2011.

7 *Al-Ahram*, January 31, 2011.

8 *Shorouk News*, February 2, 2011; *Almasry Alyoum*, January 31, 2011; and *Almasry Alyoum*, February 1, 2011.

9 *Al-Ahram*, February 1, 2011; and *Almasry Alyoum*, January 31, 2011.

10 See the blog *Popular Committees for the Defense of the Egyptian Revolution*, accessed June 26, 2023, https://leganthawrya.blogspot.com/. Also, for a discussion of the emergence and role of popular committees, see Mossallam (2011).

11 Adel Soliman, a police general, suggested that the return of the committees was dangerous because policing should be the exclusive job of the police and that members of such committees abuse their power and can act like criminals and militia (W. Ramadan 2011).

12 For a particularly good discussion of the committees and the transformation of some into NGOs, see El-Meehy (2012).

13 The irony was that the military was on the streets doing this job as a coercive power, but most protesters did not see it this way, myself included.

14 Published on Facebook on September 2, 2014, referenced here with permission.

15 To use some important historical analogies—without violating the historical specificities—to explain the nature of these committees, one can argue that the popular committees in the Egyptian Revolution were perhaps as powerful as, if not more powerful than, the Committees of Vigilance during the Paris Commune in 1871, but they were less powerful than the Soviets in the Russian Revolution in 1917, as explained and theorized by Trotsky.

In his analysis of the Paris Commune, Roger Gould interrogates the role of the Committees of Vigilance as different types of organizing. Gould proposes that these committees had the "dual purpose of safeguarding the republic and organizing the defense of the capital against the Prussian army" (1995, 141). Gould also suggests that the Committees of Vigilance, in their role of protecting Paris, saw themselves as making the "base of the democratic republic" (141).

The popular committees in Egypt were similar to the *komitehs*, armed security groups that formed spontaneously during the 1979 Iranian Revolution and deployed in neighborhoods to watch these and keep out regime thugs (see Zahedi 2019).

16 Ann Stoler (2006) presents a useful discussion on the role of contingency in relation to the United States' degrees of practicing an imperial role during the so-called war on terror.

17 The protesters had established a temporary jail in the Tahrir subway stop for a few days in the aftermath of January 28, but as these temporary jails were difficult to sustain, Tahrir protesters ended up handing their detainees—intruders and thugs who attacked the square, including intelligence officers and informants as well as police personnel they arrested—over to the military.

18 The most notable unsuccessful attempt was an attack on the Ministry of the Interior near Tahrir on January 29 and 30, 2011. Military snipers shot at activists, and the military began to guard the ministry afterward.

19 I also participated in another action on February 11, 2011, the day Mubarak was ousted. On that day, I went with a friend to Orouba Palace, the presidential palace in the Heliopolis area, in response to a call for escalation that came from revolutionaries. When I arrived around 2:00 p.m., I saw some small configurations of republican guards and the military guarding the gates of the palace. I estimated that the protesters numbered at least ten thousand. I even saw families protesting with their kids. Around 4:30 p.m., I witnessed a helicopter leaving the palace. I guessed later that it could have been the helicopter carrying Mubarak and his family to his residence in Sharm el-Sheikh. Less than an hour after I witnessed this, it was announced that Mubarak had stepped down, and a transfer of power to the military had taken place. At the time I doubted that this group of protesters was willing to storm the palace, at least if Mubarak did not step down that day, because many of the participants were families and kids. Besides, the palace was guarded by the military.

CHAPTER FOUR. THE TWO SOULS OF THE EGYPTIAN REVOLUTION

Epigraph: Essam, who currently lives in exile, has become known as the singer of the revolution. This is part of a song he composed and sang in Tahrir during the uprising.

1 For example, protesters expanded the sit-in to Qasr El Eyni Street on February 7 and occupied the area in front of the People's Assembly (the parliament) and the cabinet's headquarters. They did not, however, try to

occupy the buildings themselves, an important detail that itself is worth studying in regard to whether or not protesters were interested in seizing power.

2 Sioufi, an artist, was one of the interviewees for this book. His apartment hosted many activists and international media, which led some reporters and analysts to describe his home as the headquarters of the uprising or to describe him personally as the "guru" or the "watchdog" of the revolution (see, for example, Cohen 2011; Oehmke 2011; and Worth 2011).

3 I borrow this term from Anne Alexander. See Alexander (2011) and Alexander and Bassiouny (2014). But as discussed in the introduction, I intentionally use a modified version: two souls of the revolution.

4 For one of the best accounts on the history of coalitions and their developments leading up to the revolution, see chapter 5 of Abdelrahman (2014).

5 For more on Kefaya, see also Clarke (2011); Onodera (2009); Oweidat et al. (2008); and Shorbagy (2007a, 2007b). See also *Washington Post* (2005).

6 Because the MB has been an underground organization, it is difficult to determine its exact number of members before the revolution. Estimates are that the group had no fewer than 200,000–300,000 members in 2004. Compare this, for example, with the Revolutionary Socialists, also an underground organization, who numbered only a few hundred members at the time. Some reports show that the MB had no fewer than half a million members after the revolution, in 2013 (see Kingsley 2013).

7 For more about the NAFC, see Carnegie Endowment for International Peace (2010); and Hazzard (2010).

8 For more on the tension and the relation between the MB and the NAFC, see Abdel Aziz (2010) and Hediya (2010).

9 For an archived copy of this statement, see Al-Jamʿiyya Al-Waṭaniyya li-'l-Taghyīr (National Association for Change) 2010.

10 For example, only months before the revolution, an IMF report suggested that Egypt's economic performance was better than expected (International Monetary Fund 2010).

11 There are no documented statistics about labor strikes during the revolution, but labor organizers I spoke to estimated that there were at least 1,500 industrial actions in February 2011 alone (also mentioned in el-Hamalawy 2011a). Despite joining the revolution late, workers had high hopes and protested as an organized group not only in the last few days of the revolution but also after the ousting of Mubarak. Indeed, as a result of their actions, one of the first actions of the Supreme Council of Armed Forces (SCAF) was to issue a law banning strikes.

12 All of the fifty interviewees said they were present in Tahrir Square in various ways, such as going to the square regularly, without necessarily being part of the daily sit-in or sleeping in Tahrir.

13 The Justice and Freedom Movement preceded and should not be confused with the Freedom and Justice Party of the MB, which was banned in 2013 after the military coup.

14 Ironically, during the later transitional period, the military used the museum as a center for detaining and torturing activists, most notably in March 2011.

15 The vast expansion of the military's involvement in most aspects of social life in Egypt, especially in the aftermath of the coup in 2013 and beyond, brought corruption within the military into the public discourse. But at the time of the uprising in 2011, most activists did not see that.

16 The formation of the Independent Union of Real Estate Tax Collectors is an inspiring story. Soon after the revolution in 2011, the Egyptian Federation of Independent Trade Unions was formed. By December 2013, independent unions amounted to 1,500, with five federations. The ETUF included twenty-three general federations as of the 2006–11 union session and around 1,800 union committees (El Sharkawy and El Agati 2021). Unfortunately, soon after the military coup of 2013, the military regime began to thwart independent trade unions in several ways, including infiltrating them with spies, and the basic right to strike was outlawed by Egypt's Supreme Administrative Court on April 29, 2015 (Acconcia 2016).

17 See the website of the Egyptian Center for Economic and Social Rights (2011) for its human rights vision for Egypt.

18 The EFITU itself was initially formed in Tahrir on January 30, 2011, with four independent unions (the Independent Union of Real Estate Tax Collectors, the Retired Workers' Union, the Health Professionals Union, and the Teachers' Independent Union). The formation of the Independent Union of Real Estate Tax Collectors, the main anchor of the EFITU, has been very important in contemporary Egypt's labor history. It was the first independent trade union in Egypt's history. It was created out of a successful strike, which took place in September 2007. And it comprises a very critical segment of state employees, tax collectors, which included about 55,000 real estate tax collectors in Egypt. Due to the EFITU's significance, during the transitional period and after the military coup in 2013, state intelligence apparatuses used different strategies to infiltrate it and other key independent unions that were formed after the revolution; they also attempted to co-opt their leaders.

19 Some scholars have argued that this period can be seen as a mass strike in Rosa Luxemburg's sense (see, for example, Zemni, De Smet, and Bogaert, "Luxemburg on Tahrir Square," 2013).

20 The statement is available online at *Green Left* 2011.

21 The word *faaawyeea* has a negative connotation; it reads like "selfish demands."

22 Street kids' role in battles between police and protesters continued beyond the revolution, as they also played an important role in what are known as the

Mohamed Mahmoud battles in Egypt in November 2011 (see Sukarieh 2012; also see Fleishman 2011).

23 Note that there are discrepancies in the number of injured. I relied on narrow numbers that are documented by Daftar Ahwal, a center for archiving, documentation, and research in Cairo. Both data sets (the killed and the injured) were collected and validated by Daftar Ahwal. The data on the protesters killed in the uprising are based on sources from official authorities (court documents, especially the famous lawsuits over the killing of protesters during the revolution), as well as official statements related to these cases. The data set on the injured draws on official documents from court cases, as well as from NGOs that worked on those cases. For more on Daftar Ahwal, see https://web.archive.org/web/20220130195622/https://daftarahwal.com/en /home/.

24 Street vendors' presence in Tahrir became more contentious after Mubarak's ousting. There are grounds to believe the security apparatus under the SCAF forced many of them to spy on Tahrir protesters during the transitional period.

25 See m7mdamienrady 2011 for video footage, starting at 1:00.

26 This idea of "our image in the world" reveals how significant performance was in Tahrir. In this sense, I agree with Jeffrey Alexander (2011), who described the Egyptian revolution as performative. There was indeed a war of meanings between protesters and the regime. Also, as many scholars and analysts have rightly pointed out, actual performances were important, with different forms of art being created and performed in Tahrir (see, for example, Colla 2011; El-Khatib 2013; Lindsay 2012; Makar 2011; Pahwa and Winegar 2012; Saad 2012). Here, however, I am focusing on the performance of unity itself, a collective performance that had a particular class twist.

27 For footage of the cleanup, see TahrirSqaureEgypt 2011 and No Comment TV 2011. For further discussion of the cleanup and its symbolic significance, also see Winegar 2011.

28 I am thankful to my friend and comrade journalist Dina Samak, who alerted me to, and reminded me of, the difference between the two stages.

CHAPTER FIVE. WANING REVOLUTIONARY POSSIBILITIES

1 The hundred-day program included specific proposals about security, traffic, street cleaning, bread, and energy. See the program on Morsi's official Facebook (Morsi 2012).

2 Neither the Supreme Council of Armed Forces (SCAF) nor Morsi had made any substantive changes in the security apparatus. They repeatedly refused proposals for democratic transformation and enhanced police accountability. The SCAF introduced pseudoreform and changed the name of the State

Security Intelligence to the National Security Agency. Morsi did not make any changes in the police apparatus. During the SCAF's and Morsi's rule, the main task of the security agencies was to secure more control and expand the military's role in policing in Egypt. But in 2012 it was obvious that police brutality had expanded.

3 On January 25, 2012, the first anniversary of the uprising, Egyptians held the largest rallies since the revolution, protesting the SCAF's control of the transitional period. Egyptians chanted, "Down with military rule," as well as the revolution's main slogan, "Bread, freedom, and social justice." The rift between liberal and leftist revolutionaries on the one hand and the MB on the other that existed at the time was reflected in the protest. While the MB leaders and youth emphasized they were celebrating the one-year anniversary of the revolution, leftist actors made clear they were protesting the SCAF's control and the resistance to revolutionary reform. See Mohyi (2012).

4 On the absence of the MB from protests in Egypt during the transitional period, see Kirkpatrick (2011a). On the charge that Egypt's revolutionaries were unrealistic, see Fadel (2016, 28–39). On how sectarian logics infiltrated the political debate and electoral process, see Elmasry (2014); Hanna (2014); and Ozen (2018).

5 "Egypt: The Street Rules," cover of *Time* magazine, July 22, 2013, http://content.time.com/time/covers/asia/0,16641,20130722,00.html.

6 This was possibly one of the main paradoxes of the revolution (see A. Said 2012).

7 Mohammad Ali Kadivar (2018) is one of the few scholars who intervened with a much-needed correction to the scholarship of democratization by considering the significance of mass mobilization in the democratization process and its durability.

8 It is one thing to suggest that Egyptians did not agree on or did not have a concrete vision of the desired democracy, and another to suggest that Egyptians betrayed democracy or did not want it altogether. The latter statement is simply an ignorant, or orientalist, perspective at the least.

9 By suggesting that democracy was reduced to its very minimalist forms and that it was used as a counterrevolutionary method of containment for the revolution, I do not mean that procedural democracy and representative democracy by definition are empty forms of democratization. In short, to say that Egypt witnessed free elections for the first time in its contemporary history and that there was an emergent democracy in Egypt, albeit reduced to its shallowest content, ballotocracy, and that procedural democracy under excessive repression was a counterrevolutionary method are both true statements, as Egyptians did not have a concrete vision of democracy, which created confusion about what happened in Egypt.

10 The committee also included a member of the MB (see *Al-Ahram* 2011b).

11 On deploying sectarianism as a counterrevolutionary tool, see Al-Rasheed (2011).

12 Jessica Winegar (2012) luminously demonstrated how an empty nationalist discourse dominated during early phases of the transitional period and how this reflected middle-class logics and intersected with gender in shaping the public spaces in Egypt.

13 The SCAF was involved in feeding sectarianism throughout the transitional period, not just the MB and Islamic parties. The SCAF and the security apparatus continued to use the Mubarak regime methods of tolerating burning churches and the forced removal of Copts from Egyptian villages. The SCAF also cooperated with Salafi leaders as mediators in these incidents. In the aftermath of the coup, evidence revealed that the SCAF also released Jihadists, to fuel sectarian battles in Egypt. See Bahgat (2014).

14 The chanters were referring to Field Marshal Mohamed Hussein Tantawi, the head of the SCAF at the time, as a guardian in the Islamic sense, meaning someone who has the right to rule and earns obedience.

15 Leftist and revolutionary activists also suggested that the MB could not play the democracy game while being in coalition with Islamic extremists. For a collection of YouTube videos about that day, see https://m.youtube.com/playlist?list=PLnJKbEpCMbiG3iKGTvfeIQ2syiaEQQjza (accessed July 3, 2014).

16 In an established democracy, accountability can work through checks and balances and public opinion, and at the next election, citizens may or may not reelect officials based on their political performance and accomplishments. But in the fluid political context in Egypt, where there were no elected bodies throughout 2011 and 2012, and where the SCAF continued to rule until Morsi was elected in June 2012 and maintained legislative power after that, things were a lot messier. It is fair to say that protesters expected a lot from the first elected bodies after the revolution. Even if some of their demands were unrealistic, in the short term, protesters also aimed at empowering these bodies against the SCAF.

17 The official name of the document was "Declaration of the Fundamental Principles of the New Egyptian State." It was also known as the "Selmi Document," in reference to the deputy prime minister who announced it.

18 With the exception of the supporters of Salafi radical Hazem Salah Abu Islamiel (see *Al-Ahram* 2011b).

19 Several eyewitnesses told me that all the battles and attacks on protesters in the transitional period were under the military's direction with the assistance of the police. The Mohamed Mahmoud battles, for example, were directed by the military with the cooperation of the Central Security Forces. In addition to using live ammunition, the military and police also used CR, a banned tear gas that attacks pain-sensing nerves and can cause blocking of airways, choking, confusion, vomiting, and even death (see Rahman 2011).

20 There was always discussion in Egypt among radical actors about the difference between January 25—the revolution that was peaceful—and January 28, the date many consider the real day the uprising became a revolution. That was when the protesters defeated the police apparatus and used "unarmed collective violence," as Mohammad Ali Kadivar and Neil Ketchley (2018) put it.

21 This also established a logic that there should be "no legitimacy for killers of protesters." This was a common motto among Egyptian activists at the time. This logic was used again in the mobilization that paved the way to the coup. Graffiti on the presidential palace walls during protests against Morsi read, "The legitimacy of your ballot box is cancelled by our martyrs' coffins" (see Funaro 2012). The irony is that many protesters were killed during both the SCAF'S and Morsi's rule. But it seems that only the killing under Morsi mattered to some secular forces in their mobilizing against Morsi.

22 A common sentiment in the Mohamed Mahmoud battles was that the election was the only priority of the MB, who accused protesters in these battles of disrupting "democracy." Yet it was the Mohamed Mahmoud battles that forced army leaders, in November 2011, to concede and announce a plan for a presidential election to take place in mid-2012. Thus, from the protesters' point of view, the MB benefited from these battles, but they continued to work with the SCAF and did not challenge the SCAF and work to stop attacks against protesters. This explains the bitterness of many revolutionary youth toward the MB.

23 Some revolutionaries I talked to were skeptical of describing this assembly as a parliament of the revolution. This is because the parliament started its sessions with thanking the military for their role in the uprising and because the offices of the parliament, which were dominated by the MB and Islamists, silenced members of parliament who were critical of the military and who called for holding accountable the officers who killed revolutionaries during the uprising.

24 Some actors in Egypt suggest that the SCAF was aware of the problems in the election laws and refused to fix these problems. These actors suggest that the SCAF planned to use the litigation against the parliament. Another reason to believe that the SCAF was aware of this problem is that five of the seven parliaments under Mubarak were declared unconstitutional due to the same problem in the electoral law: the lack of equal opportunity between party candidates and individual candidates. The fact that dissolving the parliament took place a few days before transferring power to the elected president indicates that the SCAF did not want its power marginalized with two elected bodies (president and parliament). The presence of two elected bodies meant stripping the SCAF of power completely. Thus, the SCAF used the legal trenches against the parliament to dissolve it.

25 Hamdeen Sabahi, a Nasserite who identified as revolutionary, was third, with 4,820,273 votes. Abdel Menem Abu Al Fetouh, a moderate Islamist also identified as revolutionary, had 4,065,239 votes.

26 For a timeline of election events, see BBC Arabic (2012d).

27 One week into office, Morsi announced he was restituting the parliament, only to revoke his decision four days later after the SCC challenged him, suggesting it was unconstitutional (see BBC Arabic 2012d). On September 21, the Supreme Administrative Court endorsed the SCC's decision and affirmed the nullification of the parliament (see Al Jazeera 2012c).

28 The announcement of the election results was delayed by four days, which the election committee claimed was needed to investigate complaints by candidates.

29 Almost all of these trials, which took place while the SCAF was in power, ended without punishment for officers accused of killing protesters.

30 As for the "coup" reference, the Islamists meant they believed SCAF's constitutional declaration constituted a coup. This should not be confused with the military coup in July 2013 to oust Morsi.

31 On fueling sectarianism as a counterrevolutionary method in the Arab Spring, see Al-Rasheed (2011).

32 As is obvious, the demand to hold an early election was not put into force. Morsi refused concessions and refused an early election. The military had a plan that precluded having an election right after the coup. The military's plan involved hiring an interim president and preparing for continuous control by the military.

33 Here I agree with one scholar (Ketchley 2017b) that Egypt's generals used the street protests to stage the coup. However, the military would not have been able to deploy the movement to its own ends without the existence of actual outrage.

34 The mix of forces and masses in the anti-Morsi protest on June 30, 2013, was alarming. Only a few critical revolutionaries noticed this and alerted the revolutionaries of January 2011 that police and the military were guarding the protest, with pro–old regime folks joining. Groups in the June 30 protest included January 2011 revolutionaries, especially secular and civil forces within this camp, and political parties (existing ones from the Mubarak era and new parties formed after the revolution). Notable in the latter group are the Destor Party, chaired by Mohamed ElBaradei; the liberal Wafd Party; old leftist parties such as Al Tagamoa; and Nasserist parties and groups such as the Arab Nasserist Party and Al-Karama Party. This also included Christians, who were alienated by the sectarian dominance of the MB, Mubarakists, and large groups of middle-class citizens, who viewed the MB's conservative religiosity as threatening their lifestyle. This wide "coalition" was easy to fracture after the coup, enabling the military's control.

35 Big Pharaoh (@TheBigPharaoh): "A year has passed since the largest demonstration in the history of Egypt. Still, the Brotherhood does not

want to understand why [protesters] rose up against them. Demonstrations of June 30 + July 3 = a coup with popular support" (Twitter, June 30, 2014, 2:24 a.m., https://twitter.com/TheBigPharaoh/status/483496380414300160; translation by Google). Here Big Pharaoh is referring to the difference between June 30, 2013, and July 3, 2013. Interpretations of what happened on these dates are also a matter of debate in Egypt. On June 30, 2013, there were mass protests against Morsi in Egypt. And on July 3, 2013, the military announced the ousting of Morsi. Some activists in Egypt agreed and endorsed protests against Morsi, but they were not necessarily pro-coup. Big Pharaoh here is suggesting that combining what happened on June 30 and July 3 constitutes a popularly backed coup.

36 Amr Khalifa (@Cairo67Unedited): "On Jun[e] 30 2013 I termed what occured [sic] as a #RevolutionaryCoup. I was wrong. It was a #Coup but [only a] few of us had the right glasses #Egypt" (Twitter, June 30, 2014, 11:51 a.m., https://twitter.com/Cairo67Unedited/status/483638849466167296).

37 On August 14, 2013, security and military forces under the command of General Abdel Fattah el-Sisi raided two camps of protesters, mostly of Islamists and MB supporters. One camp was in al-Nahda Square in Giza, near Cairo University, and the second was in Rabaa Al-Adawiya Square in the northeast of Cairo. No fewer than 1,200 died.

38 Shukrallah wrote this as a Facebook post on June 30, 2018. The note is written in Arabic, and this is my translation. It is available at https://www.facebook .com/hani.shukrallah.1/posts/2479252175433946.

39 There has been some interesting debate among a few critical scholars of Egyptian politics about the most important foundational moment that launched Sisi's military regime and neoauthoritarianism in Egypt: the 2013 coup on July 3; the rallies to give a mandate to Sisi and the military to presumably fight terrorism, on July 26, 2013; or the Rabaa Massacre on August 14, 2013. I argue all these moments are important in different ways.

40 I am using the term *institutionalist* here cautiously. At the time (about a month and a half after the coup), Egypt had no parliament and no publicly approved constitution. But the mandate to Sisi and the military proved to be the real basis of governing in Egypt during that time in 2013.

41 The SCAF-MB partnership (despite their disagreements) was proven by documents released later. According a document published by *WikiLeaks* (2016) that includes an email from former US secretary of state Hillary Clinton to one of her aides, Jake Sullivan, on November 23, 2011, during the Mohamed Mahmoud battles, Clinton confirmed that the SCAF was working closely with the MB leaders. The MB "provides intelligence to the SCAF regarding developments in the smaller and more radical political parties. At the same time, the MB, in coordination with the Egyptian General Intelligence Directorate (GID) and Military Police forces, is working to

reduce the level of violence in demonstrations protesting extended military rule." The SCAF continued to provide a "degree of funding and information to the MB, giving it an advantage over competing secular and religious based political movements," to run in the parliamentary and presidential elections scheduled for fall 2011. According to Clinton and the document, the SCAF and the MB "represent the only two truly established political organizations in the country, and they must work together to gain full advantage from the newly developing political structure in Egypt." The SCAF's top priority was to stop protests and to ensure that they would take part in, if not regulate, political arrangements in Egypt. The MB's goal was to maximize their electoral gains and share in power.

42 For more details about the MB and its neoliberal agenda and collaboration with the World Bank and the IMF during its rule, see Gamal (2019).

43 See, for example, a letter signed by eleven civil society organizations, four political parties, two independent trade unions, and two political movements to the MB government and the IMF, protesting a new $4.8 billion IMF loan to Egypt. The letter criticized the government's acceptance of the loan and its lack of transparency ("Letter from Parties" 2012).

44 A leading expert on the MB, Khalil Al-Anani, describes the MB as *devout neoliberals*. He proposes that the MB has historically been made up of low- and lower-middle-class constituencies. Yet it adopted a market-oriented vision to appeal to world governments and foreign investors. The group's neoliberal vision, according to Al-Anani, can be explained by three factors: "the movement's pragmatism, its 'devout' bourgeoisie, and the appeal for international acceptance and recognition" (2020, 2).

45 I agree with Zeinab Abul-Magd, who emphasized the failure of most factions to hold the military-security apparatus accountable and the failure to deprivilege the officers who "capitalized on their role as security providers, bureaucrats, and entrepreneurs, presenting themselves as the nation's savior at a time of chaos. The armed forces, Egypt's wealthiest and most influential organization, exploited the political vacuum to extend its occupation of public space and to maintain dominance over civilian actors, whatever the cost" (in Hawthorne and Miller 2020, 1).

CHAPTER SIX. SQUARE ZERO

1 Maha Abdelrahman (2017) describes Sisi's Egypt as a "securocratic" state. Note that in chapter 1 I described Mubarak's Egypt as a neopatrimonial police state. While I agree completely with Abdelrahman about the centrality of the security apparatus in the functioning of the Egyptian state under Sisi, I am inclined to think of Sisi's state as a neopraetorian police state, to emphasize the centrality of the military's role in political life and security agencies under Sisi.

2 Indeed, the counterrevolutionary military regime in Egypt today, while unprecedented in Egypt itself, bears many similarities to other military or fascist regimes worldwide that came after failed or defeated revolutions, or after military coups to abort certain socialist democratic modes of governance. Without ignoring the complex historical specificities of each of these cases, some of the examples are Francisco Franco's Spain (1939–75), Augusto Pinochet's Chile (1973–90), Benito Mussolini's Italy (1922–43), and Adolf Hitler's Germany (1933–45). Interested readers can look at Campos (2004); Dülffer (1976); Elazar (2000); Ensalaco (2010); Leal (2020); Rodrigo (2012a, 2012b); and R. Sewell (2018).

3 During the final revisions of this manuscript, the second parliamentary election after the coup took place. It was held on October 24–25 and November 7–8, 2020. Mostaqbal Watan, a pro-Sisi political party known for its close relation to the security apparatuses, won about 55 percent of the seats. No other party gained more than 9 percent of the seats, and no party affiliated with the January Revolution (with the exception of the Social Democratic Party, some of whose leaders were in prison) was allowed to run in the election. This meant the continuation of Sisi's and the state's control over the main representative house in Egypt.

4 In the context of the Sisi regime, a closed circuit means that military trolls can produce news, which is then carried by the major news outlets, also controlled by the military. Trolls then recycle the news that they originally produced. Thus, the internet and news work like a closed circuit or echo chamber to one another (see *Akhbarak* 2016).

5 Mona Abaza (2017, 174) suggests that for the military regime "Tahrir is not repeatable."

6 Egyptian historian Khaled Fahmy described this period in an article titled "To Whom Does the Square Belong?" (2012).

7 I agree with Ibrahim Halawi (2019) and Jamie Allinson (2022) that counterrevolutions do not appear out of nowhere and as a reaction to revolution but are enabled by deep-rooted historical power structures and the international context. My analysis here focuses on providing an in-depth anatomy of the period from 2011 to the present, while demonstrating how the actors and actions of counterrevolution shifted constantly over time.

8 Younis, for example, states, "Bonaparte usually comes from the army. From Napoleon I and III, to Peron in Argentina, to Nasser. But that does not mean that Bonapartism is merely military rule. But in these given moments, the Bonaparte is no longer becoming a representative of the state apparatus to become a representative of the state [as a whole] and guard the social balance of the state based on the wide popular support. Especially in the case of the rise of Sisi, it was clear that his status gained from both his role as defense minister and from the popular mandate given to him. Indeed, power was

quickly transferred from the Ministry of Defense to the presidency, through elections. The election was a mere confirmation of the mandate" (2015, 19).

9 On paranoia with regard to politics in the United States, see Hofstadter (2012); Knight (2002); and O'Donnell (2000). With regard to North Korea, see French (2014).

10 See the important work of Vivienne Matthies-Boon on the significance of trauma in the aftermath of the coup and the escalated retaliation against the revolutionary youth, and on how counterrevolution deploys trauma against activists (Matthies-Boon 2017; Matthies-Boon and Head 2018).

11 Some of these actors had been released by the time I was revising this manuscript. But they, like most detainees, had never had a trial and had been detained through vague constitutional and legal loopholes of pretrial clauses. Most of these actors and other key leaders of the January Revolution were in solitary confinement.

12 As political scientist Amr Hamzawy put it, the nationalist populism of the Egyptian military regime entails constant justification that the generals are the only actors who are capable of knowing the national interests and national security and that the generals are the saviors of the nation, "as foster parents to an infant nation" (2018, 495).

13 This lecture has become an essential component of the army's education for soldiers and citizens alike in the years following the coup. I documented many instances recorded on YouTube when Colonel Al-Gamal visited schools, universities, and state-run sectors. The focus of the lecture is the army's relation to the state (see Al-Gamal 2013).

14 Sisi also continuously suggests that Egypt is fighting evil and dark powers on behalf of the world.

15 The author of the post removed it from Facebook, perhaps to keep a low profile from the Egyptian police state. For this reason, neither the name of the author nor a link to the post is given here. The last access date of the post was October 5, 2015.

16 In one of the few studies that seriously discussed the idea of fear and its complexity in the aftermath of the uprising, Talal Asad (2012) suggested that there were many sources of fear during the transitional period, all of which were fueled by military rule. This included the fear of civilians among Islamists, fear of Islamists among secularists and liberals, fear of socialists among everyone, and so on. With regard to the ideas of activists having agency and making reflections about the defeat and withdrawal from public space, see the important collection of essays of Alaa Abd El-Fattah, *You Have Not Yet Been Defeated* (2022). Abd El-Fattah is one of the most high-profile political prisoners in Egypt's revolution. In these essays, Abd El-Fattah provides critical reflections about the tension between the objective elements of defeat compared to its subjective elements.

1 A friend and comrade in the Revolutionary Socialists organization had asked me to write this a few weeks prior to the planned protest on June 30, 2013. I felt obligated to write it. I used to have organizational ties with the Revolutionary Socialists in Egypt before moving to the United States in 2004 to pursue my academic career. My relationship with the organization ended formally at the time, but I kept in touch by reading their materials and writing a few pieces through the years until the revolution.

2 In chapter 5 I also quote a 2018 post by leftist writer Hani Shukrallah, where he admits misreading the complex phenomena of the June 30 mobilization. I share the same position, as I realized that I was too naive in thinking through the complex dynamics of this mobilization and only later realized that many revolutionaries were wiser when they perceptively saw how the deep state and Mubarakists were part of this mobilization. I saw it too but did not think it was that significant.

3 As I have said earlier, the concept of lived contingency refers to how revolutionary actors practice and experience the revolution on the ground. But perhaps it may be applicable to experiencing contingency in mobilizations and contentious politics in general, especially during moments of high mobilization. The main difference between lived contingency during a revolution and during these moments of heightened mobilization is that revolutionary actors during revolutionary times go through high-risk situations that require taking daring and impromptu actions. These actions are taken under the pressure of increased uncertainties—high contingency—and are driven mainly by passion and determination. While revolutionary actors seem to have limited choices—where their decisions entail life-and-death situations— they undergo a stronger occasion of unbounding from everyday obligations (i.e., a wider range of revolutionary actions to be taken). Social movement actors, on the contrary, do not go through this intensity of lived contingency. One can argue that, compared to revolutionary actors, social movement actors practice what can be described as *calculated unbounding,* in contrast to the uncalculated or radical unbounding in the case of revolutionary actors.

4 One notable name was Major Ahmed Shoman, who announced his defection and talked to Al Jazeera during the uprising (see Al Jazeera 2011c). See also a short interview with Shoman during the Mohamed Mahmoud Street clashes in November 2011 (*Almasry Alyoum* 2011a). Also, during the transitional period, on April 8, 2011, several low-ranking officers joined the sit-in in Tahrir before the camp was stormed by the military and its intelligence apparatus, which arrested and detained these officers. This group of officers are known to close observers of the Egyptian Revolution and activists as the April 8th officers. On a rally calling for their release almost one year after the uprising, on January 13, 2012, see *Almasry Alyoum* 2012a.

5   As stated in the introduction of this book (see my third thesis with regard to defining revolutions), the separation between the social and political aspects of revolutions has become obsolete, and the dichotomy between social and political revolutions has gone too far. I cannot do justice to this broad and important discussion here. But I suggest that the dichotomy between social and political revolutions resulted from at least two main types of reasons. The first type of reason could be described as scholarly related. The best example of this reason is Theda Skocpol's famous thesis, mentioned in this book's introduction. This thesis has been popularized in the literature and dominates how scholars think of revolutions. The second type is a combination of specific historical revolutionary happenings. Some of the important cases here are the American Revolution, which entailed establishing an independent republic without necessarily changing class and race relations. Other important cases are anticolonialist revolutions, which are presumed to be revolutions to claim national sovereignty (irrespective of changing social relations). Other important historical happenings are eastern European uprisings of 1989. The latter are perceived in the literature as revolutions for Western democracy, regardless of the complexities of the socialist regimes that existed there. The literature has understood these revolutions as political only, not social. In fact, the social is not absent from these cases. I am indebted to an online discussion with many colleagues and friends on this topic, especially Cihan Tugal, Sahan Savas Karatasli, and Simeon Newman.

6   The relation between the NAC and old Cairo is very complex and cannot be reduced to protest and security. I cannot do justice to this relation in this conclusion. Also, ironically, after I finished this manuscript, Sisi on July 19, 2022, issued a presidential decree to expand the administrative boundaries of Cairo to include the NAC. The reason for this decree seems to be to avoid a constitutional challenge; according to the 2014 constitution, the government and representative councils should be located in Cairo. The amount of resources taken from the rest of Egypt and the speed of work on the NAC project, without even attending to this basic constitutional problem, prove the lack of serious research about the NAC project.

7   Recently two scholars of revolutions started an important debate on whether we are moving toward a fifth generation of scholarship on revolutions (but not there yet; Abrams 2019) or if this generation has already started (Allinson 2019). Also see Asef Bayat's (2021) insightful response to this debate. This discussion was very useful. As for where my research would fit, I will leave that to my readers. But my main concern here is to demonstrate how we can learn so much about the processes of revolution if we look at agency, contingency, and power on the ground.

8   See Achcar (2020) on the enduring inequality in the Arab world.

APPENDIX 2.

1 Only a few months before the uprising I became a naturalized US citizen and so became a dual national.

2 Sociologist Mona Abaza (2011) wrote about this phenomenon and described it as "academic tourists sight-seeing the Arab Spring" (see also El-Mahdi 2011).

3 Elsewhere I have discussed in depth my positionality and the radical difference between conducting research during the revolution and doing so in the aftermath of the military coup of 2013 (A. Said 2018).

4 Bourdieu (2003) differentiates between three kinds of reflexivities. The first is scientific reflexivity, where the researcher takes into account their social experience and applies sociological critique to their reflexivity (288). The second is narcissistic reflexivity, the reflexivity of postmodern anthropology, where some researchers—as a reaction to positivism—have become interested in simple "verging on exhibitionism" (281), which I understand as performative reflexivity. And, finally, there is egological reflexivity, in which the anthropologist "remains as remote from himself as from his object" (282).

APPENDIX 3.

1 As mentioned earlier, this project did not start as an opportunity, but it became such. Note that while the notion of *kairós*, as an opportune time, may overlap with the idea of political opportunity structure, one of the notable frameworks in social movement research, I prefer to not conflate the two. The former for me is an analytic tool for historical research. And the latter refers to a conceptual framework to study specific dynamics in social movement research.

2 I acknowledge that autoethnography may be a less accepted method for traditional anthropologists and sociologists who do qualitative research. Some of the critiques include that it simply involves studying the self, not communities or societies. Others contend that it blurs the line between the social sciences and humanities. I am aware of these critiques. My use of autoethnography in this research was limited, but I felt that the nature of this research and my location within it required some explicit thought and theorization. The advantages of drawing on my own experiences, I argue, outweigh the benefit of simply attempting to deny or ignore them.

3 I obtained institutional review board approval (IRB HUM00053086).

4 Daftar Ahwal's website can be found at https://daftarahwal.com/en/home (last accessed May 1, 2023).

references

ENGLISH REFERENCES

Abaza, Mona. 2011. "Academic Tourists Sight-Seeing the Arab Spring." *Ahram Online*, September 26, 2011. http://english.ahram.org.eg/News/22373.aspx.

Abaza, Mona. 2017. "Cairo: Restoration? And the Limits of Street Politics." *Space and Culture* 20 (2): 170–90.

Abdalla, Nadine. 2012. "Egypt's Workers: From Protest Movement to Organized Labor." *SWP Comments* (Stiftung Wissenschaft und Politik), no. 32. https://www.swp-berlin.org/fileadmin/contents/products/comments/2012C32_abn.pdf.

Abd El-Fattah, Alaa. 2022. *You Have Not Yet Been Defeated: Selected Works 2011–2021.* New York: Seven Stories.

Abdelmonem, M. Gamal. 2016. "The Abject Dream of Neo-capital: Capitalist Urbanism, Architecture and Endangered Live-Ability of the Middle East's Modern Cities." *Open House International* 41 (2): 38–46.

Abdelrahman, Maha. 2009. "'With the Islamists?—Sometimes. With the State?—Never!' Cooperation between the Left and Islamists in Egypt." *British Journal of Middle Eastern Studies* 36 (1): 37–54.

Abdelrahman, Maha. 2014. *Egypt's Long Revolution: Protest Movements and Uprisings.* New York: Routledge.

Abdelrahman, Maha. 2017. "Policing Neoliberalism in Egypt: The Continuing Rise of the 'Securocratic' State." *Third World Quarterly* 38 (1): 185–202.

Abrams, Benjamin. 2019. "A Fifth Generation of Revolutionary Theory Is Yet to Come." *Journal of Historical Sociology* 32 (3): 378–86.

Abul-Magd, Zeinab. 2012. "Occupying Tahrir Square: The Myths and the Realities of the Egyptian Revolution." *South Atlantic Quarterly* III (3): 565–72.

Abul-Magd, Zeinab. 2017. *Militarizing the Nation: The Army, Business, and Revolution in Egypt.* New York: Columbia University Press.

Abu-Lughod, Lila. 2006. "Writing against Culture." In *Anthropology in Theory: Issues in Epistemology*, edited by Henrietta L. Moore and Todd Sanders, 466–79. Malden, MA: Blackwell.

Acconcia, Giuseppe. 2016. "The Shrinking Independence of Egypt's Labor Unions." Carnegie Endowment for International Peace, September 20, 2016. https://carnegieendowment.org/sada/64634.

Achcar, Gilbert. 2013. *The People Want: A Radical Exploration of the Arab Uprising.* Berkeley: University of California Press.

Achcar, Gilbert. 2016b. *Morbid Symptoms: Relapse in the Arab Uprising.* Stanford, CA: Stanford University Press.

Achcar, Gilbert. 2020. "On the 'Arab Inequality Puzzle': The Case of Egypt." *Development and Change* 51 (3): 746–70.

Achy, Lahcen. 2010. "Concerns of Egyptian Youth: A Forgotten Majority." Carnegie Middle East Center, December 20, 2010. http://carnegie-mec.org /publications/?fa=42160.

Adam, Mohamad Salama. 2013. "Mohamed Mahmoud: The Revolutionary Romance Continues." *Mada Masr*, November 19, 2013. https://madamasr.com /en/2013/11/19/opinion/u/mohamed-mahmoud-the-revolutionary-romance -continues/.

Adly, Amr. 2012. "SCAF Strikes from the Legal Trenches." *Egypt Independent*, June 23, 2012. https://ww.egyptindependent.com/scaf-strikes-legal-trenches/.

Ahram Online. 2012a. "Egypt Population Reaches 91 Million, Grows 18 Percent in Eight Years." August 30, 2012. http://english.ahram.org.eg/News/51634.aspx.

Ahram Online. 2012b. "English Text of Morsi's Constitutional Declaration." November 22, 2012. http://english.ahram.org.eg/News/58947.aspx.

Al-Anani, Khalil. 2016. *Inside the Muslim Brotherhood: Religion, Identity, and Politics.* Oxford: Oxford University Press.

Al-Anani, Khalil. 2020. "Devout Neoliberalism?! Explaining Egypt's Muslim Brotherhood's Socio-economic Perspective and Policies." *Politics and Religion* 13 (4): 748–67.

Al-Arian, Abdullah. 2014. *Answering the Call: Popular Islamic Activism in Sadat's Egypt.* Religion and Global Politics. Oxford: Oxford University Press.

Alexander, Anne. 2011. "The Growing Social Soul of Egypt's Democratic Revolution." *International Socialism*, no. 131. http://isj.org.uk/the-growing-social-soul -of-egypts-democratic-revolution/.

Alexander, Anne, and Mostafa Bassiouny. 2014. *Bread, Freedom, Social Justice: Workers and the Egyptian Revolution.* New York: Zed.

Alexander, Jeffrey. 2011. *Performative Revolution in Egypt: An Essay in Cultural Power.* New York: Bloomsbury Academic.

Al Hussaini, Amira. 2011. "Egypt: Strike! Strike! Strike!" Global Voices, February 9, 2011. http://globalvoicesonline.org/2011/02/09/egypt-strike-strike-strike.

Ali, Khaled. 2011. "Egyptian Uprising Fueled by Striking Workers across Nation." Interview by Amy Goodman. *Democracy Now*, February 18, 2011. http://

www.democracynow.org/2011/2/18/egyptian_uprising_fueled_by_striking
_workers.

Allinson, Jamie. 2019. "A Fifth Generation of Revolution Theory?" *Journal of Historical Sociology* 32 (1): 142–51.

Allinson, Jamie. 2022. *The Age of Counter-revolution: States and Revolutions in the Middle East*. Cambridge: Cambridge University Press.

Al-Rasheed, Madawi. 2011. "Sectarianism as Counter-revolution: Saudi Responses to the Arab Spring." *Studies in Ethnicity and Nationalism* 11 (3): 513–26.

Al-Tawy, Ayat. 2013. "Egyptian Democratic Labour Congress Officially Launches." *Ahram Online*, April 25, 2013. http://english.ahram.org.eg/NewsContent/1/64/70102/Egypt/Politics-/Egyptian-Democratic-Labour-Congress-officially-lau.aspx.

Amar, Paul. 2011. "Turning the Gendered Politics of the Security State Inside Out? Charging the Police with Sexual Harassment in Egypt." *International Feminist Journal of Politics* 13 (3): 299–328.

Amar, Paul. 2013. *The Security Archipelago: Human-Security States, Sexuality Politics, and the End of Neoliberalism*. Durham, NC: Duke University Press.

Amnesty International. 2011. "State of Human Rights in the Middle East and North Africa: January to Mid-April 2011." Report 2011. https://www.amnesty.org/en/wp-content/uploads/2021/06/pol1001220011en.pdf.

Aponte, Robert. 1990. "Definitions of the Underclass: A Critical Analysis." In *Sociology in America*, edited by Herbert J. Gans, 117–37. London: Sage.

Apter, Emily. 2006. "On Oneworldedness: Or Paranoia as a World System." *American Literary History* 18 (2): 365–89.

Asad, Talal. 2012. "Fear and the Ruptured State: Reflections on Egypt after Mubarak." *Social Research* 79 (2): 271–98.

Ash, Timothy Garton. 1989a. "Revolution: The Springtime of Two Nations." *New York Review of Books*, June 15, 1989. https://www.nybooks.com/articles/1989/06/15/revolution-the-springtime-of-two-nations/.

Ash, Timothy Garton. 1989b. "Revolution in Hungary and Poland." *New York Review of Books*, August 17, 1989. http://www.nybooks.com/articles/archives/1989/aug/17/revolution-in-hungary-and-poland/.

Aspden, Rachel. 2016. "Generation Revolution: How Egypt's Military State Betrayed Its Youth." *Guardian*, June 2, 2016. https://www.theguardian.com/news/2016/jun/02/generation-revolution-egypt-military-state-youth.

Assaad, Ragui. 2008. "Unemployment and Youth Insertion in the Labor Market in Egypt." In *The Egyptian Economy: Current Challenges and Future Prospects*, edited by Hanaa Kheir-El-Din, 133–78. Cairo: American University in Cairo Press.

Assaad, Ragui, and Ghada Barsoum. 2007. "Youth Exclusion in Egypt: In Search of 'Second Chances.'" Working paper 2, Middle East Youth Initiative. https://www.meyi.org/publication-youth-exclusion-in-egypt-in-search-of-second-chances.html.

Assaad, Ragui, and Farzaneh Roudi-Fahimi. 2007. *Youth in the Middle East and North Africa: Demographic Opportunity or Challenge?* Washington, DC: Population Reference Bureau. https://www.prb.org/resources/youth-in-the-middle -east-and-north-africa-demographic-opportunity-or-challenge/.

Aya, Rod. 1979. "Theories of Revolution Reconsidered: Contrasting Models of Collective Violence." *Theory and Society* 8 (1): 39–99.

Baheyya. 2005. "The prescient yellow sign . . ." *Baheyya: Egypt Analysis and Whimsy* (blog), July 30, 2005. https://baheyya.blogspot.com/2005/07/prescient -yellow-sign-by-youth-for.html.

Bahgat, Hossam. 2014. "Who Let the Jihadis Out?" *Mada Masr*, February 16, 2014. https://madamasr.com/en/2014/02/16/feature/politics/who-let-the-jihadis -out/.

Bahgat, Hossam. 2016. "Anatomy of an Election." *Mada Masr*, March 14, 2016. https://madamasr.com/en/2016/03/14/feature/politics/anatomy-of-an -election/.

Bahgat, Hossam. 2017. "Looking into the Latest Acquisition of Egyptian Media Companies by General Intelligence." *Mada Masr*, December 21, 2017. https:// madamasr.com/en/2017/12/21/feature/politics/looking-into-the-latest -acquisition-of-egyptian-media-companies-by-general-intelligence/.

Bamyeh, Mohammed, and Sari Hanafi. 2015. "Introduction to the Special Issue on Arab Uprisings." *International Sociology* 344 (4): 343–47.

Barany, Zoltan. 2011. "The Role of the Military." *Journal of Democracy* 22 (4): 24–35.

Barany, Zoltan. 2016. *How Armies Respond to Revolutions and Why*. Princeton, NJ: Princeton University Press.

Batstone, Jade. 2014. "The Use of Strategic Nonviolent Action in the Arab Spring." *Peace Review* 36 (1): 28–37.

Bayat, Asef. 2011. "A New Arab Street in Post-Islamist Times." *Foreign Policy*, January 26, 2011. http://mideastafrica.foreignpolicy.com/posts/2011/01/26/a _new_arab_street.

Bayat, Asef. 2015. "Plebeians of the Arab Spring." *Current Anthropology* 56, no. S11 (October): S33–43.

Bayat, Asef. 2017. *Revolution without Revolutionaries: Making Sense of the Arab Spring*. Stanford, CA: Stanford University Press.

Bayat, Asef. 2021. "The Arab Spring and Revolutionary Theory: An Intervention in a Debate." *Journal of Historical Sociology* 34 (2): 393–400.

BBC News. 2011. "Egypt Unrest: 846 Killed in Protests—Official Toll." April 19, 2011. https://www.bbc.com/news/world-middle-east-13134956.

Beck, Colin J. 2014. "Reflections on the Revolutionary Wave in 2011." *Theory and Society* 43 (2): 197–223.

Beck, Colin J. 2018. "The Structure of Comparison in the Study of Revolution." *Sociological Theory* 36 (2): 134–61.

Beck, Colin J., Mlada Bukovansky, Erica Chenoweth, George Lawson, Sharon Erickson Nepstad, and Daniel P. Ritter. 2022. *On Revolutions: Unruly Politics in the Contemporary World*. Oxford: Oxford University Press.

Beinin, Joel. 2011. "Egypt's Workers Rise Up." *Nation*, February 17, 2011. http://www.thenation.com/article/158680/egypts-workers-rise.

Beinin, Joel. 2012. *The Rise of Egypt's Workers*. Washington, DC: Carnegie Endowment for International Peace. https://carnegieendowment.org/files/egypt_labor.pdf.

Beinin, Joel, and Hossam el-Hamalawy. 2007. "Strikes in Egypt Spread from Center of Gravity." *Middle East Report Online*, May 9, 2007. http://www.merip.org/mero/mero050907.

Benzecry, Claudio E., Andrew Deener, and Armando Lara-Millán. 2020. "Archival Work as Qualitative Sociology." *Qualitative Sociology* 43 (3): 297–303.

Bhuiyan, Serajul. 2011. "Social Media and Its Effectiveness in the Political Reform Movement in Egypt." *Middle East Media Educator* 1 (1): 14–20.

Bochner, Arthur P., and Carolyn S. Ellis. 2006. "Communication as Autoethnography." In *Communication as . . . : Perspectives on Theory*, edited by Gregory J. Shepherd, Jeffrey St. John, and Ted Striphas, 110–22. Thousand Oaks, CA: Sage.

Boer, Roland. 2013. "Revolution in the Event: The Problem of Kairós." *Theory, Culture and Society* 30 (2): 116–34.

Bourdieu, Pierre. 2003. "Participant Objectivation." *Journal of the Royal Anthropological Institute* 9 (2): 281–94.

Bourdieu, Pierre, and Loïc J. D. Wacquant, eds. 1992. *An Invitation to Reflexive Sociology*. Chicago: University of Chicago Press.

Brown, Wendy. 2015. *Undoing the Demos: Neoliberalism's Stealth Revolution*. Cambridge, MA: MIT Press.

Brownlee, Jason. 2012. *Democracy Prevention: The Politics of the US-Egyptian Alliance*. Cambridge: Cambridge University Press.

Brumberg, Daniel, and Hesham Sallam. 2012. "The Politics of Security Reform in Egypt." Special report, US Institute of Peace. http://www.usip.org/publications/the-politics-security-sector-reform-in-egypt.

Campos, Ismael S. 2004. "Fascism, Fascistization, and Developmentalism in Franco's Dictatorship." *Social History* 29 (3): 342–57.

Carnegie Endowment for International Peace. 2010. "National Association for Change." September 22, 2010. https://carnegieendowment.org/2010/09/22/national-association-for-change-pub-54923.

Carr, Sarah. 2015. "President Sisi's Canal Extravaganza." *Foreign Policy*, August 7, 2015. https://foreignpolicy.com/2015/08/07/sisi-dredges-the-depth-egypt-suez-canal-boondoggle/.

Carr, William Guy. (1955) 2013. *Pawns in the Game*. FBI edition. N.p.: Dauphin.

Castells, Manuel. 2018. *Rupture: The Crisis of Liberal Democracy*. Cambridge, UK: Polity.

Chang, Heewon. 2008. *Autoethnography as Method*. Walnut Creek, CA: Left Coast.

Choudhary, Alok, William Hendrix, Kathy Lee, Diana Palsetia, and Wei-Keng Liao. 2012. "Social Media Evolution of the Egyptian Revolution." *Communications of the Association for Computing Machinery* 55 (5): 74–80.

Clarke, Killian. 2011. "Saying 'Enough': Authoritarianism and Egypt's Kefaya Movement." *Mobilization: An International Journal* 16 (4): 397–416.

Clinton, Hillary. 2011. Interview by Chris Wallace. *Fox News Sunday*. January 30, 2011. Transcript published by *WikiLeaks*. https://wikileaks.wikimee.info /gifiles/attach/169/169162_Eg110130f.pdf.

Cohen, Roger. 2011. "Guru of the Revolution." *New York Times*, February 17, 2011. http://www.nytimes.com/2011/02/18/opinion/18iht-edcohen18.html.

Cole, Juan. 2011. "Egypt's Class Conflict." *Informed Comment* (blog), January 30, 2011. http://www.juancole. com/2011/01/egypts-class-conflict.html.

Colla, Elliott. 2011. "The Poetry of Revolt." *Jadaliyya*, January 31, 2011. http://www. jadaliyya.com/pages/index/506/the-poetry-of-revolt.

Colla, Elliott. 2020. "Egyptian Movement Poetry." *Journal of Arabic Literature* 51 (1–2): 53–82.

Cook, Steven A. 2017. "Egypt Goes from Bad to Worse: Under President Sisi, the Nation Longs for the Good Old Days of Mubarak." *Council on Foreign Relations Blog*, April 3, 2017. https://www.cfr.org/blog/egypt-goes-bad-worse -under-president-sisi-nation-longs-good-old-days-mubarak.

Coronil, Fernando. 1997. *The Magical State: Nature, Money, and Modernity in Venezuela*. Chicago: University of Chicago Press.

Darwisheh, Hossam. 2018. "Ruling against Revolution: The Judiciary and the Restoration of Authoritarianism in Egypt." *Middle East Review* 5:72–93.

Dawoud, Khaled. 2001. "Message to 'the Castle.'" *Al-Ahram Weekly*, September 13–19, 2001.

Denzin, Norman K. 2006. "Analytic Autoethnography, or Déjà Vu All Over Again." *Journal of Contemporary Ethnography* 35 (4): 419–28.

De Smet, Brecht. 2016. *Gramsci on Tahrir: Revolution and Counter-revolution in Egypt*. London: Pluto.

DeYoung, Karen. 2011. "Obama Administration Aligns Itself with Protests in Egypt with Call for 'Orderly Transition.'" *Washington Post*, January 31, 2011. http://www.washingtonpost.com/wp-dyn/content/article/2011/01/30 /AR2011013004401.html.

Drescher, Seymour. 1992. "'Why Great Revolutions Will Become Rare': Tocqueville's Most Neglected Prognosis." *Journal of Modern History* 64 (3): 429–54.

Dülffer, Jost. 1976. "Bonapartism, Fascism, and National Socialism." *Journal of Contemporary History* 11 (4): 109–28.

Dunne, Michele. 2011. "Egypt: Elections or Constitution First?" Carnegie Endowment for International Peace, June 21, 2011. https://carnegieendowment.org /2011/06/21/egypt-elections-or-constitution-first-pub-44744.

Economist. 2015. "The Sad State of Egyptian Liberals." October 10, 2015. https:// www.economist.com/middle-east-and-africa/2015/10/10/the-sad-state-of -egypts-liberals.

Egyptian Center for Women's Rights. 2005. "Egyptian Center for Women's Rights Campaign against Sexual Harassment." Fact sheet. https://endvawnow.org /uploads/browser/files/ecwr_harassment_campaign_fact_sheet.pdf.

Egypt Watch. 2021. "The Egyptian Regime Bought Advanced Spyware from French Companies." November 26, 2021. https://egyptwatch.net/2021/11/26/the-egyptian-regime-bought-advanced-spyware-from-french-companies/.

Einwohner, Rachel L. 2022. *Hope and Honor: Jewish Resistance during the Holocaust.* Oxford: Oxford University Press.

Elazar, Dahlia S. 2000. "Class, State, and Counter-revolution: The Fascist Seizure of Power in Italy, 1919–1922." *European Sociological Review* 16 (3): 301–21.

El Chazli, Youssef. 2016. "A Geography of Revolt in Alexandria, Egypt's Second Capital." *Metropolitics*, February 23, 2016. https://www.metropolitiques.eu/A-Geography-of-Revolt-in.html.

El-Fiqi, Mona. 2013. "Egypt on the Blacklist." *Al-Ahram Weekly*, June 11, 2013. https://www.masress.com/en/ahramweekly/102949.

El-Ghobashy, Mona. 2011. "The Praxis of the Egyptian Revolution." *Middle East Report*, no. 258, 2–13.

El-Ghobashy, Mona. 2021. *Bread and Freedom: Egypt's Revolutionary Situation.* Stanford, CA: Stanford University Press.

Elgindy, Khaled. 2012. "Egypt's Troubled Transition: Elections without Democracy." *Washington Quarterly* 35 (2): 89–104.

el-Hamalawy, Hossam. 2008. "Egypt's Tax Collectors and the Fight for Independent Trade Unions." *Socialist Worker*, December 1, 2008. https://socialistworker.co.uk/socialist-review-archive/egypts-tax-collectors-and-fight-independent-trade-unions/.

el-Hamalawy, Hossam. 2011a. "The Egyptian Revolution Continues: An Interview with Hossam El-Hamalawy." *New Socialist*, December 10, 2011. http://newsocialist.org/the-egyptian-revolution-continues-an-interview-with-hossam-el-hamalawy/.

el-Hamalawy, Hossam. 2011b. "Egypt Protests Continue in the Factories." *Guardian*, February 14, 2011. http://www.theguardian.com/commentisfree/2011/feb/14/egypt-protests-democracy-generals.

el-Hamalawy, Hossam. 2011c. "#Jan25 The Workers, Middle Class, Military Junta and the Permanent Revolution." *3arabawy*, February 12, 2011. http://www.arabawy.org/2011/02/12/permanent-revolution/.

El-Khatib, Mohamed Samir. 2013. "Tahrir Square as Spectacle: Some Exploratory Remarks on Place, Body and Power." *Theatre Research International* 38 (2): 104–11.

Ellis, Carolyn S., Tony E. Adams, and Arthur P. Bochner. 2011. "Autoethnography: An Overview." *Historical Social Research/Historische Sozialforschung* 12 (1): 273–90.

Ellis, Carolyn S., and Arthur Bochner. 2000. "Autoethnography, Personal Narrative, Reflexivity: Researcher as Subject." In *The Handbook of Qualitative Research*, edited by Norman Denzin and Yvonna Lincoln, 733–68. Thousand Oaks, CA: Sage.

El-Mahdi, Rabab. 2011. "Orientalising the Egyptian Uprising." *Jadaliyya*, April 11, 2011. https://www.jadaliyya.com/Details/23882.

Elmasry, Mohamad. 2014. "Electoral Legitimacy, Not Religious Legitimacy." *Immanent Frame* (blog), May 23, 2014. https://tif.ssrc.org/2014/05/23/electoral-legitimacy-not-religious-legitimacy/.

El-Meehy, Asya. 2012. "Egypt's Popular Committees." *Middle East Report*, no. 265. http://www.merip.org/mer/mer265/egypts-popular-committees.

El Raggal, Aly. 2019. "The Egyptian Revolution's Fatal Mistake." *Middle East Report*, no. 291. https://merip.org/2019/09/the-egyptian-revolutions-fatal-mistake/.

El Rashidi, Yasmine. 2021. "Sisi's New Cairo: Pharaonic Ambition in Ferro-Concrete." *New York Review of Books*, October 16, 2021. https://www-nybooks-com.proxy.cc.uic.edu/daily/2021/10/16/sisis-new-cairo-pharaonic-ambition-in-ferro-concrete/.

El Sharkawy, Shimaa, and Mohamed El Agati. 2021. *Independent Trade Unions: Between Political Developments and Internal Factors—Egyptian Case Study 2004–2015*. Paris: Arab Reform Initiative. https://www.arab-reform.net/publication/independent-trade-unions-between-political-developments-and-internal-factors-egyptian-case-study-2004-2015/.

El-Sherif, Ashraf. 2014. "The Egyptian Muslim Brotherhood's Failures." Carnegie Endowment for International Peace, July 1, 2014. https://carnegieendowment.org/files/muslim_brotherhood_failures.pdf.

El Shimi, Rowan. 2012. "New Layer of Anti-election Street Art on Mohamed Mahmoud Street Walls." *Ahram Online*, May 31, 2012. http://english.ahram.org.eg/NewsContent/5/0/43323/Arts—Culture/0/New-layer-of-antielection-street-art-on-Mohamed-Ma.aspx.

Eltantawy, Nahed, and Julie Wiest. 2011. "The Arab Spring: Social Media in the Egyptian Revolution: Reconsidering Resource Mobilization Theory." *International Journal of Communication* 5:1207–24.

Elyachar, Julia. 2014. "Upending Infrastructure: Tamarod, Resistance, and Agency after the January 25th Revolution in Egypt." *History and Anthropology* 25 (4): 452–71.

Ensalaco, Mark. 2010. *Chile under Pinochet: Recovering the Truth*. Philadelphia: University of Pennsylvania Press.

Ermakoff, Ivan. 2015. "The Structure of Contingency." *American Journal of Sociology* 121 (1): 64–125.

Ez-Eldin, Mansoura. 2016. "The Egyptian Revolution Five Years On: Ghosts of the Uprising." *Qantara.de*, January 26, 2016. https://en.qantara.de/node/22506.

Fadel, Mohammad H. 2014. "Can Egypt's Revolutionary Coalition Be Resurrected? Allies of Ousted President Hosni Mubarak Have Benefitted from Divisions among Backers of the 2011 Revolution." Al Jazeera, January 25, 2014. https://www.aljazeera.com/indepth/opinion/2014/01/can-egypt-revolutionary-coaliti-201412510437753102.html.

Fadel, Mohammad H. 2016. "Egyptian Revolutionaries' Unrealistic Expectations." In *Egypt beyond Tahrir Square*, edited by Bessma Momani and Eid Mohamed, 28–39. Bloomington: Indiana University Press.

Fahmy, Hazem. 2012. "An Initial Perspective on 'The Winter of Discontent: The Root Causes of the Egyptian Revolution.'" *Social Research: An International Quarterly* 79 (2): 349–76.

Farag, Fatma. 1999. "The Center of the Center." *Al-Ahram Weekly*, September 2, 1999. http://ahram.org.eg/1999/445/feature.htm.

Fillieule, Olivier. 2013. "Demobilization." In *The Wiley-Blackwell Encyclopedia of Social and Political Movements*, edited by David A. Snow, Donatella della Porta, Bert Klandermans, and Doug McAdam, 327–31. Malden, MA: Wiley-Blackwell. https://doi.org/10.1002/9780470674871.wbespm064.

Fleishman, Jeffrey. 2011. "For a Boy on the Streets of Cairo, Revolution Is His Only Hope." *Los Angeles Times*, November 27, 2011. http://articles.latimes.com/2011/nov/27/world/la-fg-egypt-homeless-boy-20111128.

Foran, John. 1993. "Theories of Revolution Revisited: Toward a Fourth Generation?" *Sociological Theory* 11 (1): 1–20.

Foran, John, and Jeff Goodwin. 1993. "Revolutionary Outcomes in Iran and Nicaragua: Coalition Fragmentation, War, and the Limits of Social Transformation." *Theory and Society* 22 (2): 209–47.

Freedom House. 2018. "Egypt: Freedom on the Net 2018 Country Report." Freedom House Country Reports. https://freedomhouse.org/country/egypt/freedom-net/2018.

French, Paul. 2014. *North Korea: State of Paranoia.* London: Zed.

Frenkel, Sheera, and Maged Atef. 2014. "Exclusive: Egypt Begins Surveillance of Facebook, Twitter, and Skype on Unprecedented Scale." *BuzzFeed News*, September 17, 2014. https://www.buzzfeednews.com/article/sheerafrenkel/egypt-begins-surveillance-of-facebook-twitter-and-skype-on-u.

Funaro, Kaitlin. 2012. "Gaber Salah, Known as 'Jika,' Dead: Thousands Rally at Funeral for Young Egyptian Activist." *Global Post*, November 26, 2012. https://www.pri.org/stories/2012-11-26/gaber-salah-known-jika-dead-thousands-rally-funeral-young-egyptian-activist.

Gaber, Yassin. 2011. "Egypt Workers Lay Down Demands at New Trade Union Conference." *Ahram Online*, March 3, 2011. http://english.ahram.org.eg/NewsContent/1/64/6901/Egypt/Politics-/Workers-lay-down-demands-at-new-trade-union-confer.aspx.

Gamal, Wael. 2019. "Lost Capital: The Egyptian Muslim Brotherhood's Neoliberal Transformation." Carnegie Middle East Center, February 1, 2019. https://carnegie-mec.org/2019/02/01/lost-capital-egyptian-muslim-brotherhood-s-neoliberal-transformation-pub-78271.

Ghannam, Jeffrey. 2011. "Social Media in the Arab World: Leading Up to the Uprisings of 2011." Washington, DC: Center for International Media Assistance. https://www.cima.ned.org/wp-content/uploads/2015/02/CIMA-Arab_Social_Media-Report-10-25-11.pdf.

Goldberg, Ellis. 2013. "Urban Structure and the Arab Spring." Unpublished paper.

Goldstone, Jack A. 1998a. "Social Movements or Revolutions? On the Evolution and Outcomes of Collective Action." In *From Contention to Democracy*, edited by Marco G. Giugni, Doug McAdam, and Charles Tilly, 125–45. Lanham, MA: Rowman & Littlefield.

Goldstone, Jack A. 2001. "Toward a Fourth Generation of Revolutionary Theory." *Annual Review of Political Science* 4 (1): 139–87.

Goldstone, Jack A. 2003. "Comparative Historical Analysis and Knowledge Accumulation in the Study of Revolutions." In *Comparative Historical Analysis in the Social Sciences*, edited by James Mahoney and Dietrich Rueschemeyer, 41–90. Cambridge: Cambridge University Press.

Goldstone, Jack A. 2009. "Rethinking Revolutions: Integrating Origins, Processes, and Outcomes." *Comparative Studies of South Asia, Africa and the Middle East* 29 (1): 18–32.

Goldstone, Jack A. 2011. "Understanding the Revolutions of 2011: Weakness and Resilience in Middle Eastern Autocracies." *Foreign Affairs*, May/June 2011. http://www.foreignaffairs.com/articles/67694/jack-a-goldstone/understanding-the-revolutions-of-2011.

Goldstone, Jack A. 2014. *Revolutions: A Very Short Introduction*. Oxford: Oxford University Press.

Goodwin, Jeff. 2001. *No Other Way Out: States and Revolutionary Movements, 1945–1991*. Cambridge: Cambridge University Press.

Goodwin, Jeff. 2003. "The Renewal of Socialism and the Decline of Revolution." In *The Future of Revolutions: Rethinking Radical Change in the Age of Globalization*, edited by John Foran, 59–71. New York: Zed.

Gould, Roger V. 1995. *Insurgent Identities: Class, Community, and Protest in Paris from 1848 to the Commune*. Chicago: University of Chicago Press.

Gramsci, Antonio. (1971) 1992. *Selections from the Prison Notebooks*. Edited and translated by Quintin Hoare and Geoffrey Nowell Smith. New York: International Publishers.

Green Left. 2011. "Egypt: Strike Wave Hits Regime." *Green Left* 867, February 10, 2011. https://www.greenleft.org.au/content/egypt-strike-wave-hits-regime.

Gunning, Jereoen, and Illan Zvi Baron. 2013. *Why Occupy a Square: People, Protests and Movements in the Egyptian Revolution*. London: C. Hurst.

Hafez, Sherine. 2019. *Women of the Midan: The Untold Stories of Egypt's Revolutionaries*. Bloomington: Indiana University Press.

Halawi, Ibrahim. 2019. "Towards a Relational Theorisation of Counterrevolution and Revolution: The Case of Modern Egypt 1805–2013." PhD diss., Royal Holloway, University of London.

Hamzawy, Amr. 2018. "Conspiracy Theories and Populist Narratives: On the Ruling Techniques of Egyptian Generals." *Philosophy and Social Criticism* 44 (4): 491–504.

Hanieh, Adam 2011. "Egypt's 'Orderly Transition'? International Aid and the Rush to Structural Adjustment." *Jadaliyya*, May 29, 2011. http://www.jadaliyya.com/pages/index/1711/egypts-%E2%80%98orderly-transition%E2%80%99-international-aid-.

Hanna, Michael Wahid. 2014. "God and State in Egypt." *World Policy Journal* 31 (2): 59–69. https://read.dukeupress.edu/world-policy-journal/article-abstract/31/2/59/52858/God-and-State-in-Egypt.

Hassan, Mohamed, and Cyrus Sassanpour. 2008. "Labor Market Pressures in Egypt: Why Is the Unemployment Rate Stubbornly High?" Paper presented at the International Conference on the Unemployment Crisis in the Arab Countries, Cairo, March 17–18, 2008. https://www.ilo.org/dyn/travail/docs/437/Hassan%20and%20Sassanpour%202008%20%E2%80%99Labor%20Market%20Pressures%20in%20Egypt%E2%80%99%20API.pdf.

Hasso, Frances S., and Zakia Salime. 2016. Introduction to *Freedom without Permission: Bodies and Space in the Arab Revolutions*, edited by Frances S. Hasso and Zakia Salime, 1–23. Durham, NC: Duke University Press.

Hawthorne, Amy, and Andrew Miller, eds. 2020. "Why Did Egyptian Democratization Fail? Fourteen Experts Respond." Project on Middle East Democracy, January 2020. https://pomed.org/wp-content/uploads/2020/01/200128b_EgyptDemocracy.pdf.

Hayano, David M. 1979. "Auto-Ethnography: Paradigms, Problems, and Prospects." *Human Organization* 38 (1): 99–104.

Hazzard, Emily Q. 2010. "Can Mohamed ElBaradei Lead Change in Egypt?" *Atlantic*, May 12, 2010. https://www.theatlantic.com/international/archive/2010/05/can-mohamed-elbaradei-lead-change-in-egypt/56613/.

Hearst, David. 2018. "The Paranoid World of Abdel Fattah el-Sisi." *Middle East Eye*, September 24, 2018. https://www.middleeasteye.net/opinion/paranoid-world-abdel-fattah-el-sisi.

Hearst, David, and Abdel Rahman Hussein. 2012. "Egypt Supreme Court Dissolves Parliament and Outrages Islamists." *Guardian*, June 14, 2012. https://www.theguardian.com/world/2012/jun/14/egypt-parliament-dissolved-supreme-court.

Herrera, Linda. 2014. *Revolution in the Age of Social Media: The Egyptian Popular Insurrection and the Internet*. London: Verso.

Hinnebusch, Raymond. 2014. "Towards a Historical Sociology of the Arab Uprising: Beyond Democratization and Post-democratization." In *Routledge Handbook of the Arab Spring*, edited by Larbi Sadiki, 39–50. New York: Taylor and Francis.

Hirschkind, Charles. 2011. "Uprising in Egypt: The Road to Tahrir." *Immanent Frame* (blog), February 9, 2011. https://tif.ssrc.org/2011/02/09/the-road-to-tahrir/.

Hofstadter, Richard. 2012. *The Paranoid Style in American Politics*. New York: Vintage.

Holmes, Amy. 2012. "There Are Weeks When Decades Happen: Structure and Strategy in the Egyptian Revolution." *Mobilization: An International Quarterly* 17 (4): 391–410.

Holmes, Amy. 2019. *Coups and Revolutions: Mass Mobilization, the Egyptian Military, and the United States from Mubarak to Sisi*. Oxford: Oxford University Press.

Howeidy, Amira. 2005a. "A Chronology of Dissent." *Al-Ahram Weekly*, June 23, 2005. https://www.masress.com/en/ahramweekly/16657.

Howeidy, Amira. 2005b. "Enough Is Not Enough." *Al-Ahram Weekly*, March 24, 2005. https://web.archive.org/web/20130223082726/http://weekly.ahram.org.eg/2005/731/eg10.htm.

Human Rights Watch. 2013. "Egypt: Security Forces Used Excessive Lethal Force." Human Rights Watch, August 9, 2013. http://www.hrw.org/news/2013/08/19/egypt-security-forces-used-excessive-lethal-force.

Immigration and Refugee Board of Canada. 2005. "Egypt: Organized Criminal Activities and Corruption in the Police Force; Government Response to These Activities and State Protection Available (January 2003–June 2005)." EGY100091.E. June 17, 2005. http://www.refworld.org/docid/440ed6f920.html.

International Monetary Fund. 2010. "Arab Republic of Egypt—2010 Article IV Consultation Mission, Concluding Statement." February 24, 2010. https://www.imf.org/en/News/Articles/2015/09/28/04/52/mcs021610.

Iskandar, Adel. 2021. "Media as Method in the Age of Revolution: Statism and Digital Contestation." In *The Oxford Handbook of Contemporary Middle Eastern and North African History*, edited by Amal Ghazal and Jens Hanssen, 342–64. Oxford: Oxford University Press.

Ismail, Salwa. 2011. "A Private Estate Called Egypt." *Guardian*, February 6, 2011. http://www.theguardian.com/commentisfree/2011/feb/06/private-estate-egypt-mubarak-cronies.

Ismail, Salwa. 2012. "The Egyptian Revolution against the Police." *Social Research: An International Inquiry* 79 (2): 435–62.

Jadaliyya. 2011. "Egypt Election Watch: Mamdouh Hamza." November 18, 2011. http://www.jadaliyya.com/pages/index/3181/mamdouh-hamza.

Jerzak, Connor. 2013. "Ultras in Egypt: State, Revolution, and the Power of Public Space." *Interface: A Journal for and about Social Movements* 5 (2): 240–62.

Kadivar, Mohammad Ali. 2018. "Mass Mobilization and the Durability of New Democracies." *American Sociological Review* 83 (2): 390–417.

Kadivar, Mohammad Ali, and Neil Ketchley. 2018. "Sticks, Stones, and Molotov Cocktails: Unarmed Collective Violence and Democratization." *Socius: Sociological Research for a Dynamic World* 4: 1–16.

Kandil, Hazem. 2012. "Why Did the Egyptian Middle Class March to Tahrir Square?" *Mediterranean Politics* 17 (2): 197–215.

Kandil, Hazem. 2014. *Soldiers, Spies, and Statesmen: Egypt's Road to Revolt*. New York: Verso.

Ketchley, Neil. 2017a. *Egypt in a Time of Revolution*. Cambridge: Cambridge University Press.

Ketchley, Neil. 2017b. "How Egypt's Generals Used Street Protests to Stage a Coup." *Washington Post*, July 3, 2017. https://www.washingtonpost.com/news/monkey-cage/wp/2017/07/03/how-egypts-generals-used-street-protests-to-stage-a-coup/.

Khondker, Hanibul Haque. 2011. "Role of the New Media in the Arab Spring." *Globalizations* 8 (5): 675–79.

Kingsley, Patrick. 2013. "Who Are the Muslim Brotherhood?" *Guardian*, April 2, 2013. https://www.theguardian.com/world/2013/apr/02/who-are-the-muslim -brotherhood.

Kirkpatrick, David. 2011a. "At a Protest in Cairo, One Group Is Missing." *New York Times*, May 27, 2011. https://www.nytimes.com/2011/05/28/world/middleeast /28egypt.html.

Kirkpatrick, David. 2011b. "Islamists Say They Have Mandate in Egypt Voting." *New York Times*, November 30, 2011. https://www.nytimes.com/2011/12/01 /world/middleeast/voting-in-egypt-shows-mandate-for-islamists.html.

Kirkpatrick, David. 2012. "Blow to Transition as Court Dissolves Egypt's Parlia- ment." *New York Times*, June 14, 2012. https://www.nytimes.com/2012/06/15 /world/middleeast/new-political-showdown-in-egypt-as-court-invalidates -parliament.html.

Kirkpatrick, David, and Mayy El Sheikh. 2012. "Citing Deadlock, Egypt's Leader Seizes New Power and Plans Mubarak Retrial." *New York Times*, Novem- ber 22, 2012. https://www.nytimes.com/2012/11/23/world/middleeast/egypts -president-morsi-gives-himself-new-powers.html.

Knight, Peter, ed. 2002. *Conspiracy Nation: The Politics of Paranoia in Postwar America*. New York: New York University Press.

Korotayev, Andrey, and Julia Zinkina. 2011. "Egyptian Revolution: A Demographic Structural Analysis." *Middle East Studies Online Journal* 2 (5). http://www .middle-east-studies.net/wp-content/uploads/2011/03/Korotayev.pdf.

Kumar, Krishan. 2007. "The Future of Revolution: Imitation or Innovation." In *Revolution in the Making of the Modern World: Social Identities, Globalization and Modernity*, edited by John Foran, David Lane, and Andreja Zivkovic, 222–35. New York: Routledge.

Kuntz, Philipp, and Mark R. Thompson. 2009. "More than Just the Final Straw: Stolen Elections as Revolutionary Triggers." *Comparative Politics* 41 (3): 253–72.

Kurzman, Charles. 2004. "Can Understanding Undermine Explanation? The Confused Experience of Revolution." *Philosophy of the Social Sciences* 34, no. 3 (2004): 328–51.

Kurzman, Charles. 2009. *The Unthinkable Revolution in Iran*. Cambridge, MA: Harvard University Press.

Kurzman, Charles. 2017. "Unruly Protest." In *Microfoundations of the Arab Uprisings: Mapping Interactions between Regimes and Protesters*, edited by Frédéric Volpi and James M. Jasper, 183–92. Amsterdam: Amsterdam University Press.

Kutay, Acar. 2022. "Neoliberalism Incites but Also Restrains Revolutionary Change in the Third World: Why Articulating Multiple Struggles Is Neces- sary to Confront Structures of Domination." *Globalizations* 19 (7): 1013–28.

LaGraffe, Daniel. 2012. "The Youth Bulge in Egypt: An Intersection of Demo- graphics, Security, and the Arab Spring." *Journal of Strategic Security* 5 (2): 65–80.

Lamont, Michèle, and Virág Molnár. 2002. "The Study of Boundaries in the Social Sciences." *Annual Review of Sociology* 28 (1): 167–95.

Landler, Mark. 2011. "Clinton Calls for 'Orderly Transition' in Egypt." *New York Times*, January 30, 2011. http://www.nytimes.com/2011/01/31/world /middleeast/31diplo.html.

Latif, Rusha. 2022. *Tahrir's Youth: Leaders of a Leaderless Revolution*. Cairo: American University in Cairo Press.

Lawson, George. 2015a. "Revolution, Nonviolence, and the Arab Uprising." *Mobilization: An International Quarterly* 20 (4): 453–70.

Lawson, George. 2015b. "Revolutions and the International." *Theory and Society* 44 (4): 299–319.

Lawson, George. 2016. "Within and beyond the 'Fourth Generation' of Revolutionary Theory." *Sociological Theory* 34 (2): 106–27.

Lawson, George. 2017. *Negotiated Revolutions: The Czech Republic, South Africa, and Chile*. New York: Routledge.

Lawson, George. 2019. *Anatomies of Revolution*. Cambridge: Cambridge University Press.

Lazard, Hamouda Chekir, and Ishac Diwan. 2012. "Crony Capitalism in Egypt." Working Paper 250, Center for International Development at Harvard University. http://www.hks.harvard.edu/var/ezp_site/storage/fckeditor/file /pdfs/centers-programs/centers/cid/publications/faculty/wp/250_Diwan _EGX%20paper.pdf

Leal, Rene. 2020. "The Rise of Fascist Formations in Chile and in the World." *Social Sciences* 9 (12): 1–17.

Lee, Eric, and Benjamin Weinthal. 2011. "Trade Unions: The Revolutionary Social Network at Play in Egypt and Tunisia." *Guardian*, February 10, 2011. http:// www.theguardian.com/commentisfree/2011/feb/10/trade-unions-egypt-tunisia.

Lefebvre, Henri. (1974) 1991. *The Production of Space*. Translated by Donald Nicholson-Smith. Malden, MA: Blackwell.

Lesch, Ann M. 2011. "Egypt's Spring: Causes of the Revolution." *Middle East Policy* 18 (3): 35–48.

"Letter from Parties, NGOs, Syndicates and Political Movements to the IMF." 2012. Egyptian Initiative for Personal Rights, November 12, 2012. https://eipr.org/en /press/2012/11/letter-parties-ngossyndicates-and-political-movements-imf.

Lim, Merlyna. 2012. "Clicks, Cabs, and Coffee Houses: Social Media and Oppositional Movements in Egypt, 2004–2011." *Journal of Communication* 62 (2): 231–48.

Lindsay, Ursula. 2011. "Corrupt and Brutal, Egypt's Police Fight for Their Survival." *Daily Beast*, November 22, 2011. http://www.thedailybeast.com/articles /2011/11/22/corrupt-and-brutal-egypt-s-police-fight-for-their-survival.html.

Lindsay, Ursula. 2012. "Art in Egypt's Revolutionary Square." *Middle East Report Online*, January 11, 2012. http://www.merip.org/mero/interventions/art -egypts-revolutionary-square.

Mahfouz, Naguib. 2007. *The Dreams of Departure: The Last Dreams Published in the Nobel Laureate's Lifetime*. Cairo: American University in Cairo Press.

Makar, Farida. 2011. "'Let Them Have Some Fun': Political and Artistic Forms of Expression in the Egyptian Revolution." *Mediterranean Politics* 16 (2): 307–12.

Malekzadeh, Shervin. 2016. "Paranoia and Perspective, or How I Learned to Stop Worrying and Start Loving Research in the Islamic Republic of Iran." *Social Science Quarterly* 97 (4): 862–75.

Malin, Carrington. 2010. "Middle East and North Africa Facebook Demographics." Spot On Public Relations, May 24, 2010. https://www.spotonpr.com/wp -content/uploads/2017/10/FacebookMENA_24May10.pdf.

Malin, Carrington. 2011a. "Egypt's Facebook Demographics." Spot On Public Relations, January 26, 2011. http://www.spotonpr.com/egypt-facebook -demographics/.

Malin, Carrington. 2011b. "Facebook Arabic Rising." Spot On Public Relations, June 8, 2011. http://www.spotonpr.com/facebook-arabic-uprising/.

Markoff, John. 2015. *Waves of Democracy: Social Movements and Political Change*. New York: Routledge.

Marshall, Katherine. 2015. "A Kairos Moment: Faith Calls to Action." *Faith in Action* (blog), September 29, 2015. https://berkleycenter.georgetown.edu/posts /a-kairos-moment-faith-calls-to-action.

Marshall, Shana. 2015. "The Egyptian Armed Forces and the Remaking of an Economic Empire." Carnegie Middle East Center Papers, April 2015. https:// carnegieendowment.org/files/egyptian_armed_forces.pdf.

Marx, Karl. (1851) 2008. *The Eighteenth Brumaire of Louis Bonaparte*. Cabin John, MD: Wildside.

Matthies-Boon, Vivienne. 2017. "Shattered Worlds: Political Trauma amongst Young Activists in Post-revolutionary Egypt." *Journal of North African Studies* 22 (4): 620–44.

Matthies-Boon, Vivienne, and Naomi Head. 2018. "Trauma as Counter-revolutionary Colonisation: Narratives from (Post) Revolutionary Egypt." *Journal of International Political Theory* 14 (3): 258–79.

Mayrl, Damon, and Sarah Quinn. 2016. "Defining the State from Within: Boundaries, Schemas, and Associational Policymaking." *Sociological Theory* 34 (1): 1–26.

McAdam, Doug. 1986. "Recruitment to High-Risk Activism: The Case of Freedom Summer." *American Journal of Sociology* 92 (1): 64–90.

McAdam, Doug, and William H. Sewell Jr. 2001. "It's about Time: Temporality in the Study of Social Movements and Revolutions." In *Silence and Voice in the Study of Contentious Politics*, edited by Ronald R. Aminzade, Jack A. Goldstone, Elizabeth J. Perry, Sidney Tarrow, and Charles Tilly, 89–125. Cambridge: Cambridge University Press.

McAdam, Doug, and Sidney Tarrow. 2010. "Ballots and Barricades: On the Reciprocal Relationship between Elections and Social Movements." *Perspectives on Politics* 8 (2): 529–42.

McAdam, Doug, and Sidney Tarrow. 2013. "Social Movements and Elections: Toward a Broader Understanding of the Political Context of Contention."

In *The Future of Social Movement Research: Dynamics, Mechanisms, and Processes*, edited by Jacquelien Van Stekelenburg, Conny Roggeband, and Bert Klandermans, 325–46. Minneapolis: University of Minnesota Press.

McAdam, Doug, Sidney Tarrow, and Charles Tilly. 2001a. *Dynamics of Contention*. Cambridge: Cambridge University Press.

McAdam, Doug, Sidney Tarrow, and Charles Tilly. 2001b. "Revolutionary Trajectories," in *Dynamics of Contention*, by Doug McAdam, Sidney Tarrow, and Charles Tilly, 193–226. Cambridge: Cambridge University Press.

Menshawy, Mustafa. 2021. "Why Is Egypt Building a New Capital? And Who Will This Multi-billion Project Benefit the Most?" Al Jazeera, July 5, 2021. https://www.aljazeera.com/opinions/2021/7/5/why-is-egypt-building-a-new-capital.

Middle East Monitor. 2019. "Rights Group: 3,185 Extrajudicial Killings in Egypt since 2013." July 4, 2019. https://www.middleeastmonitor.com/20190704-rights-group-3185-extrajudicial-killings-in-egypt-since-2013/.

Middle East News Agency. 2012. "Youth Are Quarter of Egypt's Population, and Half of Them Are Poor." *Egypt Independent*, August 12, 2012. https://www.egyptindependent.com/youth-are-quarter-egypt-s-population-and-half-them-are-poor/.

Middleton, John. 2003. "Merchants: An Essay in Historical Ethnography." *Journal of the Royal Anthropological Institute* 9 (3): 509–26.

Miller, Carolyn R. 2002. Foreword to *Rhetoric and Kairos: Essays in History, Theory, and Praxis*, edited by Phillip Sipiora and James S. Baumlin, xi–xiii. Albany: State University of New York Press.

Mohanty, Laxmi Nrusingha Prasad, and Swati Mohanty. 2005. *Slum in India*. New Delhi: APH.

Mohie, Mostafa. 2015. "Classified Report Reveals State Security's Take on Jan 25 Revolution." *Mada Masr*, January 12, 2015. https://madamasr.com/en/2015/01/12/feature/politics/classified-report-reveals-state-securitys-take-on-jan-25-revolution/.

Moss, Dana M. 2016. "Transnational Repression, Diaspora Mobilization, and the Case of the Arab Spring." *Social Problems* 63 (4): 480–98.

Mossallam, Alia. 2011. "Egypt: A Report on the Emergence and Role of 'Popular Committees.'" *Frontlines of Revolutionary Struggle*, July 4, 2011. https://revolutionaryfrontlines.wordpress.com/2011/07/04/egypt-a-report-on-the-emergence-and-role-of-popular-committees/.

Murchadha, Felix Ó. 2013. *The Time of Revolution: Kairos and Chronos in Heidegger*. London: Bloomsbury Academic.

Naber, Nadine. 2021. "The Radical Potential of Mothering during the Egyptian Revolution." *Feminist Studies* 47 (1): 62–93.

Naguib, Nefissa. 2011. "Basic Ethnography at the Barricades." *International Journal of Middle East Studies* 43 (3): 383–90.

Negri, Antonio. 2007. "Afterword: On the Concept of Revolution." In *Revolution in the Making of the Modern World*, edited by John Foran, David Lane, and Andreja Zivkovic, 252–59. New York: Routledge.

Nepstad, Sharon Erickson. 2013. "Mutiny and Nonviolence in the Arab Spring: Exploring Military Defections and Loyalty in Egypt, Bahrain, and Syria." *Journal of Peace Research* 50 (3): 337–49.

New York Times. 2011. "Egypt's Supreme Council of the Armed Forces: Statements and Key Leaders." February 14, 2011. https://archive.nytimes.com/www.nytimes.com/interactive/2011/02/10/world/middleeast/20110210-egypt-supreme-council.html?_r=0.

Nice, Pamela. 2006. "A Conversation with Alaa Al-Aswany on the 'Yacoubian Building.'" *Al Jadid* 12, nos. 56–57. http://www.aljadid.com/content/conversation.

No Comment TV. 2011. "Cleaning Up Tahrir Square—No Comment." YouTube video, 1:52, February 13, 2011. https://www.youtube.com/watch?v=c74B0OY7Y-Y.

Noureldin, Ola. 2017. "Egypt's Internet Speed among the World's Slowest, Ranking 146 out of 150." *Egypt Independent*, April 16, 2017. https://egyptindependent.com/egypt-s-internet-speed-among-world-s-slowest-ranking-146-out-150/.

NPR. 2011. "As Egypt Protests Wane, Labor Unrest Grows." February 14, 2011. http://www.npr.org/2011/02/14/133741350/egyptian-labor-unrest-grows-after-uprising.

Nunns, Alex, and Nadia Idle, eds. 2011. *Tweets from Tahrir: Egypt's Revolution as It Unfolded, in the Words of the People Who Made It.* New York: OR.

O'Donnell, Patrick. 2000. *Latent Destinies: Cultural Paranoia and Contemporary U.S. Narrative.* Durham, NC: Duke University Press.

Oehmke, Phillip. 2011. "Egypt's Man in the Moon: The Watchdog of Tahrir Square Fears the Revolution." *Spiegel*, April 29, 2011. http://www.spiegel.de/international/world/egypt-s-man-in-the-moon-the-watchdog-of-tahrir-square-fears-for-the-revolution-a-759025.html.

Onodera, Henri. 2009. "The *Kifaya* Generation: Politics of Change among Youth in Egypt." *Suomen Antropologi: Journal of the Finnish Anthropological Society* 34 (4): 44–64.

Oraby, Farah. 2018. "What Really Happened to Egyptian Democracy." *Berkeley Political Review*, April 30, 2018. https://bpr.berkeley.edu/2018/04/30/what-really-happened-to-egyptian-democracy/.

Ortmann, Stefanie, and John Heathershaw. 2012. "Conspiracy Theories in the Post-Soviet Space." *Russian Review* 71 (4): 551–64.

Oweidat, Nadia, Cheryl Benard, Dale Stahl, Walid Kildani, Edward O'Connell, and Audra K. Grant. 2008. *The Kefaya Movement: A Case Study of a Grassroots Reform Initiative.* Santa Monica, CA: RAND National Defense Research Institute. https://www.rand.org/content/dam/rand/pubs/monographs/2008/RAND_MG778.pdf.

Ozen, H. Ege. 2018. "Egypt's 2011–2012 Parliamentary Elections: Voting for Religious vs. Secular Democracy?" *Mediterranean Politics* 23 (4): 453–78.

Pahwa, Sonali, and Jessica Winegar. 2012. "Culture, State and Revolution." *Middle East Report*, no. 263. http://www.merip.org/mer/mer263/culture-state-revolution.

Paige, Jeffery. 2003. "Finding the Revolutionary in the Revolution: Social Science Concepts and the Future of Revolution." In *The Future of Revolutions: Rethinking Radical Change in the Age of Globalization*, edited by John Foran, 19–29. London: Zed.

Pankofsky, Erwin. 1939. *Studies in Iconology: Humanistic Themes in the Art of the Renaissance*. Oxford: Oxford University Press.

Pichardo Almanzar, Nelson A., and Cedric Herring. 2004. "Sacrificing for the Cause: Another Look at High-Risk/Cost Activism." *Race and Society* 7 (2): 113–29.

Population Council. 2010. *Survey of Young People in Egypt: Preliminary Report*. Cairo: Population Council. http://www.popcouncil.org/uploads/pdfs/2010PGY _SYPEPrelimReport.pdf.

Radnitz, Scott. 2016. "Paranoia with a Purpose: Conspiracy Theory and Political Coalitions in Kyrgyzstan." *Post-Soviet Affairs* 32 (5): 474–89.

Rahman, Rema. 2011. "Who, What, Why: How Dangerous Is Tear Gas?" BBC News, November 25, 2011. https://www.bbc.com/news/magazine-15887186.

Reed, Isaac Ariail. 2020. *Power in Modernity: Agency Relations and the Creative Destruction of the King's Two Bodies*. Chicago: University of Chicago Press. See esp. chap. 1, "Rector, Actor, Other."

Reed-Danahay, Deborah. 1997. Introduction to *Auto/Ethnography: Rewriting the Self and the Social*, edited by Deborah Reed-Danahay, 1–21. New York: Berg.

Reuters. 2018. "From War Room to Boardroom: Military Firms Flourish in Sisi's Egypt." May 16, 2018. https://www.reuters.com/investigates/special-report /egypt-economy-military/.

Rios, Lorena. 2015. "The Irreparable Loss of Cairo's Street Café District." *Vice*, May 27, 2015. https://www.vice.com/en/article/ypxkkw/the-irreparable-loss -of-cairos-street-cafe-district.

Ritter, Daniel P. 2015. *The Iron Cage of Liberalism: International Politics and Unarmed Revolutions in the Middle East and North Africa*. Oxford: Oxford University Press.

Rodrigo, Javier. 2012a. "Exploitation, Fascist Violence, and Social Cleansing: A Study of Franco's Concentration Camps from a Comparative Perspective." *European Review of History / Revue europeenne d'histoire* 19 (4): 553–73.

Rodrigo, Javier. 2012b. "Fascism and Violence in Spain: A Comparative Update." *International Journal of Iberian Studies* 25 (3): 183–99.

Rupp, Leila, and Verta Taylor. 1990. *Survival in the Doldrums: The American Women's Rights Movement, 1945 to the 1960s*. Columbus: Ohio State University Press.

Ryzova, Lucie. 2011. "The Battle of Cairo's Muhammad Mahmoud Street." Al Jazeera, November 29, 2011. https://www.aljazeera.com/indepth/opinion/2011 /11/2011112884946384191.html.

Saad, Abdel Rahman. 2012. *Scenes from the Heart of the Revolution*. Cairo: Al-Ahram Publications and Translations and Distributions.

Sabea, Hanan. 2013. "A 'Time out of Time': Tahrir, the Political and the Imaginary in the Context of the January 25th Revolution in Egypt." Hot Spots, *Fieldsights*, May 9, 2013. https://culanth.org/fieldsights/a-time-out-of-time

-tahrir-the-political-and-the-imaginary-in-the-context-of-the-january-25th
-revolution-in-egypt.

Said, Atef. 2012. "The Paradox of Transition to 'Democracy' under Military Rule."
Social Research 79 (2): 397–434.

Said, Atef. 2015. "We Ought to Be Here: Historicizing Space and Mobilization in
Tahrir Square." *International Sociology* 30 (4): 348–66.

Said, Atef. 2018. "Doing Research during Times of Revolution and Counter-
revolution." In *Political Science Research in the Middle East and North Africa:
Methodological and Ethical Challenges*, edited by Janine A. Clark and Francesco
Cavatorta, 83–92. Oxford: Oxford University Press.

Said, Atef. 2021. "A Sociology of Counter-revolution in Egypt." *Sociology Compass* 15
(9): e12916.

Said, Atef. 2022. "The Rise and Fall of the Tahrir Repertoire: Theorizing Temporality, Trajectory, and Failure." *Social Problems* 69 (1): 222–40.

Said, Atef, and Pete Moore. 2021. "Dialects of Hope and Despair in the Arab
Uprisings." *Middle East Report*, no. 301. https://merip.org/2021/12/dialectics-of
-hope-and-despair-in-the-arab-uprisings/.

Salvatore, Armando. 2013. "New Media, the 'Arab Spring,' and the Metamorphosis
of the Public Sphere: Beyond Western Assumptions on Collective Agency
and Democratic Politics." *Constellations* 20 (2): 217–28.

Schwedler, Jillian. 2013. "Spatial Dynamics of the Arab Uprisings." *PS: Political Science and Politics* 46 (2): 230–34.

Schwedler, Jillian. 2016. "Taking Time Seriously: Temporality and the Arab Uprisings." *POMEPS Blog*, May 2016. https://pomeps.org/2016/06/10/taking-time
-seriously-temporality-and-the-arab-uprisings/.

Seikaly, Sherene. 2019. "The Matter of Time." *American Historical Review* 124 (5):
1681–88.

Selim, Gamal M. 2015. "Egypt under SCAF and the Muslim Brotherhood: The
Triangle of Counter-revolution." *Arab Studies Quarterly* 37 (2): 177–99.

Sewell, Rob. 2018. *Germany: From Revolution to Counter-revolution*. London: Wellred.

Sewell, William H., Jr. 1996. "Historical Events as Transformations of Structures:
Inventing Revolution at the Bastille." *Theory and Society* 25 (6): 841–88.

Sewell, William H., Jr. 2001. "Space in Contentious Politics." In *Silence and Voice
in the Study of Contentious Politics*, edited by Ronald R. Aminzade, Jack A.
Goldstone, Doug McAdam, Elizabeth J. Perry, William H. Sewell Jr., Sidney
Tarrow, and Charles Tilly, 51–88. New York: Cambridge University Press.

Shadid, Anthony. 2011. "Suez Canal Workers Join Broad Strikes in Egypt."
New York Times, February 17, 2011. http://www.nytimes.com/2011/02/18/world
/middleeast/18egypt.html.

Shahine, Selim. 2011. "Youth and the Revolution in Egypt." *Anthropology Today* 27
(2): 1–3.

Shehata, Dina. 2011. "The Fall of the Pharaoh: How Hosni Mubarak's Reign Came
to an End." *Foreign Affairs*, May/June 2011. https://www.foreignaffairs.com
/articles/middle-east/2011-06-01/fall-pharaoh.

Shehata, Dina. 2012. "Youth Movements and the 25 January Revolution." In *The Arab Spring in Egypt: Revolution and Beyond*, edited by Bahgat Korany and Rabab El-Mahdi, 105–24. Cairo: American University in Cairo Press.

Shorbagy, Manar. 2007a. "The Egyptian Movement for Change—Kefaya: Redefining Politics in Egypt." *Public Culture* 19 (1): 175–96.

Shorbagy, Manar. 2007b. "Understanding *Kefaya*: The New Politics in Egypt." *Arab Studies Quarterly* 29 (1): 39–60.

Shukrallah, Hani. 2006. "The Anatomy of a Downtown Demo." *Daily News Egypt*, August 28, 2006. http://www.masress.com/en/dailynews/109395.

Simmel, Georg. 2008. "The Stranger." In *The Cultural Geography Reader*, edited by Timothy S. Oakes and Patricia L. Price, 311–15. New York: Routledge.

60 Minutes. 2011. "Revolution: Egyptians Return to Tahrir Square." CBS News, October 9, 2011. http://www.cbsnews.com/news/revolution-egyptians-return -to-tahrir-square/.

Skocpol, Theda. 1979. *States and Social Revolutions: A Comparative Analysis of France, Russia and China.* Cambridge: Cambridge University Press.

Smith, John E. 1969. "Time, Times, and the 'Right Time': Chronos and Kairos." *Monist* 53 (1): 1–13.

Soja, Edward W. 2009. "Take Space Personally." In *The Spatial Turn: Interdisciplinary Perspectives*, edited by Barney Warf and Santa Arias, 11–35. New York: Routledge.

Soliman, Samer. 2012a. "The Political Economy of Mubarak's Fall." In *The Arab Spring in Egypt: Revolution and Beyond*, edited by Bahgat Korany and Rabab El-Mahdi, 43–62. Cairo: American University in Cairo Press.

Soueif, Ahdaf. 2012. *Cairo: My City, Our Revolution.* London: A and C Black.

Springborg, Robert, and F. C. "Pink" Williams. 2019. "The Egyptian Military: A Slumbering Giant Awakes." Carnegie Middle East Center, February 28, 2019. https://carnegie-mec.org/2019/02/28/egyptian-military-slumbering-giant -awakes-pub-78238.

Stepan, Alfred C. 1988. *Rethinking Military Politics: Brazil and the Southern Cone.* Princeton, NJ: Princeton University Press.

Stoler, Ann Laura. 2006. "On Degrees of Imperial Sovereignty." *Public Culture* 18 (1): 125–46.

Stoler, Ann Laura. 2010. *Carnal Knowledge and Imperial Power: Race and the Intimate in Colonial Rule.* Berkeley: University of California Press.

Stork, Joe. 2005. "Egypt: Calls for Reform Met with Brutality." Human Rights Watch, May 25, 2005. http://www.hrw.org/news/2005/05/25/egypt-calls -reform-met-brutality.

Sukarieh, Mayssoun. 2012. "Dispatch from Mohamed Mahmoud Street: Egyptian Revolts." *Jadaliyya*, November 27, 2012. https://www.jadaliyya.com/Details /27491/Dispatch-from-Mohamed-Mahmoud-Street-Egyptian-Revolts.

Tahrir Institute for Middle East Policy. 2019. "TIMEP Brief: The Law Regulating the Press, Media, and the Supreme Council for Media Regulation." May 15, 2019. https://timep.org/reports-briefings/timep-brief-the-law-regulating-the -press-media-and-the-supreme-council-for-media-regulation/.

TahrirSqaureEgypt. 2011. "Egyptians Clean Tahrir Square and Talat Harb."
   YouTube video, 2:15, February 13, 2011. https://www.youtube.com/watch?v
   =zwxfMY7MXTI.
Tarrow, Sidney. 1993. "Cycles of Collective Action: Between Moments of Mad-
   ness and the Repertoire of Contention." *Social Science History* 17 (2): 281–307.
Taylor, Verta. 1989. "Social Movement Continuity: The Women's Movement in
   Abeyance." *American Sociological Review* 54 (5): 761–75.
Taylor, Verta, and Nicole C. Raeburn. 1995. "Identity Politics as High-Risk Activ-
   ism: Career Consequences for Lesbian, Gay, and Bisexual Sociologists."
   Social Problems 42 (2) (1995): 252–73.
Teitelbaum, Joshua. 2012. "Failing States: The Real Meaning of the Arab Upris-
   ings." Hoover Institution, Stanford University, January 11, 2012. http://www
   .hoover.org/research/failing-states-real-meaning-arab-uprisings.
Tilly, Charles. 1964. *The Vendée: A Sociological Analysis of the Counterrevolution of 1793*.
   Cambridge, MA: Harvard University Press.
Tilly, Charles. 1978. "Anthropology, History, and the Annales." *Review (Fernand
   Braudel Center)*, Winter–Spring 1978, 207–13.
Tilly, Charles. 1993. *From Mobilization to Revolution*. 2nd ed. New York: Random
   House.
Tilly, Charles. 2000. "Spaces of Contention." *Mobilization: An International Quar-
   terly* 5 (2): 135–59.
Tilly, Charles. 2004. "Social Boundary Mechanisms." *Philosophy of the Social Sciences*
   34 (2): 211–36.
Tilly, Charles. 2007a. *Democracy*. Cambridge: Cambridge University Press.
Tilly, Charles. 2007b. "History of and in Sociology." *American Sociologist* 38 (4):
   326–29.
Tilly, Charles. 2008. *Contentious Performances*. Cambridge: Cambridge University
   Press.
Tilly, Charles, and Sidney G. Tarrow. 2015. *Contentious Politics*. Oxford: Oxford
   University Press.
Time. 2013. "Cover: Egypt: The Street Rules." *Time*, July 22, 2013. http://content
   .time.com/time/covers/asia/0,16641,20130722,00.html.
Tocqueville, Alexis de. (1856) 2010. *The Old Regime and the French Revolution*.
   Norwell, MA: Anchor.
Toor, Amar. 2011. "Egypt Shuts Down Internet as Protests Intensify." *Switched*,
   January 28, 2011. http://www.switched.com/2011/01/28/egypt-shuts-down
   -internet-as-protests-intensify/.
Trotsky, Leon. (1932) 2008. *The History of the Russian Revolution*. Translated by Max
   Eastman. Chicago: Haymarket.
Trotsky, Leon. 1938. "The Question of the United Front." *New International* 4 (7):
   216–18. https://www.marxists.org/archive/trotsky/1922/02/uf.htm.
Tufekci, Zeynep, and Christopher Wilson. 2012. "Social Media and the Decision
   to Participate in Political Protest: Observations from Tahrir Square." *Journal
   of Communication* 62 (2): 363–79.

Van de Sande, Mathijs. 2013. "The Prefigurative Politics of Tahrir Square—an Alternative Perspective on the 2011 Revolutions." *Res Publica* 19 (3): 223–39.

Walsh, Declan. 2019. "Egypt's Soap Opera Clampdown Extends el-Sisi's Iron Grip to TV." *New York Times*, April 3, 2019. https://www.nytimes.com/2019/04/03/world/middleeast/sisi-egypt-soap-opera.html.

Washington Post. 2005. "Editorial: 'Kifaya' in Egypt." March 15, 2005. http://www.washingtonpost.com/wp-dyn/articles/A35379-2005Mar14.html.

Weston, Kath. 2000. "The Virtual Anthropologist." In *Is Academic Feminism Dead?: Theory in Practice*, edited by the Social Justice Group at the Center for Advanced Feminist Studies, University of Minnesota, 137–67. New York: New York University Press.

Whitehead, Laurence. 2002. *Democratization: Theory and Experience*. Oxford: Oxford University Press.

WikiLeaks. 2016. "Secret Offer to El Baradei / Muslim Brotherhood–Army Alliance" (email correspondence between Secretary of State Hillary Clinton and Deputy Chief of Staff Jake Sullivan, November 23, 2011). Hillary Clinton Email Archive. https://wikileaks.org/clinton-emails/emailid/12549.

Wilson, William Julius. 2012. *The Truly Disadvantaged: The Inner City, the Underclass, and Public Policy*. 2nd ed. Chicago: University of Chicago Press.

Winegar, Jessica. 2011. "Taking Out the Trash: Youth Clean Up Egypt after Mubarak." *Middle East Report*, no. 259. https://merip.org/2011/06/taking-out-the-trash/.

Winegar, Jessica. 2012. "The Privilege of Revolution: Gender, Class, Space, and Affect in Egypt." *American Ethnologist* 39 (1): 67–70.

World Politics Review. 2019. "'Simply Put, There's No Freedom of the Press' in Sisi's Egypt." May 20, 2019. https://www.worldpoliticsreview.com/trend-lines/27870/simply-put-there-s-no-freedom-of-the-press-in-sisi-s-egypt.

Worth, Robert F. 2011. "You Are Here: House of Coups." *New York Times Magazine*, March 4, 2011. http://www.nytimes.com/2011/03/06/magazine/06YouRHere-t.html.

Zahedi, Arya. 2019. "The Iranian Revolution at the Twilight of the Workers' Council." *Commune*, no. 4. https://communemag.com/the-iranian-revolution-at-the-twilight-of-the-workers-council/.

Zaltzman, Janine. 2012. "Egypt." Women under Siege Project, Women's Media Center, February 8, 2012. https://womensmediacenter.com/women-under-siege/conflicts/egypt.

Zemni, Sami, Brecht De Smet, and Koenraad Bogaert. 2013. "Luxemburg on Tahrir Square: Reading the Arab Revolutions with Rosa Luxemburg's *The Mass Strike*." *Antipode* 45, no. 4: 888–907.

Zhuo, Xioalin, Barry Wellman, and Justine Yu. 2011. "Egypt: The First Internet Revolt?" *Peace Magazine* 27 (3): 6–10.

003superman. 2011. "Laqaṭāt tunshar li-awwal marra :: maʿrakat kūbrī qaṣr al-nīl kāmila" [Clips released for the first time: the complete Qasr El Nile Bridge battle]. YouTube video, 27:36, June 6, 2011. https://www.youtube.com/watch ?v=NAmPedJFlFs.

Abbas, Walid. 2014. "ʿAl-lijān al-iliktrūniyya' aw ṣināʿat al-diʿāya al-siyāsiyya fī miṣr" ["Trolls" or the manufacture of political propaganda in Egypt]. *Monte Carlo Doualiya*, September 24, 2014. https://bit.ly/38koU4Z.

Abdel Aziz, Marwan. 2010. "Al-ʿAryān: jamʿ al-tawqīʿāt ʿalā bayān 'maʿan sanu-ghayyir' lā yaʿnī taḥāluf al-ikhwān maʿ al-Barādiʿī.. wa-lam nuqarrir baʿd al-badʾ fīhā" [El-Erian: "Collecting signatures for the NAFC does not mean that the MB is endorsing Baradei. We have not yet decided if we are joining the NAFC"]. *Almasry Alyoum*, June 4, 2010. https://www.almasryalyoum.com /news/details/702.

Abdel Hameed, Reem. 2012. "Al-inddibindint: manākh 'al-karāhiya' yasūd miṣr maʿ ḥiṣār al-maḥkama al-dustūriyya" [The *Independent*: Climate of "hatred" dominates Egypt with the MB siege of the Supreme Court]. *Youm7*, December 5, 2012. https://www.youm7.com/865196.

Abdel Rady, Mahmoud. 2016. "Al-dākhiliyya taqṭaʿ lisān al-ikhwān qabl 25 yanāyir.. al-qabḍ ʿalā admin 47 ṣafḥa ikhwāniyya tadʿū lil-ʿunf wa-muhājamat muʾassasāt al-dawla wa-iqtiḥām al-mabānī al-shurṭiyya.. wa-ḍabṭ awrāq takshif kharīṭat taḥarrukāt al-jamāʿāt al-irhābiyya fī dhikrā al-thawra" [The Ministry of the Interior cuts the MB's tongue before January 25: Arresting the admins of 47 Facebook pages of the MB that call for violence, attacking state institutions and police buildings. Confiscated documents reveal the planned moves of terrorist groups on the anniversary of the revolution]. *Youm7*, January 13, 2016. https://www.youm7.com/2536763.

Abdelrehim, Hosni. 2011. "Altariq alwahid" [The only road]. In *Kitāb al-thawra* [The revolution book], edited by Hosni Abdelrehim, 49–62. Cairo: Independent Publishing.

Abd Rabu, Ahmed. 2015. "Asʾila istajaddat fī sharʿiyyat al-tafwīḍ" [New questions about the legitimacy of the mandate]. *Shorouk News*, February 15, 2015. https://www.shorouknews.com/columns/view.aspx?cdate=15022015&id =b8b7daa0-a1fc-4b08-ad8d-4ac211f5d4da.

Aboul Gheit, Mohamed. 2011. "Al-fuqarāʾ awwalan yā wlād al-kalb!" [The poor first, you sons of bitches!]. *Gedarea* (blog), June 17, 2011. http://gedarea .blogspot.com/2011/06/normal-o-false-false-false.html.

Abu Ghazy, Maryam, and Emad Mubarak. 2016. *ʿAn Muḥammad Maḥmūd wa-ʾl-sirāʿ ḥawl al-ḥikāya ... taqrīr ʿan aḥdāth Muḥammad Maḥmūd 19–25 Nūfimbar 2011* [About Mohamed Mahmoud and the battle over the story: Report about the events of Mohamed Mahmoud, November 19–25, 2011]. Cairo: Association for Freedom of Thought and Expression. https://afteegypt.org/research /monitoring-reports/2016/03/24/11982-afteegypt.html.

Abu Seada, Hafez. 2011. "Al-mabādiʾ fawq al-dustūriyya" [On the supraconstitutional principles]. *Youm7*, July 21, 2011. https://www.youm7.com/459119.

Abu Yazid, Arwa. 2015. "Tansīqiyyat al-ḥurriyyāt al-miṣriyya tudīn maqtal iʿlāmī
bi-Saynāʾ" [The Egyptian Coordination of Rights and Freedoms condemns
the killing of a journalist in Sinai]. *Al-Araby Al-Jadeed*, April 28, 2015. https://
tinyurl.com/bdfu6t48.

Achcar, Gilbert. 2016a. "Hal yastaṭīʿ al-shaʿb isqāṭ al-niẓām wal-dawla lā tazāl
qāʾima? Taʾammul fī al-muʿḍila al-raʾīsiyya lil-intifāḍa al-ʿarabiyya"
[Can the people cause the regime to fall while the state remains intact?
A reflection on the main dilemma in the Arab uprisings]. Lecture at the
American University in Beirut, January 22, 2016. https://www.aub.edu.lb/ifi
/Documents/events/2015-2016/20160817_gilbert.pdf.

Agamy, Abdel Fatah. 2016. "'Wa-qālat al-ṣanādīq lil-dīn naʿam..' al-dhikrā al-
khāmisa li-shaqq ṣaff al-thawra" ["Ballots said yes to religion": The fifth anniversary of dividing the revolution]. *Tahrir News*, March 19, 2016. https://bit
.ly/3QLNYIG.

Akhbarak. 2016. "Al-Sīsī: ʿanā mumkin bi-katībatayn adkhul ʿalā al-nit wa-aʿmalhā
dāyira maqfūla'" [Sisi: "By deploying two [troll] military battalions, I can
create a closed circuit in the internet [dominate the information in the
internet"]]. April 13, 2016. https://bit.ly/2NDF8Oy.

Al-Ahram. 2011a. "'Umar Sulaymān: al-ḥiwār huwa al-ṭarīqa al-awlā li-inhāʾ
al-azma.. wa-'l-badīl huwa al-inqilāb" [Omar Suleiman: Dialog is the ideal
way to end the crisis; the alternative is a coup]. *Al-Ahram*, February 8, 2011.
https://gate.ahram.org.eg/News/38050.aspx.

Al-Ahram. 2011b. "Al-Bishrī raʾisan li-lajnat al-taʿdīlāt al-dustūriyya" [El-Bishry
to head Constitutional Review Committee]. *Al-Ahram*, February 15, 2011.
https://gate.ahram.org.eg/News/40189.aspx.

Al-Gamal, Colonel Usama. 2013. "Miṣr al-makān wal-makāna—lil-ʿaqīd Usāma
al-Gamāl" [Egypt's location and status]. YouTube video, 56:30, April 9, 2013.
https://www.youtube.com/watch?v=-Wm04vfUIqU.

Al-Hurra. 2012. "Al-ikhwān al-muslimūn: aḥkām al-maḥkama al-dustūriyya
'inqilāb kāmil al-arkān'" [Muslim Brotherhood: The Supreme Court verdict
is "a full-fledged coup"]. June 14, 2012. https://www.alhurra.com/a/202763
.html.

Ali, Mahmoud Mohamed. 2016. "Kāmil al-Wazīrī: tamm taklīf al-hayʾa al-
handasiyya lil-quwwāt al-musallaḥa bi-tanfīdh 1737 mashrūʿan tanmawiyyan
bil-dawla" [Kamel Al-Wazery: The armed forces engineering authority
was tasked with implementing 1,737 developmental projects for the state].
Shorouk News, May 12, 2016. https://www.shorouknews.com/news/view.aspx
?cdate=12052016&id=c7b8bf6b-0d40-467c-8ffe-a399118cc42c.

Al-Jamʿiyya Al-Waṭaniyya li-'l-Taghyīr [National Association for Change]. 2010.
"Bayān al-duktūr al-Barādiʿī "maʿan sanughayyir" [Dr. ElBaradei's statement "Together We Will Change"]. March 2, 2010. https://web.archive.org
/web/20100702214736/http://www.taghyeer.net/.

Al Jazeera. 2011a. "Bad' istiftā' ta'dīl al-dustūr bi-miṣr" [Referendum starts in Egypt]. March 19, 2011. https://goo.gl/qg5ijW.

Al Jazeera. 2011b. "Vīdīyū ziyārat al-liwā' Ḥasan al-Ruwaynī / qā'id al-minṭaqa al-'askariyya al-markaziyya al-ladhī khāṭab al-mutaẓāhirīn fī maydān al-taḥrīr—Al Jazeera" [Video of the visit by Major General Hassan al-Roueini, the commander of the central military region, who addressed the protesters in Tahrir—Al Jazeera]. Al Jazeera, 1:42, February 5, 2011. https://tinyurl.com/4yvy7m9b.

Al Jazeera. 2011c. "Inḍimām al-rā'id Shūmān li-ṣufūf al-muḥtajjīn fī maydān al-taḥrīr" [Major Shoman joins the ranks of the protesters in Tahrir Square]. YouTube video, 5:23, February 11, 2011. https://www.youtube.com/watch?v=DfitOJ1z6CU.

Al Jazeera. 2012a. "Al-idāriyya al-'ulyā tu'ayyid ḥall majlis al-sha'b al-miṣrī" [The Supreme Administrative Court upholds dissolution of the Egyptian parliament]. September 22, 2012. https://goo.gl/HCKdGa.

Al Jazeera. 2012b. "I'tiṣām wa-da'wa li-tawsī' al-iḥtijāj ḍidd Mursī" [Sit-ins and calls to widen protests against Morsi]. November 24, 2012. https://goo.gl/UzZpa5.

Al Jazeera. 2012c. "Al-dustūriyya tataḥaddā qarār Mursī i'ādat al-barlamān." [The Supreme Court challenges Morsi's decision to restitute the parliament]. July 10, 2012. http://goo.gl/JdGFaK.

Al Jazeera. 2012d. "Tawattur bi-miṣr qubayl i'lān ism al-ra'īs" [Tensions in Egypt prior to the announcement of the winner in the presidential election]. June 23, 2012. https://bit.ly/3KiixmV.

Al Jazeera. 2015. "Taḥdhīrāt al-Sīsī min thawrat yanāyir jadīda" [Sisi warns of a new January Revolution]. YouTube, 3:00, December 25, 2015. https://www.youtube.com/watch?v=gQH5CflJ4Vc.

Al-lijān al-sha'biyya li-'l-difā' 'an al-thawra al-miṣriyya [The Popular Committees for the defense of the Egyptian Revolution]. 2011. Homepage. https://leganthawrya.blogspot.com/.

Almasry Alyoum. 2011a. "Ḍābiṭ al-jaysh "Shūmān": "al-majlis" yaḥmī qādatah" [Army officer Shoman: The council is protecting its leaders]. YouTube video, 3:40, November 23, 2011. https://www.youtube.com/watch?v=TJzWBtvWZmI.

Almasry Alyoum. 2011b. "'Thawrat al-ghaḍab' fī 'qaṣr al-nīl'" [The "revolution of rage" at "Qasr El Nile"]. YouTube video, 9:47, January 31, 2011. https://www.youtube.com/watch?v=PujwO_iY5BU.

Almasry Alyoum. 2012a. "Masīra li-"dār al-qaḍā'" li-'l-ifrāj 'an ḍubbāṭ 8 Abrīl" [A rally to the High Court for the release of the April 8th officers]. YouTube video, 2:35, January 14, 2012. https://www.youtube.com/watch?v=fUIEUR6cJb8.

Almasry Alyoum. 2012b. "Masīrāt ilā majlis al-sha'b.. wa-'l-ishtibākāt ma' al-ikhwān amām al-barlamān" [Rallies to the parliament, and clashes with the MB in front of the parliament]. February 1, 2012. https://www.almasryalyoum.com/news/details/148337.

Almasry Alyoum. 2012c. "Miṣr fī awwal yawm barlamān khilāfāt ḥādda fī jalsat al-ijrāʾāt.. wa-muẓāharāt wa-iḥtijājāt tuḥāṣir majlis al-shaʿb" [Egypt in the first session of the new parliament: Sharp disputes inside the session while demonstrations and protests surround parliament]. January 24, 2012. https://www.almasryalyoum.com/news/details/1795410.

Almasry Alyoum. 2013. "Bil-ṣuwar.. tarmīm al-nuṣb al-tidhkārī lil-shuhadāʾ bi-maydān al-taḥrīr" [With images: Renovating the martyrs' memorial in Tahrir]. December 4, 2013. https://www.almasryalyoum.com/news/details/352380.

Almasry Alyoum. 2015. "Istiʿrāḍ jawwī li-ṭāʾirāt ḥarbiyya fī samāʾ al-qāhira" [Military planes perform aerial show in Cairo's sky]. YouTube video, 1:20, October 14, 2015. https://www.youtube.com/watch?v=Q93OvOI4nuY.

Al-Shamaaa, Rania. 2015. "Arbaʿ maʿlūmāt mukaththafa ʿan maydān al-taḥrīr: awwal miliyūniyya 1951.. wa-dahs al-mutaẓāhirīn ʿāda" [Four distilled factoids about Tahrir Square: First million-person rally in 1951 . . . and running over protesters is a common occurrence]. *Almasry Alyoum*, January 25, 2015. https://lite.almasryalyoum.com/extra/38920/.

Al-Sheikh, Haitham. 2016. "Al-qabḍ ʿalā admin ʾiksir kalābish' fī al-iskandariyya" [The arrest of the administrator of the "Break Handcuffs" Facebook page in Alexandria]. *Al-Watan News*, April 22, 2016. https://www.elwatannews.com/news/details/1116860.

Al-Shereef, Nayera. 2014. "Aḥdāth al-ittiḥādiyya.. qiṣṣat thalāthat ayyām kānat tasīr fī tijāh ḥarb ahliyya" [Al-Ittihadiya clashes: Three days that would have led Egypt to civil war]. *Masrawy*, December 4, 2014. https://goo.gl/TA32Fm.

Al-Wafd TV. 2011. "Bayān iʾtilāf quwā al-muʿāraḍa bi-ʾl-tafāwuḍ maʿ ʿUmar Sulaymān" [Coalition of Opposition Forces statement regarding negotiating with Omar Suleiman]. YouTube video, 8:00, February 3, 2011. https://www.youtube.com/watch?v=dp4oWUKkGYQ.

Al-Watan News. 2013. "Ṭāʾirāt al-jaysh taktub ism al-Sīsī fī samāʾ al-taḥrīr" [Military planes write Sisi's name in Tahrir's sky]. October 6, 2013. https://tinyurl.com/ydudynwk.

Amer, Safiyya. 2016. "Hal yudīr Ibrāhīm al-Jārī al-lijān al-iliktrūniyya lil-niẓām al-miṣrī?" [Is Ibrahim Al-Garhy running pro-regime trolls in Egypt?]. *Al-Araby Al-Jadeed*, November 6, 2016. https://bit.ly/38hhzTK.

April 6 Youth Movement. 2015. "Dhikrā ghazwat al-ṣanādīq.. awwal taṭbīq ʿamalī lil-qāʿida al-diktātūriyya al-qadīma 'farriq tasudd'" [Remembering the anniversary of the March referendum: The first practical application of the old dictatorial principle of divide and rule]. Facebook, March 19, 2015. https://www.facebook.com/shabab6april/posts/10153681777478294.

Arab 48. 2017. "Ḥarb al-lijān al-iliktrūniyya fī miṣr" [The troll war in Egypt]. April 3, 2017. https://bit.ly/2R416No.

Arab Republic of Egypt 2011. Masr al-niyāba al-ʿāmma. Ḥāfiẓat mustanadāt fī-l-jināyat raqm 1227 li-sanat 2011 qaṣr al-Nīl, al-muqayyada bi-raqm 7 li-sanat 2011 ḥaṣr taḥqīq niyābat istiʾnāf al-Qāhira. [Arab Republic of Egypt. Public prosecution. Document portfolio of felony 1227 of 2011, Qasr al-

Nil, registered under no. 7 of 2011, Listings of Cairo Appeals Prosecution Investigations.]

Armbrust, Walter. 2018. "Thawra ḍidd al-niyūlibrāliyya? Am thawra niyūlibrāliyya?" [A revolution against neoliberalism? Or a neoliberal revolution?]. In Gilbert Achcar, Lucie Ryzova, and Walter Armbrust, *Tafkīk al-thawra: dirāsāt ḥawl al-intifāḍa al-miṣriyya wal-rabī' al-arabī* [Deconstructing the revolution: Studies on the Egyptian uprising and the Arab Spring], 55–107, edited by Tamer Wagih. Cairo: Dār al-Marāyā lil-Intāj al-Thaqāfī.

Ayman, Arwa. 2012. "Nuṣūṣ al-iʿlān al-dustūrī al-mukammil fī al-yawm al-awwal li-badʾ al-ʿamal bih" [Text of the complementary constitutional declaration]. *Al-Watan News*, June 17, 2012. https://www.elwatannews.com/news/details/17978.

Azouz, Mohamed. 2007. "Muwaẓẓafū al-ḍarāʾib al-ʿaqqāriyya yuwāṣilūn al-iḍrāb wal-iʿtiṣām amām maqarr ittiḥād al-ʿummāl" [Real estate tax collectors continue their strike and sit-in in front of the headquarters of the Trade Union Federation]. *Almasry Alyoum*, November 15, 2007. https://www.almasryalyoum.com/news/details/2117902.

Basal, Mohamed. 2016. "Bil-ṣuwar.. al-Sīsī lil-muthaqqafīn: yajib tajsīr al-fajwa bayn al-tanẓīr wal-wāqiʿ al-ʿamalī.. wa-awlawiyyatunā al-ḥifāẓ ʿalā al-dawla" [With images: Sisi to intellectuals: You must bridge the gap between theorizing and practical reality: Our priority is to preserve the state]. *Shorouk News*, March 22, 2016. https://www.shorouknews.com/news/view.aspx?cdate=22032016&id=c16c013b-6103-4db0-8307-2e7b51edeb30.

Bassiouny, Moustafa. 2013. "ʿUmmāl miṣr yadfaʿūn al-thaman mujaddadan?" [Egypt's workers pay the price again?]. *Al-Akhbar*, July 27, 2013. https://al-akhbar.com/Opinion/54894.

BBC Arabic. 2011. "Lijān shaʿbiyya fī miṣr li-ḥifẓ al-amn" [Popular committees in Egypt to preserve security]. YouTube video, 1:48, January 31, 2011. https://www.youtube.com/watch?v=SMdYKY2KHSg.

BBC Arabic. 2012a. "Al-majlis al-ʿaskarī al-ḥākim fī miṣr yuṭālib bi-iḥtirām al-qaḍāʾ wasaṭ muẓāharāt ḍiddah" [SCAF urges respecting court orders amid anti-SCAF protests]. June 22, 2012. http://www.bbc.com/arabic/middleeast/2012/06/120622_scaf_egypt_demos.

BBC Arabic. 2012b. "Al-raʾīs al-miṣrī yulghī qarār ḥall al-barlamān.. wa-'l-majlis al-ʿaskarī yaʿqid ijtimāʿan ṭāriʾan" [Egyptian president restitutes the parliament, and SCAF holds an emergency meeting]. July 8, 2012. http://www.bbc.com/arabic/middleeast/2012/07/120708_egypt_parliament_decision.

BBC Arabic. 2012c. "Miṣr: al-majlis al-ʿaskarī yaḥill majlis al-shaʿb wa-'l-Katātnī yaʿtabir al-qarār ghayr dustūrī" [Egypt: SCAF dissolves the parliament, and El-Katatni considers the decision unconstitutional]. June 16, 2012. https://www.bbc.com/arabic/middleeast/2012/06/120616_egypt_parilament_scaf.

BBC Arabic. 2012d. "Intikhābāt al-riʾāsa al-miṣriyya 2012: tasalsul zamanī" [Egypt's 2012 presidential election: Timeline]. April 27, 2012. https://www.bbc.com/arabic/middleeast/2012/04/120427_egypt_election_time_line.

BBC Arabic. 2018. "Miṣr: mā al-ladhī ʿanāh al-Sīsī bi-manʿ takrār mā ḥadath mundh sabʿ sanawāt?" [Egypt: What did Sisi mean by "What happened seven years ago cannot be repeated"?]. February 1, 2018. https://www.bbc.com/arabic/interactivity-42910217.

callto Allahı. 2011. "Al-sāʿa 10 bayān ʿUmar Sulaymān bi-taklīfih bi-ʾl-tafāwuḍ maʿ al-muʿāraḍa" [10 o'clock statement by Omar Suleiman regarding his mandate to negotiate with the opposition]. YouTube video, 2:02, February 1, 2011. https://www.youtube.com/watch?v=WrnkbdGVuZQ.

Chahine, Youssef, dir. 1972. Al-asfour (The sparrow). Misr International Films, MH Films. Arabic. https://www.imdb.com/title/tt0068225/.

Che Batikha. 2012. Wathāʾiqī: al-lijān al-shaʿbiyya fi al-thawra al-miṣriyya [Documentary: the Popular Committees in the Egyptian Revolution]. Al Jazeera documentary (YouTube video posted by Che Batikha), 45:26, January 31, 2012. https://www.youtube.com/watch?v=2M_8yysRabs.

CNN Arabic. 2011. "Miṣr: Khilāf bayn al-quwā al-siyāsiyya wal-ʿaskarī ḥawl al-mabādiʾ fawq al-dustūriyya" [Egypt: Disagreement between political forces and the SCAF over the supraconstitutional principles]. December 6, 2011. http://archive.arabic.cnn.com/2011/egypt.2011/11/6/egypt.differences_pol/.

CNN Arabic. 2018. "Al-Sīsī: ʿanā mush siyāsī.. wa-baʾālī 50 sana ba-tʿallam yaʿnī eyh dawla" [Sisi: I am not a politician. I have been learning the meaning of the state for fifty years]. January 31, 2018. https://arabic.cnn.com/middle-east/2018/01/31/sisi-warns-evil-force-against-threatening-egypt-security.

Deutsche Welle. 2012. "6 Abrīl: "fawz Shafīq nihāyat al-thawra wa-taʾyīd Mursī khiyār maftūḥ"" [April 6 Movement: "Shafik's win is the end of the revolution, and endorsing Morsi is an option"]. May 30, 2012. goo.gl/jo7NsZ.

Dunqul, Amal. 1987. Al-aʿmāl al-shiʿriyya al-kāmila [Complete poetic works]. Cairo: Maktabat Madbūlī.

Eddin, Gamal Essam. 2010. "30 min kibār rijāl al-aʿmāl fi barlamān 2010" [30 businessmen tycoons in the 2010 People's Assembly]. Al-Ahram, December 7, 2010. http://gate.ahram.org.eg/News/20310.aspx.

Egypt Government, Higher Election Commission. 2011. "Al-natīja: naʿam bi-nisbat 77.3%" [The result is yes at a rate of 77.3%]. Egypt Referendum 2011. Accessed June 21, 2023. https://referendum2011.elections.eg/84-slideshow/155-result.html.

Egyptian Center for Economic and Social Rights. 2011. "Al-ʿummāl wa-ʾl-thawra al-miṣriyya: ruʾya ḥuqūqiyya" [Workers and the Egyptian Revolution: A rights-based perspective]. Egyptian Center for Economic and Social Rights, February 16, 2011. http://ecesr.org/?p=2967.

Egypt State Information Service. 2011. "Al-bayān raqm 5 li-ʾl-majlis al-aʿlā lil-quwwāt al-musallaḥa al-miṣriyya" [SCAF's statement number 5]. February 14, 2011. https://web.archive.org/web/20160401005011/http://www.sis.gov.eg/Ar/Templates/Articles/tmpArticles.aspx?ArtID=44125.

Egypt Today. 2010. "Miṣr al-Nihārda al-jalisa al-ūlā li-Barlimān. Taqrīr ʿan al-jalsah al-ūlā lil-majlis al-shaʿb" [A report on the first session of the People's Assembly]. YouTube video, 12:53, December 14, 2010. https://www.youtube.com /watch?v=nx-lFRR7wuc.

El Ayoubi, Aida, and Cairokee. 2011. "Ya El Midan" [Oh, square]. YouTube video, 5:02, November 30, 2011. https://youtu.be/eE3yaJcOp28.

El-Bishry, Tarek. 2011. "Al-khāʾifūn min al-dīmuqrāṭiyya" [Those who are scared of democracy]. *Shorouk News*, March 17, 2011. https://www.ikhwanonline.com /article/80785.

Elhady, Omar. 2011. "Muḥammad Ḥusayn Yaʿqūb: intaṣarnā fī ʿghazwat al-ṣanādīq' wal-balad baladnā.. wal-shaʿb qāl 'naʿam' lil-dīn" [Mohamed Hussain Yaakoub: We won in the ballots war, the country is ours, and the people said "yes" to religion]. *Almasry Alyoum*, March 21, 2011. https://www. almasryalyoum.com/news/details/120575.

El-Khouli, Mohamed, and Abdel Rahman Youssef. 2012. "Al-islāmiyyūn yuqirrūn: 'sharʿiyyat al-maydān hiya thawra + barlamān" [Islamists confirm "the legitimacy of the square is a revolutionary parliament"]. *Al-Akhbar*, April 14, 2012. https://al-akhbar.com/Arab/68315.

El-Merghany, Elhamy. 2009. "Al-taghayyurāt fī bunyat al-ṭabaqa al-ʿāmila al-miṣriyya" [Changes in the structure of the Egyptian working class]. *Al-Hewar Al-Motamaden*, Leftist and Socialist Research Papers, January 7, 2009. http:// www.ahewar.org/debat/show.art.asp?aid=176711.

El-Merghany, Elhamy. 2012. "Naḥw taṭwīr ʿamal al-lijān al-shaʿbiyya" [Toward developing the work of the popular committees]. *Al-Hewar Al-Motamaden*, May 1, 2012. http://www.ahewar.org/debat/show.art.asp?aid=290241&r=0.

El-Qersh, Saad. 2012. *Al-thawra al-ān: yawmiyyāt min maydān al-taḥrīr* [Revolution now: A diary from Tahrir]. Cairo: Dār al-Kutub Khān.

El Raggal, Aly. 2012. "Al-thawra wal-khanjar al-qānūnī" [The revolution and the legalistic dagger]. *Shorouk News*, June 10, 2012. https://www.shorouknews.com /columns/view.aspx?cdate=10062012&id=2fe13493-8176-4cd1-b934-c874a55d1019.

El-Shamy, May. 2016. "Fī al-yawm al-rābiʿ li-ḥabs Aḥmad Nājī.. muthaqqafūn yuṣdirūn bayān 'iftaḥū al-majāl al-ʿāmm'" [On the fourth day of Ahmed Naji's detention: Intellectuals issue "Open the Political Space" statement]. *Youm7*, February 23, 2016. https://www.youm7.com/2598590.

El-Taher, Mohamed. 2017. "ʿAn al-ḥajb wa-ʿidāʾ al-dawla lil-intarnit" [On blocking the internet and state antagonism toward the internet]. *Almasry Alyoum*, July 5, 2017. https://www.almasryalyoum.com/news/details/1157958.

El-Toukhy, Nael. 2016. "Thawra mutamaddida wa-thawriyyūn munsaḥibūn" [An expanding revolution and withdrawing revolutionaries]. *As-Safir Al-Arabi*, May 5, 2016. https://bit.ly/3cmV73k.

Essmat, Mohamed. 2010. "Kifāya.. wa-akhawātuhā" [Kefaya and its siblings]. *Shorouk News*, September 28, 2010. https://www.shorouknews.com/columns/ view.aspx?cdate=28092010&id=171512a8-8417-4b55-99f0-f29822290db5.

Fahmy, Khaled. 2011. "Maydān al-taḥrīr" [Tahrir Square]. *Khawāṭir ʿan miṣr wal-sharq al-awsaṭ wal-tārīkh* [Thoughts on Egypt, the Middle East, and history] (blog), September 11, 2011. http://tinyurl.com/y2ew3czx.

Fahmy, Khaled. 2012. "Al-maydān li-man?" [To whom does the square belong?].
Shorouk News, September 23, 2012. https://www.shorouknews.com/columns
/view.aspx?cdate=23092012&id=e9eeb0ef-0b77-4c9f-a04a-2d09d18d8f48.

Fahmy, Khaled. 2016. "Al-thawra al-muḍādda fī miṣr: dawr al-khawf wa-
taghawwul al-ajhiza al-amniyya" [The counterrevolution in Egypt: The role
of fear and the transgressions of the security apparatus]. Interview by Aly
El Raggal. *Jadaliyya*, May 22, 2016. https://www.jadaliyya.com/Details/33285.

Fayed, Omnia. 2011. "Grūb "Kullnā Khālid al-Saʿīd" miliyūn ʿuḍw" [A million
members in the "We Are All Khaled Said" group]. *Youm7*, March 8, 2011.
https://www.youm7.com/365559.

Gad, Mohamed. 2018. "Al-dawla al-miṣriyya bayn al-iḥtifāʾ bi-Gayts wa-ʿadāwat
Zūkarburg" [The Egyptian state between the celebration of Gates and
hostility toward Zuckerberg]. *Maraya Magazine* 7 (October): 19–23. https://bit
.ly/3RgtpEi.

Gamal, Wael. 2011a. "Min thawrat isqāṭ al-diktātūriyya ilā thawrat bināʾ al-niẓām
al-jadīd" [From the revolution to end dictatorship to a revolution to build
a new order]. *Shorouk News*, February 13, 2011. https://www.shorouknews
.com/columns/view.aspx?cdate=13022011&id=b8e15c51-66bb-4b91-a7e4
-72ad850c8c49.

Gamal, Wael. 2011b. "Qul ḥuqūq ijtimāʿiyya wa-lā taqul maṭālib fiʾawiyya" [Say
social rights, not partisan demands]. *Shorouk News*, February 22, 2011. https://
www.shorouknews.com/columns/view.aspx?cdate=22022011&id=83abof51
-8995-4c98-8b3c-4dfab7d00e59.

Ghoniem, Ahmed. 2013. "Al-taḥrīr yataḥawwal li-thakna ʿaskariyya.. wa 21
mudarraʿat jaysh tughliq madākhil al-maydān" [Tahrir is transformed into
a militarized zone: And 21 armored military vehicles block the entrances of
Tahrir]. *Al-Watan News*, October 5, 2013. https://www.elwatannews.com/news
/details/335114.

Ghoniem, Reda. 2015. "Al-Sīsī wa 25 yanāyir.. thawra wa-lākin" [Sisi and 25 January: A revolution, but . . .]. *Almasry Alyoum*, January 20, 2015. https://www.
almasryalyoum.com/news/details/635391.

Hafez, Ahmed Abdel. 2012. "Milyūniyya bil-iskandariyya ḍidd al-iʿlān al-dustūrī"
[One million protest in Alexandria against SCAF's constitutional declara-
tion]. Al Jazeera, June 20, 2012. http://goo.gl/bZp83w.

Hassan, Karima. 2012. "Al-ʿasharāt yataẓāharūn fī al-taḥrīr.. wa-yuʾakkidūn
ḥukm al-dustūriyya bidāyat thawra jadīda" [Dozens in Tahrir protesting,
confirming: "The Supreme Court decision will lead to another revolution"].
Almasry Alyoum, June 14, 2012. https://www.almasryalyoum.com/news/details
/186069.

Hediya, Shaaban. 2010. "Hal ibtalaʿ al-ikhwān jamʿiyyat al-Barādiʿī lil-taghyīr?"
[Did the MB swallow the NAFC?]. *Youm7*, July 16, 2010. https://www.youm7
.com/253572.

Hima zamalek. 2011. "Fatḥ al-sujūn bi-wāsiṭat al-shurṭa wa-tahrīb al-masājīn li-ʾl-
takhrīb" [Opening of the prisons by the police and releasing the prisoners

to cause vandalism]. YouTube video, 3:19, February 9, 2011. https://www.youtube.com/watch?v=bxSHvOJVzpg.

Hussein, Hassan Ahmed. 2012. "Badʾ qubūl dufʿa jadīda bi-akādīmiyyat al-shurṭa.. wal-dākhiliyya tuḥadhdhir min ʿal-wasāṭa wal-rashwa'" [New cohort is admitted in the police academy, and the Ministry of Interior warns against "favoritism and bribery"]. *Almasry Alyoum*, July 16, 2012. https://www.almasryalyoum.com/news/details/200850.

Hussein, Sherif. 2017. "Al-Sīsī: ʿAdʿū al-iʿlām li-khalq fūbiyā ḍidd fikrat suqūṭ al-dawla'" [Sisi: I ask the media to create phobia of the idea of the collapse of the state]. *Al-Watan News*, July 25, 2017. https://www.elwatannews.com/news/details/2354888.

Kamel, Yehia Mostafa. 2019. "Min waḥy al-Sīsī: alqi al-wāqiʿ warāʾ ẓahrak wa-inẓur ḥawlak muṣṭaniʿan al-barāʾa" [Sisi's inspiration: Forget about reality and pretend innocence]. *Al-Quds Al-Arabi*, December 20, 2019. https://bit.ly/3Cw7wwj.

Kamel, Yehia Mostafa. 2022. "Mutalāzimat al-rajul al-ḍaʾīl" [Little man syndrome]. *Al-Quds Al-Arabi*, October 28, 2022. https://bit.ly/3WVEzSr.

Khalifa, Mohamed. 2011. "Al-nadīm yanshur shahādāt muʿtaqalī faḍḍ iʿtiṣām al-taḥrīr ʿan taʿdhībihim wa-ṣaʿqihim wa-ijbārihim ʿalá al-zaḥf ʿarāyā" [El Nadim publishes testimonies of those imprisoned at the dispersal of the Tahrir sit-in about their torture, electrocution, and being compelled to crawl in the nude]. *Alwakei*, August 9, 2011. https://www.masress.com/alwakei/12086.

Khayal, Mohamed. 2016. "Muḥammad Rajab ākhir zaʿīm lil-aghlabiyya qabl 2011: intikhābāt barlamān 2010 warāʾ al-thawra" [Mohamed Ragab, the last majority leader before 2011: 2010 election triggered the revolution]. *Shorouk News*, January 10, 2016. https://www.shorouknews.com/news/view.aspx?cdate=10012016&id=bd0681d8-cd6f-4db3-9bad-d9d7aa5cefie.

m7mdamienrady. 2011. "Yūtūbiyā al-taḥrīr 1" [The Tahrir utopia 1]. YouTube video, 2:45, February 8, 2011. https://www.youtube.com/watch?v=rozs33CAYrU.

Marefa. n.d. "Bayānāt al-majlis al-ʿaskarī athnāʾ al-thawra al-miṣriyya 2011" [SCAF's statements during the Egyptian Revolution 2011]. Marefa.org. http://goo.gl/rQc9pz.

Markaz al-nadīm li-taʾhīl ḍaḥāyā al-ʿunf wal-taʿdhīb [El Nadim Center for Management and Rehabilitation of Victims of Violence]. 2007. "Fī qism shurṭat al-manṣūra hatk al-ʿirḍ min bāb al-mujāmala" [In Mansoura station sexual assault is complimentary]. October 4, 2007. https://web.archive.org/web/20150202011433/https://alnadeem.org/ar/node/8.

Masr Al-Jadida. 2011. "Masīra li-isqāṭ mashrūʿ qānūn tajrīm ḥaqq al-iḍrāb" [Rally to overturn proposed law to criminalize the right to strike]. Masress.com, March 27, 2011, http://www.masress.com/misrelgdida/53332.

Mehwar TV. 2016. "Al-Sīsī: matismaʿūsh kalām ḥadd ghayrī anā lā akdib wa-lā aliff wa-adūr.. anā mālīsh maṣlaḥa ghayr baladī" [Sisi: Do not listen to anybody else, I do not lie, nor do I beat around the bush. I have no interest besides my country]. YouTube, 3:34, February 25, 2016. https://www.youtube.com /watch?v=mILFp5sbHq8.

Mohyi, Mahmoud. 2012. "Ṣuḥuf: tabāṭuʾ ijrāʾāt taslīm al-sulṭa addā li-nuzūl al-miṣriyyīn marra ukhrā lil-taḥrīr" [Press: Delays in power transfer leads Egyptians to protest again in Tahrir]. *Youm7*, January 26, 2012. https://www. youm7.com/587233.

Montaser, Salah. 2013. "Intifāḍat al-jiyāʿ al-latī ghayyarat tārīkh miṣr" [The uprising of the hungry that changed the history of Egypt]. *Almasry Alyoum*, January 16, 2013. https://www.almasryalyoum.com/news/details/193297.

Morsi, Mohamed. 2012. "Khuṭṭat al-100 yawm: al-nazāfa" [The 100-day plan: cleanliness]. President Mohamed Morsi's Facebook page, June 25, 2012. https://www.facebook.com/Egypt.President.Morsi/photos/a .380573021998621/380576161998307/.

Mubarak, Hosni. 2011. "Al-khiṭāb al-akhīr li-Mubārak 10 Fibrāyir 2011." [Mubarak's last speech, February 10, 2011]. Egyptian National Media Authority. YouTube video, uploaded December 7, 2015, 16:53. https://www.youtube.com/watch?v =9_06qCKV3bE&t=183s.

Naeem, Mohammed. 2014. "Fī aḥyāʾ mithl al-muqaṭṭam kānat al-lijān al-shaʿbiyya shayʾan jāddā" [In neighborhoods such as Mokattam, the Popular Committees were something serious]. Facebook, September, 2, 2014, now archived.

Naeem, Mohamed. 2016. "Ashbāḥ Yanāyir al-latī tantaẓir al-naqd al-dhātī wal-murājaʿa" [January's ghosts await self-criticism and reassessment]. *Mada Masr*, October 18, 2016. https://bit.ly/3Cqy6at.

Naeem, Mohamed. 2021. *Tārīkh Al-ʿiṣāmīyah Wa-al-Jarbaʿah: Taʾammulāt Naqdīyah Fī al-Ijtimāʿ al-Siyāsī al-Ḥadīth*. Al-Ṭabʿah al-Ūlá. al-Qāhirah [The history of self-makers and class hoppers: Critical contemplation in political sociology]. Cairo: Markaz al-Maḥrūsah lil-Nashr wa-al-Khidmāt al-Ṣuḥufīyah wa-al-Maʿlūmāt.

Naji, Ahmed, and Ayman al-Zarqany. 2014. *Istikhdām al-ḥayāt* [The use of life]. Cairo: Manshūrāt Marsūm.

Nota Media. 2020. "Il-gadaʿ gadaʿ wi-'l-gabān gabān" [The valiant is valiant and the coward is a coward]. YouTube video, 3:19, March 17, 2020. https://www. youtube.com/watch?v=DNG3XiR3zwc.

Official Magazine of Egypt Laws [al-Jarīda al-Rasmīya] 2012. "Iʿlān dustūrī mukammal yamnaḥ al-Majlis al-ʿAskarī sulṭat al-tashrīʿ li-ḥayn intikhāb Majlis Shaʿb jadīd baʿd iqrār dustūr jadīd lil-bilād" [Complementary constitutional decree, giving SCAF legislative power]. *Official Magazine of Egypt Laws* 55 (24).

Qabil, Mohamed Safwat. 2014. "Al-maṭālib al-fiʾawiyya wal-iṣlāḥ" [Sectional demands and reform]. *Al-Ahram*, March 24, 2014. https://www.masress.com /ahram/1271902.

Qassem, Ibrahim, and Salim Aly. 2018. "Taʿarraf ʿalā 16 maḥaṭṭa marrat bihā qaḍiyyat ʿtazwīr intikhābāt al-riʾāsa 2012'" [Introducing 16 stations through which the case of fraud in the 2012 presidential election passed]. *Youm7*, April 8, 2018. https://www.youm7.com/3735433.

Ramadan, Fatma. 2011. "'Ummāl miṣr yuwāṣilūn iḍrābātahum wa-i'tiṣāmātahum lil-muṭālaba bi-ḥuqūqihim al-maslūba fī 'ahd al-ra'īs al-makhlū'" [Egypt's workers continue their strikes and sit-ins demanding their rights that were usurped in the ousted president's era]. *Tadamon Blog*, February 12, 2011. http://tadamonmasr.wordpress.com/2011/02/12/strikes.

Ramadan, Walid. 2011. "'Awdat al-lijān al-sha'biyya.. maṭlab qawmī" [The return of the popular committees as national demand]. *Al-Ahram*, June 29, 2011. https://www.masress.com/ahram/86430.

Ramzy, Hussein. 2012. "Al-ālāf fī al-ittiḥādiyya lil-muṭālaba bi-isqāṭ Mursī.. wa-shāsha li-'arḍ ṣuwar al-ishtibākāt" [Thousands in Al-Ittihadiya calling for Morsi's ousting, while showing pictures of clashes on screen]. *Almasry Alyoum*, December 9, 2012. https://www.almasryalyoum.com/news/details/260569.

Saghieh, Hazem. 2018. "Al-Sīsī 'ra'īsī'" [Sisi is my president]. *Daraj*, February 3, 2018. https://daraj.com/1170/.

Said, Atef Shahat. 2001. *Al-Ta'dhīb fī miṣr : ḥaqīqah qaḍā'iyya : yataḍamman al-taqrīr dirāsa 'an asbāb intishār al-ta'dhīb fī miṣr wa-qirā'a fī 1124 ḥukm qaḍā'ī bi-'l-ta'wīḍ 'an al-ta'dhīb* [Torture in Egypt is a judicial reality. The study includes an analysis of the spread of torture in Egypt and an examination of 1,124 lawsuits of civil compensations for torture]. Cairo: Markaz Ḥuqūq al-Insān li-Musā'adat al-Sujanā' [Center for Human Rights for the Assistance of Prisoners].

Said, Atef Shahat. 2008. *Al-ta'dhīb fī miṣr jarīma ḍidd al-insāniyya* [Torture in Egypt is a crime against humanity]. Cairo: Markaz Hishām Mubārak li-'l-qānūn [Hesham Mubarak Law Center].

Said, Atef Shahat. 2011. "Wa-mādhā ba'd al-istiftā'?" [The future beyond the referendum]. *Shorouk News*, March 18, 2011. https://urlzs.com/6mHYp.

Said, Atef Shahat. 2013. "Lā tuldagh al-thawra min juḥr marratayn: al-jaysh wal-thawra fī miṣr" [The revolution should not be fooled twice: The army and the revolution in Egypt]. *Awraq Ishtirakiyya*, June 29, 2013. https://revsoc.me/politics/l-tldg-lthwr-mn-jhr-mrtyn-ljysh-wlthwr-fy-msr/.

Said, Michael. 2011. "Ghazwat al-ṣanādīq" [The ballots war]. *Al-Hewar Al-Motamaden*, March 23, 2011. https://www.ahewar.org/debat/show.art.asp?aid=251827.

Said, Omar, and Mostafa Bassiouny. 2008. *Rāyāt al-iḍrāb fī samā' miṣr [Banners of Strikes in the Egyptian Sky]*. Cairo: Socialist Studies Center.

Salam, Amira Abdel. 2012. "Bi-'l-arqām.. nanshur natā'ij al-jawla al-ūlā min intikhābāt al-ri'āsa" [With numbers, we publish results of the first round of the presidential election." *Youm7*, May 25, 2012. https://www.youm7.com/690592.

Shaaban, Essam. 2018. "Maydān al-taḥrīr.. rāya ḍidd al-muḥtall wal-mustabidd" [Tahrir Square: A symbol against occupiers and tyrants]. *Al-Araby Al-Jadeed*, May 13, 2018. https://bit.ly/3T5zZiB.

Shorouk News. 2011a. "Al-balṭajiyya yuʿlinūn al-ḥarb ʿalá al-taghyīr" [Thugs declare war on change]. *Shorouk News*, February 3, 2011.

Shorouk News. 2011b. "Raʾūf al-Mināwī li-'l-Shurūq: khuṭṭat fatḥ al-sujūn hiya khuṭṭa muḥkama jiddan, kānat mawḍūʿa min ajl ḥimāyat tawrīth al-ḥukm" [Raouf Al-Menawy to *Shorouk News*: Opening jails was a carefully crafted plan to safeguard the succession of rule]. March 7, 2011. http://www.masress .com/kelmetna/10331.

Shukrallah, Hani. 2017. "(1) Mushkilat al-tanẓīm wa-'l-thawra wa-nihāyat ʿaṣr al-affandiyya" [The problem of organization in the revolution, and the end of the age of the Afandiyya, part 1]. *Belahmar*, May 9, 2017. https://urlzs.com /Uxoj2.

Shukrallah, Hani. 2018. Aʿtaqid anna khaṭaʾī al-jawharī fī qirāʾat 30 Yūnyū waqtahā kāna fī taṣawwurihā ka-mujarrad mawja thālitha li-'l-thawra al-miṣriyya" [I believe that my fundamental mistake in reading 30 June at the time was in imagining it as a mere third wave of the Egyptian Revolution]. Facebook, June 30, 2018. https://www.facebook.com/hani.shukrallah.1/posts /2479252175433946.

Siyam, Emad. 2010. "Kharīṭat al-iḥtijājāt al-silmiyya fī miṣr: muʾashshirāt aw-waliyya ʿalā takhalluq mujtamaʿ madanī min nawʿ jadīd" [Map of peaceful protests in Egypt: Initial indicators about the emergence of a new civil society]. In *ʿAwdat al-siyāsa: al-ḥaraka al-iḥtijājiyya al-jadīda fī miṣr* [The return of politics: The new protest movement in Egypt], edited by Dina Shahata, 49–75. Cairo: Ahram Center for Political and Strategic Studies.

Sky News Arabia. 2012. "Khams mufājaʾāt fī intikhābāt miṣr" [Five surprises in Egypt's election]. May 26, 2012. https://goo.gl/Z35FwF.

Soliman, Samer. 2012b. "Min al-tamyīz bayn al-niẓām wal-dala ilā al-tamyīz bayn al-dawla wal-mujtamaʿ" [From distinguishing between the regime and state to distinguishing between the state and society]. *Shorouk News*, February 19, 2012. https://www.shorouknews.com/columns/view.aspx?cdate=19022012&id =9a18bbc8-e46f-406c-beae-69a8453745d6.

Sorour, Safaa. 2019. "Waqāʾiʿ ʿal-tadwīr': ḍamm sujanāʾ sābiqīn li-qaḍāyā jadīda ʿaqib ikhlāʾ sabīlihim" [Recycled cases: Recently released activists are back to detention on new charges]. *Manassa*, December 19, 2019. https://almanassa .com/stories/4202.

Tariq, Muhammad. 2014. "'Garāj al-tarīr.' . . al-wāqiʿ yaṣfaʿ taṣrīḥāt al-masʾūlīn" ["Tahrir garage" . . . Reality slaps officials' statements]. *Almasry Alyoum*, July 24, 2014. https://www.almasryalyoum.com/news/details/488707.

True Egypt. 2011. "Taftīsh būks al-shurṭa min al-lijān al-shaʿbiyya bi al-iskandariyya" [Inspection of a police booth by the popular committees in Alexandria]. YouTube video, 2:25, February 14, 2011. https://www.youtube .com/watch?v=d8yL9eyCQgY.

Wagdy, Wasim. 2013. "'Tamarrud.' thawra dākhil al-thawra" ["Tamarod": A revolution inside the revolution]. *Al-Ishtiraki*, June 20, 2013. https://revsoc.me /politics/tmrd-thwr-dkhl-lthwr/.

Wageeh, Tamer. 2017. "Istiftā᾿ Mārī 2011" [On the 2011 referendum]. Face-book, March 19, 2017. https://www.facebook.com/tamerwageeh68/posts/10212369624257220.

Yassin, Ramy. 2012. "Ḥusayn Ibrāhīm zaʿīm al-aghlabiyya fī ḥiwār maʿ Al-Ahrām: narfuḍ taslīm al-sulṭa li-ra᾿īs majlis al-shaʿb" [Hussain Ibrahim, the majority leader, to *Al-Ahram*: We refuse to transfer power to the parliament Speaker]. *Al-Ahram*, January 28, 2012. http://www.ahram.org.eg/Archive/791/2012/1/27/61/127613.aspx.

Youm7. 2013. "Fī ʿīd al-ʿummāl.. 2782 iḥtijājan fī al-thalāthat ashhur al-ūlā li-2013.. muqāranatan bi-2210 ʿām 2010.. wa-ziyādat al-ghaḍab yundhir bi-ʿinfijār ʿummālī.᾿ wa-taḥsīn al-awḍāʿ wa-taṭbīq ḥadd adnā wa-aqṣā lil-ujūr wal-ḥurriyyāt al-naqābiyya abraz al-maṭālib" [On International Workers' Day, 2,782 labor protests in the first three months of 2013, compared to 2,210 in 2010. Escalating anger foreshadows "labor upheaval." The most prominent demands are improved working conditions, implementing minimum and maximum wage rates, and union organizing freedoms]. May 1, 2013. https://www.youm7.com/1044586.

Younis, Sharif. 2015. "Sharʿiyyat al-tafwīḍ: al-judhūr wal-ma᾿āl" [The legitimacy of the mandate: Roots and repercussions]. *Al-Malaf Al-Masry Magazine* 15. Al-Ahram Center for Political and Strategic Studies.

Youssef, Abdul Rahman. 2011. *Yawmiyyāt thawrat al-ṣabbār* [Memoirs of the Cactus Revolution]. Cairo: Dār al-Shāʿir li-᾿l-Nashr wa-᾿l-Tawzīʿ.

Zidan, Fatima. 2010. "Al-barlamān al-muwāzī yaʿkis khaybat amal al-muʿāraḍa al-ḍaʿīfa" [The parallel parliament reflects the disappointment of the "weak" opposition]. *Almasry Alyoum*, December 14, 2010. https://www.almasryalyoum.com/news/details/99724.

index

Page numbers in italics refer to figures.

battles (continued)

    over Tahrir, 190. *See also* Camel Battle; Mohamed Mahmoud Street: battles; Qasr El Nile Bridge: battle

Bayat, Asef, 20, 22–24, 127, 139, 194, 265n14, 286n7

Beinin, Joel, 41, 138

bloggers, 37, 46, 51–54, 113–14, 180; Supreme Council of Media and, 183; virtual making of Tahrir Square and, 61, 69

blogging, 51–52

blogs, 52–54, 183

Bonapartism, 180, 196, 283n8. *See also* Sisi, Abdul Fatah

boundaries, 58; of the Egyptian Revolution, 29, 58, 64, 100, 111; revolutions and, 3, 17; social, 83; of Tahrir Square, 5, 61, 83, 86, 88, 100–101

bourgeoisie, 48, 172, 198, 282n44

Caesarism, 180, 196–97. *See also* Sisi, Abdul Fatah

Cairo, 1–2, 5–8, 12, 14, 42, 44, 65; American embassy in, 32; cafés in, 182; class differences in, 107–8; downtown, 5, 36–37, 39–41, 46, 76, 267n9, 269n1, 270n13; greater, 263n3, 264n5; injured in, 140–41; Mahalla workers solidarity protest in, 52; main squares of, 89; martyrs in, 139, 141–42; militarization of, 190; old, 218–19, 286n6; policing in, 187; popular committees in, 95, 98–99, 104; protests against Morsi's constitutional declaration in, 168; Rabaa Massacre and, 192; State Security Intelligence headquarters in, 18; strikes in, 134; working-class sit-ins in, 123. *See also* Nasr City; Qasr El Nile district; 6th of October City

Cairo University, 44, 61, 128, 191, 281n37

Camel Battle, 14, 58, 72, 75, 84, *102*, 133, 195; Gheit and, 140

capitalism: crony, 48, 125; digital, 222; neoliberal, 27

censorship, 54, 126, 178–79; internet, 183, 187

Central Security Forces (riot police), 14, 32–33, 38, 40, 42, 268n17, 269nn1–2, 278n19

checkpoints, 13, 105, 222; army, 89; citizen, 2; popular committees and, 88, 92–93, 97; revolutionary, 64, 84; security, 187, 192

clashes, 1, 6–7, 58–63, 71, 78, 148, 163, 269n2; Al-Ittihadiya Palace, 169; football games and, 72; Mohamed Mahmoud Street, 192, 285n4; Tahrir Square and, 29, 60–61, 63

class, 4, 207, 224; antagonism, 107; bourgeois, 198; capitalist, 17; coalitions, 129; composition, 108, 116, 124, 130, 139; conflict, 212; differences, 107–8; divisions, 90; participation, 5; popular committees and, 88, 96, 99; power, 176; privilege, 115; relations, 286n5; status of military officers, 216; structures, 26, 123, 126; unity, 144, 276n25; upper, 19; water and, 75. *See also* middle class; working class

complicity, 203, 205, 208; of elites, 5

conspiracy theories, 199, 201

constitution (Egyptian), 14, 54, 119, 141, 156–57, 166, 175, 281n40; dissolution of 2012, 172; MB-sponsored, 174, 176; Mubarak's amendment of, 53; new, 115, 123, 136, 149, 157, 161–62, 166–67, 174, 176, 182, 286n6

constitutional assembly, 14, 157–58, 161, 166–68, 175

contention, 12, 34–35, 154; electoral, 151

contingency, 8, 10–11, 22, 177, 212, 217, 285n3, 286n7; revolutionary, 15, 264n7; revolutionary boundary and, 100; US war on terror and, 273n17. *See also* lived contingency

Corniche El Nile, 7, 63, 148

corruption, 40, 82, 89; Cairo Transport Authority and, 134; electoral, 52; funding and, 95; globalization and, 27; military and, 275n15; Mubaraks and, 130–31; police, 49, 53; privatization and, 136; state 115, 176

counterrevolution, 12, 17, 21–22, 26–27, 30, 172, 180, 193–94, 225, 265n16, 266n19, 283n7; democratic consensus and, 116, 223; French, 196; internet and, 188–89; political space and, 182, 203, 208; role of, 4, 24; trauma and, 284n10; victory of, 174; vulnerability to, 177 coup, 209, 280n30; Free Officers, 44–45, 197, 267n12; revolutionary victory as, 23. *See also* military coup of July 2013

cronyism, 27; Mubarak's, 48, 115

cross-class coalitions/alliances, 4, 116–18, 122, 125–26, 129, 145, 217

curfew, 1, 58, 63, 124, 133

demobilization, 193, 203

democracy, 24, 28, 34, 69, 116, 157, 160, 166, 169, 185, 192, 223–25, 277n8; battles over, 3; demands for, 17–18, 115, 118; electoral, 145, 149–50, 156; established, 278n16; Free Officers coup and, 44–45; July Republic and, 219; Kefaya campaign for, 52; liberal, 126; meaning of, 177, 214, 224; military regime's crackdown on, 180; Muslim Brotherhood (MB) and, 278n15; representative, 155, 277n9; republican regime's lack of, 46; technology and, 222; transition to, 21, 23, 29, 154, 156, 158; Western, 286n5. *See also* procedural democracy

Democratic Front Party, 71, 73, 128, 161

democratic revolution, 23, 95, 115–16

democratization, 22, 34, 150–52, 157, 193, 223–24, 277n9; de-democratization, 34, 193; elections without, 5, 30, 150–51, 175, 223; equality and, 28; failure of, 176–77; mass mobilization and, 277n7

dictatorship, 33, 47, 137

digital spaces, 3, 17, 22, 55, 182, 185–86, 208, 222–23

dissent, 182, 204; counterrevolution's war on, 186; internet and, 185, 187; political, 33–35, 49; public, 33–34; social media and, 29, 35; technology and, 222

Egyptian Bar Association headquarters, 37, 39–40

Egyptian Federation of Independent Trade Unions (EFITU), 134, 137–38, 275n17

Egyptian High Court Building, 39, 41

Egyptian Movement for Change (Kefaya), 39, 51–52, 54, 72, 117–22, 125, 127–28, 274n5; National Association for Change and,

270n11; protests organized by, 267n10, 268n17. *See also* Youth for Change

Egyptian Museum, 63, 131

Egyptian Popular Committee in Solidarity with the Palestinian Intifada (EPCSPI), 31–32, 36

Egyptian state, 48–49, 125, 176, 179, 282n1

Egyptian Trade Union Federation (ETUF), 132, 134, 138

El-Adly, Habib, 48–49

ElBaradei, Mohamed, 53, 122, 280n34

El-Bishry, Tarek, 156–57

elections, 22, 154, 165–67, 173, 284n8; army and, 174; boycotts of, 40; corrupt, 122; early, 152; free, 17, 175, 208, 277n9; low participation in, 205; media and, 119; organizing for, 150; political space and, 35; presidential, 38, 53, 120, 149, 165, 167, 282n41; rigged, 156; unions and, 55; without democratization, 5, 30, 150–51, 175, 223

electoral laws, 174–75, 279n24

El-Ghobashy, Mona, 20, 159, 174, 202, 264n6, 269n4, 271n26

El-Hamalawy, Hossam, 37, 41, 123–24, 134, 145

elites, 22, 117, 163, 271n20; defection of, 19; liberal, 5, 18, 171; political, 5, 153, 194; secular, 176; state, 49

equality, 28, 151, 220

Ermakoff, Ivan, 10

Facebook, 51–54, 69, 99, 183, 185–88, 203, 268n20; government surveillance of, 187, 207, 284n15; wars, 13. *See also* We Are All Khaled Said (WAAKS)

Fahmy, Khaled, 207, 283n6

Fatah, Israa Abdel, 52, 200

Fayez, Mohamed, 91, 94–95, 104

fear, 1, 199–201, 221, 284n16; military counterrevolutionary regime and, 181, 203, 206–8, 219; of popular committees, 95

food: collected for Palestinians, 31; Tahrir Square and, 47, 58, 71, 74, 76–78, 80, 105, 270nn16–17

fraternization, 10–11, 22, 111

free markets, 5, 17, 27–28, 153, 223

Friday of Rage, 59, 62–63, 68, 185

Gamal, Wael, 17, 137
Garden City, 63, 148
General Intelligence Directorate (GID), 174, 183, 28n41
Ghoneim, Wael, 53–54, 270n6
Giza, 65, 139; al-Nahda Square in, 28n37
globalization, 27, 214
Goldstone, Jack, 18–19, 23, 26, 28, 117
Goodwin, Jeff, 23, 150
governance, 4, 142, 283n2

Hamza, Mamdouh, 126, 271n18
Hasso, Frances, 13, 28
Hazemoon, 168, 191
Heliopolis, 63, 166, 169, 273n20
Hinnebusch, Raymond, 48, 176
Hisham Mubarak Law Center (HMLC), 76, 270n16
Holmes, Amy, 20, 264n6, 265n15, 269n4
honorable citizens, 157, 206
human rights, 23, 53, 88, 270n15; abuses, 76; international, 162; movement, 49; NGOs, 43; reports, 181; Sisi and, 179–80

Independent Union of Real Estate Tax Collectors, 42, 132, 138, 275n17
intelligence apparatuses, 5, 153, 196, 202; EFITU and, 275n17; electoral process and, 174; expansion of, 180; formal political space and, 184–85; media and, 173, 183–84; military, 285n4; Tamarod campaign and, 170
International Monetary Fund (IMF), 123, 176, 209, 274n10, 282nn42–43
internet, 51, 186–89, 283n4; activism, 35, 187; cafés, 183; shut down of, 68–69, 80, 92; spaces, 185
Iraq: shutting down internet in, 189; war in, 37, 46, 51–52, 128, 206
Islamists, 121, 128–29, 148–50, 161, 166, 168, 28n37, 284n16; militant, 49; National Association for Change and, 270n11; parliament and, 279n23; political, 17, 159, 164; public hatred of, 175; Rabaa Massacre and, 206; regime and, 204; SCAF and, 190, 280n30
Ismail, Khedive, 5, 267n12

Justice and Freedom Movement, 73, 128, 275n13

Ketchley, Neil, 10, 20, 22, 269n4, 278n20, 280n33
King Farouk I, 6, 44
Kurzman, Charles, 9, 12, 14, 28

labor, 63, 104, 132, 134; division of, 77; gendered division of, 5; movement, 266–67n9; organizing, 138; protests, 41, 133; strikes, 3, 123, 137, 266–67n9, 274n11
legitimacy, 117, 156, 168, 173; constitutional, 165; crises, 220; for killers of protesters, 279n21; Mubarak regime's lack of, 122, 136; revolutionary, 161, 165
Lenin, Vladimir, 11, 131, 215
liberals, 17, 137, 153, 161; fear of Islamists and, 284n16; Morsi and, 168; National Association for Change and, 270n11; as pro-state intellectuals, 206; in RYC, 129, 146
lived contingency, 9, 11, 16, 21–22, 111, 211–12, 220–21, 285n3

Mahalla, 6–7, 123–25
Mahmoud Bassiouny Street, 63–64
Mansour, Adly, 171, 173
martyrs, 12, 113, 116, 120, 186, 279n21; class makeup of, 130, 139–42; demographics of, 29; families of, 192; justice for, 190, 192; pictures of, 73, 155, 163
media, 40, 58, 81–82, 95, 104–5, 144, 164, 184, 187, 189, 205–6, 271n24, 271n27; campaigns, 80; commentators, 78; conventional, 180, 183; digital, 85; Egyptian, 140; elections and, 119; government, 89, 137, 159; hostile, 142; independent, 91; intelligence apparatus and, 173; international, 105, 134, 146, 171, 274n2; mainstream, 51, 54, 159, 163; MB youth and, 149; news, 65; public, 118, 201; role of, 115; Sisi and, 200–201; state-run, 191, 197. See also social media
middle class, 144–45, 195; complacency of, 125; lower, 130; military officers as, 107; police officers from, 49; poor, 127

Middle East, 264n10; Facebook and, 51; uprisings in, 127

military coup of July 2013, 3, 21, 149, 153–54, 169–77, 188, 204–7, 211, 215, 223, 265n15, 280–81n35; anti-Morsi coalition and, 280n34; closure of political space and, 30, 179–85, 222; counterrevolution and, 266n19; EFITU and, 275n17; elections and, 280n32, 283n3; Freedom and Justice Party (of the MB) and, 275n13; militarization after, 190, 192, 270n13; mobilization for, 20, 186, 279n21; revolutionary youth and, 200; SCAF and, 186, 278n13; Sisi and, 196–98, 201–2, 208–9, 281n39; sovereignty and, 8; street protest and, 280n33; trauma and, 199, 284n10; US support for, 224. *See also* Muslim Brotherhood (MB)

Military Intelligence and Reconnaissance Administration, 55, 174, 183, 270n16

militia, 41–42; civilian, 92, 107; Mubarak's, 58, 63, 78; revolutionary, 19; ruling party, 90; Supreme Council of Media, 183

Ministry of the Interior, 6, 10, 93, 186–87, 272n3; attack on, 273n19; confrontations near, 60; practice of offering bribes, 268n16; stand-in at, 40

mobilization, 20, 58, 73–74, 118, 127, 131, 164–66, 185, 188–89, 193–94, 223; Arab Spring and, 23; contingency and, 285n3; cross-class, 123; electoral politics and, 149, 152, 162; against exclusionary politics of MB, 200; Facebook and, 52–53; history of, 55–56; July 2013, 173; June 30, 172, 285n2; limitations of, 43; mass, 19, 22, 277n7; of the Muslim Brotherhood (MB), 170; polarization and, 161; political, 70, 150; popular committees and, 97; revolutionary, 4, 30, 64, 152–56, 166, 175–77, 189, 193, 212; social media and, 53, 66–67, 222; Supreme Council of Media and, 183; Tahrir Square and, 9, 46, 76–78, 82–83, 86, 100–101, 103; Tamarod campaign and, 169; WAAKS Facebook page and, 186; of the working class, 123, 134

modernization, 27, 220

Mogamma, 6, 32, 148

Mohamed Mahmoud Street, 63, 182, 270n17; battles, 162–63, 175, 192, 275n21, 278n19, 279n22, 281n41, 285n4

momentum, 24, 122, 170, 217; movement's dwindling, 37; of rallies, 38; revolutionary, 4, 152, 154, 172, 188, 195, 216; shifts, 18; of street power, 158

Moore, Pete, 18, 213

Morsi, Mohamed, 148, 162, 165–69, 176, 188, 190, 195, 278n16, 279n27, 280n32; Facebook of, 276n1; mobilization/protest against, 20, 211, 223, 279n21, 280–81nn34–35; ouster of, 118, 170–71, 191, 197, 280n30, 281n35; presidency of, 3, 170; security apparatus and, 272n1, 276n2

mosques, 6, 36–38, 75

Mubarak, Gamal, 48, 50, 108, 120, 125–26, 155, 195, 271n18

Mubarak, Hosni, 2, 10, 39, 48–50, 57, 78, 87–89, 101, 146, 165, 175, 196, 211; army and, 11; authoritarianism of, 54–55, 69, 121, 128–29; autocratic rule of, 32–33; bribery under, 268n16; conspiracy and, 201; constitutional amendment by, 53; criticism of, 53, 55; detention of, 76; economic elites and, 117; Egyptian Trade Union Federation (ETUF) and, 132; military and, 19, 216; mobilization against, 20; as modern-day pharaoh, 209; Muslim Brotherhood (MB) and, 23; ouster of, 3, 5, 8–9, 17–18, 47, 58, 63, 69–70, 72, 75, 79–81, 84, 86, 90, 94, 97, 103–4, 108, 109–13, 118–19, 126, 129–31, 133–37, 143–45, 150, 155–56, 163, 186, 190–91, 195, 206–7, 216–17, 273n20, 274n11, 276n23; police apparatus of, 59; political economy of, 122; pro-democracy judges prosecuted by, 46, 52, 54; regime of, 4, 6, 13, 21, 27, 35, 37–38, 82–83, 108, 115–16, 121, 123, 125, 128, 169, 180, 188, 193, 215, 223, 266n19, 278n13; security apparatus of, 62, 120; supporters of, 270n16. *See also* Suleiman, Omar

Muslim Brotherhood (MB), 5, 18, 72–73, 77, 101, 126, 163, 166, 191, 194–95, 215, 265n13, 274n6; constitution, 174, 176; denunciation of strikes, 137; exclusionary politics of, 162, 177, 200; Freedom and Justice

Muslim Brotherhood (continued)

party, 70–71, 164, 180, 275n13; government, 282n43; Kefaya and, 121–22; media and, 173; military and, 153–54, 171, 175–76, 196; Morsi and, 165, 168–69, 280n34; Mubarak and, 23; NAFC and, 274n8; neoliberalism of, 282n42, 282n44; parliamentary elections and, 164; revolutionaries and, 148–49, 161, 277nn3–4, 278n15, 279nn22–23; SCAF and, 157–61, 165, 190, 195, 204, 277n13, 279n22, 281–82n41; security forces and, 172; Sisi and, 281n37; Suleiman and, 81; Supreme Council of Media and, 183; Tamarod campaign and, 170; WAAKS Facebook page and, 186; workers and, 146; Younis on, 197; youth of, 128, 149

mutual recognition, 29, 58, 80

Naeem, Mohamed, 16, 18, 99, 219–20
Nahda Square, 191, 281n37
Nasr City, 92, 191
Nasser, Gamal Abdel, 6, 55, 131–32, 157, 203, 265n13, 266n26; Bonapartism and, 283n8; coup of, 197–98, 267n12; funeral of, 267n11; welfare state and, 125
Nasserists, 121, 128, 270nn11–12
National Association for Change (NAFC), 72–73, 115, 118, 122, 126–27, 156, 270n11, 274n7; Muslim Brotherhood (MB) and, 274n8. See also Egyptian Movement for Change (Kefaya)
National Democratic Party (NDP), 155; headquarters, 6, 62, 110
Negm, Ahmed Fou'ad, 47, 267n13
new administrative capital (NAC), 209, 218–19, 286n6
Nile delta, 6, 52, 90, 101, 103
nongovernmental organizations (NGOs), 43, 54–55, 76, 119, 189, 206, 272n13, 276n22
nonviolence, 22, 61–62, 218

Omar Makram Mosque, 6, 75, 267n11
ontology, 9; processual, 220; relational, 22; of revolution, 25

organizing, 5, 52, 54, 66, 72, 213, 273n16; for elections, 150; freedom of, 118; labor, 138; power and, 225; pro-democracy, 53; skills, 102; union, 134; youth, 117

Paige, Jeffery, 212–13
Palestinians, 31–32; solidarity with, 35–38
paranoia, 199–200, 202; counterrevolution and, 193; of military counterrevolutionary regime, 181, 209; political, 180; politics in the United States and, 284n9; state control and, 187
paranoid regime, 30, 180–81, 193, 199, 202, 204
paranoid state, 201–2
parliament, 149–50, 167–68, 184, 218, 281n40; alternative, 122, 155–56; dissolution of, 154, 156, 164, 166, 168, 175, 279n24, 279–80n27; first post-uprising, 161–65, 195, 279n23; intelligence, 174; protests in front of, 41–42, 60, 110–11, 123, 274n1; revolutionaries marching to, 14, 149; Tahrir banner demands and, 113, 119; Tahrir Square's proximity to, 82. See also Muslim Brotherhood (MB); popular committees
peasants, 49, 103, 117, 140–42, 198
polarization, 19, 146, 153, 162, 169, 173, 189; digital space and, 185–86; mobilization and, 153, 161
police, 1, 34–36, 49, 54–55, 62, 64–65, 70–72, 107, 271n1; academy, 268n16; anger toward, 100; apparatus, 57–60, 65, 83, 88, 102, 140, 215, 269n5, 276n2, 278n20; arrest of, 14, 92, 94, 97, 273n18; betrayal by, 93; brutality, 27, 50, 53, 67, 89, 276n2; communications, 63; corruption, 53; defeat of, 68, 83, 90, 215, 269n5, 278n20; generals, 174, 272n3, 272n12; harassment, 114; honorable citizens and, 206; informal, 93–94, 102; military and, 61, 170, 278n19, 280n34; Mohamed Mahmoud Street battles and, 163; Mubarak and, 55, 57–58, 79; Muslim Brotherhood (MB) and, 148; plainclothes, 38–39, 50, 268n17; popular committees and, 95; power, 216; repression, 32, 40, 267n10; sexual harassment of female

protesters, 38–39, 50; sexual violence against female protesters, 39, 268n17; Sisi and, 173–74; state, 10, 29, 33, 48, 50, 122, 125, 282n1, 284n15; street kids and battles between protesters and, 275n21; Tahrir Square occupation and, 74–75, 78, 88, 191; torture, 33, 71; violence, 28, 37, 43–44, 57, 139; withdrawal of, 88, 91. *See also* Central Security Forces (riot police)

police stations, 36, 90, 92, 94, 131; battles, 64, 140–41; burning of, 62, 97, 110; police withdrawal from, 269n5; protests in front of, 41

policing, 79, 187, 216–17; brutal, 214; military and, 2, 93, 276n2; popular committees and, 96–97, 107–9, 272n12; revolutionaries and, 19; state and, 27, 99; of Tahrir Square, 55

political desertification, 181, 202–3, 209

political parties, 54–55, 72, 81, 120–21, 280n34, 282n43; Muslim Brotherhood (MB) and radical, 281n41; restrictions on, 151; young Egyptians and, 127

political revolutions, 17, 26–27, 218, 224, 286n5

political space, 180–82, 193, 203, 205, 215, 219, 222–23; closure of, 3, 30, 179, 181, 185, 197–98, 202, 206, 208; control of, 33; electoral/constitutional, 157; formal, 3, 22, 55–56, 179, 184–85, 208, 222; public, 35–36, 38–39, 43, 50, 54, 56, 66; street, 22

politics, 11, 27, 52, 55, 88, 97, 129, 205, 224; changes in, 126; coalition, 117, 128; constitutional, 149–52; contentious, 34, 83, 150, 181, 193, 285n3; counterrevolutionary, 195; electoral, 30, 146, 149–52, 157, 162, 199, 223; Egyptian, 149, 173, 176, 281n39; formal, 35–36, 54–56; Gamal Mubarak and, 125; hatred of, 208; internet and, 51; MB's exclusionary, 162, 169, 177, 200; of mutual blame, 215; paranoia and, 284n9; party, 45, 149; post-Islamic, 194; public, 34, 151; radical, 155; reform-minded, 122; regional, 35–36; street, 35–36, 43, 50, 55–56, 161, 182, 185, 222; of street protest, 29, 35; of Tahrir, 74; young people and, 127

popular committees, 2–3, 19, 29, 82, 84, 87–100, 102, 104–9, 111, 136, 216, 263n1, 272nn11–13, 272–73n16

Popular Committees to Defend the Revolution, 94–95, 104

postcolonial state, 35, 43; formation, 6; military and, 217

poverty, 27, 126–27, 137, 140, 214; line, 141

power, 4, 20, 30, 50, 58, 79, 156–57, 175, 187; abuse of, 94–95, 272n12; of activists, 102; ambivalence about, 12; of arrest, 97, 106–7; centers of, 18, 34, 42, 82, 151; crisis of, 198; dual, 106–7, 216; of elected bodies, 146; military, 108–9, 154, 197, 202, 272n14, 273n20; Mubarak and, 53, 120, 180; Muslim Brotherhood (MB) and 176–77, 195, 282n41; patrimonial, 48; people, 33; practices of, 2, 11, 88–89, 116, 212, 217, 221; presidential, 265n13; purchasing, 125; relations, 161; of revolutionaries, 172; revolutionary, 99; SCAF and, 149, 154, 159, 162, 165–68, 186, 195, 278n16, 279n24, 280n29; seizing, 14–15, 19, 21, 23, 109–11, 116, 152, 213–14, 217–18, 221, 225, 274n1; Sisi and, 180, 188, 196, 199, 203, 209; state, 19, 100, 110–11, 213, 221; street, 158; symbolic, 84, 190, 222; symbols of, 90; Tahrir Square and, 6, 8, 46, 101, 105–6, 190; testing, 10–11, 93; transfer of, 164; vacuums, 90, 92

privatization, 115, 131, 136, 146

procedural democracy, 141, 151, 153–55, 161–62, 175–76, 223, 277n9; free markets and, 5, 17, 28, 153

protest, 1, 7, 9, 16, 32, 58, 176, 205; conventional narrative about, 149; criminalization of, 175; cycles of, 26; forms of, 40–41; locations, 12; methods, 42; million-person, 267n11; in old Cairo, 219, 286n6; organizers, 206; political, 50, 56, 150, 203; pro-democracy, 51; reform and, 121; repertoires of, 39, 43; sites of, 35, 40; social media and, 185, 189, 268n19; tactics, 33, 36, 38, 55, 67; Tahrir Square and, 3, 33, 35, 43–44, 46–47, 65, 86, 142, 266n3, 270n8. *See also* street protests

Press Syndicate, 37, 39–40

Tamarod campaign, 169–71, 176, 211
Tarrow, Sidney, 34, 69, 151
terrorism, 173, 180, 183, 206, 208, 281n39
Tilly, Charles, 12, 18–19, 34, 83, 151, 173
torture, 49–50, 53, 71, 88, 93, 179, 267n15
Trotsky, Leon, 106–7, 109, 117, 215–16, 272n16
TV channels, 126, 183
Twitter, 51, 54, 171, 183, 189, 270n7; accounts calling for ElBaradei's presidency, 53; government surveillance on, 187; role in uprisings, 268n20; wars, 13

unbounding, 11, 15, 264nn11–12, 285n3
uncertainties, 11, 16, 30, 155, 158, 177, 208–9, 220–21, 285n3; in electoral politics, 152; mutual, 10–11, 21, 131
underclass, 115, 139, 141
unity, 118, 142, 146, 159, 161; of demands, 163; performative, 104, 144, 218, 276n25

violence, 40, 42–43, 74, 76, 173, 181, 202, 204–5, 212, 218–19, 223; authoritarian, 191; of clashes, 269n2; collective, 22, 62, 266n21, 269n4, 278n20; in demonstrations, 281n41; family, 266n6; gender and, 39, 268n17; from Israeli authorities, 36; in jails, 65; military and, 109, 199; police, 28, 37, 139, 163, 268n17; popular committees

and, 92; against protesters, 89; sectarian, 206; state, 188; symbolic, 190, 192–93; Tahrir Square and, 1, 60–61, 63
virtual making of Tahrir, 29, 58, 66, 69

Wafd Party, 162, 164, 280n34
Wagdy, Adel, 79, 101
War of Attrition, 47, 267n14
war on terror, 49, 208, 273n17
We Are All Khaled Said (WAAKS), 67, 185–86
West Bank, 31, 37
Winegar, Jessica, 5, 277n12
workers, 52–53, 130, 137–42, 146, 274n11; cinema, 73; constitutional assembly and, 168; Nasser and, 198; protests and, 18, 49, 117, 123–24, 132–36, 176; without salaries, 138; sit-ins organized by, 46; Tahrir Square and, 125, 133–34; textile, 7. See also strikes
working class, 124, 130–34, 145; soldiers as, 107
World Bank, 123, 176, 282n42
writers, 131, 178–79, 192, 200, 209, 224; collective reflection and, 172; pro-government, 137; Supreme Council of Media and, 183

Yahoo Groups, 52, 54
Younis, Sharif, 197, 283n8
Youth for Change, 121, 127, 266n4